Social Entrepreneurship

Social entrepreneurship differs from traditional forms of entrepreneurship in that the primary goal of the social venture is to address social problems and needs that are as yet unmet. The driving force of such ventures is social value creation. This new textbook aims to provide a comprehensive, cutting-edge resource for students, introducing them to the unique concerns and challenges that face social ventures through a comparison with the principles of traditional entrepreneurship. The book consists of fourteen chapters covering all aspects of venture creation and management—from writing a business plan, to financing, people management, marketing, and social impact measurement.

Social Entrepreneurship uses real-life examples and sources to expose students to contemporary developments in the field, encouraging them to think critically about the issues faced by social ventures across the globe, and experiential exercises and assignments are included to provide students with hands-on experience in creating and managing their own social ventures. Also containing review and application questions, illustrative cases, definitions of key terms, and a comprehesive companion website, *Social Entrepreneurship* is the essential guide to this rapidly emerging field.

Visit the companion website at www.routledge.com/cw/beugre to find:

For Instructors

- PowerPoint slides
- Instructor's manual
- Multiple-choice questions

For Students

- Extra illustrative cases
- Web links
- Links to video

Constant Beugré is Professor of Management at Delaware State University, USA, where he teaches classes in organizational behavior, leadership, and entrepreneurship. He has published five books and more than 70 refereed journal articles, book chapters, and conference proceedings.

Finally a true textbook for my social entrepreneurship class! This text provides comprehensive coverage of this emerging discipline along with supplements needed to provide students with the knowledge and skills needed to become social entrepreneurs. In addition to a comprehensive text covering needed content, other valued aspects of the text are the international focus of the book, the cases, and the thought questions provided.

Charles A. Rarick, *Purdue University Northwest, USA*

This book is a much welcome entry into the family of social enterprise books. It addresses critical gaps in the provision of social enterprise teaching and will be a valuable tool in the hands of an ever increasing number of students of social entrepreneurship. The book and the accompanying website are innovative in nature and broaden the scope for increased social entrepreneurial activity. Its structure is unique; blending the philosophy of deep and constructive learning by taking the student on a captivating journey that informs, questions and provokes critical reflection. Students will find this book to be a relevant resource in the creation of social value.

Charles Oham, *Senior Lecturer, University of Greenwich, UK*

An excellent introduction to key concepts, illuminated by relevant and inspiring real world examples, *Social Entrepreneurship* is an invaluable resource for experienced and aspiring social entrepreneurs alike. This book will support anyone interested in studying or addressing societal challenges through the means of a social venture, and the perils of losing sight of the complexities and pitfalls involved in attempting to do so.

Michael Roy, *Glasgow Caledonian University, UK*

Social Entrepreneurship

Managing the Creation of Social Value

Constant Beugré

Routledge
Taylor & Francis Group

NEW YORK AND LONDON

First published 2017
by Routledge
711 Third Avenue, New York, NY 10017

and by Routledge
2 Park Square, Milton Park, Abingdon, Oxon OX14 4RN

Routledge is an imprint of the Taylor & Francis Group, an informa business

© 2017 Constant Beugré

Library of Congress Cataloging-in-Publication Data
Names: Beugrâe, Constant D., author.
Title: Social entrepreneurship: managing the creation of social value /
by Constant Beugre.
Description: Abingdon, Oxon; New York, NY: Routledge, 2017.
Identifiers: LCCN 2016006272 | ISBN 9780415817370 (pbk.) |
ISBN 9780415817363 (hardback) | ISBN 9780203442609 (ebk)
Subjects: LCSH: Social entrepreneurship.
Classification: LCC HD60 .B478 2017 | DDC 658.4/08—dc23
LC record available at http://lccn.loc.gov/2016006272

ISBN: 978-0-415-81736-3 (hbk)
ISBN: 978-0-415-81737-0 (pbk)
ISBN: 978-0-203-44260-9 (ebk)

Typeset in Sabon
by codeMantra

This book is dedicated to my lovely twins, Jane-Victoria and Constant Jr. They very much make my life meaningful.

Contents

Preface

A Book for Future Social Change Agents

Social entrepreneurship is becoming a burgeoning field of study. Universities around the globe are introducing and teaching courses on social entrepreneurship within entrepreneurship programs at or outside business schools. Universities, such as Duke University and New York University in the United States, Oxford University in the UK, and many others, operate centers of social entrepreneurship. However, although social entrepreneurship is coming of age and is now widely taught, there are few conventional textbooks on the topic. Thus, the purpose of this textbook is to help fill this gap. In so doing, the book extensively expands the topic of social entrepreneurship in guiding students from understanding social entrepreneurship as a discipline to measuring the impact of social ventures.

A Book about Social Entrepreneurship as Social Value Creation

As the title indicates, social entrepreneurship is about the creation of social value. Social value can be created by adopting several forms of social ventures—purely philanthropic, hybrid, or for-profit. The ultimate goal of a social venture is to address a social need. This book builds on the latest research in the field to present a coherent learning tool for students. The inclusion of research from different parts of the world makes social entrepreneurship a global phenomenon. This textbook represents an effective teaching tool for social entrepreneurship educators by including several pedagogical features, such as review questions, application questions, and application cases with accompanying discussion questions at the end of each chapter. In addition, the companion website is a friendly teaching and learning tool. Students can use it as an effective learning tool and instructors can use it to prepare for teaching and assessing student learning.

Educator's Companion

To facilitate the use of this textbook for undergraduate or graduate classes on social entrepreneurship, an "Educator's Companion" was created. This includes: Chapter Outline and Lecture Notes; PowerPoint Presentation Slides; Case Teaching Notes; Audiovisual Listing; Test Bank; and Companion Website.

Chapter Outlines and Lecture Notes

The purpose of the chapter outlines and the lecture notes is to serve as guides to instructors. They represent adequate tools that facilitate the instructor's preparation. Of course, instructors can modify them, depending on the learning objectives of their respective courses.

PowerPoint Presentation Slides

The PowerPoint slides also serve as a teaching tool for instructors. Of course, they can be edited by instructors, depending on the themes they want to focus on in class.

Case Teaching Notes

Brief teaching notes are available to instructors. They represent guidelines that instructors can rely on to lead class discussions for each case.

Audiovisual Listing

The audiovisual listing provides a list of videos of social entrepreneurs or social ventures that instructors can use in class to illustrate particular topics.

Test Bank

The test bank presents a set of multiple-choice and essay questions at the end of each chapter. Instructors can use them to assess student learning.

Companion Website

The website, which was specifically designed for this textbook, represents a valuable tool for instructors. All teaching materials are posted on the website, which is easily accessible to instructors who use this textbook for their classes in social entrepreneurship.

Student's Companion

This book is written for students, and to make it easier for them to understand social entrepreneurship and the challenges of becoming a social agent. It can be used at both the undergraduate and graduate levels. Each chapter is written with the student in mind. The following pedagogical features have been included to facilitate the learning process.

Review Questions

Each chapter includes ten review questions that help students to assess their understanding of the chapter. Answering these questions will help students to evaluate their understanding. The responses may also help instructors to assess whether their students understand the material.

Application Questions

Each chapter also includes five application questions that are intended to help students apply their theoretical knowledge of the chapter. The purpose of these application questions is to challenge students to apply their knowledge. Indeed, it is often said that "What we do with what we know is more important than what we know." Thus, students should be able to apply their knowledge. After all, social entrepreneurship is about action.

Application Cases

Each chapter also includes two cases of "real-life" social ventures. By discussing these cases first-hand, students will be able to understand how social entrepreneurs navigate and manage the creation of social value. The cases include social entrepreneurs from around the world, with social ventures from Africa, Asia, Europe, Latin America, and the United States all represented. To some extent, the geographic coverage of the cases gives a global flavor to the development of social entrepreneurship and the emergence of social entrepreneurs as a new breed of social agents.

Companion Website

The website includes pedagogical materials that students can use to improve their learning experience.

Acknowledgments

Working on this book has been a collective endeavor. Several colleagues and reviewers have contributed to this final product. I would like to take this opportunity to thank them. Especially, my gratitude goes to all of the reviewers who have provided invaluable feedback. Their comments, suggestions, and criticisms have helped to improve this textbook. I would also like to thank the editors, Mike Travers and Sharon Golan, for keeping me on track and reminding me of the importance of meeting deadlines. Any shortcomings are mine.

Constant D. Beugré, Ph.D.
Dover, DE, December 31, 2015

About the Author

Constant D. Beugré is Professor of Management at Delaware State University, College of Business, where he teaches courses in entrepreneurship, organizational behavior, and decision-making at the undergraduate level and organizational leadership and behavior in the MBA program. Dr. Beugré earned a Ph.D. in Management from Rensselaer Polytechnic Institute and a Ph.D. in Industrial and Organizational Psychology from the University of Paris X Nanterre. His research interests include organizational justice, entrepreneurship, and organizational neuroscience. Dr. Beugré has published five books and more than 70 refereed journal articles and conference proceedings. His publications have appeared in academic outlets, such as *Organizational Behavior and Human Decision Processes, Decision Sciences, International Journal of Human Resource Management, International Journal of Manpower, Journal of Applied Behavioral Science, Journal of Applied Social Psychology, Research in the Sociology of Organizations,* the *International Journal of Entrepreneurial Venturing,* and the *Africa Journal of Management.*

Chapter 1

The Nature of Social Entrepreneurship

Learning Objectives

1 Define social entrepreneurship.
2 Differentiate social entrepreneurship from commercial entrepreneurship.
3 Explore the characteristics of social ventures.
4 Identify the multidimensional nature of social entrepreneurship.
5 Describe social entrepreneurship as a global phenomenon.

This first chapter defines social entrepreneurship, delineates it as a field of study and presents a typology of social ventures. The chapter also describes the similarities and differences between social and commercial entrepreneurship. Finally, the chapter analyzes social entrepreneurship as a global phenomenon. The chapter is intended to help students develop a deep understanding of social entrepreneurship and social ventures.

1 The Nature of Social Entrepreneurship

Social entrepreneurship can be better understood if one has a clear understanding of commercial entrepreneurship. Therefore, it is important to provide a definition of commercial entrepreneurship before discussing social entrepreneurship. Doing so is important because several entrepreneurship scholars have contended that any definition of the term "social entrepreneurship" must start with the word "entrepreneurship." The word "social" simply modifies entrepreneurship.[1] In this book, the terms "social venture" and "social enterprise" are used interchangeably, although social enterprise may have a slightly different connotation across countries. For example, in the United States, the concept of social enterprise includes organizations that fall within a continuum from profit-oriented businesses engaged in socially beneficial activities (corporate philanthropies or corporate social responsibility) to dual-purpose businesses that mediate profit goals with social objectives (hybrids) to nonprofit organizations engaged in mission-supporting activity (social-purpose organizations). In Western Europe, the concept of social enterprise is roughly drawn along the same continuum but with variations between two streams of thought—a focus on the social impact of productive activities, and the inclusion of social cooperatives in the taxonomy of social ventures.[2] The main factor, however, is that the social venture addresses a social mission.[3]

1.1   Defining and Understanding Entrepreneurship

The concept of entrepreneurship is not new. It has been around for more than 200 years. The word itself derives from the French word *entreprendre*, which literally means "to undertake." One of the early French writers on entrepreneurship was Jean-Baptiste Say, who noted that the entrepreneur shifts economic resources out of an area of lower productivity and into an area of higher productivity and greater yield.[4] Translated into the business language of today, Say's definition implies that entrepreneurs create value. Joseph Schumpeter continued on the path set by Say and defined entrepreneurs as innovators who drive the "creative–destruction" process and their function is to reform or revolutionize the pattern of production.[5]

Today, entrepreneurship is commonly defined as the relentless pursuit of opportunity without regard to resources currently controlled.[6] In this regard, entrepreneurship is concerned with the discovery and exploitation of profitable opportunities. Hence, entrepreneurial opportunities are those situations in which new goods, services, raw materials, and organizing methods can be introduced and sold at greater than their cost of production.[7] This implies that entrepreneurship is a process rather than a static state of affairs or an occupation. Other scholars have construed entrepreneurship as a way of thinking, reasoning, and acting that is opportunity obsessed, holistic in approach, and leadership balanced.[8] Thus, entrepreneurship is not limited to the creation of new businesses.

It is a mindset and a type of behavior that can manifest itself in several areas, commercial or social. This is in line with the early works of Jean-Baptiste Say and Joseph Schumpeter, who focused more on the entrepreneur as an innovator and an agent of change rather than a person who necessarily starts a new business.[9] Hence, entrepreneurship can occur any time one or several individuals engage in an activity that adds value to what already exists. This way of thinking has led some entrepreneurship scholars to consider social entrepreneurship as a subfield of entrepreneurship and to advocate that no specific theory tailored to social entrepreneurship is needed; rather, existing theories of entrepreneurship could inform the understanding and practice of social entrepreneurship.[10]

1.2   Defining Social Entrepreneurship

Social entrepreneurship is still emerging as an area of academic inquiry, so much so that its theoretical underpinnings have not been adequately explored, and the need for contributions to theory and practice is pressing.[11] This probably explains why social entrepreneurship scholars have not settled on a unified definition. Some scholars even argue that social entrepreneurship is still a contested concept; as a consequence, a universal definition of the concept that would be accepted among all contributors to the debate is hardly possible.[12] Is social entrepreneurship an application of commercial entrepreneurship to the social sector or is it a field in itself? There are debates about whether social entrepreneurship is really different from entrepreneurship as we know it. There are perhaps as many definitions of social entrepreneurship as there are authors who attempt to define it. This has led some scholars to argue that social entrepreneurship is poorly defined and has become an immense tent into which all manners of socially beneficial activities fit.[13] What sets social entrepreneurship apart is its focus on social needs. However, some social entrepreneurship scholars argue that since the concepts of novelty and profitability are recurrent in the definition of entrepreneurship, any definition of social entrepreneurship must include both terms.[14]

The economic dimension in social entrepreneurship is a means to an end—which is the social value. Regardless of the country and governance mechanisms, the definition of social entrepreneurship should include the following four elements:

- address a particular social need;
- be centered on the creation of social value;
- emphasize social impact; and
- acknowledge that the means to attain the social mission can include purely philanthropic, hybrid, or market-orientated mechanisms.

Despite the lack of a clear definition, most authors tend to agree that the main driver of social entrepreneurship is the social problem being addressed.[15] As a consequence, the particular organizational form a social venture takes should depend on which format would most effectively mobilize the resources needed to address that problem. Social entrepreneurship is also conceived as an innovative, social value-creating activity that can occur within or across the nonprofit, business, or government sectors.[16]

This conceptualization of social entrepreneurship is broad and encompasses the creation of new social ventures as well as a focus on social needs within existing commercial or governmental organizations. Other authors highlight the multidimensional nature and moral inclination of social entrepreneurship and contend that it involves the expression of entrepreneurially virtuous behavior to achieve the social mission, a coherent unity of purpose and action in the face of moral complexity, the ability to recognize social value-creating opportunities, and key decision-making characteristics of innovativeness, proactiveness, and risk-taking.[17] A more comprehensive definition of social entrepreneurship is offered by Mair and Marti:

> First, we view social entrepreneurship as a process of creating value by combining resources in new ways. Second, these resource combinations are intended primarily to explore and exploit opportunities to create social value by stimulating social change or meeting social needs. And third, when viewed as a process, social entrepreneurship involves the offering of services and products but can also refer to the creation of new organizations. Importantly, social entrepreneurship … can occur equally well in a new organization or an established organization, where it may be labeled social intrapreneurship. Like intrapreneurship in the business sector, social intrapreneurship can refer to either new venture creation or entrepreneurial process innovation.[18]

This definition helps to capture the essence of social entrepreneurship as a process through which individuals, organizations, or communities take actions whose outcomes add social value. Social entrepreneurship can also be a process within an existing organization where actions are taken to meet social needs. The construct of *corporate social entrepreneurship* is used to refer to social entrepreneurship occurring within established for-profit companies.

Although entrepreneurship itself is not new, the concept of social entrepreneurship is, and

- addresses social problems or needs that are unmet by private markets or governments;
- is driven by social value creation; and
- is not antinomic of market forces.

Very often, social entrepreneurship works *with* market forces, not *against* them. Social entrepreneurship is also a global phenomenon. Examples of social ventures abound in both developed and developing countries. Most social entrepreneurship scholars agree that the term "social" refers to the fact that social entrepreneurs develop products and services that cater directly to basic human needs that remain unsatisfied by current economic and social institutions.[19] The social mission is at the core of social entrepreneurship. Social value creation occurs when an organization achieves equivalent social benefits with fewer dollars or creates greater social benefits for comparative costs.[20] Thus, a social benefit is a solution to a social problem that accrues to society or a targeted segment of the population as opposed to an individual or specific organization.[21]

1.3   Typology of Social Ventures

A social enterprise is created to solve a social problem or address a market or government failure, while operating in a financially sound manner. Social enterprises have "social" missions that focus on creating systemic and sustainable change while addressing the needs of others. Dees coined the term, "social enterprise spectrum" to describe the different forms social ventures could take. According to Dees, social enterprises range from *purely philanthropic* to *purely commercial* with a social purpose.[22] Along this spectrum lies a variety of social enterprises.

1.3.1   Purely Philanthropic Social Ventures

Purely philanthropic enterprises ask for gifts and grants from donors and then provide free services and goods to beneficiaries. They rely on external sources of funding and are sustainable only when these external sources continue to fund their ventures. Physicians for Human Rights, a social venture based in New York City (www.physiciansforhumanrights.org) and Médecins Sans Frontières (Doctors Without Borders; www.doctorswithoutborders. org/?ref=donate-header) could be considered as philanthropic social ventures. Physicians for Human Rights focuses on investigating human rights abuses around the world, whereas Médecins Sans Frontières is most present where dire medical problems persist, including in armed conflict areas. For example, the organization played an instrumental role in tackling the Ebola outbreak in Guinea, Liberia, and Sierra Leone in West Africa in 2014.

As indicated earlier, to accomplish their mission, purely philanthropic social ventures receive their funding from external sources. They also rely extensively on volunteers who have the appropriate skills and the dedication to serve. However, one must acknowledge that the resource limitations facing purely philanthropic organizations could lead them to explore other social models to be sustainable over time. This is particularly important in a period of shrinking resources and reduced donations. In addition, in countries where the philanthropic culture is poorly developed or nonexistent, purely philanthropic social ventures may not be sustainable unless they receive government support. In such countries, there are just not enough individual philanthropists to donate to such social ventures.

1.3.2   Purely Commercial Social Ventures

Purely commercial enterprises are market-driven and provide economic value by supplying goods and services to customers who pay market prices. They pay market-rate wages, purchase market-rate materials, and use resources that are priced at market rates. A social venture may take the form of a purely commercial business but its profits are used to address social needs. For example, a social venture may be created to address a particular social need. However, in doing so, the social venture may be run as a commercial venture. Such a business model could help to address the social need without depending on donors or government grants. Some social needs fit in such a formula, whereas others do not. For-profit social ventures are legally incorporated as for-profit entities and designed to serve a social purpose while making a profit.[23]

Because of this dual purpose, for-profit social ventures must focus on a double bottom line, addressing social issues while adding economic value at the same time. Their success is measured in terms of both economic value and social impact. As such, they are different from purely philanthropic social ventures. In a for-profit social venture, the product is the vehicle of the venture, the beneficiary can pay most of the price, and the social mission is embedded in the company's overall mission. An illustrative example of a for-profit social venture is TOMS shoes. The company sells shoes for profit. In addition to this main activity, though, it donates shoes to barefoot children in developing and emerging countries. Its business model works as follows: for each pair of shoes sold, the company donates a pair of shoes to be distributed to the beneficiaries.

1.3.3   Hybrid Social Ventures

As discussed earlier, social enterprises can take several forms. They can be purely social—relying on grants or donations—or they can have a combination of earned income in the form of charging fees and relying on grants and donations. Social purpose business ventures are hybrid enterprises straddling the boundary between the for-profit business world and social mission-driven public and nonprofit organizations. Thus, they do not fit wholly in either sphere.[24] The concepts of hybrid organizing and hybrid organizations best describe such social ventures. Hybrid organizing refers to the activities, structures, processes, and meanings by which organizations make sense of and combine multiple organizational forms.[25]

In hybrid social ventures, both social value creation and economic value creation are core organizational activities. Hence, a social enterprise that combines the organizational forms of both business and charity at its core is an ideal type of hybrid organization.[26] For example, a social venture can focus on addressing a particular social issue where the beneficiaries do not pay for the services received. However, the same social venture can sell products aimed at making a profit. Examples of hybrid organizations include the OneWorld Health Institute created by Victoria Hale (see the application case below) and the Aravind Eye Hospital in India, which performs cataract surgery. The OneWorld Health Institute performs research and development on drugs for diseases that afflict people in developing countries. These drugs are sold at low prices to those who need them and the revenues generated by these sales are used to further its mission of making the drugs available to poor populations. The Aravind Eye Hospital has developed a tiered pricing model based on patients' ability to pay. Hence, relatively wealthy patients subsidize the vision-saving surgery for poorer patients.[27]

These different forms of social venture indicate that social entrepreneurship need not be confined to a specific area. Social value creation can occur in a for-profit venture, a non-profit venture or a venture combining some forms of for-profit and nonprofit activities. Recognizing this view, some authors argue that social entrepreneurship is an innovative, social value-creating activity that can occur within or across nonprofit, business, and public sectors.[28] The profit is then reinvested in the social venture to help accomplish its mission. However, focusing on commercial operations could undermine a social venture's social mission. Although market-based income provides benefits in terms of reducing reliance on external sources of funding and increasing self-reliance, it also exposes the social venture to market risk and legitimacy loss. The pursuit of market-based income can dilute the social mission.[29] Thus, it is important for managers in the social sector to balance the search for earned income with the pursuit of the social mission. Hence, managing hybrid social ventures is a balancing act. As several scholars have argued, the tension between social missions and meeting the demands of a market economy is best managed through communication.[30]

According to Dees, a prominent social entrepreneurship scholar, five major reasons explain the shift from a purely philanthropic funding for social ventures to an earned income model:

1   A new pro-business zeitgeist has made for-profit initiatives in the social sector more acceptable.
2   Many nonprofit leaders are looking to deliver social goods and services in ways that do not create dependency on their constituencies.
3   Nonprofit leaders are searching for the holy grail of financial sustainability. They view earned income-generating activities as more reliable funding sources than donations and grants.
4   The sources of funds available to nonprofits are shifting to favor more commercial approaches.
5   Competitive forces are leading nonprofit managers to consider commercial alternatives to traditional sources of funding.[31]

1.3.4   Corporate Social Entrepreneurship

Social ventures can also be created by established for-profit companies. This trend has led to the emergence of the concept of corporate social entrepreneurship (CSE), which is defined as "the process of extending the firm's domain of competence and corresponding opportunity set through innovative leveraging of resources, both within and outside its direct control, aimed at the simultaneous creation of economic and social value."[32] Corporate social entrepreneurship emerges from three conceptual frameworks: entrepreneurship, corporate entrepreneurship, and social entrepreneurship.[33] The concepts of entrepreneurship and social entrepreneurship have already been defined in this chapter. They represent the theoretical foundations of corporate social entrepreneurship. Corporate entrepreneurship refers to the "presence of innovation with the objective of rejuvenating or redefining organizations, markets, or industries in order to create or sustain competitive superiority."[34] Starbucks is an example of a company practicing corporate social entrepreneurship.[35] It treats social value creation as part of its core mission and business model.

Corporate social entrepreneurship is not another form of social responsibility but represents a process for advancing the development of corporate social responsibility.[36] The concept of corporate social entrepreneurship is a radical departure from Milton Friedman's assertion that the social responsibility of business is to increase profits.[37] In examining social entrepreneurship in Germany, some authors concluded that social innovation has developed as a result of intrapreneurship: that is, social innovations originated within the established organizational field and not as a result of challenges from new actors.[38] Corporate social entrepreneurship is not guided by economics but it may be championed as a result of personal morality inspired by employees' own socially oriented personal values.

Corporate social entrepreneurship is an indication that businesses can be forces for good. Hence, addressing social issues may not necessarily require the creation of new social ventures. This idea was developed in a TED talk by Michael Porter, a professor of strategic management at Harvard Business School. Porter argues that businesses profit from solving solution problems.[39] His argument is challenged to some extent by the renowned philosopher Michael Sandel, also of Harvard University. In his book *What Money Can't Buy*, Sandel argues that business is corrupting every aspect of human life and there are situations where the market is not necessarily efficient or the main means to use.[40] Contrasting the views of Porter and Sandel is interesting insofar as it helps to explain the role of established for-profit corporations in social entrepreneurship. The TED talk debate between the two scholars illustrates their arguments for and against the role of business in addressing social problems.[41]

2   Comparing Commercial and Social Entrepreneurship

Current research on social entrepreneurship indicates that it focuses on creating social value—that is, fulfilling a particular social need—whereas commercial entrepreneurship focuses on creating economic value. Like business entrepreneurship, social entrepreneurship recognizes and acts upon what others miss: opportunities to improve systems, create solutions, and invent new approaches.[42] Wealth is just a means to an end for social entrepreneurs, whereas for business entrepreneurs wealth creation is the way to measure value creation.[43] In social entrepreneurship, social value creation appears to be the primary objective, while economic value creation is often a by-product that allows the organization to achieve sustainability and self-sufficiency.[44] Thus, the ways in which social and commercial ventures measure their value creation differ in terms of purely focusing on economic value creation, social value creation, or a combination of the two. Although commercial ventures can also address social needs, the fundamental purpose of social entrepreneurship is to create social value for the public good, whereas commercial entrepreneurship aims to create profitable operations resulting from private gains.[45]

In some ways, every entrepreneur is a social entrepreneur because a successful entrepreneur creates wealth, and without wealth there is no surplus that may be used to fulfill unmet social needs. The difference between a social entrepreneur and a business entrepreneur is best summarized by Pierre Omidyar, founder and chairman of the online auction giant eBay: "I think of myself as an entrepreneur, and I have a social view, but I don't call myself a social entrepreneur."[46] This quote indicates two things. First, by creating eBay, Omidyar acted as a business entrepreneur because his goal was to create financial value. Second, by donating money, he acted not as a social entrepreneur but as a philanthropist because social entrepreneurs are involved in the actual creation and management of the social venture, unlike philanthropists, who only provide resources to help address social issues.

At the start of a social venture lies the desire to fulfill a social need. However, at the start of a business venture lies the desire to exploit a business opportunity, although doing so may lead to solving social problems. These apparent differences between social entrepreneurship and business entrepreneurship should not overshadow the similarities between them. In fact, the distinction between commercial and social entrepreneurship is not a dichotomy but a continuum.[47] On this continuum, social ventures focus more on social

Table 1.1 Commercial versus social entrepreneurship

	Focus	*Interest*	*Metric for effectiveness*
Commercial entrepreneurship	Economic activity to generate value for entrepreneur(s) and investors	Focus on profitable opportunities	Profit Shareholder value
Social entrepreneurship	Social value for recipient of social goods	Focus on opportunities that add social value	Social change Social needs met Social impact

issues than commercial ventures do. Today, however, the boundaries between commercial and social entrepreneurship are blurred. To the extent that social ventures can be profit-seeking and still continue their social missions, focusing on the differences between social and commercial ventures may seem irrelevant. As indicated previously, social ventures come into existence as a result of market or government failure; and the same can be said of commercial ventures. Both commercial and social entrepreneurship are dynamic processes rather than static occupations. The difference, however, lies in the core mission. Table 1.1 summarizes the focus and metrics in comparing commercial and social entrepreneurship.

3   Social Entrepreneurship: A Global Phenomenon

The meaning, practice, and governance of social entrepreneurship could vary from country to country. Contrary to the United States, in Europe the term "social enterprise" encompasses a variety of organizations, such as cooperatives, associations, mutual societies, and even foundations.[48] For instance, in Belgium, France, Germany, and Ireland, social entrepreneurship often refers to third-sector nonprofit ventures financed by government agencies, whereas in the United Kingdom it refers to independent-sector for-profit or nonprofit ventures that use quasi-market mechanisms to increase efficiency in service.[49] In Southern European countries, such as Italy, Portugal, and Spain, social entrepreneurship refers to multi-stakeholder work integration programs for groups that are typically excluded from the labor market.[50] In Denmark, Norway, and Sweden, the term "social enterprise" is often used to describe worker cooperatives in the childcare and healthcare sectors, whereas in the United States it encompasses a variety of organizations from for-profit businesses to hybrid organizations and philanthropic organizations with a social purpose.[51]

Social entrepreneurship activities also occur in developing and emerging countries in Africa, Asia, the Middle East, and Latin America. In these parts of the world, the development and management of social ventures are influenced by a variety of factors, including colonial history, cultural and social values, ethnic identity, religious beliefs, and government support (or lack thereof).[52] For example, an analysis of the factors underlying the development of social entrepreneurship in Indonesia highlights three main factors:

- perceived degree of economic empowerment by indigenous groups as a result of social entrepreneurship;
- Islamic identity of social enterprises; and
- social activism.[53]

Likewise, a study of social ventures in sub-Saharan Africa shows that ethnic identity and acute poverty levels influence self-perceptions and activity choices, whereas colonial history influences only self-perceptions.[54]

The form that social ventures take in a country depends on their institutional environments. The role of the external environment in social entrepreneurship is discussed further in Chapter 4. It is worth acknowledging that although the achievements of individual social entrepreneurs have been highlighted by social entrepreneurship organizations, such as Ashoka, the Skoll Foundation, the Schwab Foundation, and CNN in its annual series *CNN Heroes*, social entrepreneurial ventures can be started by collectives, such as a group of individuals, established companies, or entire communities. These communities often create community-based enterprises that address social issues. A community-based enterprise is the result of a process in which the community acts entrepreneurially to create and operate a new enterprise embedded in its existing social structure.[55] In such a context, the community acts as an entrepreneur to create a venture that addresses endemic issues that the community faces, thereby making social entrepreneurship a collaborative and collective endeavor.[56]

The current trend for most social ventures around the world is toward hybridization to help meet their social missions. For example, a recent study in Cambodia showed that most social ventures in the country now tend to combine donations/grants and earned-income activities. This is particularly important because the earned-income activities allow these social ventures to rely less on grants and donations and help to improve their governance in terms of more professional management practices, greater financial rigor, and improved accounting practices, transparency, and accountability.[57]

These differences in meaning across borders sometimes make the concept of social entrepreneurship confusing. However, one unifying conceptualization of social entrepreneurship is that social ventures address social issues that are prevalent in a particular country or community. The model of social venture used, be it purely philanthropic, purely commercial, or a hybrid form, may depend on the prevailing institutional environment of a country. Some entrepreneurship scholars have noted that the success of a social venture largely depends on the local political, social, and cultural contexts, all of which influence how the local community perceives a social problem and its proposed solution.[58] It is also possible that the emergence of social entrepreneurship may be influenced by the particular institutional environment. Despite the growing interest and increasing prevalence of social entrepreneurship, there is currently no or very limited data available to assess the nature and incidence of social entrepreneurship across the world, nor its antecedents and consequences.[59]

Lepoutre and colleagues conducted a survey in 49 countries to assess the prevalence of social entrepreneurship activity using part of the GEM (Global Entrepreneurship Monitor) survey.[60] They used the social entrepreneurship equivalent of the total early-stage entrepreneurial activity (TEA), which captures the percentage of the adult population (age 18–64) that is actively involved in entrepreneurial start-up activity. They found that the average social entrepreneurship activity rate across all 49 countries was 1.9 percent but ranged from 0.2 to 4.9 percent. This low prevalence indicates that the creation of social ventures is still a relatively new phenomenon in most countries and unevenly distributed across countries (see Table 1.2).

The rate of new social venture creation is relatively high in the United States compared to the rest of the world. This could be due to the generally vibrant entrepreneurial culture

Table 1.2 Prevalence levels of nascent, new, established, and early-stage social entrepreneurial activity (SEA) by country and region[61]

Region/country	SE nascent	SE new	SE established	SEA
North America				
United States	2.90	1.69	0.84	4.15
Caribbean				
Dominican Republic	0.76	1.84	0.98	2.59
Jamaica	1.15	2.41	3.27	3.50
Average	0.95	2.12	2.13	3.05
Latin America				
Argentina	2.21	2.30	3.31	4.32
Brazil	0.21	0.16	0.03	0.37
Chile	1.77	0.85	0.41	2.60
Colombia	2.60	1.31	1.18	3.83
Ecuador	0.39	0.12	0.21	0.50
Guatemala	0.17	0.32	0.05	0.43
Panama	0.86	0.43	0.38	1.29
Peru	3.45	0.49	0.13	3.94
Uruguay	1.89	0.75	0.64	2.57
Venezuela	3.77	0.32	0.30	4.09
Average	1.73	0.70	0.66	2.39
Africa				
South Africa	1.32	0.74	0.31	2.01
Uganda	0.98	1.94	1.41	2.70
Average	1.15	1.34	0.86	2.35
Western Europe				
Belgium	1.03	0.82	1.24	1.78
Finland	1.17	1.58	2.42	2.71
France	1.63	0.87	0.32	2.31
Germany	0.54	0.32	0.88	0.72
Greece	1.30	0.65	0.92	1.95
Iceland	2.34	2.07	1.86	4.24
Italy	0.86	0.42	1.26	1.22
Netherlands	0.60	0.45	0.51	1.02
Norway	0.64	1.00	0.57	1.58
Spain	0.37	0.19	0.36	0.55
Switzerland	2.39	0.46	1.48	2.84
United Kingdom	0.79	1.48	2.05	2.18
Average	1.14	0.86	1.16	1.93
Eastern Europe				
Bosnia and Herzegovina	0.60	0.24	0.09	0.83
Croatia	1.32	1.56	1.56	2.85
Hungary	2.15	1.27	0.59	3.31
Latvia	1.49	0.56	0.83	1.99
Romania	1.39	0.34	0.82	1.73
Russia	0.39	0.46	0.38	0.86
Serbia	0.40	0.74	0.62	1.14
Slovenia	1.34	0.90	1.40	2.19
Average	1.13	0.76	0.79	1.86

Region/country	SE nascent	SE new	SE established	SEA
Middle East & North Africa				
Algeria	1.23	0.53	0.11	1.77
Israel	0.95	1.35	1.80	2.24
Iran	1.07	0.34	0.58	1.41
Jordan	0.39	0.40	0.19	0.70
Lebanon	0.49	0.45	0.55	0.95
Morocco	0.26	0.27	0.40	0.39
Saudi Arabia	0.07	0.18	0.00	0.24
Syria	0.69	0.25	0.04	0.94
United Arab Emirates	2.46	2.70	1.35	4.93
West Bank and Gaza Strip	0.19	0.19	0.09	0.38
Average	0.78	0.67	0.51	1.39
South-East Asia				
China	1.53	1.36	1.12	2.89
Hong Kong	0.20	0.37	0.46	0.51
Malaysia	0.20	0.00	0.02	0.20
South Korea	0.40	0.41	0.56	0.81
Average	0.58	0.53	0.54	1.10

in the United States. It could also be explained by the prevalence of other support mechanisms, such as a culture of philanthropism and the existence of social venture capitalists and social angels. It could also be due to the form that social ventures take in some countries. For instance, in other parts of the world, such as Europe, cooperatives and non-governmental organizations (NGOs) play critical roles in addressing social issues. Hence, such organizations might not have been captured by the GEM survey. Knowledge spillover may also transform the way social ventures are managed. For instance, when social entrepreneurs have opportunities to learn from other well-run social ventures or for-profit organizations, they may benchmark these practices to improve their internal operations. A study conducted in the United Kingdom indicates that knowledge spillover helps social enterprises transform themselves into more market-driven, businesslike social enterprises.[62]

Summary

There are as many definitions of social entrepreneurship as there are authors who have attempted to define it. However, the consensus seems to be that social entrepreneurship addresses longstanding social needs. Although social entrepreneurship bears similarities with commercial entrepreneurship, it differs from it in some respects. Social enterprises can take several forms, ranging from purely philanthropic, relying solely on external funding, to purely commercial, seeking profit while addressing social issues. Between these two extremes lies a variety of social ventures. Social entrepreneurship is a global phenomenon that is not limited to a single country or region of the world.

Key Terms

Commercial entrepreneurship; commercial social ventures; corporate social entrepreneurship; entrepreneurship; hybrid social ventures; purely philanthropic social ventures; social entrepreneurship; social ventures

Review Questions

1 What is a hybrid social venture and how is it different from a purely philanthropic one?
2 Identify the differences between commercial and social entrepreneurship. Are these differences compelling enough to separate the two disciplines? Explain.
3 Identify the similarities between commercial and social entrepreneurship. Do you think that these similarities should lead to considering the two disciplines as similar? Should social entrepreneurship be considered a subfield of entrepreneurship (yes or no)? Explain.
4 Describe and discuss the factors that make a given venture social.
5 Explain the concept of corporate social entrepreneurship.
6 Describe the different types of social ventures.
7 Comment on Pierre Omidyar's statement "I think of myself as an entrepreneur, and I have a social view, but I don't call myself a social entrepreneur."
8 Identify some of the reasons why social entrepreneurship is becoming a global phenomenon.
9 Visit the website of OneWorld Health (http://onehealth.org), an organization created by Victoria Hale. Would you describe this organization as a social venture? Explain.
10 Discuss the following statement: "To some extent, all ventures are social ventures because society tends to benefit from them. Even commercial ventures have a positive social impact."

Application Questions

1 After reading the chapter, think about a problem that bothers you in your community or in the world in general. Identify the social problem and develop a social concept to address it. What type of social venture do you think would be appropriate to address the social problem(s) identified? Explain your choice.
2 Watch Michael Porter's YouTube video Why business can be good at solving social problems (www.youtube.com/watch?v=0iIh5YYDR2o). Do you think business plays a positive role in addressing social issues (yes or no)? Explain.
3 Identify three social ventures in your area. Classify these social ventures along the spectrum of purely philanthropic to purely commercial.
4 Visit the websites of the following social enterprises: Ashoka, a US-based foundation (www.ashoka.org), and the Young Foundation of the United Kingdom (http://youngfoundation.org/). Discuss the extent to which these two organizations are similar and/or different. Discuss the social impacts of these two organizations.
5 Watch the TED talk debate on YouTube between Professor Michael Porter and Professor Michael Sandel, both of Harvard University (www.youtube.com/watch?v=2yzzt9XXIO8). What is your position regarding the role of business in society? With which professor do you agree? Explain.

Application Case 1: Victoria Hale and the Creation of the OneWorld Health Institute

Victoria Hale, then a researcher in a pharmaceutical company, observed the following dire statistics: about 90 percent of the planet's disease burden falls on the developing world, yet only 3 percent of the research and development expenditure of the pharmaceutical industry is directed toward those ailments. The rest goes toward treating diseases of the rich. Such a concern may have been perceived as an unmet social need that triggered a sense of injustice. Hale decided to create a social venture to address this issue. Her ultimate goal is to bring much-needed medicine to those who are less likely to have the money to afford it. By so doing, she helps solve a social problem.

In 2000, Hale founded the OneWorld Health Institute to help tackle the discrepancy she had observed with Ahvie Herskowitz as her partner. OneWorld Health received 501(c)(3) tax-exempt status the following year to become the first nonprofit pharmaceutical company in the United States. Hale knew from her work as a scientist in the pharmaceutical and biotechnology industries, and subsequently as an official at America's Food and Drug Administration, that numerous promising drug-development projects—particularly for diseases of the poor—are dropped for lack of funding. She reasoned that there was a gap in the market—between academically inclined university departments and fully fledged pharmaceutical firms—for an organization that would identify such orphans, get their owners to donate the intellectual property if they were still in patent, raise development funding from noncommercial sources, and arm-twist researchers to contribute their expertise to the development process pro bono.[63] Her premise was simple: identify research on neglected diseases that has been completed but has not passed the profit hurdle; next, persuade the companies that own the research to donate the information to her institute in return for attractive tax write-offs and public-relations benefits; then use grant money and donations to distribute affordable drugs among those who desperately need them.[64]

For Victoria Hale, the status quo was the lack of medicine for poor people, and the better alternative was giving poor people access to affordable medicine. Poor people who needed the medicine the most did not have access to it. This sense of perceived injustice led her to create the OneWorld Health Institute out of a moral imperative. Moreover, the point of departure for starting this venture was Hale's realization that a certain social need was not met by appropriate institutions, such as the market and/or government.

The success of the OneWorld Health Institute has been recognized worldwide. ABC News featured Victoria Hale and the institute (see the video link: www.youtube.com/watch?v=jA0tsJB8cQM). Hale's work has also been recognized by several organizations and foundations. In 2004, she received the Schwab Fellowship of the World Economic Forum, awarded by the Schwab Foundation for Social Entrepreneurship. In 2005, she received the Economist Innovation Award for Social and Economic Innovation, from *The Economist* magazine. In 2007, she was one of *Glamour* magazine's Women of the Year for her work developing and providing pharmaceutical care to the world's poor. The OneWorld Health Institute is now an affiliate of PATH, a global health organization which intends to transform global health through innovation.

Discussion Questions

1 Identify the reasons that led Victoria Hale to start the OneWorld Health Institute.
2 Do some research on how the OneWorld Health Institute finances its activities and determine whether it is a purely philanthropic, a purely commercial, or a hybrid form of social venture.
3 Identify some of the factors that explain the success of the OneWorld Health Institute.
4 Watch the OneWorld Health Institute video at www.youtube.com/watch?v=jA0tsJB8cQM and visit the website of PATH (www.path.org). Would you contribute financially to this social venture if you were asked to do so?

Application Case 2: Cinepop: Bringing Movies to the People

Is going to the movie theater a privilege or a right that even people who are poor or who live in rural areas or shanty towns in cities should also enjoy? The economic evidence suggests that poor people do not have access to movie theaters because of the price of movie tickets and the lack of disposable income. To address this issue, Ariel Zylbersztejn, a native of Mexico and an entertainment 'master', launched Cinepop (www.cinepop.com.mx) in Mexico in 2004. Cinepop offers free outdoor movie screenings to low-income families in Mexico. Zylbersztejn realized that over 90% of people had no access to the movies because of the high price of movie tickets. Therefore he explored the idea of bringing the movies to the people. Indeed, he pondered the following question. If people cannot go to the movies, why not bring the movies to them.[1]

Cinepop operates as a for-profit social venture. It offers free outdoor movies on giant inflatable screens. Cinepop's business model consists of using sponsorship from large, medium-size and small corporations to fund its operations and generate a profit. In return, the corporations use Cinepop's events as promotional venues to expose their products, sell some of them and directly communicate with potential customers. The events are a means of reaching bottom-of-the pyramid customers. Cinepop also benefits from the support of local governments that provide the venues, usually, public places in the communities where the events are held. The local governments also provide electrical hook-ups, security, and sanitation services. In return, these local governments can use the venues to promote social issues, such as health and diet. Cinepop also provides them with a database that they can use to understand the needs of these communities.

Cinepop has three key stakeholders, the beneficiaries who do not pay for the movies, the sponsoring corporations that use the venues to promote their products or services, and the local governments that promote social issues. The events also help create an emotional connection for beneficiaries and a tailored value proposition for each stakeholder. Cinepop has clear incentives for each partner and can demonstrate to some extent measurable benefits for each of them.[2]

For example, sponsors can use the venues to brand themselves and even sell their products. A slight refinement of Cinepop's business model consists now in the addition of the Opportunity Tent, a form of mobile mall in which companies buy a three-by-three-meter space to promote products and services. More than 20,000 people per week come through the Opportunity Tent and are offered health, housing, clothing, micro-credit, consulting, and coaching services.[3]

Although viewing movies may not be perceived as a basic need or an endemic social problem, such as poverty, that must be alleviated, it is appropriate to acknowledge that Cinepop helps these families experience moments of entertainment and happiness. The events bring together family and community members and could represent a morale booster. Cinepop provides bottom-of-the pyramid customers the opportunity to enjoy the amenities that life offers.

Zylbersztejn received several awards for the success of his social venture including being named the Social Entrepreneur of the Year in 2006 by the Schwab Foundation. In 2009, he was invited to participate in the World Economic Forum's Global Agenda on the future of entertainment. Cinepop was named the most innovative company in Mexico in 2007.[4]

Cinepop has reached more than 10 million people and has an annual budget of more than 21 million dollars. It has 100% of earned income. Frilled with the success of Cinepop in Mexico, Zylbersztejn is now exploring the possibility of scaling his social venture in other countries, such as Brazil, China and India.

Discussion Questions

1 Explain Cinepop's business model.
2 Identify Cinepop's key stakeholders. What does each of these stakeholders gain from Cinepop's activities?
3 Identify the potential challenges of scaling Cinepop's in the three countries identified in the case. How can these potential challenges be addressed?
4 What other benefits do you think offering free movies provide to the beneficiaries? Explain.

References

1 Bringing movies to the masses: The Cinepop model (December 9, 2009). *http://www8.gsb.columbia.edu/chazen/publication/517*. (pp. 1–4). [Retrieved on April 11, 2016].
2 Social enterprise: Cinepop/Hormiga. *http://reports.weforum.org/social-innovation-2013/cinepop-hormiga*. [Retrieved on April 11, 2016].
3 Bringing movies to the masses: The Cinepop model (December 9, 2009). *http://www8.gsb.columbia.edu/chazen/publication/517*. (pp. 1–4). [Retrieved on April 11, 2016].
4 Ariel Zylbersztejn. *http://www.schwabfound.org/content/ariel-zylbersztejn*. [Retrieved on April 11, 2016].

Notes

1 Martin, R. L., & Osberg, S. (2007). Social entrepreneurship: The case for a definition. *Stanford Social Innovation Review, 5*(2), 28–39.
2 Kerlin, J. A. (2006). Social enterprise in the United States and Europe: Understanding and learning from the differences. *Voluntas, 17*, 247–263.
3 Stevens, R., Moray, N., & Bruneel, J. (2014). The social dimension and mission of social enterprises: Dimensions, measurement, validation, and relation. *Entrepreneurship Theory and Practice, 39*(5), 1051–1082; Newbert, S. L., & Hill, R. P. (2014). Setting the stage for paradigm development: A small-tent approach to social entrepreneurship. *Journal of Social Entrepreneurship, 5*(3), 243–269.
4 Say, J. B. (1971 [1880]). *A treatise of political economy or the production, distribution, and consumption of wealth*. Translated from the 4th edition. New York: Augustus M. Kelley.
5 Schumpeter, J. A. (1934). *The theory of economic development*. London: Oxford University Press; Schumpeter, J. A. (1942). *Capitalism, socialism, and democracy*. New York: Harper & Brothers.
6 Stevenson, H. H., & Jarillo, J. C. (1990). A paradigm of entrepreneurship: Entrepreneurial management. *Strategic Management Journal, 11*, 17–27.
7 Shane, S., & Vankataraman, S. 2000. The promise of entrepreneurship as a field of research. *Academy of Management Review, 25*(1), 217–226.
8 Timmons, J., & Spinelli, S. (2007). *New venture creation: Entrepreneurship for the 21st century*. New York: McGraw-Hill/Irwin.
9 Say, J. B. (1971 [1880]). *A treatise of political economy or the production, distribution, and consumption of wealth*. Translated from the 4th edition. New York: Augustus M. Kelley; Schumpeter, J. A. (1934). *The theory of economic development*. London: Oxford University Press; Schumpeter, J. A. (1942). *Capitalism, socialism, and democracy*. New York: Harper & Brothers.

10   Dacin, P. A., Dacin, M. T., & Matear, M. (2010). Social entrepreneurship: Why we don't need a new theory and how we move forward from here? *Academy of Management Perspectives*, 24(3), 37–57.

11   Austin, J., Stevenson, H., & Wei-Skillern, J. (2006). Social and commercial entrepreneurship: Same, different, or both? *Entrepreneurship Theory and Practice*, 30, 1–22; Short, J., Moss, T. W., & Lumpkin, G. T. (2009). Research in social entrepreneurship: Past contributions and future opportunities. *Strategic Entrepreneurship Journal*, 3, 161–194.

12   Choi, N., & Majumdar, S. (2014). Social entrepreneurship as an essentially contested concept: Opening a new avenue for systematic future research. *Journal of Business Venturing*, 29(3), 363–376.

13   Martin, R. L., & Osberg, S. (2007). Social entrepreneurship: The case for a definition. *Stanford Social Innovation Review*, 5(2), 28–39.

14   Santos, F. M. (2012). A positive theory of social entrepreneurship. *Journal of Business Ethics*, 111(3), 335–351.

15   Austin, J., Stevenson, H., & Wei-Skillern, J. (2006). Social and commercial entrepreneurship: Same, different, or both? *Entrepreneurship Theory and Practice*, 30, 1–22.

16   Austin, J., Stevenson, H., & Wei–Skillern, J. (2006). Social and commercial entrepreneurship: Same, different, or both? *Entrepreneurship Theory and Practice*, 30, 1–22.

17   Mort, S., Weerawardena, J., & Carnegie, K. (2003). Social entrepreneurship: Toward conceptualization. *International Journal of Non-profit and Voluntary Sector Marketing*, 8(1), 76–88.

18   Mair, J., & Marti, I. (2006). Social entrepreneurship research: A source of explanation, prediction, and delight. *Journal of World Business*, 41(1), 36–44, at p. 37.

19   Seelos, C., & Mair, J. (2005). Social entrepreneurship: Creating new business models to serve the poor. *Business Horizons*, 48, 241–246.

20   Porter, M. E., & Kramer, M. R. (1999). Philanthropy's new agenda. *Harvard Business Review*, 77(6), 121–131.

21   Thompson, J. (2002). The world of the social entrepreneur. *International Journal of Public Sector Management*, 15(5), 412–431; Thompson, J., Alvy, G., & Lees, A. (2000). Social entrepreneurship: A new look at the people and the potential. *Management Decision*, 38(5), 328–338.

22   Dees, J. G. (1998). Enterprising nonprofits. *Harvard Business Review*, January–February, 55–67.

23   Dees, J. G., & Anderson, B. B. (2003). Sector blending: Blurring the lines between profit and for–profit. *Society* (Social Sciences and Modern Society), 40(4), 16–27.

24   Hockerts, K. (2006). Entrepreneurial opportunity in social purpose business ventures. In J. Mair, J. Robinson, & K. Hockerts (Eds.), *Social Entrepreneurship* (pp. 142–154). New York: Palgrave Macmillan.

25   Battilana, J., Sengul, M., Pache, A., & Model, J. (2015). Harnessing productive tensions in hybrid organizations: The case of work integration social enterprises. *Academy of Management Journal*, 58(6), 1658–1685; Battilana, J., & Lee, M. (2014). Advancing research on hybrid organizing: Insights from the study of social enterprises. *Academy of Management Annals*, 8(1), 397–441; Pache, A. C., & Santos, F. (2012). Inside the hyrbid organization: Selective coupling as a response to conflicting institutional logics. *Academy of Management Journal*, 56(4), 972–1001; Battilana, J., & Borado, S. (2010). Building sustainable hybrid organizations: The case of commercial microfinance organizations. *Academy of Management Journal*, 53(6), 1419–1440.

26   Battilana, J., & Lee, M. (2014). Advancing research on hybrid organizing: Insights from the study of social enterprises. *Academy of Management Annals*, 8(1), 397–441.

27   Battilana, J., & Lee, M. (2014). Advancing research on hybrid organizing: Insights from the study of social enterprises. *Academy of Management Annals*, 8(1), 397–441.

28   Austin, J. (2006). Three avenues for social entrepreneurship research. In J. Mair, J. Robinson, & K. Hockerts (Eds.), *Social Entrepreneurship* (pp. 22–33). New York: Palgrave Macmillan; Wei-Skillern, J., Austin, J. E., Leonard, H., & Stevenson, H. (2007). *Entrepreneurship in the social sector*. Thousand Oaks, CA: Sage.

29 Gras, D., & Mendoza-Abarca, K. I. (2014). Risky business? The survival implications of exploiting commercial opportunity by nonprofits. *Journal of Business Venturing*, 29(3), 392–404.

30 Sanders, M. L. (2015). Being nonprofit-like in a market economy: Understanding the mission–market tension in nonprofit organizing. *Nonprofit and Voluntary Sector Quarterly*, 44(2), 205–222; Battilana, J., & Lee, M. (2014). Advancing research on hybrid organizing: Insights from the study of social enterprises. *Academy of Management Annals*, 8(1), 397–441; Stevens, R., Moray, N., & Bruneel, J. (2014). The social dimension and mission of social enterprises: Dimensions, measurement, validation, and relation. *Entrepreneurship Theory and Practice*, 39(5), 1051–1082; Battilana, J., & Borado, S. (2010). Building sustainable hybrid organizations: The case of commercial microfinance organizations. *Academy of Management Journal*, 53(6), 1419–1440.

31 Dees, J. D. (1998). *The meaning of social entrepreneurship*. Palo Alto, CA: Graduate School of Business.

32 Austin, J. E., Leonard, H. B., Refico, E., & Wei-Skillern, J. (2006). Social entrepreneurship: It's for corporations, too. In A. Nicholls (Ed.), *Social entrepreneurship: New models of sustainable social change* (pp. 169–180, at p. 170). Oxford: Oxford University Press.

33 Austin, J. E., & Refico, E. (2009). Corporate social entrepreneurship. *Harvard Business School Working Paper* 09–101.

34 Covin, J. G., & Miles, M. P. (1999). Corporate entrepreneurship and the pursuit of competitive advantage. *Entrepreneurship Theory and Practice*, 23(3), 47–63, at p. 48.

35 Austin, J. E., & Ravis, C. (2002). Starbucks and conservation international. *Harvard Business School Case* 303–055. Boston: HBS Division of Research.

36 Austin, J. E., & Refico, E. (2009). Corporate social entrepreneurship. *Harvard Business School Working Paper* 09–101.

37 Friedman, M. (1970). The social responsibility of business is to increase its profits. *New York Times Magazine*, September 13.

38 Grohs, S., Schneiders, K., & Heinze, R. G. (2015). Social entrepreneurship versus intrapreneurship in the German social welfare state: A study of old-age care and youth welfare services. *Nonprofit and Voluntary Sector Quarterly*, 44(1), 163–180.

39 Porter, M. Why business can be good at solving social problems. www.youtube.com/watch?v=0iIh5YYDR2o.

40 Sandel, M. (2012). *What money can't buy?* New York: Farrar, Straus, & Giroux; Sandel, M. What money can't buy. The moral limits of markets. www.youtube.com/watch?v=GvDpYHyBlgc.

41 Debate: The Michael (Porter) v. Michael (Sandel) business enlightenment roadshow. *www.youtube.com/watch?v=2yzzt9XXIO8.*

42 Stevens, R., Moray, N., & Bruneel, J. (2014). The social dimension and mission of social enterprises: Dimensions, measurement, validation, and relation. *Entrepreneurship Theory and Practice*, 39(5), 1051–1082.

43 Dees, J. D. (1998). *The meaning of social entrepreneurship*. Palo Alto, CA: Graduate School of Business.

44 Seelos, C., & Mair, J. (2005). Social entrepreneurship: Creating new business models to serve the poor. *Business Horizons*, 48, 241–246.

45 Stevens, R., Moray, N., & Bruneel, J. (2014). The social dimension and mission of social enterprises: Dimensions, measurement, validation, and relation. *Entrepreneurship Theory and Practice*, 39(5), 1051–1082; Austin, J., Stevenson, H., & Wei-Skillern, J. (2006). Social and commercial entrepreneurship: Same, different, or both? *Entrepreneurship Theory and Practice*, 30, 1–22.

46 *Economist, The.* (2006). The rise of the social entrepreneur. February 25, 11–13, at p. 12.

47 Austin, J., Stevenson, H., & Wei-Skillern, J. (2006). Social and commercial entrepreneurship: Same, different, or both? *Entrepreneurship Theory and Practice*, 30, 1–22.

48 Gras, D., & Mendoza-Abarca, K. I. (2014). Risky business? The survival implications of exploiting commercial opportunity by nonprofits. *Journal of Business Venturing*, 29(3), 392–404;

Defourny, J., & Nyssens, M. (2010). Social enterprise in Europe: At the cross-roads of market, public policies and third sector. *Policy and Society*, 29(3), 231–242.

49   Spear, R., & Bidet, E. (2005). Social enterprise for work integration in 12 European countries: A descriptive analysis. *Annals of Public and Cooperative Economics*, 26(2), 195–231.

50   Salamon, L. M., Solokowski, S. W., & List, R. (2004). *Global civil society*. Baltimore, MD: Center for Civil Society Studies, Institute for Policy Studies, Johns Hopkins University.

51   Kerlin, J. A. (2006). Social enterprise in the United States and Europe: Understanding and learning from the differences. *Voluntas*, 17, 247–263.

52   Lanteri, A. (2015). The creation of social enterprises: Some lessons from Lebanon. *Journal of Social Entrepreneurship*, 6(1), 42–69; Khieng, S., & Dahles, H. (2015). Commercialization in the Non-profit sector: The emergence of social enterprise in Cambodia. *Journal of Social Entrepreneurship*, 6(2), 218–243; Rivera-Santos, M., Holt, D., Littlewood, D., & Kolk, A. (2015). Social entrepreneurship in sub-Saharan Africa. *Academy of Management Perspectives*, 29(1), 72–91; Idris, A., & Hati, R. H. (2013). Social entrepreneurship in Indonesia: Lessons from the past. *Journal of Social Entrepreneurship*, 4(3), 277–301.

53   Idris, A., & Hati, R. H. (2013). Social entrepreneurship in Indonesia: Lessons from the past. *Journal of Social Entrepreneurship*, 4(3), 277–301.

54   Rivera-Santos, M., Holt, D., Littlewood, D., & Kolk, A. (2015). Social entrepreneurship in sub-Saharan Africa. *Academy of Management Perspectives*, 29(1), 72–91.

55   Peredo, A. M., & Chrisman, J. J. (2006). Toward a theory of community-based enterprise. *Academy of Management Review*, 31(2), 309–328.

56   Montgomery, A. W., Dacin, P. A., & Dacin, M. T. (2012). Collective social entrepreneurship: A collaboratively shaping social good. *Journal of Business Ethics*, 111(3), 375–388.

57   Khieng, S., & Dahles, H. (2015). Commercialization in the non-profit sector: The emergence of social enterprise in Cambodia. *Journal of Social Entrepreneurship*, 6(2), 218–243.

58   Borzaga, C., & Spear, R. (2004). *Trends and challenges for co-operatives and social enterprises in developed and transition countries*. Trento: Fondazione Cariplo.

59   Trivedi, C., & Stokols, D. (2011). Social enterprises and corporate enterprises: Fundamental differences and defining features. *Journal of Social Entrepreneurship*, 20(1), 1–32.

60   Lepoutre, J., Justo, R., Terjesen, S., & Bosma, N. (2013). Designing a global standardized methodology for measuring social entrepreneurship activity: The global entrepreneurship monitor social entrepreneurship study. *Small Business Economics*, 40, 693–714.

61   Lepoutre, J., Justo, R., Terjesen, S., & Bosma, N. (2013). Designing a global standardized methodology for measuring social entrepreneurship activity: The global entrepreneurship monitor social entrepreneurship study. *Small Business Economics*, 40, 693–714.

62   Ko, W. W., & Liu, G. (2015). Understanding the process of knowledge spillovers: Learning to become social enterprises. *Strategic Entrepreneurship Journal*, 9(3), 263–285.

63   *Economist, The*. (2005). Hale and healthy. April 14, 69–70.

64   Overholt, A. (2003). Health and the profit motive. *Fast Company*, 67, 38.

Chapter 2

Social Entrepreneurs
Mindset, Characteristics, and Competencies

Learning Objectives

1 Discuss the entrepreneurial mindset and its relevance to social entrepreneurship.
2 Discuss the nature of social entrepreneurs.
3 Identify the individual characteristics of social entrepreneurs.

This chapter focuses on social entrepreneurs as individuals who are eager to bring social change in their respective communities. It describes the mindset of social entrepreneurs, their nature, and their characteristics. The chapter is divided into three sections. The first section discusses the social entrepreneur's mindset. The second presents and discusses a typology of social entrepreneurs. The third identifies individual characteristics that might influence the likelihood of someone becoming a social entrepreneur.

I Understanding the Entrepreneurial Mindset

This section describes the entrepreneurial mindset and explores its relevance for social entrepreneurship. The concept of entrepreneurial mindset has been used to describe how commercial entrepreneurs think and act compared to managers and other non-entrepreneurs. However, it has not focused on social entrepreneurship and the extent to which it could be used to describe the inner thinking of social entrepreneurs. A mindset is a particular way of seeing the world and things around us. In entrepreneurship, a mindset is a particular way of looking at opportunities and how business should (or should not) be conducted.

McGrath and MacMillan define the entrepreneurial mindset as a way of thinking about business that captures the benefits of uncertainty and contend that the entrepreneurial mindset takes hold when the following five characteristics are displayed:

- passionate pursuit of opportunities;
- pursuit of opportunities with discipline;
- pursuit of only the best opportunities;
- a focus on adaptive execution; and
- engagement with the energies of everyone.[1]

Other entrepreneurship scholars have attempted to operationalize the concept of the entrepreneurial mindset by identifying a set of values and characteristics that set entrepreneurs apart.[2] In such characterizations, the entrepreneurial mindset also includes the ability to adapt one's thinking process to a changing context and task demands.[3] An entrepreneurial mindset is both an individualistic and a collective phenomenon to the extent that it is important for individual entrepreneurs as well as for managers and employees in established firms to think and act entrepreneurially.[4]

Carol Dweck, a psychologist, identifies two types of mindset: a *fixed* mindset and a *growth* mindset. A fixed mindset refers to a view that one's talents and abilities comprise a set of traits. A growth mindset refers to a view that one's abilities can be developed through effort, dedication, and hard work.[5] It is possible that one can be trained to move from a fixed mindset to a growth mindset. The importance of the growth mindset is that it helps people believe that they can change their environment and improve their own abilities by taking action. This orientation toward a growth mindset led Ireland and colleagues to define the entrepreneurial mindset as a growth-oriented perspective through which individuals promote flexibility, creativity, continuous innovation, and renewal.[6] This indicates that the entrepreneurial mindset can be developed and is not necessarily an innate faculty that one possesses.

The literature on the entrepreneurial mindset could lead to the identification of four key elements:

- entrepreneurial thoughts;
- entrepreneurial choices;
- entrepreneurial actions; and
- entrepreneurial outcomes.

Entrepreneurial thoughts invoke the cognitive processes that lead to the discovery or creation of entrepreneurial opportunities. This element addresses such questions as "How do entrepreneurs think? How are they able to translate situations into viable opportunities?" (The creation or discovery of social entrepreneurial opportunities is discussed in Chapter 5.) As discussed in Chapter 1, entrepreneurship is not limited to the creation of new ventures. Therefore, the entrepreneurial mindset could guide employee behavior in corporations. In this regard, an entrepreneurial mindset could help employees be more innovative and add value to their organization. It could also lead them to spearhead corporate social entrepreneurial initiatives.

The second element, choice, implies that the entrepreneur has to decide which opportunities to pursue and which ones to disregard or delay. The ability to pursue the "right" opportunities is one of the characteristics of effective entrepreneurs. The third element relates to the entrepreneur's actions. Indeed, the entrepreneur has to act on the opportunities. His or her actions would lead to the creation of a new venture that adds economic or social value, thereby leading to the fourth element—outcomes—which could include the number of successful new ventures, the economic or social value added, or the contribution to economic growth. Although this characterization of the entrepreneurial mindset was discussed with respect to commercial entrepreneurship, it could easily apply to social entrepreneurship, too. For example, social entrepreneurs may look at social problems as opportunities to introduce social change.

2   Who Is a Social Entrepreneur?

Social entrepreneurs focus on solving social problems.[7] Dees (who unfortunately passed away on December 20, 2014) was one of the earliest scholars in social entrepreneurship and contended that social entrepreneurs play the role of change agents in the social sector by:

- adopting a mission to create and sustain social value (not just private value);
- recognizing and relentlessly pursuing new opportunities to serve that mission;
- engaging in a process of continuous innovation, adaptation, and learning;
- acting boldly without being limited by current resources; and
- exhibiting heightened accountability to the constituencies served and the outcomes created.[8]

The main question, then, is whether social entrepreneurs are different from other types of entrepreneurs, especially commercial entrepreneurs. Social entrepreneurs are considered as people with new ideas to address major problems who are relentless in the pursuit of their vision. They simply refuse to take "no" for an answer and will not give up until they have spread their ideas as far as they possibly can.[9] They tend to display the following characteristics:

- passion;
- vision for change;
- ethical fiber;
- creativity;
- caring and compassion; and
- morality.

It is worth mentioning that these characteristics are not so different from those found in studies on commercial entrepreneurs. Indeed, many of the attributes and talents of social and business entrepreneurs are similar: both are innovative and possess high amounts of energy, tenacity, and resilience; and both are driven by a vision to which they remain passionately committed.[10] Both types of entrepreneurs recognize when a part of society is stuck and they provide new ways to free it.[11] Many traits and behaviors of successful social entrepreneurs mirror those of business entrepreneurs. Their leadership and personal qualities are quite similar.[12] The three key attributes of social entrepreneurs—vision, leadership, and determination—also characterize business entrepreneurs.[13] Perhaps social entrepreneurs tend to communicate their vision in more moral terms, driven by a desire for social justice.[14] A social entrepreneur is a social innovator who adds value to people's lives by pursuing a social mission, using the processes, tools, and techniques of business entrepreneurship.[15] The social entrepreneur is considered as a moral agent, whereas the commercial entrepreneur is perceived as an economic agent.[16] Social entrepreneurs are one species of the genus entrepreneur; they are entrepreneurs with social missions.[17]

Sharir and Lerner studied the parallel between social and commercial entrepreneurs and found that, like commercial entrepreneurs, social entrepreneurs were driven by a combination of motives, including the desire for self-fulfillment, occupational independence, and opportunities for creativity. However, they also had other motives, including personal rehabilitation, a desire to find solutions for individual distress, and a sense of obligation to their community or affiliation.[18]

Social entrepreneurs are different from philanthropists because they create and run social ventures, whereas philanthropists provide resources to help social ventures accomplish their missions, but they are not themselves involved in their management. Philanthropy is an unconditional transfer of cash or other assets to an entity or a settlement or cancellation of its liabilities in a voluntary, nonreciprocal transfer by another entity acting other than as an owner.[19] For example, Warren Buffett, the legendary investor who donated 90 percent of his fortune to the Bill and Melissa Gates Foundation in 2006, is an example of a philanthropist rather than a social entrepreneur. By contrast, Muhammad Yunus, who pioneered microcredit through the Grameen Bank, and Martin Burt of the Fundacion Paraguaya, which is dedicated to fighting poverty in Paraguay through education, small-scale enterprise, and health, are examples of social entrepreneurs. It is worth acknowledging that social entrepreneurs might not be a homogeneous group. For example, individuals who start social movements to address workplace issues, such as sweatshops, may be considered as social entrepreneurs. Likewise, social entrepreneurs may be found in civil society, government agencies, and nonprofit organizations. How, then, are social entrepreneurs identified? The answer is by their goals.

Although a business entrepreneur's behavior may be self-directed, it may also have positive effects on others. There are countless examples of successful business entrepreneurs who donate financial resources to address social problems. For example, Mark Zuckerberg, the founder of Facebook, donated $100 million to the State of New Jersey to support its public schools. Likewise, the creation of a social venture may carry some personal benefit for the social entrepreneur under certain conditions. The example of the most famous social entrepreneur, Muhammad Yunus, is illustrative in this regard. His social venture, the Grameen Bank, has not only helped to address poverty issues in Bangladesh but has made Yunus himself world famous and gained him the 2006 Nobel Peace Prize. Fame or winning a Nobel Prize, however, was not the ultimate motive for commencing this social venture. Rather, they are by-products of the social venture's success. Zahra and colleagues have proposed a typology of social entrepreneurs, including social bricoleurs, social constructionists, and social engineers. Table 2.1 compares the three types. Social bricoleurs focus on discovering and addressing small-scale local social needs. Social constructionists exploit opportunities and market failures. They do so by attempting to satisfy needs that have not been met by governments or the markets. Finally, social engineers recognize systemic problems within existing social structures and address them by introducing revolutionary change.[20]

Table 2.1 Typology of social entrepreneurs[21]

Type	Social bricoleurs	Social constructionists	Social engineers
Theoretical inspiration	Hayek	Kirzner	Schumpeter
What do they do?	Perceive and act upon opportunities to address local social needs. They are motivated and have the expertise and resources to address such needs.	Build and operate alternative structures to provide goods and services, addressing social needs that governments, agencies, and businesses cannot.	Create newer, more effective social systems designed to replace existing ones when they are ill-suited to address significant social needs.
Scale, scope, and timing	Small scale, local in scope— often episodic in nature.	Small to large scale, local to international in scope, designed to be institutionalized to address ongoing social needs.	Very large scale— that is, national to international—in scope and seek to build lasting structures that will challenge existing order.

Type	Social bricoleurs	Social constructionists	Social engineers
Why are they necessary?	Knowledge about social needs and the abilities to address them are widely scattered. Many social needs are indiscernible, easily misunderstood from afar, requiring local agents to detect and address them.	Laws, regulation, political acceptability, inefficiencies, and/or lack of will prevent existing governmental and business organizations from addressing many important social needs effectively.	Some social needs are not amenable to amelioration within existing social structures. Entrenched incumbents can thwart actions to address social needs that undermine their own interests and source of power.
Social significance	Collectively, their actions help maintain social harmony in the face of social problems.	They mend the social fabric where it is torn, address acute social needs within existing broader social structures, and help maintain social harmony.	They seek to rip apart existing social structures and replace them with new ones. They represent an important force for social change in the face of entrenched incumbents.
Effect on social equilibrium	Atomistic actions by local social entrepreneurs move closer to a theoretical "social equilibrium."	Addressing gaps in the provision of socially significant goods and services creates new "social equilibriums."	Fractures existing social equilibrium and seeks to replace it with a more socially efficient one.
Source of discretion	Being on the spot with the skills to address local problems not on others' "radars." Local scope means they have limited resource requirements and are fairly autonomous. Small scale and local scope allow for quick response times.	They address needs left unaddressed and have limited/no competition. They may even be welcomed and seen as a "release valve," preventing negative publicity/social problems that may adversely affect existing governmental and business organizations.	Popular support to the extent that existing social structures and incumbents are incapable of addressing important social needs.
Limits to discretion	Not much aside from local laws and regulations. However, the limited resources and expertise they possess limit their ability to address other needs or expand geographically.	Need to acquire financial and human resources necessary to fulfill mission and institutionalize as a going concern. Funder demands oversight. Professional volunteers and employees are needed to operate organization.	Seen as fundamentally illegitimate by established parties that see them as a threat, which brings scrutiny and attempts to undermine the ability of the social engineers to bring about change. The perceived illegitimacy will inhibit the ability to raise financial and human resources from traditional sources. As a consequence, they may become captive of the parties that supply much-needed resources.

3 Characteristics of Social Entrepreneurs

Without ignoring Gartner's advice that asking "who is an entrepreneur is the wrong question" (see below), it is worth acknowledging that current research evidence suggests that, to some extent, personality traits affect entrepreneurial intentions. That is not to say that entrepreneurs are born with specific traits that make them become who they are and that those who do not have these traits cannot become entrepreneurs. The reality is more complex than one could imagine. Recent research in entrepreneurship shows that personality traits affect entrepreneurial intentions.[22] For example, a study on the impact of creative personalities on new venture creation found that creative people are more likely than others to identify business opportunities and start businesses.[23] Another study focusing on the role of the 'Big Five' personality model on social venture creation found that personality dimensions, such as agreeableness, openness to experience, and conscientiousness, have a positive influence on social entrepreneurship dimensions. Of these, agreeableness seems to have a particularly positive influence on social vision, social innovation, sustainability, social networking, and financial returns.[24]

Thus, this section explores some of the individual characteristics associated to venture formation. In the context of social entrepreneurship, are there characteristics that set social entrepreneurs apart from non-social entrepreneurs? To address this question, this section relies on the extant literature on the role of individual characteristics in entrepreneurship. The individual characteristics that are discussed below include:

- autonomy or independence;
- the need for achievement;
- risk propensity;
- self-efficacy;
- goal setting and drive;
- passion; and
- alertness.

These characteristics were selected because most studies in entrepreneurship tend to agree on their influence on entrepreneurial activity. To the extent that there are similarities between commercial and social entrepreneurship, understanding the impact of these characteristics could inform our understanding of who is likely to become a social entrepreneur.

3.1 Autonomy/Independence and Social Entrepreneurship

Independence or autonomy entails the ability to take responsibility to use one's own judgment as opposed to blindly following the assertions of others. Entrepreneurs take responsibility for pursuing an opportunity that did not exist before. In a study on the motivation of women entrepreneurs conducted in the United States, it was found that independence was an important factor motivating women to start their own ventures;[25] and several other studies have supported the view that the desire to be one's own boss is one of the main drivers of entrepreneurial activity.[26]

Autonomy is embedded in the need for power, which refers to the desire to be in charge, to take control.[27] Can this need for power be a driver of social entrepreneurship? Researchers have not studied the impact of this need on the motivation to become a social entrepreneur. However, to the extent that any entrepreneurial activity requires that one takes personal initiative, it is understandable that the desire to be in charge is an important motivator of entrepreneurial behavior, including social entrepreneurial behavior. The desire for autonomy has been identified as one of the individual characteristics that both social and commercial entrepreneurs have in common, along with other characteristics, such as the tendency to take risks and self-efficacy.[28] McClelland identifies two types of power: *personalized* power and *socialized* power.[29] The former refers to power used for personal aggrandizement and gain, whereas the latter refers to power used to advance a cause that benefits the group or the community. The definition of social entrepreneurship provided in Chapter 1 puts a particular emphasis on addressing social needs or taking action that benefits others. In this regard, one could speculate that socialized power could be a better predictor of social entrepreneurial behavior than personalized power. This is not to say that some social entrepreneurs cannot be motivated by individualized power.

3.2 Need for Achievement and Social Entrepreneurship

In his book *The Achieving Society*, David McClelland identifies the need for achievement as one of the main drivers of entrepreneurship and prosperity of societies and defines it as the desire to attain an inner feeling of personal accomplishment, which is satisfied primarily by an intrinsic sense of success and excellence rather than extrinsic rewards.[30] The achievement motive involves undertaking difficult rather than easy tasks, accepting personal rather than shared responsibility for performance and its outcomes, and coping with uncertainty of outcomes. In entrepreneurship, this translates into certain behaviors, such as taking calculated risks, solving problems rather than relying on conventional solutions, and satisfying the need for success rather than avoiding failure.[31] It also pushes entrepreneurs to persist in the face of difficulties.[32]

McClelland later contended that the need for achievement is culturally acquired and is a key psychological attribute of entrepreneurs.[33] Organizational psychologists and organizational behavior and entrepreneurship scholars have studied the impact of the need for achievement on individual behaviors. They have found that the need for achievement explains the willingness to strive for success and the attainment of lofty goals. Thus, the need for achievement could explain certain people's tendency to engage in entrepreneurial activities. After all, entrepreneurs are required to *think big* and, indeed, some entrepreneurs do just that. Bill Gates and the late Steve Jobs, who between them revolutionized the computer industry, are fine examples of entrepreneurs who thought big.

In a longitudinal study, McClelland found that 83 percent of entrepreneurs in business scored high in needing achievement as college sophomores, whereas 79 percent of nonentrepreneurs scored low.[34] Studies conducted in different cultures have also indicated a positive link between the need for achievement and entrepreneurship. For example, two studies show that Chinese people who score high on the need for achievement tend to be motivated to start their own businesses.[35] Similar results were found in Singapore, where male entrepreneurs reported greater need for achievement when compared to female employees (although both samples reported above-average scores when measured for need for achievement).[36] These studies are consistent with those conducted in the United States and other Western countries, which suggests that the link between need for achievement and entrepreneurial activity is universal.

The results of two meta-analyses have supported the impact of need for achievement on entrepreneurship. The first meta-analysis on achievement motivation difference between entrepreneurs and managers found that the former exhibited higher achievement motivation than the latter. The difference was even greater when the analysis was restricted to venture founders and managers.[37] The second meta-analysis supported McClelland's contention of a positive relationship between achievement motivation and performance in an entrepreneurial role.[38] Although the need for achievement influences entrepreneurial behavior, the percentage of variance explained was relatively small, varying from 4–6 percent.

The need for achievement might influence social venture creation. One study that aimed to determine the motivation of social entrepreneurs found that they rated contribution to the community as their primary motive, along with flexibility and achievement, and some desire to emulate role models, while they showed minimum concern for material benefits and status.[39] The desire to make a difference and accomplish something special to help others could lead a social entrepreneur to start and grow a social venture. To the extent that individuals with a high need for achievement would have moderate propensities to take risks, there could be a relationship between the need for achievement and risk propensity.

3.3   Risk Propensity and Social Entrepreneurship

Risk-taking appears to be one of the most distinctive features of entrepreneurial behavior, since creating new ventures is by definition a risky business.[40] Thus, to pursue an entrepreneurial venture, a person must be willing to take risks or at least tolerate some type of risk. Risk is often viewed in classical economics as a function of the variation in the distribution of possible outcomes, the associated outcomes, likelihoods, and their subjective values.[41] The tendency to take risks is often referred to as "risk propensity." Two types of literature have dominated research on the concepts of risk and risk propensity. The first, drawn from classical economics, assumes that entrepreneurs have a high risk propensity.[42] The second is grounded in classical motivation theory, where the focus is on achievement motivation.[43] The latter assumes that both entrepreneurs and managers score high on the need for achievement; therefore, there should be little or no difference in the risk propensity that they display. Risk propensity is interesting to study in social entrepreneurship because the entrepreneurial process involves a dose of risk and uncertainty. Entrepreneurship scholars define risk propensity as the ability to deal with uncertainties and the degree of readiness to bear risk, and consider it as a motivational force that explains the tendency to engage in entrepreneurial activities.[44]

In fact, in deciding to become an entrepreneur, an individual risks financial well-being, career advancement, family relations, and psychological health.[45] A meta-analysis comparing the risk propensity of entrepreneurs and managers found a significant difference between the two. Entrepreneurs had a higher risk propensity than managers. The authors concluded that their results were influenced by the definition of entrepreneur that was used in the various studies. In this meta-analysis, the samples of entrepreneurs were divided between *growth-oriented* entrepreneurs and *income-oriented* entrepreneurs. The former were more focused on growing their business ventures, whereas the latter were more concerned about generating income for themselves and their families. The authors found that growth-oriented entrepreneurs had a higher risk propensity compared to income-oriented entrepreneurs.[46] An empirical study that was intended to measure the effects of risk propensity on entrepreneurial activity was conducted on a sample of 71 Bangladeshi immigrant entrepreneurs and 62 non-entrepreneurs living in the Greater London area. The key finding of this study was that Bangladeshi immigrant entrepreneurs displayed higher scores for risk propensity, need for achievement, and internal locus of control compared to non-entrepreneurs.[47]

Entrepreneurship scholars have also sought to determine whether entrepreneurs differ from managers in regard to risk propensity. The findings have been mixed: some studies found a difference between managers and entrepreneurs, whereas others did not. Two reasons could probably explain the lack of conclusive differences between managers and entrepreneurs. First, to some extent, the activities of managers may be closely related to what entrepreneurs do. Managers may be engaged in activities that require innovativeness, risk-taking, and uncertainty. These aspects are all common in the tasks of the entrepreneur. Second, entrepreneurs may not consider their own actions as risky, because they accept risk as a given and focus on controlling the outcomes at any given level of risk, framing their problem spaces with personal values, and assuming greater personal responsibility for the outcomes.[48] In this regard, risk propensity may be confounded with self-efficacy.

Can risk propensity influence the creation of social ventures? What types of risks do social entrepreneurs take? Although the literature on social entrepreneurship has yet to discuss the risk propensity of social entrepreneurs, knowledge already gleaned from commercial entrepreneurship could shed light on the impact of risk propensity on social venture creation. Despite the fact that the findings on the impact of risk propensity on business venture creation are sometimes inconsistent, one trend seems to emerge: the risk propensity of entrepreneurs tends to be greater than that of non-entrepreneurs. To the extent that the creation of any type of venture, commercial or social, entails some type of risk, one could conclude that risk propensity could positively influence the creation of social ventures. Social entrepreneurs risk income, reputation, and psychological well-being when they start their social ventures. The failure of a social venture could undermine the reputation and psychological well-being of a social entrepreneur. Moreover, engaging in social entrepreneurial activity, which does not necessarily provide financial rewards, could lead to an opportunity cost: the social entrepreneur could have reaped more financial rewards if he/she had started a for-profit business rather than a social venture.

3.4 Self-efficacy and Social Entrepreneurship

Self-efficacy refers to the belief in one's ability to muster and implement the necessary personal resources, skills, and competencies to attain a certain level of achievement on a given task.[49] Entrepreneurship scholars have used the construct of entrepreneurial self-efficacy (ESE) to account for the belief entrepreneurs have in their capabilities to start and grow their own ventures. Entrepreneurial self-efficacy refers to the strength of a person's belief that he/she is capable of successfully performing the various roles and tasks of entrepreneurship.[50] This definition could be extended to social entrepreneurship, where self-efficacy could be defined as the belief an individual has that he/she possesses the skills and competencies required to launch and manage a social venture successfully. Self-efficacy has been shown to be a robust predictor of an individual's performance in a task, and it helps to explain why people of equal ability can perform differently.[51] It is based on individuals' self-perceptions of their skills and abilities, and people are motivated by perceived self-efficacy, rather than by objective ability, and their perceptions affect both their affective states and their behaviors.[52]

Research on the impact of entrepreneurial self-efficacy on entrepreneurial activity found that self-efficacy influences entrepreneurial intentions. Individuals with higher entrepreneurial self-efficacy had higher entrepreneurial intentions.[53] Entrepreneurs who display high self-efficacy are likely to exert more effort for a greater length of time, persist through setbacks, and develop better plans and strategies for the task than those who do not. When entrepreneurs are confident in their abilities to perform the tasks necessary to start and run a new venture, they are more likely to attempt those tasks and continue to succeed.[54] Entrepreneurs with high levels of self-efficacy will also take negative feedback in a more positive manner and use that feedback to improve their performance.[55]

Self-efficacy can positively influence social entrepreneurial activity to the extent that individuals who believe that they can successfully perform the functions involved in the creation and management of social enterprises would be likely to start such ventures. In fact, people can be trained to develop social entrepreneurial self-efficacy. An educational experiment designed to increase social entrepreneurial self-efficacy has indicated that as students participate in successful projects that require initiative, provide opportunities to implement solutions, and have observable social impacts, their identification with the social entrepreneurial community increases and they start to develop social entrepreneurial self-efficacy.[56]

3.5   Goal Setting, Drive, and Social Entrepreneurship

According to Kurt Lewin, goal-directed motivation has the following four features:

- the organism desires some change in its experience;
- a force of some magnitude exists, drawing the organism toward the goal;
- if a barrier prevents direct access to the goal, alternative routes will be sought; and
- the force disappears when the goal is reached.[57]

Addressing a social issue is the ultimate goal of the social entrepreneur. An ultimate goal is an end in itself and not just an intermediate means for reaching some other goal.[58] Goals are mental representations of what the future could be, enabling individuals, such as entrepreneurs, not to give up.[59] Goal-setting theory, developed by Edwin Locke, proposes that specific and challenging goals lead to higher performance than easy or vague goals. Goals provide direction and clarity to entrepreneurial efforts and represent self-regulated processes.[60] In management and entrepreneurship, goals are also related to vision. A vision is a projected mental image of what a leader or an entrepreneur intends to achieve and represents a distant general goal. This distant goal is motivational to the extent that the individual will strive to accomplish it.

A positive relationship between vision and performance has been found by several entrepreneurship and management scholars.[61] Entrepreneurs have visions of the companies that they want to build and these visions include images of growing their businesses, fame, and personal wealth. In social entrepreneurship, goals and/or visions may be related to the social venture's impact on the beneficiaries and/or the community.

The effort displayed to accomplish a goal is also known as *drive*, which refers to the willingness to invest effort, both the effort of thinking and the effort involved in bringing one's ideas into reality.[62] There are generally four aspects of drive:

* ambition;
* goals;
* energy; and
* persistence.

Ambition influences the degree to which entrepreneurs seek to create something great, important, and significant when they pursue opportunities. The nature of the entrepreneurial ambition may include making money or the desire to create something new, from conception to actuality.[63] Goals are important because they direct entrepreneurs' actions and channel their energy. Achieving high goals requires enormous energy and stamina. When goal-directed energy is sustained over time, it is called persistence or tenacity.[64] This is a key element of the entrepreneurial process. It is also related to entrepreneurial drive. Social entrepreneurs must have the drive to engage in entrepreneurial activities that focus on solving social problems. Without drive, they cannot sustain such endeavors.

3.6   Passion and Social Entrepreneurship

Passion is a key driver of entrepreneurial action.[65] Anecdotal evidence and testimonies from several successful entrepreneurs, such as Bill Gates, Michael Dell, the late Steve Jobs, and many others, indicate that passion and entrepreneurial drive are the cornerstones of entrepreneurial success. Scholars view passion as the main ingredient of entrepreneurship. For example, Cardon and colleagues note that "entrepreneurship can be thought of as a tale of passion"[66] and Smilor contends that "passion is perhaps the most observed phenomenon of the entrepreneurial process."[67] An interesting question, however, is to identify the object of entrepreneurial passion. In other words, what are entrepreneurs passionate about? In the case of social entrepreneurship, are social entrepreneurs passionate about starting and growing their social ventures or the social impact of their social ventures, which is to make a difference in the lives of the beneficiaries?

Some authors equate passion with love—love of the activity performed. For example, Shane and colleagues note that egoistic passion is a central motive of entrepreneurial behavior because the true or rational egoist passionately loves the work—the process of building an organization and making it profitable.[68] Passion is a strong inclination toward an activity that people like, that they find important, and in which they invest time and energy.[69] When entrepreneurs are passionate about tasks and activities, they enjoy doing them and experience self-identity reinforcement from doing them regardless of the ultimate outcome or success of that task engagement.[70] As studied by social psychologists, passion is a motivational construct that is task-specific. It is a psychological state characterized by intense positive emotional arousal, internal drive, and full engagement with personally meaningful work activities.[71]

Three themes emerge from the study of entrepreneurial passion:

* the content of passion is an intense positive emotion;
* the empirical referents or objects of passion usually involve venture-related opportunities, tasks, or activities; and
* passion has a motivational effect that stimulates entrepreneurs to overcome obstacles and remain engaged.[72]

The focus here is on functional passion as opposed to dysfunctional passion, which can interfere with entrepreneurial effectiveness. Entrepreneurial passion is a complex pattern of psychological, brain, and bodily responses activated and maintained by an entrepreneur's passion that, when regulated, aid in motivating coherent and coordinated goal pursuit.[73] Passion contributes to an entrepreneur's ability to adapt to changing and challenging environments and fosters creativity and recognition of new patterns that are critical in opportunity exploration and exploitation.[74]

Despite the importance of entrepreneurial passion, there is scant theory to explain its effects on entrepreneurial activity. To compensate for these limitations, Cardon and collaborators proposed a model of entrepreneurial passion, which suggests that entrepreneurial passion leads to goal-directed cognitions, such as goal challenge, goal commitment, and goal striving, which in turn facilitate entrepreneurial behaviors.[75] Such entrepreneurial behaviors include creative problem-solving, persistence, and absorption, and they enhance entrepreneurial effectiveness in terms of opportunity recognition, venture creation, and growth.[76] Although Cardon's model has not been empirically tested as yet, it represents an important step in developing a theory of entrepreneurial passion. It could easily be applied to social entrepreneurship because social entrepreneurs do not become wealthy as a result of starting and running social ventures.

In social entrepreneurship, passion may intervene at two levels: as a self-regulating mechanism leading the social entrepreneur to commit fully to the social venture; and as a persuasive mechanism, helping the social entrepreneur to convince donors that the cause is worth funding. Promoters of social ventures are required to make compelling cases for the causes they pursue. Passion can facilitate the funding process because it may give some confidence to potential investors that the entrepreneur is committed to the venture. This is particularly important for social ventures when they solicit funding from social venture capitalists or social venture angels.[77]

3.7 Alertness and Social Entrepreneurship

Alertness is an attitude of receptiveness to available, but hitherto overlooked, opportunities and leads people to discover what could add value to the human experience.[78] Entrepreneurial alertness is construed as a cognitive process that allows an individual to recognize and exploit entrepreneurial opportunities. Thus, those who are entrepreneurially alert would be more likely to discover and exploit new venture opportunities compared to those who are not. The literature on commercial entrepreneurship often contends that alertness plays a critical role in people's ability to discover entrepreneurial opportunities. As with commercial ventures, alertness is a dispositional factor that could also facilitate the discovery of social entrepreneurial opportunities. In fact, the process of discovering commercial entrepreneurial opportunities may not after all be so much different from that of discovering social venture opportunities.

Alertness in social entrepreneurship could manifest itself as the attitude consisting of seeing social problems as opportunities rather than as social ills with which one is condemned to live. Entrepreneurship scholars have identified three components of alertness:

- scanning the environment;
- association and connection; and
- evaluation and judgment.

The first dimension deals with constantly scanning the environment and searching for new information, changes, and shifts that have been overlooked by other individuals and involves the use of existing knowledge, preparedness, and sensitivity to new opportunities.[79] The second dimension, association and connection, implies putting together disparate pieces of information and building them into coherent alternatives. It consists of understanding how people cognitively respond to and process new information clues. Finally, the third dimension, evaluation and judgment, consists of assessing whether the changes and shifts in the market or information would lead to a business opportunity with profit potential.

Alertness can be facilitated by the possession of prior knowledge. As a consequence, entrepreneurs who have prior experience in a particular industry are more likely to discover opportunities for new ventures pertaining to that industry. In fact, entrepreneurship scholars have found that the possession of prior knowledge influences the likelihood of discovering entrepreneurial opportunities.[80] For social ventures, it could well be that a social entrepreneur's familiarity with certain industries or social problems could facilitate the process of identifying ways to address those social problems. Moreover, a person who has prior experience of creating and managing a social venture could develop the skills needed to spot social entrepreneurial opportunities.

Table 2.2 summarizes the key points of the individual characteristics described above. Although most studies on the impact of these individual characteristics have focused on entrepreneurs creating for-profit ventures, their understanding could help to shed light on the characteristics of social entrepreneurs. They are not specific to a particular form of entrepreneurship and can influence both commercial and social entrepreneurial intentions and actions. However, we must keep in mind that individual characteristics may lead to negative outcomes if pushed to the extreme.[81] For example, positive attributes, such as energy, self-confidence, need for achievement, and independence, may sometimes devolve naturally into aggressiveness, narcissism, ruthlessness, and irresponsibility.[82] It is therefore important to focus on skills and competencies in addition to assessing the role

Table 2.2 Individual characteristics and social entrepreneurial actions

Dispositional characteristics	Actions leading to social entrepreneurship
Autonomy/independence	Being a social entrepreneur helps a person to manage their own venture. It also helps them to become their own boss.
Goal setting/drive	Goal setting allows the social entrepreneur to focus on the direction set for the social venture. Drive leads a person to pursue a given course of action. It is important in motivating someone to start and sustain a social venture.
Need for achievement	Being a social entrepreneur help a person to realize their full potential.
Passion	Passion allows the social entrepreneur to pursue the social opportunity relentlessly.
Risk propensity	The desire to take moderate risk influences entrepreneurial behavior.
Self-efficacy	Believing that one has the capacity to engage successfully in a course of action influences entrepreneurial activity.
Entrepreneurial alertness	Being alert to social opportunities leads social entrepreneurs to seek opportunities where others see only intractable problems. Prior experience and knowledge can improve alertness, leading a social entrepreneur to spot opportunities in familiar terrain.

of individual characteristics in social entrepreneurial education. As Gartner admonished entrepreneurship scholars more than two decades ago, research should focus on what the entrepreneur does, not who the entrepreneur is.[83]

3.8   From Individual Characteristics to Competencies

Entrepreneurial competencies are defined as underlying elements, such as specific knowledge, social roles, and skills which result in venture birth, survival, and/or growth.[84] They are seen as important to business growth and success.[85] Bird, one of the first entrepreneurship scholars to work on entrepreneurship competencies, draws a distinction between competency as contributing to excellence in performance and competency as a minimum standard, baseline, or threshold.[86] For example, the competency required to start a new venture would be considered as baseline, whereas the competency required to ensure the growth and survival of the new venture would be termed competency contributing to excellence in performance.

Research on entrepreneurial competencies has led to the identification of a set of factors that are deemed likely to influence the likelihood of starting and running a new venture. These include:

- opportunity recognition competencies;
- relationship competencies;
- conceptual competencies;
- organizing competencies;
- strategic competencies; and
- commitment competencies.[87]

Opportunity recognition competencies are related to recognizing and developing market opportunities through various means. The ability to recognize, envision, and act on opportunity, and the willingness and capacity to generate intense effort are at the core of the entrepreneurial process.[88] Relationship competencies refer to the extent to which the entrepreneur is able to build social interactions and leverage them to raise the resources needed to start and run the new venture. Entrepreneurship scholars have found that entrepreneurs who have higher social competence have greater financial success than those who do not have it.[89] Social entrepreneurs need social competence to raise the funds that are needed to start and run their social enterprises and to navigate the multitude of stakeholders successfully.

Conceptual competencies relate to the ability to display such behaviors as decision-making, absorbing and understanding complex information, risk-taking, and innovativeness. Organizing competencies are related to the organization of different internal and external human, physical, financial, and technological resources, including team-building, leading employees, training, and controlling.[90] This competency is closely related to a managerial competency. Strategic competencies are related to setting, evaluating, and implementing the strategies of the new venture. Finally, commitment competencies drive the entrepreneur to move forward. Without strong commitment, an entrepreneur cannot pursue the venture, especially in the face of difficulties.

To some extent, these entrepreneurial competencies—especially those that relate to organization and strategy—are related to managerial competencies.[91] The competencies discussed above are presented in Table 2.3. Although studied in commercial entrepreneurship, they are equally relevant to the creation and management of social ventures.

Table 2.3 Entrepreneurial competency framework[92]

Opportunity competencies	Relationship competencies	Conceptual competencies	Organizing competencies	Strategic competencies	Commitment competencies
Competencies related to recognizing and developing market opportunities through various means	Competencies related to person-to-person or individual-to-group interactions, such as building a context of cooperation and trust, using contacts and connections, persuasive ability, communication and interpersonal skill	Competencies related to different conceptual abilities, which are reflected in the behaviors of the entrepreneur, such as decision skills, absorbing and understanding complex information, risk-taking, and innovativeness	Competencies related to the organization of different internal and external human, physical, financial, and technological resources, including team-building, leading employees, training, and controlling	Competencies related to setting, evaluating, and implementing the strategies of the firm	Competencies that drive the entrepreneur to move ahead with the business

Summary

This chapter has discussed the entrepreneurial mindset, the nature, and the characteristics of social entrepreneurs. Individual characteristics, such as autonomy or independence, the need for achievement, drive, passion, the propensity to take risks, self-efficacy, alertness, and goal setting are discussed. These individual characteristics could explain the creation intentions and actions of both commercial and social ventures.

Key Terms

Alertness; autonomy; competency; creativity; drive; entrepreneurial mindset; fixed mindset; goal-setting theory; growth mindset; independence; need for achievement; need for power; passion; risk propensity; self-efficacy

Review Questions

1 Describe the entrepreneurial mindset and explain how it might affect the likelihood of an individual engaging in social entrepreneurship.
2 Do you think that having a high need for achievement could lead to success in starting and running a social venture (yes or no)? Explain.
3 Explain how goals affect an individual's tendency to engage in social entrepreneurial activities.
4 "If entrepreneurship is a mindset, then to some extent we are all entrepreneurs." Do you agree or disagree with this statement? Explain.

5 Identify the key competencies discussed in the text and explain how they could lead to the creation and effective management of a social venture.
6 Explain the role that risk propensity could play in social entrepreneurship.
7 Explain the role of passion in launching and managing a social venture.
8 Discuss the importance of risk-taking and risk propensity in social venture creation.
9 Explain the role of self-efficacy in creating and running a social venture.
10 Do you think that alertness plays a critical role in the discovery or creation of social entrepreneurial opportunities (yes or no)? Explain.

Application Questions

1 Watch Victoria Hale's video at www.youtube.com/watch?v=bEEY7OFTp_0 and identify the characteristics that she thinks social entrepreneurs should exhibit. What do you think about her advice? Would it be useful to you? Explain.
2 Develop a competency model for social entrepreneurs based on this chapter. What competencies would you add to this model? Explain why you think these competencies are important in starting and running a social venture.
3 Suppose that you are asked to facilitate a workshop whose purpose is to develop the entrepreneurship competencies of participants. Which competencies would you cover and why?
4 Explain the role passion could play in starting and running a social venture. Give examples where passion could be a good thing for a social entrepreneur. Do you see a downside to having passion? Give an example.
5 Suppose you are a member of a panel judging a social venture business plan competition. What elements would you consider important in determining whether a social entrepreneur is passionate about his/her venture during the presentation?

Application Case 1: Aakar Innovations[93]

Sombodhi Ghosh and Jaydeep Mandal, two friends, saw a problem in India and decided to create Aakar Innovations (www.aakarinnovations.com), a social venture, to address an issue relating to women's health. They found that many women in India did not use menstruation hygiene items for one or a combination of four reasons:

* awareness;
* affordability;
* availability; and
* disposability.

Because of these reasons and traditional Indian taboos, women were using traditional means that could lead to infections, maternal complications, and even cancer. To remedy these problems, the pair started Aakar Innovations, which manufactures sanitary napkins for rural and poor women. It is worth mentioning that their initiative was inspired by Arunachalam Muruganantham's idea of making sanitary pads in India. According to the findings of a comprehensive nationwide survey carried out by AC Nielsen and reviewed and endorsed by Plan India, only 12 percent of the 355 million menstruating women in India use sanitary napkins; and usage in rural areas is even lower, at 2–3 percent.

Most of these women are poor and cannot afford the sanitary napkins sold by multinationals, such as Procter & Gamble. Thus, Aakar Innovations is facilitating the production of low-cost sanitary napkins in rural areas using agri-wastes, including banana fiber, bagasse, bamboo, and water hyacinth. The napkins are marketed under the brand name Anandi—meaning "joy and happiness"—and are priced at 40 percent less than the cheapest regular sanitary napkins sold by mainstream manufacturers. Aakar Innovations supplies the machines to the women, sets up production centers, supplies raw materials, offers technical support, and advises on marketing. The napkins are safe and sterilized by ultraviolet light and meet all of the quality requirements of the BIS (Bureau of Indian Standards).

Aakar Innovations is a hybrid social venture. Its non-profit arm—Aakar Social Ventures—is involved in community engagement, capacity-building, and increasing awareness of menstrual hygiene. Its for-profit component manufactures the sanitary napkin machines and sells them to rural women. On its website, Aakar Innovations claims that it transforms lives by distributing high-quality, compostable sanitary pads to girls and women throughout rural India. It also identifies the problem it intends to solve and the solution it provides. The problem is embarrassment and low self-esteem as a result of not using sanitary pads during menstruation. The napkins provide a solution because they are cheaper than the commercial alternatives and produced by the women themselves.

Discussion Questions

1 Identify the problem(s) that Aakar Innovations is solving. How effective has it been in finding a solution?
2 Do some research on Aakar Innovations' two founders, Sombodhi Ghosh and Jaydeep Mandal. What competencies do you think they possess? How did these competencies help them start Aakar Innovations? How will these competencies help them grow and scale Aakar Innovations?
3 Watch Aakar Innovations' video at www.youtube.com/watch?v=40C32F_K4eE. How has Aakar Innovations affected the lives of the beneficiaries of its services?
4 What role do you think passion played in the creation of Aakar Innovations?

Application Case 2: Ciudad Saludable[94]

Albina Luiz, a social entrepreneur from Lima, Peru, has an impressive résumé. She was the only woman in her class at the National University of Engineering in Lima, where she majored in industrial engineering. She then went on to earn a Master's degree in Ecology and Environmental Management from the Ricardo Palma University and a Ph.D. in Chemistry from Ramon Llull University in Barcelona, Spain. At an early age, she started to work on waste issues in Lima. In 2001, she founded a social venture, Ciudad Saludable (Healthy City), to address the issue of waste collection. Ciudad Saludable started its work in the neighborhood of El Cono Norte in Lima and then expanded throughout the city and eventually to other cities. It now covers 20 cities, employs about 150 people, and serves over 3 million residents in Peru.

Ciudad Saludable recruits microentrepreneurs who are generally from the community to collect and process the garbage. This helps to solve two critical issues at once: it removes garbage and provides a cleaner environment; and it reduces unemployment. Each of these microbusinesses is charged a monthly fee of $1.50. Ciudad Saludable has organized more than 1,500 waste collectors, creating employment and improving health and living conditions for over 6 million people in rural and poor urban regions in Bolivia, Brazil, Colombia, Mexico, Venezuela, and India in addition to Peru.

These efforts have led to recognition of Ciudad Saludable as a leader in waste management around the world. Ruiz herself and Ciudad Saludable have received a number of honors, including a 1995 fellowship from the Ashoka Foundation, a 2006 fellowship from the Skoll Foundation, the 2007 Energy Globe Award, the 2006 Dubai International Award for Best Practices to Improve the Living Environment, the 2006 Global Development Network Award, and the 2006 Bravo Award from Latin Trade as Environmentalist of the Year in Latin America. Ruiz's ultimate goal is to change the way people think. She sees opportunities where most people see problems.

Discussion Questions

1　How would you describe Albina Ruiz? What traits best characterize her?
2　List Albina Ruiz's chief competencies.
3　What type of social change has Albina Ruiz brought to Peru?
4　Watch Ciudad Saludable's video at www.youtube.com/watch?v=x0LgwcAsNB4. What impresses you about this social venture?

Notes

1　McGrath, R. G., & MacMillan, I. (2000). *The entrepreneurial mindset.* Boston: Harvard Business School Press.
2　Haynie, J. M., Shepherd, D., Mosakowski, E., & Early, P. C. (2010). A situated metacognitive model of the entrepreneurial mindset. *Journal of Business Venturing, 25,* 217–229.
3　Pollard, V., & Wilson, E. (2013). The entrepreneurial mindset in creative and performing arts higher education in Australia. *Artivate: A Journal Entrepreneurship in the Arts, 3*(1), 3–22; Bruwer, J. P. (2012). The entrepreneurial mindset profile of South African small medium and micro enterprises (SMMEs) in the Cape metropole. *African Journal of Business Management, 6*(15), 5383–5388; Shepherd, D. A., Patzelt, H., & Haynie, J. M. (2010). Entrepreneurial spirals: Deviation-amplifying loops of an entrepreneurial mindset and organizational culture. *Entrepreneurship Theory and Practice, 34*(1), 59–82; Haynie, J. M., & Shepherd, D. A. (2007). Exploring the entrepreneurial mindset: Feedback and adaptive decision-making. *Frontiers of Entrepreneurship Research, 27*(6), 1–15; Ireland, R. D., Hitt, A. M., & Simon, G. D. (2003). A model of strategic entrepreneurship: The construct and its dimensions. *Journal of Management, 29*(6), 963–989.
4　Ireland, R. D., Hitt, A. M., & Simon, G. D. (2003). A model of strategic entrepreneurship: The construct and its dimensions. *Journal of Management, 29*(6), 963–989.
5　Dweck, C. (2006). *The new psychology of success.* New York: Random House.
6　Ireland, R. D., Hitt, A. M., & Simon, G. D. (2003). A model of strategic entrepreneurship: The construct and its dimensions. *Journal of Management, 29*(6), 963–989.
7　Sastre-Castillo, M. A., Peris-Ortiz, M., & Danvila-Del Valle, I. (2015). What is different about the profile of the social entrepreneur? *Nonprofit Management & Leadership, 25*(4), 349–369; Dees, J. G. (1998). Enterprising nonprofits. *Harvard Business Review,* January–February, 55–67.
8　Dees, J. D. (1998). *The meaning of social entrepreneurship.* Palo Alto, CA: Graduate School of Business, Stanford University.
9　Borstein, D. (2004). *How to change the world: Social entrepreneurs and the power of new ideas.* Oxford: Oxford University Press.
10　Roberts, D., & Woods, C. (2000). Changing the world on a shoestring: The concept of social entrepreneurship. *University of Auckland Business Review,* Autumn, 45–51.

11   Drayton, W. (2002). The citizen sector: Becoming as entrepreneurial and competitive as business. *California Management Review, 44*(3), 120–132.

12   Drayton, W. (2002). The citizen sector: becoming as entrepreneurial and competitive as business. *California Management Review, 44*(3), 120–132.

13   Drucker, P. F. (1989). What business can learn from nonprofits. *Harvard Business Review, 67*, 88–93.

14   Roberts, D., & Woods, C. (2000). Changing the world on a shoestring: The concept of social entrepreneurship. *University of Auckland Business Review*, Autumn, 45–51.

15   Kickul J., & Lyons, T. S. (2012). *Understanding social entrepreneurship: The relentless pursuit of mission in an ever changing world*. New York: Routledge.

16   Hemingway, C. A. (2005). Personal values as a catalyst for corporate social entrepreneurship. *Journal of Business Ethics, 60*, 233–249.

17   Dees, J. D. (1998). *The meaning of social entrepreneurship*. Palo Alto, CA: Graduate School of Business, Stanford University.

18   Sharir, M., & Lerner, M. (2006). Gauging the success of social ventures initiated by individual social entrepreneurs. *Journal of World Business, 41*, 6–20.

19   Financial Accounting Standards Board. (1993). *Accounting for contributions received and contributions made*. Norwalk, CT: Financial Accounting Standards Board.

20   Zahra, S. A., Gedajlovic, E., Neuman, D. O., & Shulman, J. M. (2009). A typology of social entrepreneurs: Motives, search processes and ethical challenges. *Journal of Business Venturing, 24*, 519–532.

21   Zahra, S. A., Gedajlovic, E., Neuman, D. O., & Shulman, J. M. (2009). A typology of social entrepreneurs: Motives, search processes and ethical challenges. *Journal of Business Venturing, 24*, 519–532.

22   Espiritu Olmos, R., & Sastre-Castillo, M. A. (2015). Personality traits versus work values: Comparing psychological theories on entrepreneurial intention. *Journal of Business Research, 68*(7), 1595–1598; Shane, S., & Nicolaou, N. (2015). Creative personality, opportunity recognition and the tendency to start businesses: A study of their genetic predispositions. *Journal of Business Venturing, 12*(4), 11–31; Nga, K. H. N., & Shamuganathan, G. (2011). The influence of personality traits and demographic factors on social entrepreneurship start up intentions. *Journal of Business Ethics, 95*, 259–282.

23   Shane, S., & Nicolaou, N. (2015). Creative personality, opportunity recognition and the tendency to start businesses: A study of their genetic predispositions. *Journal of Business Venturing, 12*(4), 11–31.

24   Nga, K. H. N., & Shamuganathan, G. (2011). The influence of personality traits and demographic factors on social entrepreneurship start up intentions. *Journal of Business Ethics, 95*, 259–282.

25   Hirisch, R. D. (1985). The woman entrepreneur in the United States and Puerto Rico: A comparative study. *Leadership and Organizational Development Journal, 5*(5), 3–8.

26   McClelland, D. (1961). *The achieving society*. Princeton, NJ: Van Nostrand; Hirisch, R. D. (1985). The woman entrepreneur in the United States and Puerto Rico: A comparative study. *Leadership and Organizational Development Journal, 5*(5), 3–8; Lumpkin, G. T., & Dees, G. G. (1996). Clarifying the entrepreneurial orientation construct and linking it to performance. *Academy of Management Review, 21*, 135–172.

27   McClelland, D. (1965). Need achievement and entrepreneurship: A longitudinal study. *Journal of Personality and Social Psychology, 1*, 389–392.

28   Bargsted, M., Picon, M., Salazar, A., & Rojas, Y. (2013). Psychosocial characterization of social entrepreneurs: A comparative study. *Journal of Social Entrepreneurship, 4*(3), 331–346.

29   McClelland, D. (1961). *The achieving society*. Princeton, NJ: Van Nostrand.

30   McClelland, D. (1961). *The achieving society*. Princeton, NJ: Van Nostrand; Atkinson, J. W. (1964). *Motives in fantasy: Action and society*. Princeton, NJ: Van Nostrand.

31   Sagie, A., & Elizur, D. (1999). Achievement motive and entrepreneurial orientation: A structural analysis. *Journal of Organizational Behavior, 20*(3), 375–387.

32   Wu, S., Matthews, L., & Dagher, G. K. (2007). Need for achievement, business goals, and entrepreneurial persistence. *Management Research News*, 30(2), 298–941.

33   McClelland, D. C. (1978). Managing motivation to expand human freedom. *American Psychologist*, 33, 201–210.

34   McClelland, D. (1965). Need achievement and entrepreneurship: A longitudinal study. *Journal of Personality and Social Psychology*, 1, 389–392.

35   Lau, C. M., & Busenitz, L. W. (2001). Growth intentions of entrepreneurs in a transitional economy: The People's Republic of China. *Entrepreneurship Theory and Practice*, 26(1), 5–20; Taormina, R. J., & Lao, S. K. M. (2007). Measuring Chinese entrepreneurial motivation: Personality and environmental influences. *International Journal of Entrepreneurial Behavior & Research*, 13(4), 200–221.

36   Lee, J. (1997). The motivation of women entrepreneurs in Singapore. *International Journal of Entrepreneurial Behavior & Research*, 3(2), 93–110.

37   Stewart, Jr., H. W., & Roth L. P. (2007). A meta-analysis of achievement motivation differences between entrepreneurs and managers. *Journal of Small Business Management*, 45(4), 401–421.

38   Collins, C. J., Hanges, P. J., & Locke, E. A. (2004). The relationship of achievement motivation to entrepreneurial behavior: A meta-analysis. *Human Performance*, 17(1), 95–117.

39   Jayawarna, D., Rouse, J., & Kitching, J. (2011). Entrepreneur motivations and life course. *International Small Business Journal*, 31(1), 34–56.

40   Das, T. K., & Teng, B. S. (1997). Time and entrepreneurial risk behavior. *Entrepreneurship Theory and Practice*, Winter, 69–88.

41   March, J. G., & Shapira, Z. (1987). Managerial perspectives on risk and risk taking. *Management Science*, 33(1), 1404–1418; Yates, F., & Stone, E. R. (1992). The risk construct. In J. F. Yates (Ed.), *Risk-taking behavior* (pp. 1–25). Chichester: Wiley.

42   Knight, F. H. (1964 [1921]). *Risk, uncertainty and profit*. New York: Augustus M. Kelly; Yates, F., & Stone, E. R. (1992). The risk construct. In J. F. Yates (Ed.), *Risk-taking behavior* (pp. 1–25). Chichester: Wiley.

43   Atkinson, J. W. (1957). Motivational determinants of risk taking behavior. *Psychological Review*, 64(6), 359–372; McClelland, D. (1961). *The achieving society*. Princeton, NJ: Van Nostrand.

44   Brockhaus, R. H. (1980). Risk taking propensity of entrepreneurs. *Academy of Management Journal*, 23(3), 509–520; Shane, S., Locke, E. A., & Collins, C. J. (2003). Entrepreneurial motivation. *Human Resource Management*, 13, 257–279.

45   Liles, P. R. (1974). *New business ventures and entrepreneur*. Homewood, IL: Richard D. Irwin, Inc.

46   Stewart, W. H., & Roth, P. L. (2007). A meta-analysis of achievement motivation differences between entrepreneurs and managers. *Journal of Small Business Management*, 45(4), 401–421.

47   Amhed, S. U. (1985). nAch, risk-taking propensity, locus of control and entrepreneurship. *Personality and Individual Differences*, 6(6), 781–782.

48   Sarasvathy, D. K., Simon, H. A., & Love, L. (1998). Perceiving and managing business risks: Differences between managers and bankers. *Journal of Economic Behavior and Organization*, 33, 207–225.

49   Bandura, A. (1997). *Self-efficacy: The exercise of control*. New York: Freeman.

50   Chen, C. C. Greene, P. G., & Crick, A. (1998). Does entrepreneurial self-efficacy distinguish entrepreneurs from managers? *Journal of Business Venturing*, 13(4), 295–316.

51   Shane, S., Locke, E. A., & Collins, C. J. (2003). Entrepreneurial motivation. *Human Resource Management*, 13, 257–279.

52   Markham, G., Balkin, D., & Baron, R. A. (2002). Inventors and new venture formation: The effects of general self-efficacy and regretful thinking. *Entrepreneurship Theory and Practice*, 27(2), 149–165; Wilson, F., Kickul, J., & Marlino, D. (2007). Gender, entrepreneurial self-efficacy, and entrepreneurial career intentions: Implications for entrepreneurial education. *Entrepreneurship Theory and Practice*, 31(3), 387–406.

53 Bargsted, M., Picon, M., Salazar, A., & Rojas, Y. (2013). Psychosocial characterization of social entrepreneurs: A comparative study. *Journal of Social Entrepreneurship*, 4(3), 331–346; Chen, C. C. Greene, P. G., & Crick, A. (1998). Does entrepreneurial self-efficacy distinguish entrepreneurs from managers? *Journal of Business Venturing*, 13(4), 295–316; Boyd, N. G., & Vozikis, G. S. (1994). The influence of self-efficacy on the development of entrepreneurial intentions and actions. *Entrepreneurship Theory and Practice*, 18(4), 63–77.

54 Cardon, M. S., & Kirk, C. P. (2015). Entrepreneurial passion as mediator of the self-efficacy to persistence relationship. *Entrepreneurship Theory and Practice*, 39(5), 1027–1050.

55 Shane, S., Locke, E. A., & Collins, C. J. (2003). Entrepreneurial motivation. *Human Resource Management*, 13, 257–279.

56 Smith, I. A., & Woodworth, W. P. (2012). Developing social entrepreneurs and social innovations: A social identity and self-efficacy approach. *Academy of Management Learning & Education*, 11(3), 390–407.

57 Lewin, K. (1951). *Field theory in social science*. New York: Harper & Row.

58 Batson, C. D., & Shaw, L. L. (1991). Evidence for altruism: Toward a pluralism of prosocial motives. *Psychological Inquiry*, 2, 107–122.

59 Collins, J. C., & Porras, J. (1991). Organizational vision and visionary organizations. *California Management Review*, 34, 30–52; Perwin, L. (2003). *A science of personality*. Oxford: Oxford University Press.

60 Locke, A. E., & Latham, P. G. (1990). *A theory of goal setting and performance*. Englewood Cliffs, NJ: Prentice-Hall; Latham, P. G., Locke, E. A. (1991). Self-regulation through goal setting. *Organizational Behavior and Human Decision Processes*, 50(2), 212–247; Cardon, M. S., Wincent, J., Singh, J., & Drnovsek, M. (2009). The nature and experience of entrepreneurial passion. *Academy of Management Review*, 34(3), 511–532.

61 Baum, J. R., & Locke, E. A. (2004). The relationship of entrepreneurial traits, skill, and motivation to subsequent venture growth. *Journal of Applied Psychology*, 89, 1173–1182.

62 Shane, S., Locke, E. A., & Collins, C. J. (2003). Entrepreneurial motivation. *Human Resource Management*, 13, 257–279.

63 Shane, S., Locke, E. A., & Collins, C. J. (2003). Entrepreneurial motivation. *Human Resource Management*, 13, 257–279.

64 Shane, S., Locke, E. A., & Collins, C. J. (2003). Entrepreneurial motivation. *Human Resource Management*, 13, 257–279.

65 Murnieks, C. Y., Mosakowski, E., & Cardon, M. S. (2014). Pathways of passion: Identity centrality, passion, and behavior among entrepreneurs. *Journal of Management*, 40(6), 1583–1606.

66 Cardon, M. S., Zietsma, C., Saparito, P., Matherne, B. P., & Davis, C. (2005). A tale of passion: New insights into entrepreneurship from a parenthood metaphor. *Journal of Business Venturing*, 20(1), 23–45, at p. 23.

67 Smilor, R. W. (1997). Entrepreneurship: Reflections on a subversive activity. *Journal of Business Venturing*, 12, 341–346, at p. 341.

68 Shane, S., Locke, E. A., & Collins, C. J. (2003). Entrepreneurial motivation. *Human Resource Management*, 13, 257–279.

69 Vallerand, R. J., Blanchard, C., Mageau, G. A., Koestner, R., Ratelle, C., Leonard, M. Gagne, M., & Marsolais, J. (2003). Les passions de l'ame: On obsessive and harmonious passion. *Journal of Personality and Social Psychology*, 85, 756–767.

70 Cardon, M. S., & Kirk, C. P. (2015). Entrepreneurial passion as mediator of the self-efficacy to persistence relationship. *Entrepreneurship Theory and Practice*, 39(5), 1027–1050.

71 Pertulla, K. M. (2003). The POW factor: Understanding passion for one's work. Paper presented at the Annual Academy of Management, Seattle, August 1–6.

72 Cardon, M. S., Wincent, J., Singh, J., & Drnovsek, M. (2009). The nature and experience of entrepreneurial passion. *Academy of Management Review*, 34(3), 511–532.

73 Cardon, M. S., Wincent, J., Singh, J., & Drnovsek, M. (2009). The nature and experience of entrepreneurial passion. *Academy of Management Review*, 34(3), 511–532.

74 Baum, R., Locke, E. A., & Smith, K. G. (2000). A longitudinal model of a multi-dimensional model of venture growth. *Academy of Management Journal, 44,* 292–303; Baron, R. A. (2008). The role of affect in the entrepreneurial process. *Academy of Management Review, 33,* 328–340.

75 Cardon, M. S., Wincent, J., Singh, J., & Drnovsek, M. (2009). The nature and experience of entrepreneurial passion. *Academy of Management Review, 34*(3), 511–532.

76 Kirzner, I. (1973). *Competition and entrepreneurship.* Chicago: University of Chicago Press; Kirzner, I. (1979). *Perception, opportunity, and profit.* Chicago: University of Chicago Press.

77 Mitteness, C., Sudek, R., & Cardon, M. S. (2012). Angel investor characteristics that determine whether perceived passion leads to higher evaluations of funding potential. *Journal of Business Venturing, 27*(5), 592–606.

78 Kirzner, I. (1973). *Competition and entrepreneurship.* Chicago: University of Chicago Press; Kirzner, I. (1979). *Perception, opportunity, and profit.* Chicago: University of Chicago Press.

79 Tang, J., Kacmar, K. M., & Busenitz, L. 2012. Entrepreneurial alertness in the pursuit of new opportunities. *Journal of Business Venturing, 27,* 77–94.

80 Venkataraman, S. (1997). The distinctive domain of entrepreneurship research: An editor's perspective. In J. Katz & R. Brockhaus (Eds), *Advances in entrepreneurship, firm emergence, and growth, 3,* 119–138. Greenwich, CT: JAI Press; Baron, R. A. (2006). Opportunity recognition as pattern recognition: How entrepreneurs "connect the dots" to identify new business opportunities. *Academy of Management Perspectives, 20*(1), 104–119.

81 DeNisi, A. S. (2015). Some further thoughts on the entrepreneurial personality. *Entrepreneurship Theory and Practice, 39*(5), 997–1003; Miller, D. (2015). A downside to the entrepreneurial personality. *Entrepreneurship Theory and Practice, 39*(1), 1–8; Simon, M., & Shrader, R. C. (2012). Entrepreneurial actions and optimistic overconfidence: The role of motivated reasoning in new product introductions. *Journal of Business Venturing, 27*(3), 291–309; Hayward, M. L., Shepherd, D. A., & Griffin, D. (2006). A hubris theory of entrepreneurship. *Management Science, 52*(2), 160–172.

82 DeNisi, A. S. (2015). Some further thoughts on the entrepreneurial personality. *Entrepreneurship Theory and Practice, 39*(5), 997–1003.

83 Gartner, W. B. (1988). "Who is an entrepreneur?" is the wrong question. *American Journal of Small Business, 12*(4), 11–32.

84 Man, T., Lau, T., & Chan, K. F. (2002). The competitiveness of small and medium enterprises: A conceptualization with focus on entrepreneurial competencies. *Journal of Business Venturing, 17*(2), 123–142; Bird, B. (1995). Towards a theory of entrepreneurial competency. *Advances in Entrepreneurship, Firm Emergence and Growth, 2,* 51–72.

85 Mitchelmore, S., & Rowley, J. (2010). Entrepreneurial competencies: A literature review and development agenda. *International Journal of Entrepreneurial Behavior & Research, 16*(2), 92–111.

86 Bird, B. (1995). Towards a theory of entrepreneurial competency. *Advances in Entrepreneurship, Firm Emergence and Growth, 2,* 51–72.

87 Man, T., Lau, T., & Chan, K. F. (2002). The competitiveness of small and medium enterprises: A conceptualization with focus on entrepreneurial competencies. *Journal of Business Venturing, 17*(2), 123–142.

88 Chandler, G. N., & Jansen, E. (1992). The founder's self-assessed competence and venture performance. *Journal of Business Venturing, 7*(3), 223–236.

89 Baron, R. A., & Markman, G. D. (2000). Beyond social capital: How social skills can enhance entrepreneurs' success. *Academy of Management Perspectives, 14*(1), 106–116.

90 Man, T., Lau, T., & Chan, K. F. (2002). The competitiveness of small and medium enterprises: A conceptualization with focus on entrepreneurial competencies. *Journal of Business Venturing, 17*(2), 123–142.

91 Boyatzis, R. E. (1982). *The competent manager: A model for effective performance.* New York: Wiley & Sons.

92 Man, T., Lau, T., & Chan, K. F. (2002). The competitiveness of small and medium enterprises: A conceptualization with focus on entrepreneurial competencies. *Journal of Business Venturing*, *17*(2), 123–142.

93 Sources for this whole section: *The Economist*. Social entrepreneurship in India: Cut from a different cloth. www.economist.com/node/21586328/print, retrieved on October 22, 2014; Vibeke Venema, V. (2014).The Indian sanitary pad revolutionary. BBC News. www.bbc.com/news/magazine-26260978, retrieved on December 14, 2014; Aakar Innovations. www.aakarinnovations.com, retrieved on October 22, 2014.

94 Sources for this whole section: PBS. Meet the new heroes. www.pbs.org/opb/thenewheroes/meet/p_ruiz.htm, retrieved on October 22, 2014 [no longer available]; Skoll Foundation. Ciudad Saludable. http://skoll.org/organization/ciudad-saludable/, retrieved on March 22, 2016; Ciudad Saludable. www.ciudadsaludable.org, retrieved on March 22, 2016.

Chapter 3

Social Entrepreneurial Motivations

Learning Objectives

1 Explain social entrepreneurial motivations.
2 Discuss compassion as a driver of social entrepreneurship activities.
3 Describe the role of moral engagement in explaining social entrepreneurial motivation.
4 Explain the link between social entrepreneurship and social justice.

Why do some people engage in social entrepreneurial activities while others do not? Why do some people devote their time, lives, and even financial resources to pursuing ventures that address social needs rather than seeking profit for themselves and their families? Are these people motivated by altruism or a type of enlightened self-interest? This chapter addresses those questions. In so doing, it focuses on the motivations of individual social entrepreneurs. It does not consider the effect of external factors on the creation of social ventures, as that is the subject of Chapter 4. The construct of social entrepreneurial motivation (SEM) is used to explain why some people decide to become social entrepreneurs. This construct is embedded in the concept of entrepreneurial motivation, which focuses on the reasons why people start business ventures.

Explaining the motivation to become a social entrepreneur is important "because motivation plays an important part in the creation of new organizations; thus, theories of organizational creation that fail to address this notion are incomplete."[1] Moreover, the development of entrepreneurship theory requires consideration of the motivations of people making entrepreneurial decisions.[2] Studying the motivations of social entrepreneurs is important because entrepreneurship involves human agency, and the entrepreneurial process occurs because people act to pursue opportunities. Moreover, people differ in their willingness and abilities to act on these opportunities.[3]

The chapter is divided into four sections. The first reviews the concept of entrepreneurial motivation as discussed in the literature on commercial entrepreneurship and relates it to social entrepreneurship. The second explores compassion as a motivator of social entrepreneurship. The third discusses the role of moral engagement in social entrepreneurship. Finally, the fourth analyzes the extent to which the quest for social justice could represent a driver of social entrepreneurial intentions and actions.

I Entrepreneurial Motivations and Social Entrepreneurship

To understand why people decide to start social ventures, it is important to have a better grasp of the research into entrepreneurial motivation. Entrepreneurial motivation is defined as possessing the drive to found a new business. As motivation plays an important role in all human actions, it plays a critical role in the entrepreneurial process. This is important to remember when trying to understand why some people engage in activities geared toward helping others. Motivation may be the spark that transforms a latent intention into real action and, therefore, the missing link between intention and action.[4] Entrepreneurial motivation is a dynamic concept because the entrepreneur's motives may change over time or during the course of the venture. For example, an entrepreneur may be motivated by autonomy when starting the venture. However, as the venture grows and becomes profitable (or otherwise), the entrepreneur may be more motivated by financial gain (or by survival).

Entrepreneurship scholars have attempted to explain the reason why people start business ventures. This began with two closely related explanations of entrepreneurial motivation—the *push theory* and the *pull theory*.[5] The push theory suggests that people are pushed into entrepreneurship by *negative* external forces, such as job dissatisfaction, difficulty finding employment, insufficient salary, or inflexible work schedule. This type of entrepreneurship is sometimes equated with *entrepreneurship by necessity*. In such situations, people engage in entrepreneurship because they have few other options available to them. Some entrepreneurship scholars contend that necessity motives for starting new businesses play a major role in developing countries and a lesser role in developed countries.[6]

For social entrepreneurship, one could speculate that social venture creation would be more prevalent in developed countries than developing areas. The main reason could be that the institutional environment in developed countries is more conducive to social venture creation. For example, the social entrepreneur may be able to secure third-party funding from foundations, corporations, individual philanthropists, social venture capitalists, or social angels. Another reason could be that relatively more people in developed countries are able to satisfy their basic needs. This is particularly important because social ventures are not generally created to make social entrepreneurs wealthy or to address their basic financial needs.

The pull theory, to the contrary, contends that people are attracted into entrepreneurial activities because they seek independence, self-fulfillment, wealth, and other *desirable* outcomes. Early conceptualizations of entrepreneurial motivations focused on this theory.[7] People engage in entrepreneurial activities because of economic factors, and most entrepreneurial activities in developed countries have been characterized as stemming from pull factors. Using Global Entrepreneurship Monitor (GEM) data from 2005 and 2006 on 29 countries, Hessels and colleagues found that entrepreneurial activity was more influenced by the autonomy/independence motive in developed countries than in developing ones. However, the necessity-driven motive was prompting more entrepreneurial activities in developing countries.[8]

Another study, focusing on entrepreneurs in Japan and their contemporaries in Silicon Valley, found that the former were more society-oriented, meaning that they were searching for social recognition, while the latter were more motivated by individualistic factors, such as personal achievement and the accumulation of personal wealth.[9] This difference could be explained by the cultures of the two countries. The Japanese culture tends to be collectivistic, whereas the US culture is recognized as individualistic. In a collectivistic culture, people tend to emphasize group harmony, and adherence to the group norm is an important aspect of social life. In this case, social recognition could be a form of social validation. In an individualistic culture, however, people tend to be more oriented toward self-fulfillment.

Could the push theory and the pull theory of entrepreneurship explain social entrepreneurial motivations? Arguably, social entrepreneurs might not be motivated by the desire to satisfy basic needs, such as physiological and safety needs,[10] to the extent that the satisfaction of such needs requires tangible outcomes that social ventures are not intended to deliver. The study of the motivation of social entrepreneurs has received scant attention in the literature.[11] However, a few authors have attempted to explain the reasons why people decide to become social entrepreneurs.

A study conducted on a sample of 18 social bricoleurs (small-scale social entrepreneurs) from eight countries found that the motivation to become a social entrepreneur included pull factors, such as an awareness of social injustice, and push factors, such as job dissatisfaction. The study also found that the social bricoleurs' motivations were similar across countries. For example, when referring to the present or the future, many social entrepreneurs sought scalability (an expansion of their vision and actions evolving from small-scale organizations to larger organizations that serve multiple populations and needs) as an important factor.[12] Another study conducted on a sample of 30 Israeli social entrepreneurs using life-story analysis methodology found that most of them were motivated by pull factors, such as prosocial behaviors based on past or current life events. The others were motivated by push factors, such as job dissatisfaction and a search for meaning in life.[13]

Sharir and Lerner studied the parallel between social and commercial entrepreneurs and found that, like commercial entrepreneurs, social entrepreneurs were driven by a combination of motives, including the desire for self-fulfillment, occupational independence, and opportunities for creativity. However, the social entrepreneurs also displayed some motives that were not found among their commercial counterparts, such as personal rehabilitation, a compulsion to find solutions to individual distress, and a sense of obligation to community or affiliation.[14] A central difference between commercial entrepreneurship and social entrepreneurship is that social entrepreneurs are driven primarily by a motivation to *create* value for society, not to *capture* value.[15] A recent study shows that social entrepreneurs are motivated by five factors:

- personal fulfillment;
- helping society;
- nonmonetary focus;
- achievement orientation; and
- proximity to social problems.[16]

Another study found that an individual's general social appraisal is the most important antecedent of social entrepreneurial intention. Social appraisal refers to the tendency to be oriented toward social values. Thus, individuals with high levels of social appraisal are more likely to engage in social entrepreneurship.[17] Likewise, a study conducted in Portugal shows that social entrepreneurs were motivated by altruism, passion, the influence of role models, past volunteering experience, and a willingness to create and innovate.[18] In other words, social entrepreneurs tend to engage in prosocial motivations. If the goal of social ventures is to address social issues, then focusing on tangible resources, such as financial resources, cannot be a primary driver of the social entrepreneur. Other factors, such as compassion, moral engagement, and the quest for social justice, could explain the tendency for some people to engage in social entrepreneurship. These three types of motivation are discussed in detail below.

2 Compassion and Social Entrepreneurship

According to the *Oxford English Dictionary*, the word "compassion" stems from the Latin *compati*, which means to suffer with.[19] The modern meaning of compassion, as studied by psychologists, philosophers, and now management scholars, also encompasses the notion of suffering. Suffering with a victim is likely to lead someone to take action in order to address that victim's suffering. Compassion is characterized by an orientation and an emotional connection linking an individual to a suffering community and serves as a powerful motivator for action, compelling individuals to alleviate others' suffering.[20] The late Mother Teresa, founder of the Missionaries of Charity, who devoted her life to caring for the poor in Kolkata, India, epitomized compassion.

Miller and colleagues have proposed a conceptual model to explain the role of compassion in fostering social entrepreneurial behavior. Their model views compassion as the main driver of social entrepreneurship. Social venture creation cannot rely solely on self- or family-oriented motives because this organizational form rarely leads to the direct accumulation of private wealth.[21]

Compassion is recognized as an essential element of human behavior to the extent that it guides how individuals act toward others. More than two hundred years ago, Adam Smith emphasized its role by noting:

> How selfish soever man may be supposed, there are evidently some principles in his nature, which interest him in the fortune of others, and render their happiness necessary to him, though he derives nothing from it except the pleasure of seeing it. Of this kind is pity or compassion, the emotion we feel for the misery of others, when we either see it, or are made to conceive it in a very lively manner.[22]

Using the theory of moral sentiments, Yiu and colleagues posit that some Chinese entrepreneurs are altruistically motivated to promote a morally effective economic system by engaging in social entrepreneurial activities. Focusing on China's Guangcai (Glorious) Program, a social entrepreneurship project initiated by private entrepreneurs to combat poverty and contribute to regional development, the authors found that private entrepreneurs were motivated to participate in social entrepreneurship programs if they had suffered distressing experiences themselves, including limited educational opportunities, unemployment, rural poverty, or startup location hardship.[23] These prior experiences led them to connect personally and emotionally with those who were in need, and thus express a form of compassion.

2.1 Compassion as a Determinant of Social Entrepreneurship

Miller and colleagues note that compassion, through orientation toward and emotional connection with others, acts as a prosocial motivator of cognitive and affective processes that are considered preconditions for undertaking social entrepreneurship. These processes include:

- integrative thinking;
- inducing prosocial judgments regarding the costs and benefits of social entrepreneurship; and
- fostering commitment to alleviate others' suffering.[24]

Integrative thinking is a critical antecedent of social entrepreneurship because it enables an individual to combine social and economic goals. In other words, it allows individuals to discover that social and economic goals are not mutually exclusive.

Although these processes increase the likelihood of social entrepreneurial behavior, they do not act in isolation. Compassion-triggered cognitions and emotions do not by themselves lead to social venture creation. Rather, such processes are more likely to foster social entrepreneurship when used in institutional settings that are favorable to social entrepreneurship.[25] Compassion results in the creation of a social venture when paired with institutional factors that channel it toward social entrepreneurship.[26] Thus, the external environment determines whether compassion would be likely to foster social entrepreneurial activities. In other words, compassion is a necessary but not sufficient condition for social entrepreneurship to emerge in a given society.

Miller and colleagues argue that compassion acts as a prosocial motivator fundamentally through its orientation toward and emotional connection with others who are suffering. Prosocial motivation is the desire to increase one's efforts to benefit other people.[27] Compassion motivates social entrepreneurial activity through four mechanisms:

- it directs one's attention from self-concern to concern for others and their suffering;[28]
- it increases one's belief in the significance of others' suffering and one's understanding of the issues contributing to it;
- it encourages a concerted response for the benefit of others; and
- it can make others' suffering personally relevant and generalize such concerns to others.[29]

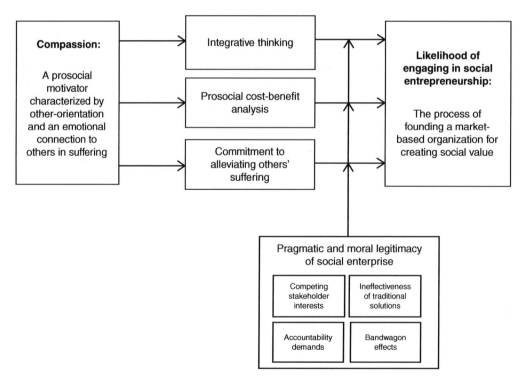

Figure 3.1 How compassion encourages social entrepreneurship.[30]

This model, which attempts to explain the role of compassion in the creation of social ventures, has not been empirically tested, and some authors have criticized it for not fully explicating social entrepreneurs' motivation by arguing that compassion is a questionable choice in a study of social entrepreneurship for three reasons.[31] First, compassion is a poorly distinguished concept because it is only a borderline emotion[32] that overlaps with more basic concepts, such as empathy, and it can be fleeting.[33] Second, compassion can have many negative consequences. Third, compassion does not appear to be a basis for differentiating which individuals will engage in social entrepreneurship and which will not, since it "lies at the core of what it means to be human."[34] Despite these shortcomings, though, the model of entrepreneurial compassion remains a useful step in explaining the role of compassion in social entrepreneurship.

3   Moral Engagement and Social Entrepreneurship

In an earlier study, I proposed a model of moral engagement to explain why some people decide to become social entrepreneurs.[35] The model draws on Bandura's theory of moral disengagement.[36] However, it departs from the latter by focusing on positive moral agency. If humans can commit atrocities and inhumane acts against other human beings, they can also engage in positive actions that benefit others. Before explaining the key assumptions of the moral engagement model, it is important to understand the main assumptions of Bandura's theory of moral disengagement.

3.1   Bandura's Theory of Moral Disengagement

Bandura developed his theory of moral disengagement to explain why people engage in cruel and inhumane acts. He contends that the exercise of moral agency has dual aspects—*inhibitive* and *proactive*.[37] The inhibitive form is manifested in the power to refrain from behaving inhumanely, whereas the proactive form is expressed in the power to behave humanely. The latter form is an expression of proactive morality rooted in social obligation. Moral agency is embedded in a broader sociocognitive self-theory encompassing self-organizing, proactive, self-reflective, and self-regulatory mechanisms rooted in personal standards linked to self-sanction.[38] Several moral agency mechanisms must be activated for people to engage in cruel and inhumane acts against their fellow human beings. To engage in cruelty, perpetrators morally dissociate themselves from their victims. Moral disengagement centers on the following aspects:

- the reconstrual of the conduct itself so that it is not viewed as immoral;
- the operation of the agency of action so that perpetrators can minimize their role in causing harm;
- the consequences that flow from actions; and
- how the victims of maltreatment are regarded by devaluing them as human beings and blaming them for what is being done to them.[39]

The four cognitive mechanisms that perpetrators of inhumane acts go through are:

- moral justification;
- euphemistic labeling;
- advantageous comparison; and
- displacement of responsibility.[40]

In moral justification, the perpetrator reconstructs the motive of the inhumane action. In euphemistic labeling, the perpetrator uses language that reduces the inhumane aspect of the behavior. Euphemistic language is used to make harmful conduct "respectable" and to reduce personal responsibility.[41] For example, calling civilian casualties "collateral damage" is a form of euphemistic labeling. In advantageous comparison, the perpetrator compares the inhumane acts to others to legitimize them. Such comparison leads to some degree of exoneration. In displacement of responsibility, the perpetrator obscures or minimizes his/her role in the harm caused. This can be done when the actions are committed in a group, when the perpetrator receives orders from a higher authority, or when the harmful conduct is collective.

3.2 The Model of Moral Engagement

The moral engagement model I propose also draws from the literature on moral mandates.[42] A moral mandate is a selective self-expressive stand on a specific issue, not a generalized orientation toward the world.[43] People have a moral mandate when they have a strong attitude that they see as rooted in moral conviction. These attitudes rooted in moral convictions could influence social entrepreneurs' reactions toward unmet social needs. Thus, the *moral mandate effect* may help to explain social entrepreneurs' perceptions of unmet social needs to the extent that commitment to a moral mandate allows perceivers to classify the actions of institutions, authorities, ingroup or outgroup members, and even themselves into the mutually exclusive categories of legitimate thought or deed versus fundamental transgression.[44]

As illustrated in Figure 3.2, the model of moral engagement suggests that the existence of social needs triggers feelings that personal moral mandates have been violated. These feelings subsequently trigger a moral engagement response to act. The model suggests that a moral engagement response influences the creation of social ventures. As a consequence, moral engagement is the main determinant of social venture creation. Moral engagement motivates a social entrepreneur to act and serves both as a motive and as a justification for action. A recent study found that social entrepreneurs were motivated by empathy with marginalized people and a feeling of moral obligation.[45] To some extent, these findings lend support to the model of moral engagement. Individuals who become social entrepreneurs may think that they have a moral obligation to address social needs and provide some form of comfort to those who are socially disenfranchised.

Moral engagement refers to the extent to which social entrepreneurs are deeply committed to their ideals and feel morally obligated to pursue them. The construct of moral

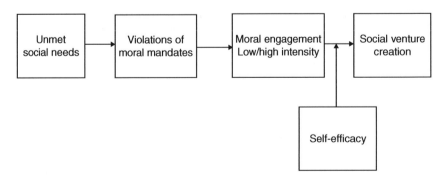

Figure 3.2 The model of social entrepreneurs' moral engagement.[46]

engagement is particularly important for social entrepreneurs because it conveys the intention that addressing a particular social problem is "the right thing to do." In developing a strong sense of moral engagement, social entrepreneurs are more motivated to help others than to fulfill their selfish interests. Moral engagement emphasizes the sense of duty. People are motivated to act on the basis of an internalized sense of duty and uphold moral norms.[47]

The construct of moral engagement encompasses two components: *inner-directed* moral engagement and *outer-directed* moral engagement. The former refers to the extent to which the person is morally obligated to fulfill his/her own goals and objectives, whereas the latter refers to the extent to which the person feels obligated to meet others' expectations. In the case of social entrepreneurs, inner-directed moral engagement would translate into a desire to feel morally compelled to engage in activities that may make a difference regardless of social approval. Outer-directed moral engagement would occur whenever the social entrepreneur is compelled to act because of societal expectations.[48]

Moral engagement is a dynamic construct that can be represented on a continuum ranging from low to high. Thus, the model proposes the construct of *intensity of moral engagement*,[49] which refers to the strength of a social entrepreneur's moral commitment and determination to create a social venture. It is possible that individuals who experience a higher intensity of moral engagement would be more likely to create social ventures compared to those who express a lower intensity of moral engagement. The model acknowledges the existence of boundary conditions, such as self-efficacy. Being morally engaged could foster social entrepreneurship if individuals believe in their capacity to undertake such ventures. Like the model of compassion described earlier, the moral engagement model has not been empirically validated. Nonetheless, it represents an interesting attempt to explain the motivation underlying social venture creation.

4 Social Justice as a Motivator of Social Entrepreneurship

Is social entrepreneurship a response to perceived social injustice? This question is interesting when one tries to understand the reason why people decide to become social entrepreneurs. To the extent that the purpose of a social venture is to address a social need, the existence of that social need may be construed as an injustice that needs to be addressed. Thus, the social entrepreneur acts to correct a perceived wrong. Social entrepreneurs could be motivated by their own life experiences or by historical awareness of social injustice and inequality.[50] Research on organizational justice contends that for an injustice to occur there must be someone who can be held accountable. If there is no one to blame, then injustice has not occurred.[51] In the case of social injustice, governments, market forces, or institutions could be blamed for the plight of the poor and the needy. The perception of social injustice may trigger a moral response that motivates the social entrepreneur to act.

Reactions to social injustices are implied in the model of moral engagement. The unmet social needs could be construed as a result of perceived social injustice, which triggers a deontic response—that is, a moral obligation to act. The victims of the social injustice are humanized by the would-be social entrepreneurs. As Bandura suggested, humanization can arouse empathic sentiments and a strong sense of social obligation linked to evaluative self-sanction that motivates action on others' behalf irrespective of one's self-interest or even at one's own peril.[52]

Social entrepreneurial activities occur as a result of market or government failure. Hence, the social entrepreneur acts to address the social issue that is not otherwise addressed by market of government initiatives. One of the reasons that could motivate a social entrepreneur to do so could be the quest for social justice. An individual could frame a social issue in such a way that addressing it becomes a means to redress an apparent injustice. This gives an impetus to the social entrepreneur or other individuals to join him or her. The quest for social justice can be a powerful motivator for an individual to become a social entrepreneur. Social entrepreneurs have a strong sense of justice.[53] They also tend to be altruistic, morally outraged by injustice, and sensitive to issues of equity.[54] A study conducted on a group of six prominent social entrepreneurs in the UK found that they were motivated by social justice, sustainable futures, doing something worthwhile, making a difference, and knowing that others breathe easier because of their actions.[55] These could all be considered as altruistic motives.

Social entrepreneurs engage in social ventures because they want to redress perceived social injustices. Using equity theory could help explain the drive for social entrepreneurship. Equity theory contends that people compare the ratio of their inputs/outputs to that of another person. When the two ratios are unequal, the person experiences feelings of inequity and is motivated to restore equity.[56] In the case of social entrepreneurship as a desire to redress perceived injustices, the individual who starts the social venture is not necessarily the victim of a perceived injustice. Rather, he/she sees that others are being socially *victimized*. As a result, he/she feels compelled to take action.

The example of the best-known social entrepreneur, Muhammad Yunus, is illustrative of this desire to restore social justice. As a young economics professor at Chittagong University in Bangladesh in 1976, Yunus lent $27 out of his own pocket to a group of poor craftsmen in the nearby town of Jobra. To boost the impact of that small sum, Yunus served as guarantor for a larger loan from a bank, and thereby launched a village-based enterprise called the Grameen Project. In doing so, he started an industry, known as microcredit. The Grameen Bank is now a powerful financial institution: it has lent more than $5.1 billion to 5.3 million people and is a leading advocate for the world's poor.

The bank is built on Yunus's conviction that poor people can be both reliable borrowers and avid entrepreneurs. Grameen has spread the idea of microcredit throughout Bangladesh, the rest of Southern Asia, and elsewhere in the developing world. One of his first moves was to focus on women because they are most likely to think of the family's needs. This was a radical step in a traditional Muslim society, and it took Yunus six years to reach his initial goal of a 50–50 gender distribution among borrowers. Today, though, 96 percent of Grameen's borrowers are women. "If banks made large loans, he made small loans. If banks required paperwork, his loans were for the illiterate. Whatever banks did, he did the opposite," explained Sam Daley-Harris, director of the Microcredit Summit Campaign. "He's a genius."[57] In 2006, Yunus was awarded the Nobel Peace Prize because of his efforts to address social issues and empower the poor.

Another example is that of Gram Vikas, a social venture located in Orissa, India. The purpose of this project is to help communities in rural villages gain access to clean water and set up and maintain water-supply and sanitation systems as a basis for improving health, restoring dignity, empowering women, and breaking the vicious circle of poverty.[58] By its actions, Gram Vikas also intends to combat social injustice.

Summary

This chapter has discussed what motivates people to start social ventures. It builds on the literature on entrepreneurial motivation to discuss why people decide to become social entrepreneurs. Three types of motivation—compassion, moral engagement, and the quest for social justice—are deemed to motivate the creation of social ventures specifically.

Key Terms

Compassion; entrepreneurial motivation; moral engagement; pull theory; push theory; social entrepreneurial motivation; social justice

Review Questions

1 Explain how the pull and push approaches contribute to social entrepreneurial motivations. Do these two approaches differ in explaining social and commercial entrepreneurial motivations?
2 Do you agree with the assumption that social entrepreneurs have a strong sense of social justice (yes or no)? Explain.
3 Do you think that entrepreneurship by necessity could apply to the creation of social ventures (yes or no)? Explain.
4 How do you think moral engagement might explain the motivation to become a social entrepreneur?
5 Explain the role of compassion in social entrepreneurship. Do you think that social entrepreneurs are more compassionate than commercial entrepreneurs? Explain.
6 Compare the models of compassion and moral engagement. Do you think they represent acceptable models for explaining the creation of social ventures? Could these models be used to explain commercial entrepreneurship?
7 Discuss the role of moral mandates in social venture creation.
8 Identify examples of prosocial motivations that social entrepreneurs display.
9 Discuss whether moral disengagement can prevent people from becoming social entrepreneurs.
10 Do you agree with the assumption that social entrepreneurship is a reaction to perceived social injustice? Should governments be held responsible for the social problems that plague their countries (yes or no)? Explain.

Application Questions

1 Watch the video in which Victoria Hale explains her motivations for starting the One-World Health Institute at www.youtube.com/watch?v=2aVBDYx9Hmw. What were the main drivers of her desire to start her social venture?
2 List the five most important things you wish to achieve in life. Identify the actions you might take to achieve them. What emotions would you feel if you achieved them? What emotions would you feel if you failed to achieve them?
3 Do some research on Muhammad Yunus and the Grameen Bank. Identify and discuss the motivations that led Yunus to start the Grameen Bank as a social venture.
4 Review the moral engagement model introduced in this chapter. Can people be trained to display a high degree of moral engagement?
5 Grace Hightower De Niro, the philanthropist wife of Robert De Niro, launched Grace Hightower & Coffees of Rwanda in January 2013.[59] It is a for-profit operation that aims to boost growers' incomes by paying above "fair trade" prices for beans and then selling them to US stores. Hightower De Niro says the idea arose when she heard Rwanda's president, Paul Kagame, requesting "'trade not aid.' I thought that was really inspiring."[60] What do you think motivated Hightower De Niro to start this venture? How does the company fulfill its social mission?

Application Case 1: Dignified Mobile Toilets[61]

DMT Mobile and Portable Toilets Ltd.

Dignified Mobile Toilets
World Economic Forum

Dignified Mobile Toilets (DMT) is a social enterprise that was the first organization to offer a mobile toilet service in Nigeria. Isaac Durojaiye, who was deeply concerned about health and environmental issues, launched the venture in 1992 after observing that there were only about 500 functional public toilets in the whole country, whose population at the time was 130 million people. Moreover, even this small number of public toilets was poorly maintained. Durojaiye came up with the idea for DMT after thinking about how to deliver an essential service in a manner that was both self-sustaining and would simultaneously lift providers out of poverty. The company's mobile toilets are made of high-quality plastic and are available for sale, rent, or lease. DMT maintains the toilets and its specialized trucks evacuate the human waste twice a week from each one. The toilets are usually situated in public parks, at bus stops, or in any other location where demand is likely to be high. Durojaiye explained, "We are performing a major social service as we are eliminating the need for people to defecate in public places." DMT also runs a "Basic Toilet for Schools" scheme, through which schools are offered mobile toilets at discounted rates, and the company has donated 100 toilets to public schools in the states of Lagos and Ogun.

Each mobile toilet serves about 100 people a day, with the fee set at 20 Nigerian naira per use, which amounts to about $15 per day—a good sum of money by Nigerian standards. Businesses can pay to advertise their products on the toilet doors, which generates about 20 percent of DMT's revenue. Sixty percent of each toilet's total revenue goes to the toilet manager, while 40 percent returns to the company to sustain its operations. The company is currently planning to recycle the waste to generate bio-gas, electricity, and fertilizer for farmers.

According to Durojaiye, before DMT was created, the workers who disposed of human waste in Nigeria were ashamed to do the job, so much so that they covered their faces so that nobody would recognize them. This changed with the launch of DMT. As Durojaiye put it, "I named it Dignified to show the world that there is dignity in the business. There is nothing to be ashamed about human waste, it is a reality. We all have to answer the call of nature."

In 2008, Durojaiye became one of five Ashoka-Lemelson fellows, who were recognized for developing innovative sanitation business models. Unfortunately, he died on April 3, 2012, at the age of just 50. Despite his premature death, DMT now operates in all of Nigeria's major cities and it continues to grow and prosper.

Discussion Questions

1   Identify some of the motivations behind the creation of DMT.
2   Discuss the motivations to start DMT from the perspective of the compassionate model of social entrepreneurship.
3   Discuss the motivations to start DMT from the perspective of the moral engagement model of social entrepreneurship.
4   Watch the video about Isaac Durojaiye and DMT at www.youtube.com/watch? v=XjTGm3YQR4s. Describe the problem(s) that DMT is solving.
5   Do some research on DMT's plans to transform human waste into gas and electricity. What other uses might DMT find for recycled human waste?

Application Case 2: Aduna: Transforming the Baobab Fruit into a Global Product

There are many different social ventures created in Africa in order to improve the lifestyle of its citizens. Some social ventures raise awareness and seek help from those who are willing, while others are created to generate revenue and create a profit so that the citizens can make money for themselves. Aduna was founded by Andrew Hunt and Nick Salter in 2011. Their goal is to help rural small farm holders to generate revenue and make a profit, thereby improving their lives. On its website, Aduna underlines that its mission is to create demand for under-utilized natural products from small-scale producers in rural Africa.[1]

During a trip in Senegal a French-speaking country in West Africa, Salter had the opportunity to taste a drink made from a baobab fruit. The baobab fruit is one of the most dense-nutrient fruits. Its seeds contain vitamin C, thiamin, potassium, calcium, and vitamin B6.[2] Salter realized that the baobab fruit could be turned into a major product. Salter had heard about Andrew Hunt as a person who was also currently working on transforming the idea of the baobab fruit into a drink. He then contacted him. Salter had met Andrew Hunt before. Andrew Hunt had spent time before in The Gambia, West Africa, on a business trip where the baobab tree also existed. Andrew Hunt and Nick Salter started to brainstorm ideas about how they could make the product and globalize it. Their goal was to use the baobab tree to create and provide a sustainable income to between 8 to10 million different rural households.[3]

Salter and Hunt recognized that more than 25% of the world's botanical species come from Africa, but only less than 1% ever reach the shelves of beauty and health retailers.[4] They wanted to create a marketing brand that took complete advantage of the benefits that the unique natural products actually had. They strived to provide these products to consumers, while also making a direct contribution to the large number of small-scale producers who cultivate these products. By doing this they are able to accomplish their ultimate mission, which is promoting the positivity and vibrancy of Africa that they have personally seen through their own eyes.

Aduna's business model consisted of creating a demand for a natural product produced by small-scale farmers, improving the lives of these farmers and generating a profit. The natural products from the baobab tree were considered as "super-ingredients." This process is beneficial for the farmers because these super-ingredients already grow in the wild on their land, while other super-ingredients used to make different products can effortlessly be cultivated by small farmers. Aduna invests heavily in marketing in order to promote and raise the awareness for using these super-ingredients. In addition to creating awareness, Aduna also promotes and educates consumers on the health benefits of using these natural products. They sell them as organic powders and raw energy bars in beauty and health stores throughout the world. This creates global markets for the products. Aduna is having a significant impact by improving the community. For example, it is working in partnership with government and community associations in Ghana to create a supply chain where more than 1,200 women and families are buying the raw materials, processing them and selling them to Aduna. In Senegal and Ethiopia, more than 4,400 women are part of Aduna's supply chain.[5]

Aduna's products are sold in retail stores in the United Kingdom and elsewhere. Retail stores, such as Whole Food Market, Liberty, and Holland and Barrett in the United Kingdom carry its products. It is also making products from the Moringa tree and has introduced the Aduna super-cocoa, the first cocoa product with a European-approved claim for health effects in 2015. As a result of its success, Aduna won the United Kingdom's Business Angels' Association Award (UKBAA) and the Global Sourcing Council's Innovative Sourcing Award.

Discussion Questions

1   Why do you think Aduna has been so successful?
2   What changes, if any, would you make to Aduna's social venture plan?
3   If you were in charge, would you work on the expansion of this social venture?
4   Can you think of other areas, products or geographic locations where Aduna could expand?

References

1   http://aduna.com/ [Retrieved on April 14, 2016].
2   Aduna creates a market for baobab tree. *http://www.theguardian.com/sustainable-business/2015/apr/30/aduna-creates-a-market-for-baobab-fruit*. [Retrieved on April 15, 2016].
3   http://aduna.com/pages/supporting-small-scale-producers-aduna [Retrieved on April 14, 2016].
4   http://aduna.com/pages/our-story-aduna [Retrieved on April 14, 2016].
5   Aduna creates a market for baobab tree. *http://www.theguardian.com/sustainable-business/2015/apr/30/aduna-creates-a-market-for-baobab-fruit*. [Retrieved on April 15, 2016].

Notes

1 Herron, L., & Sapienza, H. J. (1992). The entrepreneur and the initiation of new venture launch activities. *Entrepreneurship Theory and Practice*, 17(1), 49–55, at p. 49.
2 Shane, S., Locke, E. A., & Collins, C. J. (2003). Entrepreneurial motivation. *Human Resource Management*, 13(2), 257–279.
3 Shane, S., Locke, E. A., & Collins, C. J. (2003). Entrepreneurial motivation. *Human Resource Management*, 13(2), 257–279.
4 Carsrud, A., & Brannback, M. (2011). Entrepreneurial motivations: What do we still need to know? *Journal of Small Business Management*, 49(1), 9–26.
5 Schjoedt, L., & Shaver, K. G. (2007). Deciding on an entrepreneurial career: A test of the pull and push hypotheses using the panel study of entrepreneurial dynamics data. *Entrepreneurship Theory and Practice*, 31(5), 733–752; Segal, G., Borgia, D., & Schoenfeld, J. (2005). The motivation to become an entrepreneur. *International Journal of Entrepreneurial Behavior and Research*, 11(1), 42–57; Gilad, B., & Levine, P. (1986). A behavioral model of entrepreneurial supply. *Journal of Small Business Management*, 24(4), 45–54.
6 Gilad, B., & Levine, P. (1986). A behavioral model of entrepreneurial supply. *Journal of Small Business Management*, 24(4), 45–54; Williams, C. C. (2008). Beyond necessity-driven versus opportunity-driven entrepreneurship: A study of informal entrepreneurs in England, Russia and Ukraine. *International Journal of Entrepreneurship and Innovation*, 9(3), 157–165; McMullen, J. S., Bagby, D. R., & Palich, L. E. (2008). Economic freedom and the motivation to engage in entrepreneurial action. *Entrepreneurship Theory and Practice*, 32(5), 875–895.
7 Amit, R., & Muller, E. (1995). Push and pull entrepreneurship (two types based on motivation). *Journal of Small Business and Entrepreneurship*, 12(4), 64–80; Kirkwood, J. (2009). Motivational factors in a push–pull theory of entrepreneurship. *Gender in Management: An International Journal*, 24(5), 346–364.
8 Hessels, J., van Gelderen, M., & Thurik, R. (2008). Entrepreneurial aspirations, motivations, and their drivers. *Small Business Economics*, 31(3), 323–339.
9 Suzuki, K., Kim, S. H., & Bae, Z. T. (2002). Entrepreneurship in Japan and Silicon Valley: A comparative study. *Technovation*, 22, 595–606.
10 Maslow, H. A. (1943). A theory of human motivation. *Psychological Review*, 50(4), 370–396; Maslow, H. A. (1954). *Motivation and personality*. New York: Harper.
11 Germak, A. J., & Robinson, J. A. (2014). Exploring the motivation of nascent social entrepreneurs. *Journal of Social Psychology*, 5(1), 5–21.
12 Yitshaki, R., & Kropp, F. (2011). Becoming a social entrepreneur: Understanding motivations using life story analysis. *International Journal of Business and Globalization*, 7(3), 319–331.
13 Yitshaki, R., & Kropp, F. (In press). Motivation and opportunity recognition of social entrepreneurs. *Journal of Small Business Management*.
14 Sharir, M., & Lerner, M. (2006). Gauging the success of social ventures initiated by individual social entrepreneurs. *Journal of World Business*, 41, 6–20.
15 Santos, F. (2012). A positive theory of social entrepreneurship. *Journal of Business Ethics*, 111(3), 335–351.
16 Germak, A. J., & Robinson, J. A. (2014). Exploring the motivation of nascent social entrepreneurs. *Journal of Social Psychology*, 5(1), 5–21.
17 Baierl, R., Grichnik, D., Sporrle, M., & Welpe, I. M. (2014). Antecedents of social entrepreneurial intentions: The role of an individual's general social appraisal. *Journal of Social Entrepreneurship*, 5(2), 123–145.
18 Braga, J. C., Proença, T., & Ferreira, M. R. (2014). Motivations for social entrepreneurship: Evidences from Portugal. *Tekhne, Review of Applied Management Studies*, 12(1), 11–21.
19 *Oxford English Dictionary* (1989). 2nd edition. Oxford: Oxford University Press.
20 Lazarus, R. S. (1991). Progress on a cognitive–motivational–relational theory of emotion. *American Psychologist*, 46(8), 819–834; Nussbaum, M. (1996). Compassion: The basic social emotion.

Social Philosophy and Policy, 13, 27–58; Goetz, J. L., Keltner, D., & Simon-Thomas, E. (2010). Compassion: An evolutionary analysis and empirical review. *Psychological Bulletin, 136*(3), 351–374; Batson C. D. (1987). Prosocial motivation: Is it ever truly altruistic? *Advances in Experimental Social Psychology, 20*, 65–122; Batson, C. D., & Shaw, L. L. (1991). Evidence for altruism: Toward a pluralism of prosocial motives. *Psychological Inquiry, 2*(2), 107–122.

21 Miller, T. L., Grimes, M. G., McMullean, J. S., & Vogus, T. J. (2012). Venturing for others with heart and head: How compassion encourages social entrepreneurship. *Academy of Management Review, 37*(4), 616–640.

22 Smith, A. (1759). *The theory of moral sentiments*. London: Henry G. Bohn, at p. 1.

23 Yiu, D. W., Wan, W. P., Ng, F. W., Chen, X., & Su, J. (2014). Sentimental drivers of social entrepreneurship: A study of China's Guangcai. *Management and Organization Review, 10*(1), 55–80.

24 Miller, T. L., Grimes, M. G., McMullean, J. S., & Vogus, T. J. (2012). Venturing for others with heart and head: How compassion encourages social entrepreneurship. *Academy of Management Review, 37*(4), 616–640.

25 Miller, T. L., Grimes, M. G., McMullean, J. S., & Vogus, T. J. (2012). Venturing for others with heart and head: How compassion encourages social entrepreneurship. *Academy of Management Review, 37*(4), 616–640; Grimes, M. G., McMullen, J. S., Vogus, T. J., & Miller, T. L. (2013). Studying the origins of social entrepreneurship: Compassion and the role of embedded agency. *Academy of Management Review, 38*(3), 460–463.

26 Grimes, M. G., McMullen, J. S., Vogus, T. J., & Miller, T. L. (2013). Studying the origins of social entrepreneurship: Compassion and the role of embedded agency. *Academy of Management Review, 38*(3), 460–463.

27 Grant, A. M. (2008). Does intrinsic motivation fuel the prosocial fire? Motivational synergy in predicting persistence, performance, and productivity. *Journal of Applied Psychology, 93*, 48–58.

28 Solomon, R. C. (1998). The moral psychology of business: Care and compassion in the corporation. *Business Ethics Quarterly, 8*, 515–533.

29 Miller, T. L., Grimes, M. G., McMullen, J. S., & Vogus, T. J. (2012). Venturing for others with heart and head: How compassion encourages social entrepreneurship. *Academy of management Review, 37*(4), 616–640.

30 Miller, T. L., Grimes, M. G., McMullen, J. S., & Vogus, T. J. (2012). Venturing for others with heart and head: How compassion encourages social entrepreneurship. *Academy of Management Review, 37*(4), 616–640, at p. 620.

31 Arend, J. R. (2013). A heart–mind–opportunity nexus: Distinguishing social entrepreneurship for entrepreneurs. *Academy of Management Review, 38*(2), 313–315.

32 Lazarus, R. S. (1991). Progress on a cognitive–motivational–relational theory of emotion. *American Psychologist, 46*(8), 819–834.

33 Miller, T. L., Grimes, M. G., McMullean, J. S., & Vogus, T. J. (2012). Venturing for others with heart and head: How compassion encourages social entrepreneurship. *Academy of Management Review, 37*(4), 616–640.

34 Kanov, J. M., Maitlis, S., Worline, M. C., Dutton, J. E., Frost, P. J., & Lilius, J. M. (2004). Compassion in organizational life. *American Behavioral Scientist, 47*(6), 808–827, at p. 808.

35 Beugré, C. D. (2014). Exploring the motivation to create social ventures: A model of moral engagement. *International Journal of Entrepreneurship Venturing, 6*(1), 37–50.

36 Bandura, A. (1999). Moral disengagement in the perpetration of inhumanities. *Personality and Social Psychology Review, 3*(3), 193–209.

37 Bandura, A. (1999). Moral disengagement in the perpetration of inhumanities. *Personality and Social Psychology Review, 3*(3), 193–209.

38 Bandura, A. (1999). Moral disengagement in the perpetration of inhumanities. *Personality and Social Psychology Review, 3*(3), 193–209.

39 Bandura, A. (1999). Moral disengagement in the perpetration of inhumanities. *Personality and Social Psychology Review*, 3(3), 193–209.

40 Bandura, A. (1999). Moral disengagement in the perpetration of inhumanities. *Personality and Social Psychology Review*, 3(3), 193–209.

41 Bandura, A. (1999). Moral disengagement in the perpetration of inhumanities. *Personality and Social Psychology Review*, 3(3), 193–209.

42 Blasi, A. (1980). Bridging moral cognition and moral action: A critical review of the literature. *Psychological Bulletin*, 88(1), 1–45; Aquino, K. F., & Reed, II, A. (2002). The self-importance of moral identity. *Journal of Personality and Social Psychology*, 83(6), 1423–1440; Skitka, L. J., Bauman, C. W., & Sargis, E. G. (2005). Moral conviction: Another contributor to attitude strength or something more? *Journal of Personality and Social Psychology*, 88(6), 895–917; Mullen, E., & Skitka, L. J. (2006). Exploring the psychological underpinnings of the moral mandate effect: Motivating reasoning, group differentiation, or anger? *Journal of Personality and Social Psychology*, 90(4), 629–643.

43 Skitka, L. J. (2002). Do the means justify the ends, or the ends sometimes justify the means? A value protection model of justice reasoning. *Personality and Social Psychology Bulletin*, 28(5), 588–597.

44 Skitka, L. J. (2002). Do the means justify the ends, or the ends sometimes justify the means? A value protection model of justice reasoning. *Personality and Social Psychology Bulletin*, 28(5), 588–597; Mullen, E., & Skitka, L. J. (2006). Exploring the psychological underpinnings of the moral mandate effect: Motivating reasoning, group differentiation, or anger? *Journal of Personality and Social Psychology*, 90(4), 629–643.

45 Hockerts, K. (2015). The social entrepreneurial antecedents scale (SEAS): A validation study. *Social Enterprise Journal*, 11(3), 260–280.

46 Beugré, C. D. (2014). Exploring the motivation to create social ventures: A model of moral engagement. *International Journal of Entrepreneurship Venturing*, 6(1), 37–50.

47 Kahneman, D., Knestch, J. L., & Thaler, R. H. 1986. Fairness and the assumptions of economics. *Journal of Business*, 59(4), 285–300; Montada, L. (1998). Justice: Just a rational choice? *Social Justice Review*, 11(2), 81–101.

48 Beugré, C. D. (2014). Exploring the motivation to create social ventures: A model of moral engagement. *International Journal of Entrepreneurship Venturing*, 6(1), 37–50.

49 Beugré, C. D. (2014). Exploring the motivation to create social ventures: A model of moral engagement. *International Journal of Entrepreneurship Venturing*, 6(1), 37–50.

50 Van Ryzin, G. G., Grossman, S., Dipadova-Stocks, L., & Bergrud, E. (2009). Portrait of the social entrepreneur: Statistical evidence from a US panel. *Voluntas: International Journal of Voluntary and Nonprofit Organizations*, 20(2), 129–140.

51 Folger, R. (2001). Fairness as deonance. In S. Gilliland, D. D. Steiner, & D. Skarlicki (Eds.), *Theoretical and cultural perspectives on organizational justice* (pp. 3–33). Greenwich, CT: Information Age Publishing.

52 Bandura, A. (1986). *Social foundations of thought and action: A social cognitive theory*. Englewood Cliffs, NJ: Prentice-Hall.

53 Kickul, J., & Lyons, T. S. (2012). *Understanding social entrepreneurship: The relentless pursuit of mission in an ever changing world*. New York: Routledge.

54 Anderson, A. R. (1998). Cultivating the garden of Eden: Environmental entrepreneuring. *Journal of Organizational Change Management*, 11(2), 135–144.

55 Christopoulos, D., & Vogi, S. (2015). The motivation of social entrepreneurs: The roles, agendas and relations of altruistic economic actors. *Journal of Social Entrepreneurship*, 6(1), 1–30.

56 Adams, S. J. 1965. Inequity in social exchange. In L. Berkowitz (Ed.), *Advances in Social Experimental Psychology* (2, pp. 267–299). New York: Academic Press.

57 Gangerni, J. (2005). Muhammad Yunus: Microcredit missionary. *Business Week*, December 16, 16.

58 Pless, N. M., & Appel, J. (2012). In pursuit of dignity and social justice: Changing lives through 100% inclusion: How Gram Vikas fosters sustainable rural development. *Journal of Business Ethics, 111*(3), 389–411.

59 Grace Hightower & Coffees of Rwanda. www.coffeeofgrace.com.

60 VanderMey, A. (2013). Rwanda's new buzz. *Fortune, 168*(1), 20–21.

61 Source for this whole section: Olukoya, S. (2006). Answering the call of nature in Lagos. BBC, November 16. http://newsvote.bbc.co.uk/mpapps/pagetools/print/news.bbc.co.uk/2/hi/africa/6133556.stm, retrieved on June 10, 2013.

Chapter 4

The External Environment of Social Ventures

Learning Objectives

1 Discuss the impact of the external environment on entrepreneurial activity.
2 Assess the external environment of social ventures.
3 Describe the role of institutional environment on social venture creation.
4 Discuss the tools used to analyze the external environment of social entrepreneurship.

It is well documented that entrepreneurship is the outcome of both internal and external factors. This chapter focuses on the role of external factors in the creation of social ventures, now that Chapters 2 and 3 have discussed the role of internal factors. It is organized into three main sections. The first discusses the role of the external environment on entrepreneurship. This discussion should help students to understand how the external environment facilitates or impedes the creation of new business ventures. With this understanding, students are equipped to assess the role of the external environment on social venture creation, which is discussed in the second section. This section uses the institutional environment of entrepreneurship and the PEST model as conceptual frameworks to explain how environmental forces shape social entrepreneurial activity in a given country. The final section discusses the traditional strategic management tools that can be used to analyze the external environment of social ventures.

I Understanding the External Environment of Entrepreneurship

I.I The Macro-Environment of Entrepreneurship

Context is important in understanding entrepreneurship.[1] It determines when, how, and why entrepreneurship happens; it can be an asset or a liability that shapes entrepreneurship; but, equally, entrepreneurship may influence context, too.[2] Entrepreneurs can bring about social change by being engaged and working with the community in which they are embedded.[3] Viewed from this angle, entrepreneurship could be construed as a socially embedded process.[4] The social problems prevailing in a particular country may influence the likelihood of creating social ventures to address them. For example, Safeena Husain created Educate Girls (www.educategirls.in) in 2007 to address the issue of girls' education in rural India, which is a significant problem there and in other developing and emerging areas. Such a venture would not be created in the United States or Western Europe, where girls' education is not an endemic social problem.

As the saying goes, *no man is an island*. This adage could be extended to entrepreneurship by arguing that no *entrepreneur is an island* and surely *no firm is an island*. The implication of this saying is that entrepreneurs and the firms they create always operate in environments that shape them. In discussing the impact of the external environment on social venture creation, it is important to bear in mind that to date little attention has focused on understanding the macro-level factors that influence the prevalence of social ventures. However, research in social entrepreneurship will advance quickly if it utilizes the knowledge gained in the study of commercial entrepreneurship.[5] Thus, social entrepreneurship scholars should build their theories by relying on the strong tradition of entrepreneurship theory and research to the extent that social entrepreneurs are one species of the genus entrepreneur.[6] This is particularly important because social entrepreneurs use both for-profit and nonprofit organizational forms.

Generally, three broad types of environment affect entrepreneurship:

- political;
- economic; and
- sociocultural.

The political environment includes factors such as government policies, the stability of the political system, democracy, and rules of law, and it can facilitate or impede entrepreneurial activity. Studies using Global Entrepreneurship Monitor (GEM) survey data found that government policies tend to influence entrepreneurial activity. Specifically, governments that provide strong property rights facilitate entrepreneurial activities, whereas entrepreneurial activities tend to be limited where corruption and weak property rights prevail.[7] Other studies have found that specific government policies, such as expenditure on welfare programs, affect the creation of both commercial and social ventures.[8] The economic environment of a country includes the state of the economy in general (growth or recession), exchange rates, monetary policy, the financial system as well as the level of employment or unemployment and capital availability. The sociocultural environment includes the value system of the country, demographic factors, culture and traditions, and lifestyle.

Research has recently added a fourth type of environment—the technological environment—to create the acronym PEST (political, economic, social, and technological). The PEST model will be used to explore the role of the four environmental factors in social venture creation in Section 2. However, it is important to understand the concept of institutional environment and its role in entrepreneurship. The external environment has recently been reconceptualized as the institutional environment, and entrepreneurship scholars are using the construct of institutional profile to describe the external forces that influence new venture creation in a given country.[9]

1.2   Institutional Profile and Entrepreneurship

A country's institutional environment comprises relatively stable rules, social norms, and cognitions that guide, constrain, and liberate domestic economic activity.[10] It sets the framework for market transactions by defining the alternative courses of action that are open to firms.[11] Institutions structure human interactions and are made up of formal constraints (laws, rules, constitutions), informal constraints (norms, behaviors, conventions, self-imposed codes of conduct), and their enforcement characteristics, and form the

Table 4.1 Description of Scott's institutional profile of a country

Regulatory	Normative	Cognitive
Laws, regulations, rules set by legal and formerly recognized institutions	Social norms, values, and beliefs influence the relative social desirability of entrepreneurship as an occupational choice	Availability of expertise and knowledge Perceptions and shared mental models

incentive structure of a society. In consequence, the political and economic institutions are the underlying determinants of economic performance.[12]

Scott provided an interesting classification of the institutional environment encompassing three dimensions:

- normative;
- cognitive; and
- regulatory.[13]

These three dimensions are illustrated in Table 4.1. They were further operationalized by Kostova, who introduced the concept of a three-dimensional institutional profile to explain how a country's government policies (regulatory dimension), widely shared social knowledge (cognitive dimension), and value system (normative dimension) affect domestic business activity.[14] Normative institutions reflect the degree to which a country's residents admire entrepreneurs and entrepreneurial activity.[15] Society's attitude toward entrepreneurs and entrepreneurship influences the level of entrepreneurial activity. A positive attitude toward entrepreneurs and entrepreneurship facilitates the creation of new ventures, whereas a negative attitude inhibits entrepreneurial activity. The cognitive dimension of the institutional environment refers to shared mental models through which people interpret information. It reflects the knowledge and skills possessed by people in a given country as well as the framework they use to categorize and evaluate information.[16] Its influence and legitimacy in a society rest on the common frame of reference or interpretation of a given situation, which are adopted and shared between individuals.[17] The normative environment encourages people to become entrepreneurs, but it takes a strong cognitive and regulatory environment for firms to obtain the resources and legitimacy necessary to secure external investors.[18]

Entrepreneurship scholars have shown that general perceptions of technological uncertainty and attitudes toward risk influence entrepreneurial activity and innovation. As discussed in Chapter 2, risk propensity plays a positive role in fostering entrepreneurship. Thus, a country where people have a tendency to tolerate risk could be a fertile ground for entrepreneurship and innovation. A good example is the United States, which is considered as an innovation-driven economy. By contrast, in cultures where uncertainty and unknown outcomes of individual behavior are perceived negatively, the appreciation of entrepreneurship is lower.[19] Institutional characteristics significantly influence the allocation of entrepreneurial effort. The type of activity in which entrepreneurs engage is likely to influence the potential contribution of entrepreneurship to economic growth and prosperity. Analyzing data from 40 countries collected between 2002 and 2004, Bowen and De Clerq found that the allocation of entrepreneurial effort toward high-growth activities was positively related to a country's financial and educational activities targeted at entrepreneurship and negatively to a country's level of corruption.[20]

The regulatory dimension of the institutional environment consists of laws, regulations, and government policies that promote certain behaviors and restrict others.[21] These factors influence economic growth and set the basic *rules of the game*.[22] Supportive regulatory environments are crucial for the development of entrepreneurial activities. For example, most countries whose regulatory environments are weak tend to have fewer entrepreneurial activities than those whose regulatory environments are strong. In such countries, the informal economy tends to dominate economic activity. Two striking examples are Africa and Latin America, where the informal economy accounts for more than 70 percent of the economic activity in each case. In fact, the instability of the regulatory dimension may lead to corruption. As a case in point, the regulatory environment in Russia explains the low level of entrepreneurship development as measured in terms of both number of startups and number of existing business owners.[23] Most entrepreneurship scholars acknowledge that institutional environments that promote regulation foster the rate of general entrepreneurial activity in a country more than any other factor.[24]

The three pillars identified by Scott could differ from country to country and affect entrepreneurial activity. In some countries, institutional support may be weak and resources very limited. Examples of such countries are found in Africa, Asia, the Middle East, and Latin America. Many entrepreneurs in developing and emerging economies face ecologies that provide neither specialized resources and institutional support nor good general financial, educational, political, or legal infrastructure.[25] Yet, social entrepreneurs in such regions leverage the limited resources that are available to start social ventures that address specific social needs. They often do so by partnering with those located in richer countries or with local governments and development agencies. For example, the Acumen Fund, Ashoka, and the Skoll Foundation provide fellowships to social entrepreneurs based in developing and emerging countries to enhance their capabilities and improve the impact of their social ventures.

Entrepreneurship scholars have studied the impact of the three institutional pillars on entrepreneurial activity in specific countries. For example, Spencer and Gomez drew from the construct of institutional profile to identify normative, cognitive, and regulatory institutional structures that could influence entrepreneurial activity in a given country. They found that cognitive institutions explained the prevalence of small firms in a country as well as the number of new firms listed on the country's stock exchange. Normative institutions were marginally associated with the most basic form of entrepreneurship—self-employment—but not with more advanced forms. The authors also found that per capita GDP explained basic forms of entrepreneurship.[26] Other studies support their findings. For example, Stenholm and colleagues studied the impact of the external environment in 63 countries at various levels of economic development. They found that differences in institutional arrangements were associated with variance in both the rate and the type of entrepreneurial activity across countries. For the formation of innovative, high-growth new ventures, the regulatory environment matters very little, while for high-impact entrepreneurship an institutional environment filled with new opportunities created by knowledge spillovers and the capacity necessary for high-impact entrepreneurship matters most.[27]

In addition to formal institutions, informal institutions play an important role in entrepreneurship. This is especially evident in China, a country where political connections facilitate access to resources and opportunities and provide private protection for property rights.[28] The effects of these political connections are stronger in Chinese regions with weak market and legal institutions.[29] When formal institutions are weak, informal institutions tend to play a critical role in business transactions. In an unstable and weakly structured environment, informal networks often play a key role in helping entrepreneurs mobilize resources, win orders, and cope with the constraints imposed by highly bureaucratic structures and often unfriendly officials.[30] A recent study found that the informal institutions in former Eastern Bloc countries, especially Bulgaria, tend to impede entrepreneurial activity. Williams and Vorley used the concept of institutional asymmetry to explain the discrepancy between the formal and the informal institutions and note that despite efforts to reform formal institutions to make entrepreneurial activity easier, informal institutions have undermined their impact as the culture remains averse to entrepreneurial activity.[31]

Baumol argues that the external environment facilitates the type of entrepreneurship that emerges in a particular society. He uses the term "rules of the game" to indicate the extent to which what is valued and rewarded in a given society influences the emergence of a particular type of entrepreneurship.[32] He also notes that the productive contribution of a society's entrepreneurial activities varies much more because of their allocation between productive activities, such as innovation, and largely unproductive activities, such as rent seeking or organized crime. This allocation is heavily influenced by the relative payoffs society offers to such activities. Most governments around the globe now understand their own roles in facilitating (or impeding) economic performance. Thus, they are enacting policies that are conducive to spurring entrepreneurship and innovation and improving economic performance. There is, then, an increasing tendency for governments around the world to promote entrepreneurship.[33]

The Global Entrepreneurship Monitor (GEM) explores the role of entrepreneurship in national economic growth, unveiling detailed national features and characteristics associated with entrepreneurial activity. The collected data are harmonized by a central team of experts, guaranteeing quality and facilitating cross-national comparisons. GEM has three objectives:

- to measure differences in the level of entrepreneurial activity between countries;
- to uncover factors leading to appropriate levels of entrepreneurship; and
- to suggest policies that may enhance the national level of entrepreneurial activity.

Unlike other entrepreneurship data sets that measure newer and smaller firms, GEM studies measure, at the grassroots level, the behavior of individuals with respect to starting and managing a business. This approach provides a more detailed picture of entrepreneurial activity than is found in official national registry data sets.[34]

An institutional environment that facilitates commercial entrepreneurship is likely to be conducive to the emergence of social entrepreneurship. For example, a country where it is relatively easy to do business could provide incentives for social entrepreneurship to emerge. Using the GEM methodology of Total Entrepreneurial Activity (TEA) in 49 countries, Lepoutre and colleagues found that countries with higher rates of commercial entrepreneurship tended to have higher rates of social entrepreneurial activity. They also found that the form of capitalism prevailing in a country can affect social entrepreneurship. For example, countries with liberal capitalism, such as the United States, tend to have higher rates than countries with cooperative economies, such as most of Western Europe.[35] However, when rules are cumbersome and corruption rampant, social entrepreneurs may not receive many incentives. To the extent that some social ventures rely on donations, an economy that is uncompetitive may not have the ability to develop a strong business sector that can support some types of social venture.

The next section explores the role of the four factors included in the PEST model in entrepreneurship with a particular emphasis on social entrepreneurship. Indeed, the institutional environment defines, creates, and limits social opportunities and thus affects the speed and scope of social entrepreneurship.[36]

2   The PEST Model and Social Entrepreneurship

A PEST analysis consists of assessing the impact of four key factors—political, economic, social, and technological—on a company (see Table 4.2). It is generally used in strategic management, particularly when performing environmental scanning. Although entrepreneurship scholars have suggested that these factors influence entrepreneurship in a given country, only scarce attention has been devoted to the study of their impact on the emergence of social entrepreneurship. Nonetheless, findings from studies on commercial entrepreneurship could enhance our understanding of these factors' impact on social venture creation in a given country.

2.1   Political Environment and Social Entrepreneurship

The political environment includes factors such as tax policy, labor laws, environmental laws, trade restrictions, democracy, political stability, rule of law, and political risk. It is generally believed that governments influence the propensity of entrepreneurship and innovation. A supportive government tends to facilitate the emergence of entrepreneurial and innovation ecology. A study conducted in 47 countries using GEM data found that social/political variables accounted for 76 percent of the variance in explaining social entrepreneurial activity. The study also found that the single greatest determinant of social entrepreneurial activity was the degree of female participation in the labor force.[37] Other findings of a multi-country study showed that government, economic factors, and the availability of capital explained the macro-level differences among countries. They also found that the size of the government, the quality of the monetary policy, and overall financial environment were strong predictors of entrepreneurship.[38] Such factors also affect entrepreneurial activity in rural areas. A particular example of this effect was found in a study examining the role of macro-environmental factors in rural entrepreneurship in China.[39]A large government provides a safety net to citizens who

Table 4.2 PEST model and commercial and social entrepreneurship

Political factors	Economic factors	Social factors	Technological factors
Tax policy	Economic growth	Culture	R&D activity
Labor law	Interest rates	Traditions	Automation
Environmental law	Exchange rates	Religion(s)	Rate of technological
Trade restrictions	Inflation rates	Religious tolerance	change
Tariffs	State of economy	Lifestyle	Use of technology
Democracy	Standard of living	Value system	Types of technology
Political stability	Economic risk	Norms	
Political risk	Structure of industry	Population demographics	
Rule of law	Market size		
	Availability of investment capital		

may not have an incentive to engage in entrepreneurial activities and needs to finance itself through taxes.

Understanding their role in wealth creation and economic prosperity, many governments around the world are taking measures to create business-friendly environments. Some do this by encouraging entrepreneurship education in the belief that it is a sure means to stimulate economic activity. As a consequence, there is an increased tendency for government policies to promote entrepreneurship for its apparent benefits.[40] Government support for social entrepreneurship also tends to make a difference. A study of jurisdictions in the United States with populations over 50,000 found that municipalities facilitate social entrepreneurship by increasing awareness of social problems and then help social entrepreneurs to acquire resources, coordinate with other organizations, and implement their social programs. Nearly three-quarters of cities provided active or moderate support, which was positively associated with the perceived effectiveness of nonprofit organizations in their communities.[41]

2.2   Economic Environment and Social Entrepreneurship

The impact of the economic environment on the prevalence of entrepreneurship has been recognized in the literature. It has been documented that although entrepreneurs may play a key role in addressing basic social needs in developing and emerging countries, they are often burdened by a lack of environmental munificence.[42] The attractiveness of social entrepreneurship in a country frequently exists as a result of information about existing material and human resources. In other words, countries where material resources are available may have more social entrepreneurial activity than those that lack such resources.

Zacharakis and colleagues conducted policy-capturing experiments on 119 venture capitalists (VCs) across three countries, representing distinct economic institutions: US, mature market economy; South Korea, emerging economy; and China, transitional economy. The results showed that VCs in rules-based market economies (US) relied more on market information than VCs in emerging economies (South Korea) and those in transitional economies (China). However, VCs in China weighed human capital factors more heavily than either US or Korean VCs.[43] These findings suggest that, although professional institutions may dictate which information is included in VC decision policies, the extent to which that information is emphasized is determined partly by the economic institution in which the decision-maker operates.

The existence of entrepreneurs in a given community also influences the likelihood of engaging in entrepreneurial activity. People who reside in highly entrepreneurial neighborhoods are more likely to become entrepreneurs themselves and invest more in their own businesses, even though their entrepreneurial profits could be lower and their alternative job opportunities more attractive. In other words, peer effects create nonpecuniary benefits from entrepreneurial activity and play an important role in the decision to become an entrepreneur.[44] Taxation also affects entrepreneurial activity. Studies conducted in the United States showed that more individuals become self-employed when personal income is relatively more taxed than corporate income. In OECD (Organization for Economic Cooperation and Development) countries, there are large cross-country differences in startup costs, which affect the degree of entry into entrepreneurship.[45] Because social entrepreneurs often operate in resource-constrained environments, they are usually compelled to use creative approaches to attract resources and to apply these resources in novel ways to the challenges they face.[46]

Generally, entrepreneurship scholars have found a positive relationship between the economic environment of a country and entrepreneurial activity. Economic stability, capital availability, and reduced personal income taxes are all positively related to new venture creation.[47] A recent analysis of venture activity in 68 countries spanning the period from 1996 to 2006 found that formal institutions—operationalized as a set of political, economic, and contractual rules that regulate individual behavior and shape human interaction—had a positive effect on the level of venture capital activity, but this effect was weaker in more uncertainty-avoidance and collectivistic societies.[48] These findings indicate that the existence of formal institutions in a country fosters venture capital activity, which is essential in funding new startups. To some extent, formal institutions reduce the level of uncertainty inherent within new venture creation activity.

The economic environment has been operationalized as economic freedom to facilitate cross-country comparisons. A study using data from the GEM on 29 countries found that economic factors, such as the size of the government, the quality of the monetary policy, and overall financial environment, were strong predictors of entrepreneurship. It was also found that access to sound money (rate and variability of inflation) was important in facilitating both opportunity and necessity entrepreneurship. Government's share in total consumption positively affected necessity entrepreneurship, while government consumption, transfers, subsidies, and the extent of taxation were negatively associated with opportunity entrepreneurship.[49] Research has also indicated that the recent economic recession that started in 2008 had a positive impact on social venture creation in the United States. During this recession, factors such as low cost of skilled labor, less expensive supplies, tax benefits, as well as new internet tools, blogs, and social networks made it easier for people to engage in social entrepreneurial activities.[50]

2.3   Social Environment and Social Entrepreneurship

As indicated in Table 4.2, the social environment includes factors such as culture, the value system, traditions, religious belief(s), and demographics as well as attitudes toward entrepreneurship. Research has underlined the important role of culture in influencing entrepreneurial activity. This research has specifically noted that norms and values influence the relative desirability of entrepreneurship as an occupational choice.[51] Likewise, attitudes, beliefs, and expectations of a social reference group influence individuals' entrepreneurial intentions.[52] It has also been found that the appreciation of entrepreneurship is lower in cultures where uncertainty and unknown outcomes of individuals' behavior are perceived negatively.[53] Tiessen presents a theoretical framework linking national culture—specifically, individualist and collectivist orientations—to entrepreneurship. He suggests that both orientations affect the functions of entrepreneurship to the extent that entrepreneurship requires two activities—generating variety through innovation or new ventures, and leveraging resources internally or by establishing external ties. Individualistic orientation allows individuals to generate ideas for new ventures, whereas collectivistic orientation facilitates the leveraging of the resources needed to exploit these opportunities.[54]

Shane examined the per capita number of invention patents granted to nationals of 33 countries in 1967, 1971, 1976, and 1980 and compared this data with an index of the values of power distance (social hierarchy) and individualism, compiled from a survey of 88,000 employees at IBM undertaken by Geert Hofstede in the late 1960s and early

1970s.[55] His results showed that individualistic and non-hierarchical societies are more inventive than other societies.[56] In a subsequent study, Shane examined the preferences of a sample of 4,405 individuals from 43 organizations from 68 countries on four innovation roles:

- organizational maverick;
- network facilitator;
- transformational leader; and
- organizational buffer.

The results show a positive association between uncertainty acceptance and these four roles. In other words, uncertainty-acceptance cultures may be more innovative than uncertainty-avoidance cultures.[57]

Several studies have also found a positive relationship between individualism and entrepreneurship and innovation. A recent analysis of independent data sets of culture and innovation from 62 countries spanning more than two decades shows that most measures of individualism have a strongly significant and positive effect on innovation, even when controlling for major policy variables.[58] Innovation is directly related to entrepreneurship. A society that is innovative is more likely to be entrepreneurial. Perhaps individualistic societies may have a competitive edge over collectivistic ones because they not only provide a more tolerant environment for would-be innovators but also offer more social incentives for such individuals to innovate.[59] Individualistic societies emphasize personal freedom, which encourages individuals to think and act creatively to discover for themselves what works or does not work, whereas collectivistic societies tend to impede communication upwards through the social hierarchy, overcentralize authority, rely on rules and procedures, and resist the radical social changes that often accompany innovation.[60]

Urbano and colleagues studied the emergence of social entrepreneurship in Catalonia. They found that the institutional environment affected the creation of social ventures. In particular, informal institutions had more impact on social venture creation than formal institutions because they affected both the implementation and the emergence of social enterprises.[61] The social climate prevailing in a country could also have an impact on perceptions of entrepreneurs and entrepreneurship. The set of values that indicates the acceptance of entrepreneurship in a country may lead to the removal of regulatory barriers that could impede it.[62] The emergence of social entrepreneurship can be affected by the entrepreneurship climate in a given country. Social entrepreneurship can flourish only in a strong entrepreneurial climate. It founders in a weak entrepreneurial environment. For example, the United States is considered as one of the most entrepreneurial countries in the world, and social entrepreneurship flourishes there, too. By contrast, in most African countries the entrepreneurial climate could be considered as weak. Consequently, social ventures do not flourish in these environments. (Of course, this is not to say that there are no social ventures in Africa.)

2.4 Technological Environment and Social Entrepreneurship

The PEST model contends that the technological environment influences firms' strategies and operations. Extended to social entrepreneurship, one could argue that the technological environment influences social venture creation in several ways. First, technology, especially information technology, facilitates increased awareness of the existence of social problems not only locally but in other parts of the world. Second, technology can facilitate the creation of social ventures because social entrepreneurs can easily use the internet to advertise their social ventures. Third, technology facilitates partnerships among social entrepreneurs located in various parts of the world.

Advances in information technology have increased awareness of social problems around the world and facilitated interactions between social ventures located in different geographic areas. Increased public awareness of a social problem acts as an external added incentive, which makes engagement appear more worthy because of an added social component.[63] These interactions have also encouraged the founding of many social ventures.[64] Technology has also created a sense of shared responsibility in addressing social problems. Because people now have easy access to what is happening in different parts of the world, they are compelled to take action when they see human suffering. For example, many people saw the effects of the Boxing Day tsunami in December 2004, the Haiti earthquake in 2010, and Hurricane Katrina in 2005 on television or online. Such awareness creates a natural response among many concerned individuals. Even actions by established companies that violate ethical practices are easily publicized. For instance, the Western media has widely publicized the plight of Pakistani children who work in sweatshops to produce soccer balls, making it very difficult for the multinational corporations that operate the factories not to take action.[65]

Technology can also affect the types of social ventures that are created. For example, Application Case 1 at the end of this chapter describes the establishment of Ushahidi, a nonprofit technology venture in Nairobi, Kenya, that addresses the issue of power outage and weak interconnectivity. Realizing that most electrical power systems in Africa are extremely unreliable, the founders created a device—the BRCK—which allows users to connect to the internet without an electricity supply. Institutions and the technology employed determine the transaction and transformation costs that add up to the costs of production.[66] Technology can reduce the costs of starting and operating social ventures. By the same token, entrepreneurs who have been successful in creating technology ventures are now turning into social entrepreneurs. For example, highly successful technology-turned-social entrepreneurs like Jeffrey Skoll and Pierre Omidyar of eBay, Bill Gates of Microsoft, and Larry Page and Sergey Brin of Google have inspired other entrepreneurs to turn their attention to tackling today's global social problems.[67]

3   Tools for Analyzing Social Ventures' External Environment

3.1   Environmental Scanning

Environmental scanning is a strategic management tool that is used to analyze the external environment of a firm. This five-step process involves:

- identifying the environmental scanning needs of the firm;
- gathering the information needed by the focal firm;
- analyzing the information;
- communicating the results to concerned parties; and
- making informed decisions.

Sources of information for environmental scanning are both external and internal. External sources of information include printed materials and experts in the field and industry as well as the media. Internal sources include organization-specific information, such as personal contacts, internal reports and memos, committee meetings, managers, and employees.[68]

Environmental scanning can help a firm identify the driving forces in the industry in which it operates. Driving forces represent major causes of changing industry and competitive conditions. For a company to formulate its strategic plan, it needs to identify the driving forces in the industry in which it operates. Generally, three to four driving forces must be identified and their impact on the industry over a period of one to three years must be assessed. Examples of driving forces include: increasing globalization, internet opportunities, regulatory policies/government legislation, changing societal concerns, attitudes, and lifestyles, and changes in the degree of uncertainty and risk. Then the firm must assess the impact of these driving forces on the industry in which it operates.

An interesting question is whether this strategic management tool could be applied to social entrepreneurship. Because the purpose of social ventures is not to generate profits for stakeholders but rather to address social issues, applying a competitive tool might sound odd. However, at close examination, one may find it useful to apply this tool to social ventures. It is important for social entrepreneurs to understand the landscape in which their ventures will operate. For instance, will a social venture in a particular area, such as healthcare, succeed? What are the driving forces in this particular area? What are the critical success factors? Addressing these questions is important for social entrepreneurs, especially when the social venture combines a social mission with a profit-generating bottom line.

3.2   Competitive Intelligence

Competitive intelligence is a strategic management tool that is used to garner useful information about the competition, the market, and the technology that can be utilized by managers to make strategic decisions.[69] It can be used by entrepreneurs to learn about their potential competitors and the industry they are about to enter. Social entrepreneurs can also use competitive intelligence to collect information about social needs to address and the potential competitive landscape of social ventures that address similar needs. This is particularly important when the social venture has a hybrid or a for-profit form of organization. Garnering information about key stakeholders can also help social entrepreneurs build a competitive advantage and ensure the sustainability of their ventures.

Competitive intelligence is an important tool for information gathering about the business environment. It has even become a profession. Not only do major companies, such as General Motors and British Petroleum, have competitive intelligence units, but competitive intelligence analysts have formed a professional society known as Strategic and Competitive Intelligence Professionals (SCIP). This has more than 5,000 members, offers competitive intelligence certification, and organizes regular seminars and an annual conference. It also publishes an academic journal, *Competitive Intelligence and Management*. Most information related to the competition can be garnered through legitimate means that do not involve spying activities. For example, a company can learn from its competitors by talking to their customers, suppliers, and even employees, reading their annual reports, or browsing the internet for any useful information.

Competitive intelligence involves collecting information, analyzing and interpreting the information, distributing and storing the information, and responding to the information. A survey conducted on a sample of 55 CEOs (chief executive officers) and 82 CIOs (chief information officers) found that most respondents believed that spending time and resources on competitive intelligence activities was appropriate for their companies.[70] Although competition among social ventures is not as fierce as in the commercial sector, social ventures do compete for resources, donors, and government attention. Thus, using competitive intelligence can help them acquire useful information about their key stakeholders. Competitive intelligence is about taking action. The information garnered is useful only when it is acted upon.

3.3   Benchmarking

Despite fierce competition, organizations can learn from one another. A technique that allows this to happen is benchmarking, which refers to the process of comparing one's own business processes and performance metrics with the industry's best or with best practices from other industries. Formally defined, benchmarking is a systematic, continuous process of measuring and comparing an organization's business processes against the leaders in an industry to gain insights that will help the organization take action to improve its performance.[71] It allows organizations not to waste time and resources reinventing the wheel. Companies often benchmark others on three dimensions—quality, time, and cost.

Although there is no universal way of conducting benchmarking, practitioners and scholars agree on the importance of following seven steps in the benchmarking process:

- identify problem areas;
- identify industries that have similar processes;
- identify organizations that are leaders in those areas;
- survey leading organizations for measures and practices;
- visit the leading organizations to identify best practices;
- implement best practices; and
- evaluate and make adjustments when necessary.

Benchmarking can be considered as an entrepreneurial tool to the extent that it enables entrepreneurs to learn from best practices. Such a learning tool results in the identification of opportunities that can be transformed into commercial or social ventures.

John Saul proposes the application of benchmarking to social businesses and nonprofits.[72] By using benchmarking, social ventures can learn not only from other high-quality social ventures but also from high-performing commercial businesses. Benchmarking offers nonprofit organizations a systematic and reliable tool to manage and improve performance by studying the best solutions to common problems.[73] For example, KaBOOM, a nonprofit that builds playgrounds in US inner cities, used benchmarking by studying how businesses built easy-to-maintain websites and then used the same method to reduce its own web development costs.[74]

Although the literature on social entrepreneurship has paid scant attention to benchmarking as a management tool, one must acknowledge that it is essential in helping social entrepreneurs learn from existing best practices. But what are best practices? They can be conceived as innovative processes, including methods, policies, or programs of top-performing organizations that make them leaders in a particular industry. Social ventures can use benchmarking to compare themselves to the best in a particular area or to learn from the best practices in both social and commercial entrepreneurship.

3.4   Applying Porter's Five Forces Model to Social Ventures

In 1980, Michael E. Porter developed the five forces model, which remains one of the foundations of competitive analysis and strategic management to this day.[75] The model is ubiquitous and always takes a prominent place in any textbook on strategic management. The five forces identified by Porter are illustrated in Figure 4.1. They comprise:

- intensity of rivalry among existing firms;
- threats of new entrants;
- pressure from substitute products;
- bargaining power of buyers; and
- bargaining power of suppliers.

The joint influence of these five forces determines the intensity of the competition in a given industry. The greater the strength of the five forces, the lower the expected profitability in a given industry will be. In social entrepreneurship, one may speculate that the greater the strength of the five forces, the lower will be the expected sustainability of the social venture operating in a given sector. According to Porter, if a firm

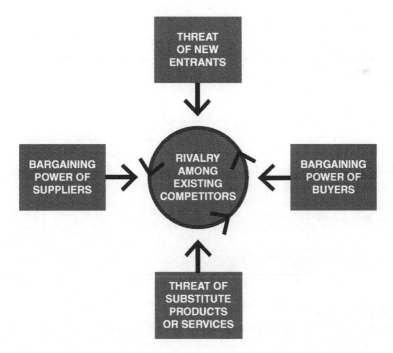

Figure 4.1 Porter's five forces model.

knows the effect of each competitive force, it can take offensive or defensive action to address it.[76]

A social venture can compete with other social ventures or commercial ventures that engage in corporate social responsibility (CSR) or corporate social entrepreneurship. Thus, it makes perfect sense to apply Porter's five forces model to social entrepreneurship. Despite the fact that social ventures address social needs, they compete for resources, grants, donors, volunteers, and government contracts. What does this competitive environment look like? What are the forces that shape it? Can the five forces model help us to understand the social venture's competitive landscape? Competitors include any social ventures that provide similar services. These ventures compete to acquire much-needed financial resources from benefactors, grants, government contracts, corporate and foundation sponsorships, and for volunteers. The second force, called beneficiaries, equates to buyers in the traditional five forces model. However, in social ventures, most "buyers" are unable to purchase specific products or services themselves, so it is appropriate to call them beneficiaries instead. Most of the time, these beneficiaries do not have strong bargaining power over the focal social venture. The third force is suppliers. Social ventures that make products interact with the suppliers of raw materials. Such suppliers could have strong bargaining power when they are few in number and have a vested interest in the social needs addressed by the social venture. The fourth force, substitute products, may not operate in quite the same manner as in the traditional five forces model. Here, the beneficiaries may not have the choice to choose alternative services because they are often needy. The fifth force, threats of new entrants, refers to the possibility that new social ventures may enter the "social market" to provide similar products or services. Such entry may erode the competitive advantage of existing social ventures.

As depicted in Figure 4.1, the five forces model can effectively apply to social ventures. Thus, social entrepreneurs must analyze the external environment and the competitive landscape in which their venture will operate. Failure to understand it could lead to disastrous consequences.

Summary

This chapter discussed the role of the external environment in the emergence of social ventures. In so doing, it explored the role of the institutional environment on social venture creation. It also discussed the PEST model in assessing the impact of the external environment on social venture creation. Finally, the chapter assessed the relevance of strategic management tools, such as benchmarking, competitive intelligence, environmental scanning, and the five forces model, in social entrepreneurship.

Key Terms

Benchmarking; competitive intelligence; environmental scanning; formal institutions; Global Entrepreneurial Monitor; informal institutions; institutional environment; institutional profile; normative dimension; PEST model; political factors; Porter's five forces model

Review Questions

1 Discuss how the three components of the institutional environment could facilitate the emergence of social entrepreneurship in a given country.
2 Discuss how the three components of the institutional environment could impede the emergence of social entrepreneurship in a given country.
3 Explain why the United States is a relatively fertile ground for the emergence of social ventures.
4 Identify at least three elements that could be included in the normative component of the institutional environment. Explain how they could affect social venture creation.
5 Discuss the application of Porter's five forces model to social entrepreneurship. How could it help social entrepreneurs to understand their competitive environment?
6 How can social entrepreneurs use benchmarking effectively to learn from the best in their respective sectors?
7 Do you think that social entrepreneurs need to conduct competitive intelligence?
8 How can environmental scanning help social entrepreneurs?
9 Discuss the PEST model and its influence on understanding social venture environments.
10 Discuss the extent to which the external environment could have similar or differential effects on social and commercial entrepreneurship.

Application Questions

1 Visit the website of the Global Entrepreneurship Monitor (www.gemconsortium.org). Select two countries that are ranked among the top five for social entrepreneurship. Identify what characteristics facilitate the emergence of social entrepreneurship in these countries. Select two countries that are ranked at or near the bottom when it comes to social entrepreneurship. Identify the characteristics that are similar among these countries and explain why they impede social entrepreneurship.
2 Visit the website of the Global Competitiveness Index (www.weforum.org/issues/global-competitiveness). Perform an analysis of the top five countries in the ranking. Which characteristics make these countries more competitive than the others? Explain.
3 The Ease of Doing Business Index, compiled by the World Bank, ranks countries on ten dimensions. Visit the website (www.doingbusiness.org/rankings) and consider the latest rankings. Identify some of the reasons why sub-Saharan African countries are faring poorly compared to those from other parts of the world. If you were a consultant to a government from a sub-Saharan African country, what advice would you give to foster commercial and social entrepreneurship? Be specific.
4 Select a country other than your country of birth, citizenship, or current residency. Analyze that country's external environment using the PEST model. Explain how each of the four factors of the model could facilitate or impede social entrepreneurship in the country.
5 Select a social venture you are familiar with and apply Porter's five forces model. To what extent does this model allow you to increase your understanding of the competitive landscape of this social enterprise?

Application Case 1: BRCK—Africa's Answer to the Internet[77]

The BRCK Device
BRCK Inc.

Ushahidi (www.brck.com) is a nonprofit technology venture located in Nairobi, Kenya. BRCK—or backup generator to the internet—is Africa's answer to the internet. Realizing that most people do not have access to electricity and that connectivity is essential to productivity and a better social life, the founders of Ushahidi developed the concept of BRCK. Ushahidi (the name means "testimony" in Swahili) is a nonprofit technology company that builds open-source software and digital tools to help people in the developing world use information more effectively. The project began in 2008 when engineers David Kobia, Juliana Rotich, and Erik Hersman built a crowdsourced mapping platform in response to post-election violence in Kenya. In such a situation, timely access to information can mean survival, yet maintaining reliable connectivity proved to be exceedingly difficult (watch the video at www.youtube.com/watch?v=qsJYrwzfd6w for more details of the company and the project).

BRCK works much like a cell phone by intelligently and seamlessly switching between ethernet, wifi, and 3G or 4G mobile phone networks. It gains connectivity through a standard SIM card and/or ethernet or wifi connections, and has a smart battery that seamlessly kicks in for eight hours if the power is interrupted. The BRCK connects to the BRCK Cloud, a website that can be accessed from anywhere to check how network connections and electricity supply are performing on the device you are using. You can also manage alerts and applications remotely from your phone or computer, and gather data reported from attached sensors or computers. The BRCK has 16GB of memory on board that can be linked to Dropbox and other connected devices and applications. It is small and designed to be the easiest possible networking device to set up. It can connect up to 20 devices with a wifi signal that can cover several rooms.

The BRCK not only provides connectivity for workers on the ground but also allows information to flow continuously from sensors in one location that can be monitored remotely and securely. In this way, Ushahidi hopes to create robust bridges between sites and sensors in Africa, India, Indonesia, and elsewhere to the BRCK Cloud and then to anywhere in the world. According to Ethan Zuckerman, Director of the MIT Center for Civic Media, the BRCK is the equivalent of a backup generator for the internet, a battery wired to an access point, mated to a GSM modem, designed so that your coded session does not have to end when the power goes out.

On its website, Ushahidi notes that the BRCK is the easiest, most reliable way to connect to the internet from anywhere in the world, even if there is no electricity supply. All kinds of jobs require steady connectivity, even when infrastructure is spotty due to poor wireless connections, intermittent power, or devices that cannot share connections. The device is physically robust and able to connect to multiple networks, represents a hub for all local devices, and has enough backup power to survive blackouts, which are common problems in most African countries. It can also be useful in developed countries, especially during natural disasters, when electricity and internet connections are often unavailable.

The BRCK is priced at $249.99. In addition, Ushahidi manufactures and distributes similarly low-cost tablets known as Kio kits to elementary schools in parts of Kenya with poor infrastructure.

Discussion Questions

1 Using the PEST model, identify the factors that led to the creation of the BRCK device.
2 What social needs is the BRCK device addressing?
3 Devise pricing options that could make this product affordable to most people in rural areas of Africa, East Asia, and Latin America.
4 Which institutional factors would facilitate or impede the diffusion of this technology in developing countries?

Application Case 2: Global Health Corps[78]

Global Health Corps (GHC) is a nonprofit enterprise co-founded by Barbara Bush, daughter of former President George W. Bush, to tackle global health issues. Barbara Bush was struck by what she saw when she arrived in Africa in 2003, at a time when her father was unveiling a plan to combat AIDS. Hundreds of people were waiting in the streets for antiretroviral drugs that had been readily available in the United States for years. As Barbara Bush declared, "I think that enraged me … and that experience really is what opened me up to considering global health as a career path for myself." Thereafter, she worked for the Red Cross Children's Hospital in Cape Town, South Africa, and interned with UNICEF in Botswana.

Armed with this experience, she started Global Health Corps in 2008 with her twin sister, Jenna Bush Hager, and four others. She is the CEO of GHC and sits on the boards of other organizations, such as Covena House International and Friends of the Global Fight against AIDS, Tuberculosis, and Malaria. GHC offers fellowships to young professionals and recent college graduates in health organizations in the United States and Africa for a year to improve access to healthcare.

On its website (http://ghcorps.org), GHC describes its mission "to mobilize a global community of emerging leaders to build the movement for health equity. We are building a community of change makers who share a common belief. Health is a human right." The organization provides opportunities for young professionals from diverse cultural and professional backgrounds to work on global health issues in Burundi, Malawi, Rwanda, Uganda, the United States, and Zambia. For example, architects in Rwanda designed better air-flow systems at a health center to prevent the spread of tuberculosis. The plan is now to implement this system across the country. Meanwhile, in Malawi, supply-chain experts reduced the problem of running out of prescription drugs in one district by 28 percent. GHC expects its fellows—of which there have been more than 450 thus far—to go on to occupy leadership positions in the field of global health.

Discussion Questions

1 Describe the experience that led to the creation of Global Health Corps.
2 Would this experience have triggered the same interest in you (yes or no)? Explain.
3 Use some of the concepts introduced in this chapter to describe Barbara Bush's motivation to start Global Health Corps.
4 Visit the website of Global Health Corps (http://ghcorps.org) and read the mission and vision statements. What do they tell you about the organization?
5 Watch the video at www.youtube.com/watch?v=JVYhPhmfTQ4 and discuss the process of creating Global Health Corps. Was this an unconventional way of starting a social venture (yes or no)? Explain.

Notes

1 McKeever, E., Jack, S., & Anderson, A. (2015). Embedded entrepreneurship in the creative re-construction of place. *Journal of Business Venturing, 30*(1), 50–65; Zahra, S. A., Wright, M., & Abdelgawad, S. G. (2014). Contextualization and the advancement of entrepreneurship research. *International Small Business Journal, 32*(5), 479–500; Zahra, S. A., & Newey, & Li, Y. (2014). On the frontiers: The implications of social entrepreneurship for international entrepreneurship. *Entrepreneurship Theory and Practice, 38*(1), 137–158; Welter, F. (2011). Contextualizing entrepreneurship: Conceptual challenges and ways forward. *Entrepreneurship Theory and Practice, 35*(1), 165–184.
2 Welter, F. (2011). Contextualizing entrepreneurship: Conceptual challenges and ways forward. *Entrepreneurship Theory and Practice, 35*(1), 165–184.
3 McKeever, E., Jack, S., & Anderson, A. (2015). Embedded entrepreneurship in the creative re-construction of place. *Journal of Business Venturing, 30*(1), 50–65.
4 Granovetter, M. (1985). Economic action and social structure: The problem of embeddedness. *American Journal of Sociology, 91*(3), 481–510.
5 Griffiths, D. M., Gundry, K. L., & Kickul, R. J. (2013). The socio-political, economic, and cultural determinants of social entrepreneurship activity: An empirical examination. *Journal of Small Business and Enterprise Development, 20*(2), 341–357.
6 Dees, G., Emerson, J., & Economy, P. (2001). *Enterprising nonprofits: A toolkit for social entrepreneur.* Hoboken, NJ: Wiley.
7 Estrin, S., Mickiewicz, T., & Stephan, U. (2013). Entrepreneurship, social capital, and institutions: Social and commercial entrepreneurship across nations. *Entrepreneurship Theory and Practice,*

37(3), 479–504; Estrin, S., Korosteleva, J., & Mickeiwicz, T. (2012). Which institutions encourage entrepreneurial growth aspirations? *Journal of Business Venturing, 24*(4), 564–580.

8 Mendoza-Abarca, K. I., Anokhin, S., & Zamudio, C. (2015). Uncovering the influence of social venture creation on commercial venture creation: A population ecology perspective. *Journal of Business Venturing, 30*(6), 793–807.

9 Busenitz, L. M., Gomez, C., & Spencer, J. W. (2000). Country institutional profiles: Unlocking entrepreneurial phenomena. *Academy of Management Journal, 43*(5), 994–1003.

10 Scott, W. R. (1995). *Institutions and organizations.* Thousand Oaks, CA: Sage Publications.

11 North, D. C. (1990). *Institutions, institutional change and economic performance.* Cambridge: Cambridge University Press.

12 Munoz, P., & Dimov, D. (2015). The call of the whole in understanding the development of sustainable ventures. *Journal of Business Venturing, 30*(4), 632–654; Valdez, M. E., & Richardson, J. (2013). Institutional determinants of macro-level entrepreneurship. *Entrepreneurship Theory and Practice, 37*(5), 1149–1175; Katre, A., & Salipante, P. (2012). Start-up social ventures: Blending fine-grained behaviors from two institutions for entrepreneurial success. *Entrepreneurship Theory and Practice, 36*(5), 967–994; Norton, C. D. (1994). Economic performance through time. *American Economic Review, 84*(3), 359–368.

13 Scott, W. R. (1995). *Institutions and organizations.* Thousand Oaks, CA: Sage Publications.

14 Kostova, T. (1997). Country institutional profile: Concept and measurement. *Academy of Management Best Paper Proceedings,* 180–189.

15 Spencer, J. W., & Gomez, C. (2004). The relationship among national institutional structure, economic factors, and domestic entrepreneurial activity: A multicountry study. *Journal of Business Research, 57*(10), 1098–1107.

16 Spencer, J. W., & Gomez, C. (2004). The relationship among national institutional structure, economic factors, and domestic entrepreneurial activity: A multicountry study. *Journal of Business Research, 57*(10), 1098–1107.

17 Scott, W. R. (1995). *Institutions and organizations.* Thousand Oaks, CA: Sage Publications.

18 Busenitz, L. M., Gomez, C., & Spencer, J. W. (2000). Country institutional profiles: Unlocking entrepreneurial phenomena. *Academy of Management Journal, 43*(5), 994–1003.

19 Bowen, H. P., & De Clerq, D. (2008). Institutional context and the allocation of entrepreneurial effort. *Journal of International Business Studies, 39*(4), 747–767; Thomas, A., & Mueller, S. (2000). A case for comparative entrepreneurship: Assessing the relevance of culture. *Journal of International Business Studies, 31*(2), 287–301.

20 Bowen, H. P., & De Clerq, D. (2008). Institutional context and the allocation of entrepreneurial effort. *Journal of International Business Studies, 39*(4), 747–767.

21 Spencer, J. W., & Gomez, C. (2004). The relationship among national institutional structure, economic factors, and domestic entrepreneurial activity: A multicountry study. *Journal of Business Research, 57*(10), 1098–1107.

22 Baumol, W. J. (1990). Entrepreneurship: Productive, unproductive, and destructive. *Journal of Political Economy, 98*(5), 893–921.

23 Aidis, R., Estrin, S., & Mickiewicz, T. (2008). Institutions and entrepreneurship development in Russia: A comparative perspective. *Journal of Business Venturing, 23*(6), 656–672.

24 Stenholm, P., Acs, Z. J., & Wuebker, R. (2013). Exploring country-level arrangements on the rate and type of entrepreneurial activity. *Journal of Business Venturing, 28*(1), 176–193.

25 George, G., & Prabhu, G. N. (2000). Developmental financial institutions as catalysts of entrepreneurship in emerging economies. *Academy of Management Review, 25*(3), 620–629.

26 Spencer, J. W., & Gomez, C. (2004). The relationship among national institutional structure, economic factors, and domestic entrepreneurial activity: A multicountry study. *Journal of Business Research, 57*(10), 1098–1107.

27 Stenholm, P., Acs, Z. J., & Wuebker, R. (2013). Exploring country-level arrangements on the rate and type of entrepreneurial activity. *Journal of Business Venturing, 28*(1), 176–193.

28 Smallborne, D., & Welter, F. (2001). The distinctiveness of entrepreneurship in transition economies. *Small Business Economics, 16*(4), 249–262.

29 Zhou, W. (2013). Political connections and entrepreneurial investment: Evidence from China's transition economy. *Journal of Business Venturing*, 28(2), 299–315.

30 Smallborne, D., & Welter, F. (2001). The distinctiveness of entrepreneurship in transition economies. *Small Business Economics*, 16(4), 249–262.

31 Williams, N., & Vorley, T. (2015). Institutional asymmetry: How formal and informal institutions affect entrepreneurship in Bulgaria. *International Small Business Journal*, 33(8), 840–861.

32 Baumol, W. J. (1990). Entrepreneurship: Productive, unproductive, and destructive. *Journal of Political Economy*, 98(5), 893–921.

33 Minniti, M., & Levesque, M. (2008). Recent developments in the economics of entrepreneurship. *Journal of Business Venturing*, 23(6), 603–612; O'Connor A. (2013). A conceptual framework for entrepreneurship education policy: Meeting government and economic purposes. *Journal of Business Venturing*, 28(4), 546–563.

34 www.gemconsortium.org.

35 Lepoutre, J., Justo, R., Terjessen, S., & Bosma, N. (2013). Designing a global standardized methodology for measuring social entrepreneurship activity: The Global Entrepreneurship Monitor social entrepreneurship study. *Small Business Economics*, 40(3), 693–714.

36 Urbano, D., Toedano, N., & Soriano, D. R. (2010). Analyzing social entrepreneurship from an institutional perspective: Evidence from Spain. *Journal of Social Entrepreneurship*, 1(1), 54–69.

37 Griffiths, D. M., Gundry, K. L., & Kickul, R. J. (2013). The socio-political, economic, and cultural determinants of social entrepreneurship activity: An empirical examination. *Journal of Small Business and Enterprise Development*, 20(2), 341–357.

38 Griffiths, M., Kickul, J., & Casrud, A. (2009). Government bureaucracy, transactional impediments, and entrepreneurial intentions. *International Small Business Journal*, 27(5), 626–645; Griffiths, M., Gundry, L. Kickul, J., & Fernandez, A. (2009). Innovation ecology as a precursor to entrepreneurial growth: A cross-country empirical investigation. *Journal of Small Business and Enterprise Development*, 16(3), 375–390; Bjornskov, C., & Foss, N. J. (2008). Economic freedom and entrepreneurial activity: Some cross-country evidence. *Public Choice*, 134(3), 307–328.

39 Poon, P. S., Lianxi, Z., & Chan, T. C. (2009). Social entrepreneurship in a transitional economy: A critical assessment of rural Chinese entrepreneurial firms. *Journal of Management Development*, 28(2), 94–108.

40 O'Connor, A. (2013). A conceptual framework for entrepreneurial education policy: Meeting government and economic purposes. *Journal of Business Venturing*, 28(4), 546–563.

41 Korosec, R. L., & Berman, E. M. (2006). Municipal support for social entrepreneurship. *Public Administration Review*, 66(3), 448–462.

42 Baker, T., Gedajlovic, E., & Lutbakin, M. (2005). A framework for comparing entrepreneurship processes across nations. *Journal of International Business Studies*, 36(5), 492–504.

43 Zacharakis, A., McMullen, J., & Shepherd, D. A. (2007). Venture capitalists' decision making across three countries: An institutional theory perspective. *Journal of International Business Studies*, 38(5), 691–708.

44 Giannetti, M., & Simonov, A. (2004). On the determinants of entrepreneurial activity: Social norms, economic environment and individual characteristics. *Swedish Economic Policy Review*, 11(2), 269–313.

45 Djankov, S., La Porta, R., Lopez-de-Silanes, F., & Shleifer, A. (2002). The regulation of entry. *Quarterly Journal of Economics*, 117(1), 1–37; Djankov, S., Ganser, T., McLiesh, C., Ramalho, R., & Shleifer, A. (2008). The effect of corporate taxes on investment and entrepreneurship. *American Law and Economics Association Annual Meetings*, Paper 80, 1–54.

46 Griffiths, M. D., Gundry, L. K., & Kickul, J. R. (2013). The socio-political, economic, and cultural determinants of social entrepreneurship activity: An empirical examination. *Journal of Small Business and Enterprise Development*, 20(2), 341–357.

47 Shane, S. (2004). *A general theory of entrepreneurship: The individual–opportunity nexus*. Northampton: Edward Elgar.

48 Li, Y., & Zahra, S. A. (2012). Formal institutions, culture, and venture capital activity: A cross-country analysis. *Journal of Business Venturing, 27*(1), 95–111.

49 Bjornskov, C., & Foss, N. J. (2008). Economic freedom and entrepreneurial activity: Some cross-country evidence. *Public Choice, 134*(3), 307–328.

50 Stenholm, P., Acs, Z. J., & Wuebker, R. (2013). Exploring country-level arrangements on the rate and type of entrepreneurial activity. *Journal of Business Venturing, 28*(1), 176–193.

51 Van Putten, II, P., & Green, R. D. (2011). Does it take an economic recession to advance social entrepreneurship? *Research in Business and Economics Journal, 3*(1), 1–10.

52 Krueger, N. F., Reilly, M. D., & Carsrud, A. L. (2000). Competing models of entrepreneurial intentions. *Journal of Business Venturing, 15*(5–6), 411–432.

53 Mueller, S., & Thomas, A. (2001). Culture and entrepreneurial potential: A nine country study of locus of control and innovativeness. *Journal of Business Venturing, 16*(1), 51–75.

54 Tiessen, H. J. (1997). Individualism, collectivism and entrepreneurship: A framework for international comparative research. *Journal of Business Venturing, 12*(5), 367–384.

55 Hofstede, G. (1991). *Culture and organizations: Software of the mind.* New York: McGraw-Hill; Hofstede, G. (2001). *Culture's consequences: Comparing values, behaviors, institutions, and organizations across nations.* Thousand Oaks, CA: Sage Publications.

56 Shane, S. (1992). Why do some societies invent more than others? *Journal of Business Venturing, 7*(1), 29–46; Shane, S. (1993). Cultural influences on national rates of innovation. *Journal of Business Venturing, 8*(1), 59–73.

57 Shane, S. (1995). Uncertainty avoidance and the preference for innovation championing roles. *Journal of International Business Studies, 26*(1), 47–68.

58 Taylor, M. Z., & Wilson, S. (2012). Does culture still matter? The effects of individualism on national innovation rates. *Journal of Business Venturing, 27*(2), 234–247.

59 Taylor, M. Z., & Wilson, S. (2012). Does culture still matter? The effects of individualism on national innovation rates. *Journal of Business Venturing, 27*(2), 234–247.

60 Taylor, M. Z., & Wilson, S. (2012). Does culture still matter? The effects of individualism on national innovation rates. *Journal of Business Venturing, 27*(2), 234–247.

61 Urbano, D., Toedano, N., & Soriano, D. R. (2010). Analyzing social entrepreneurship from an institutional perspective: Evidence from Spain. *Journal of Social Entrepreneurship, 1*(1), 54–69.

62 Cuervo, A. (2005). Individual and environmental determinants of entrepreneurship. *International Entrepreneurship and Management Journal, 1*(3), 293–311.

63 Dorado, S., & Ventresca, M. J. (2013). Crescive entrepreneurship in complex social problems: Institutional conditions for entrepreneurial engagement. *Journal of Business Venturing, 28*(1), 69–82.

64 Barendsen, L., & Gardner, H. (2004). Is the social entrepreneur a new type of leader? *Leader to Leader, 34,* 43–50.

65 Kahn, F. R., Munir, A. K., & Willmott, M. (2007). Dark side of institutional entrepreneurship: Soccer balls, child labor and postcolonial impoverishment. *Organization Studies, 28*(7), 1055–1077.

66 Norton, C. D. (1994). Economic performance through time. *American Economic Review, 84*(3), 359–368.

67 Zahra, S. A., Rawhouser, H. N., Bhame, N., Neubaum, D. O., & Hayton, J. C. (2008). Globalization of social entrepreneurship opportunities. *Strategic Entrepreneurship Journal, 2*(2), 117–131.

68 Albright, K. S. (2004). Environmental scanning: Radar for success. *Information Management Journal,* May–June, 38–44.

69 Ghoshal, S., & Westner, D. E. (1991) Organizing competitor analysis systems. *Strategic Management Journal, 12*(1), 17–31.

70 Vedder, R. G., Vanecek, M. T., Guynes, C. S., & Cappel, J. J. (1999). CEO and CIO perspectives on competitive intelligence. *Communications of the ACM, 42*(8), 109–116.

71   Camp, R. C. (1995). *Business process benchmarking: Finding and implementing business practices.* Milwaukee, WI: ASQC Quality Press; Drew, S. A. W. (1997). From knowledge to action: The impact of benchmarking on organizational performance. *Long Range Planning,* 30(3), 427–441; Saul, J. (2004). *Benchmarking for nonprofits: How to measure, manage, and improve performance.* St. Paul, MN: Fieldstone Alliance Publishing Center.

72   Saul, J. (2004). *Benchmarking for nonprofits: How to measure, manage, and improve performance.* St. Paul, MN: Fieldstone Alliance Publishing Center.

73   Saul, J. (2004). *Benchmarking for nonprofits: How to measure, manage, and improve performance.* St. Paul, MN: Fieldstone Alliance Publishing Center.

74   Saul, J. (2004). *Benchmarking for nonprofits: How to measure, manage, and improve performance.* St. Paul, MN: Fieldstone Alliance Publishing Center.

75   Porter, M. E. (1980). *Competitive strategy.* New York: The Free Press/Macmillan; Porter, M. (2008). The five forces that shape strategy. *Harvard Business Review,* 86(1), 78–93.

76   Porter, M. E. (1980). *Competitive strategy.* New York: The Free Press/Macmillan.

77   Sources for this whole section: Kosner, W. A. (2013). BRCK keeps the internet on when the power goes off even in Africa. *Forbes,* May 5. www.forbes.com/sites/anthonykosner/2013/05/05/brck-keeps-the-internet-on-when-the-power-goes-off-even-in-africa, retrieved on July 14, 2013; Kickstarter. BRCK—your backup generator for the internet. www.kickstarter.com/projects/1776324009/brck-your-backup-generator-for-the-internet, retrieved on March 23, 2016.

78   Source for this whole section: Christoffersen, J. (2014). Why Barbara Bush started Global Health Corps. *Christian Science Monitor,* June 28. www.csmonitor.com/World/Making-a-difference/Latest-News-Wires/2014/0628/Why-Barbara-Bush-started-Global-Health-Corps, retrieved on November 11, 2014.

Chapter 5

Discovering Opportunities for Social Ventures

Learning Objectives

1 Explain the nature of entrepreneurial opportunities.
2 Discuss the application of discovery and creation theories to social entrepreneurial opportunities.
3 Describe the uniqueness of social venture opportunities.
4 Explain how entrepreneurial opportunities are found.

The recognition of opportunities to create or innovate is the initiation point of the entrepreneurial process.[1] Consequently, this chapter discusses the nature of entrepreneurial opportunity and particularly social venture opportunity. The chapter is divided into three major sections. The first section discusses the nature of entrepreneurial opportunity. The second explores the process through which entrepreneurial opportunities come into being. The third analyzes social entrepreneurial opportunities.

I Entrepreneurial Opportunities

It is well understood in the literature and practice of entrepreneurship that at the start of a new venture lies an opportunity, which itself is preceded by an idea. Every commercial or social venture starts with an idea. Hence, before discussing entrepreneurial opportunities, it is important to explain the concept of idea.

1.1 What Is an Idea?

Ideas are merely "grist for the mill" and commodities of the entrepreneurial process.[2] Although they are the point of departure of the entrepreneurial process, ideas are not opportunities in themselves. They are inert and have no real value in and of themselves.[3] We know that ideas are the seeds of the entrepreneurial process but they must be acted upon to be useful. Because ideas are important to the entrepreneurial process, it is worth knowing where they originate. Entrepreneurship scholars have identified at least five sources of ideas:

- personal experiences;
- hobbies;

- accidental discovery;
- systematic search; and
- awareness created by media, personal, and professional networks.[4]

The personal life experiences of an individual may provide useful insights for entrepreneurial ideas. The same is true for personal hobbies (activities that people enjoy doing). People may also discover ideas through serendipity, which refers to the accidental discovery of ideas. Very often, scientists discover useful ideas when researching into something else. A prominent example of serendipity in science is Alexander Fleming's discovery of penicillin in 1928: Fleming mistakenly left open a *Staphylococcus* bacteria culture that was then contaminated by a mold—penicillin—which killed the bacteria. In business, serendipity is often referred to as the unexpected windfall of a business decision. People can also actively look for ideas. They do this by conducting research to find ideas that may stick for a business venture. Finally, people can generate ideas by exposure to the media or through their personal and professional networks. An example of a professional network that may prove useful for idea generation is the *idea bath*, a gathering of experts in a particular field or industry to discuss trends and tease out ideas that may be useful for launching new ventures and/or adding new features to existing products.[5] Next time that you think about starting a new venture, you may want to explore one or more of these sources.

Longenecker and colleagues have identified three types of entrepreneurial idea: Type A, Type B, and Type C.[6] Type A ideas involve identifying a new market for an existing product or service. An example is expanding the use of cellular phones to rural areas in Africa, Latin America, or South East Asia. Type B ideas involve the creation of an entirely new product or service. An example is the creation of the iPad—an entirely new product introduced by Apple in April 2010. Type C ideas involve the creation of new processes for producing and delivering existing products and services. An example is the reengineering process that allows companies to restructure their internal processes to deliver better services or improve the quality of their existing products. Information technology can help companies to exploit Type C ideas. Thus, opportunity recognition involves movement from an idea to an opportunity. This process is described as transforming caterpillars into butterflies.[7] Table 5.1 illustrates the three types of idea discussed above.

1.2   What Is an Opportunity?

As with several concepts in the field of entrepreneurship, there are several definitions of the concept of entrepreneurial opportunity. However, some definitions stand out compared

Table 5.1 Three types of business idea

Type A ideas	Type B ideas	Type C ideas
Involves identifying a new market for an existing product or service.	Involves identifying entirely new products or services.	Involves creating new processes for producing or delivering existing products or services.
Example: Expand the sales of cell phones to rural areas in Africa or South East Asia.	Example: Apple's launch of the iPad in 2010.	Example: Re-engineering a company's processes to be more efficient and responsive to customers.

to others. Entrepreneurial opportunities are situations in which new goods, services, raw materials, and organizing methods can be introduced and sold at greater than the cost of their production.[8] An opportunity is also defined as a future situation that is considered desirable and feasible.[9] An opportunity occurs when there is both supply and demand for the idea.[10] The common thread of these definitions is that opportunities must be profitable and feasible. Entrepreneurial opportunities occur as a result of changes in a variety of parts of the value chain. For example, Schumpeter suggested five different foci of changes:

- those that stem from the creation of new products or services;
- those that stem from the discovery of new geographical markets;
- those that emerge from the creation or discovery of new raw materials;
- those that emerge from new methods of production; and
- those that are generated from new ways of organizing.[11]

Entrepreneurship scholars have identified some characteristics that opportunities should have in order to remain viable business opportunities. For example, Timmons and Spinelli identified four characteristics of a business opportunity:

- ability to add value to the customer;
- adding value by solving a customer's problem or fulfilling a customer's need;
- ability to capture a market and generate profits; and
- compatibility with the skill set of the entrepreneur who pursues it.[12]

These four characteristics imply that the opportunity must add value to the customer's experience and must generate profit for the entrepreneur, who must have the skills that are necessary to pursue it successfully. This description of an entrepreneurial opportunity is similar to the one proposed by Gartner and Bellamy, who also identified four aspects of an opportunity:

- customers;
- consideration;
- connection; and
- commitment.[13]

The *customer* is any individual who will buy the company's products or use its services. An opportunity does not exist unless there are customers who are interested—or might be interested—in the products or services that the new venture will offer. *Consideration* addresses the question of whether the entrepreneur's specific goods or services provide significant value to the customer. Here, the entrepreneur must focus on the value proposition of the opportunity. Unless the opportunity solves a particular problem for the customer, it cannot be considered as viable. Assuming that the opportunity adds value to the customer's experience, the next step is to consider how to *connect* with this customer. How does an entrepreneur identify and reach specific customers? In marketing, this is often called the distribution channel (see Chapter 9). Finally, the entrepreneur must indicate that he/she is *committed* to transforming the opportunity into reality. In other words, is the entrepreneur committed to the idea and willing to execute it to create an actual business? The entrepreneur's commitment is important because exploiting the opportunity will require constant effort and dedication. Without a strong commitment, the entrepreneur will not overcome the obstacles that always stand in the path of a new venture. Opportunities do not exist unless these four aspects are considered.[14] Opportunities must also be attractive, timely, durable, and anchored in a product, service, or business that creates or adds value for its buyer or end-user.[15] As opportunities are discussed and refined, they must be translated into business concepts

1.3   From an Opportunity to a Business Concept

A business concept refers to a set of favorable events involving customers, consideration, connection, and commitment (the four Cs) that have the potential to become a successful business.[16] According to Gartner and Bellamy, to evaluate a business concept, one must address the following questions:

- Does this story hold up?
- Does it make sense?
- Do the four characteristics of the story fit together?[17]

How these three questions are answered will determine whether the idea is a business opportunity or just an idea. For example, the entrepreneur must ensure that there are customers whose needs or wants will be addressed. No venture can subsist without customers. The opportunity must add value to the customer and the entrepreneur should have a means of bringing the product to the customer or delivering the service. Finally, the entrepreneur must devote resources, time, and effort to the venture. For example, Dell's business concept was to sell customized computers direct to customers by bypassing the middle men. Will the concept hold to create a new venture? It seems that Dell's concept of bypassing the middle men and selling direct to customers made sense. It became Dell's core business model until it was copied by the company's competitors. With the advent of the internet, selling direct to the customer is now part of the core business model of most computer manufacturers.

1.4   From a Business Concept to a Social Venture Concept

What is the business concept of social enterprises? Addressing this question is important because social ventures start with an idea, just as business ventures do. The idea should then be translated into an opportunity, which can be acted upon. The opportunity for a social venture should be viable for the social entrepreneur to pursue it. Thus, the social venture concept should follow the four Cs of the commercial enterprise—customers, consideration, connection, and commitment. In a social enterprise, however, the *customer* is the individual who will benefit from the service. This customer may or may not pay for the product or the service. For instance, a social enterprise that focuses on distributing food to the needy may have homeless people as its customers. However, they will not pay for the food. Here, *consideration* means that the product or service should make a difference in the lives of the customers.

Connection refers to the extent to which the social entrepreneur will deliver the product or service to the beneficiaries. Finally, as in commercial entrepreneurship, the social entrepreneur should be *committed* to the venture. Once the social entrepreneur has determined whether the social concept is a viable one, he/she must identify the best set of strategies to help the venture sustain itself while also helping to solve a particular social problem.

Idea ⟶ Opportunity ⟶ Business Concept

Figure 5.1 Evolution of an idea to a business concept.

The social venture will not last or will not accomplish its mission unless it navigates this process successfully.

In any case, a business concept or a social venture concept must be tested. Chapter 7 provides the tools for doing this. For now, though, we turn to the sources of entrepreneurial opportunities. Figure 5.1 provides a visual representation of how an idea evolves into a business concept.

2   How Are Entrepreneurial Opportunities Found

Research on how entrepreneurial opportunities come into being can be explained by two theories—the *discovery theory* and the *creation theory*. Both of these assume that entrepreneurs wish to generate and exploit opportunities[18] and recognize that opportunities exist when imperfections in a market or industry exist.[19] However, they diverge on several points, as illustrated in Figure 5.2. For example, discovery theory assumes that opportunities are exogenous, independent of the entrepreneur, and represent objective phenomena. The implication is that entrepreneurship is about a systematic search for opportunities. In creation theory, however, opportunities are not assumed to be objective phenomena formed by exogenous shocks to an industry or market.[20] Rather, this theory assumes they are created by the actions, reactions, and behaviors of entrepreneurs.[21] Thus, entrepreneurs do not search; they act.[22] Entrepreneurs make use of socially constructed rules to discern the attractiveness of an opportunity. Specifically, their use of rules regarding opportunity novelty, resource efficiency, and worst-case scenarios significantly influences their evaluation of opportunities.[23]

Combining the discovery and creation theories led to the creation of the four-quadrant framework for teaching entrepreneurial opportunity discovery and creation advocated by Babson College, one of the leading institutions of entrepreneurship education in the United States (and indeed the world; see Figure 5.2). The framework posits four ways through which entrepreneurial opportunities emerge:

- systematic search;
- alertness;
- idea generation; and
- design thinking.

	Discovery	Creation
Active	1. Systematic search	3. Idea generation
Passive	2. Alertness	4. Design thinking

Figure 5.2 Methods for opportunity discovery or creation.

Both discovery and creation can be either active or passive. For the sake of clarity and simplicity, the remaining part of this section will focus on these four ways of discovering or creating entrepreneurial opportunities.

2.1 Systematic Search

In the active phase of the discovery process, would-be entrepreneurs are involved in a systematic search for new business opportunities. They do this by building on their competencies and personal and professional experiences. This process is a narrow one since the opportunities are limited to the entrepreneur's background, competencies, and experience. Research on opportunity recognition found that prior experience, particularly in a given industry, represents an asset that leads people to discover business opportunities in that industry.[24] When people work in a given industry, it is easier for them to discover underserved needs in that industry. They may then take action to fill those needs. People may also build professional and social networks in that industry, and these may later become sources of novel business ideas.

Experience is not limited to working in a particular industry. It also involves having prior experience as an entrepreneur (repeat or habitual entrepreneurs). Research has shown that experienced entrepreneurs exhibit an ability to recognize patterns.[25] Using a sample of 630 participants from the United Kingdom, Ucbasaran and colleagues found that more experienced entrepreneurs identified more opportunities than less experienced entrepreneurs.[26] This is perhaps explained by the fact that habitual entrepreneurs accumulate experience, which can then be leveraged to identify new business opportunities. Through experience, people acquire prototypes that serve as templates for concepts, such as opportunity identification.[27] A prototype of an opportunity may include such features as novelty, practicality, market appeal, and the ease with which necessary resources can be obtained.[28] Thus, experienced entrepreneurs are more able to "connect the dots" than novice entrepreneurs.[29] Experience also facilitates the recognition of patterns and clues leading to opportunity identification.[30] The concept of pattern recognition draws from Herbert Simon's work on creativity.[31] In his work, Simon describes pattern recognition as a creative process that is not simply logical but intuitive and inductive, and he argues that it involves the creative linking of two or more chunks of experience, know-how, and contacts. Simon suggests that it takes ten or more years for someone to accumulate the 50,000 "chunks" of experience that will enable them to be highly creative and recognize patterns.

Using one's experience as a source of business opportunities can lead to what entrepreneurship scholars have labeled the *corridor principle*, which basically states that once an entrepreneur starts a firm, he/she begins a journey down a path where corridors leading to new venture opportunities become apparent.[32] Despite its obvious benefits, experience is not a panacea in opportunity identification. It can sometimes lead entrepreneurs to rely on heuristics and biases. The relationship between experience and performance can also plateau,[33] and greater levels of experience can be associated with liabilities as well as assets.[34] Experience can also limit the range of opportunities. For example, having experience in a particular industry or technology can limit an entrepreneur's scope of opportunities because he/she may see opportunities only in that industry or technology. A recent study investigating the role of individual differences in opportunity evaluations found that people with technological experience emphasized fewer opportunity dimensions than those with management or entrepreneurial experience.[35]

A particular form of experience is prior knowledge. Research has shown that this influences opportunity identification.[36] For example, entrepreneurship scholars have found that prior knowledge of a particular market increases the likelihood of discovering an opportunity in that market.[37] Shane examined the role of prior information in opportunity recognition. He found that some individuals have a better capacity to recognize opportunities than others because they have better access to pertinent information and are then better able to utilize that information. In other words, access to information and the capacity to utilize it effectively are key determinants of opportunity recognition. In addition, individuals with prior knowledge make faster decisions when dealing with opportunities and tend to rely on heuristics.[38] To some extent, prior knowledge and personal experience can be considered as the prism through which entrepreneurs make sense of the world. For example, Wood and colleagues found that an entrepreneur's related knowledge, motivation to evaluate the opportunity, prior failure, and fear of failure shape perceptions of opportunity attractiveness. They also contend that entrepreneurs individuate exogenous opportunity formation—that is, the entrepreneur interprets external clues based on his/her cognitive resources.[39] This perspective implies that "entrepreneurial opportunities could be in the eye of the beholder." An individual's cognitive resources play an important role in the formation of opportunity beliefs. Entrepreneurs use prior knowledge as a starting point for identifying an opportunity and then to gather the resources that are necessary to pursue that opportunity. Prior knowledge can be leveraged by paying attention to one's surroundings. This is often referred to as being alert to opportunities.

2.2 Alertness

In the passive phase, the discovery process relies mostly on alertness. Although it is broader than the systematic search process, alertness implies that the opportunities are out there and entrepreneurs have to be vigilant in order to find them. Alertness is defined as an individual's ability to identify opportunities that have been overlooked by others.[40] The conceptualization of alertness as an important determinant of opportunity identification has evolved since the early works of Kirzner. For example, Tang and colleagues conceptualize alertness as a three-dimensional construct comprising:

- scanning and searching for new information;
- connecting previously disparate information; and
- evaluating whether the new information represents an opportunity.[41]

Strategies for increasing alertness include varying the way we do things, increasing the novelty in the situation, viewing situations from different perspectives, turning work into play, and drawing distinctions. Table 5.2 illustrates the evolution and refinement of the concept of alertness.

Considering alertness as an important determinant of opportunity discovery implies that opportunities exist in the external environment, waiting to be discovered. It also implies that entrepreneurship occurs when people are displaced from their regular business routines by political, cultural, or economic factors.[42] As we learned in Chapter 4, the forces in the external environment that lead to opportunity recognition or discovery include economic forces, social forces, technological advancements, and political and regulatory changes. Economic factors may include unexpected occurrences (economic crises), incongruities, and changes in the industry or market. These forces have the potential to disrupt the market and lead to the creation of new businesses or business models.

Table 5.2 Developing views of entrepreneurial alertness[43]

	Early Kirzner	Later Kirzner	Recent developments
Role of markets	Disequilibrium gaps to be identified	Adjustments of opportunities to fit the market	Opportunities emerge from macro changes
Role of knowledge and preexisting conditions	Helpful to the extent that it triggers the "Aha" moment	Prior knowledge can be expanded to pursue opportunities further	Prior knowledge and information processing inform observations and feasibility assessment
Alert scanning and search	Passive; a unique preparedness	Passive and active; pursue specific opportunities	Cognitive capacity (e.g., creativity, intelligence) and personal fit
Alert association and scanning	Lying dormant waiting to be identified	Still lying dormant but room for creativity and further development	Initial insights heighten sensitivity and can produce further search and processing
Alert evaluation and judgment	Largely unaddressed, assumed that entrepreneurs would act on opportunities	Evaluations of opportunities can evolve over time	Combining beliefs/ insights and desires for a judgment on venture prospects; distinction between first- and third-person opportunities

Social forces, such as demographic changes and changes in societal perceptions and lifestyles, could also disrupt the market. For example, the population is aging in most Western countries. This demographic change could generate opportunities to create ventures geared toward older people. The same is true for the changing perceptions relating to same-sex marriage in most Western countries. Technological changes also influence opportunity discovery. New knowledge and processes could revolutionize the way people interact as well as the needs and wants they pursue. Finally, the regulatory environment could affect the opportunity recognition process. Factors in the external environment affect not only the opportunity recognition process but also the process of starting and managing a social venture.

Systematic search and alertness both draw on the discovery theory of entrepreneurial opportunity. Discovery opportunities may be considered as perceptual phenomena and therefore represent automatic responses to external stimuli. These external stimuli may be market imperfections. Signal detection theory can prove useful in helping us to understand the link between ideas and opportunities.[44] This theory describes the relationship between perception and reality when it comes to opportunity, recognizing that people sometimes see opportunities that are not there or fail to see those that are present.[45] Building on this theory, Brooks has identified four conditions related to opportunity recognition: hit, miss, false alarm, and correct rejection.[46] When a person perceives an opportunity that actually exists, that is a hit. When a person does not perceive an opportunity that actually exists, that is a miss. When a person perceives an opportunity that does not actually exist, that is a false alarm. Finally, when a person does not see an opportunity that does not actually exist, that is a correct rejection.[47] Figure 5.3 illustrates these four conditions.

Presence of Opportunity   Absence of Opportunity

	Presence of Opportunity	Absence of Opportunity
Seen	Hit	False Alarm
Overlooked	Miss	Correct Rejection

Figure 5.3 Conditions related to opportunity recognition.

2.3 Idea Generation

The creation process also includes an active and passive phase. During the active phase, would-be entrepreneurs actively take steps to generate business ideas. They can do this by using idea-generation techniques, such as brainstorming or focus groups. The most popular techniques are briefly discussed below. Major textbooks on organizational behavior, management, and industrial/organizational behavior provide in-depth analysis of these idea-generation techniques.

2.3.1 Brainstorming

The use of brainstorming in generating business ideas has been advocated by several entrepreneurship researchers and it features prominently in several entrepreneurship textbooks.[48] This technique is widely used in other fields of management to generate new ideas. It generally consists of gathering a group of people in a room to generate ideas about a specific topic. It can be either formal or informal. In entrepreneurship, it may even consist of one would-be entrepreneur or a team of entrepreneurs sitting down to generate ideas about possible business opportunities. It could also be useful in generating social venture ideas. To facilitate the generation of novel ideas, brainstorming sessions do not generally allow criticism.

2.3.2 Focus Groups

A focus group would usually consist of five to ten people who are familiar with a particular topic. In entrepreneurship, using a focus group can be a follow-up to a brainstorming session. Once the idea for a particular business opportunity has been generated, a focus group can be used to refine it and answer specific questions pertaining to this opportunity. Focus groups are often conducted by trained moderators whose primary goals are to facilitate the discussion and keep the participants focused.

2.3.3 Other Techniques

Other techniques to generate business ideas include library or internet research, customer advisory board meetings, if the venture is already in existence, and day-in-the-life research. The latter consists of the entrepreneur observing his/her own habits as a customer or beneficiary of public services as well as observing other customers' behaviors. Knowledge gleaned from such observations could lead to new business ideas. When using day-in-the-life research, the entrepreneur acts as an anthropologist. Companies such as Quicken, Quickbooks, and TurboTax all practice day-in-the-life research by routinely sending teams of testers to the homes and businesses of their end-users to see how their products are working and for insights that may lead to new product ideas.[49]

This creation phase draws from the effectuation theory of entrepreneurial opportunity.[50] Effectuation theory emphasizes creativity and suggests that the entrepreneur acts as an imaginative actor who seizes contingent opportunities and exploits any and all means at hand to fulfill a plurality of current and future aspirations, many of which are shaped and created through the very process of economic decision-making and are not given a priori.[51] It contends that entrepreneurs create something with what they have at their disposal. The creation theory of business opportunity posits that entrepreneurs seek to optimize the gains of a large number of stakeholders and in so doing identify opportunities post hoc.[52] Opportunity creation is an iterative process. In creation theory, entrepreneurs do not search for opportunities, because opportunities are not objective entities existing in the external environment. Instead, entrepreneurs generate opportunities, act, and observe how consumers and markets respond to their actions.[53] Entrepreneurs' actions are therefore the source of opportunities in creation theory. Opportunities do not exist until they are created.

2.4   Design Thinking

In the passive phase, would-be entrepreneurs are likely to use design thinking, which consists of using ethnographic methods, such as observation, to come up with new ways of solving problems. Although design thinking has a relatively long history in the sciences, design, and architecture,[54] it has only recently come to prominence in management and entrepreneurship education. Now, though, some scholars are calling for the integration of design thinking in business schools' curricula.[55]

Design thinking is an iterative, exploratory process involving visualization, experimenting, creating, and prototyping of models, and then gathering feedback. It is an approach for dealing with complex, ill-defined problems[56] that is construed as a cognitive style, a process, or a resource. As a cognitive style, design thinking refers to how people conceive their world and take action to improve it. In doing so, they may be creative, generating ideas that are totally new or improving existing ones. As a process, design thinking is a methodology by which individuals generate new ideas or reformulate older ones to tackle complex and ill-structured problems. It is, then, a problem-solving methodology. After all, entrepreneurs create and exploit opportunities to solve problems. As a resource, design thinking can be considered as a tool that organizations use to improve their performance. Several companies, such as Pepsico, are using it to spur innovation and better address their customers' needs.[57] Using assumptions of the creation theory of entrepreneurship, design thinking can be used by entrepreneurs to create new business opportunities. An example of the result of design thinking is Apple's iPod. According to Herbert Simon, a design thinking process may have seven stages: define; research; ideation; prototype; choose; implement; and learn.[58] The content of these steps is illustrated in Table 5.3.

Design thinking is particularly suited to address so-called "wicked problems."[59] These are wicked in the sense that they are ill-defined or tricky, rather than malicious.[60] With ill-defined problems, both the problem and the solution are unknown at the outset of the problem-solving exercise. By contrast, with well-defined problems, the problem is clear from the beginning and the solution should be found through the application of some

Table 5.3 Elements of design thinking[61]

Define	Research	Ideation	Prototype	Choose	Implement	Learn
Decide what issue you are trying to resolve. Agree on who the audience is. Prioritize this project in terms of urgency. Determine what will make this project successful. Establish a glossary of terms.	Review the history of the issue; remember any existing obstacles. Collect examples of other attempts to solve the same issue. Note the project supporters, investors, and critics. Talk to your end-users; that brings you the most fruitful ideas for later design. Take into account thought leaders' opinions.	Identify the needs and motivations of your end-users. Generate as many ideas as possible to serve these identified needs. Log your brainstorming session. Do not judge or debate ideas. During brainstorming, have one conversation at a time.	Combine, expand, and refine ideas. Create multiple drafts. Seek feedback from a diverse group of people, including your end-users. Present a selection of ideas to the client. Reserve judgment and maintain neutrality. Create and present actual working prototype(s).	Review the objective. Set aside emotion and ownership of ideas. Avoid consensus thinking. Remember: the most practical solution isn't always the best. Select the powerful ideas.	Make task descriptions. Plan tasks. Determine resources. Assign tasks. Execute. Deliver to client.	Gather feedback from the consumer. Determine if the solution met its goals. Discuss what could be improved. Measure success; collect data. Document.

technical knowledge.[62] Social entrepreneurs often face wicked problems because social problems tend to be complex and there is rarely a simple—or even a correct—solution to them.

3   The Nature of Social Entrepreneurial Opportunities

3.1   Defining Social Entrepreneurial Opportunities

The definition of social entrepreneurial opportunities is made difficult by the combination of economic and social value creation. This is particularly true for hybrid social ventures that combine economic and social value creation. Under these conditions, a social entrepreneurial opportunity is one that is likely to solve a social problem while generating a profit. A need gap must exist for a social opportunity to be meaningful and relevant. According to Zahra and colleagues, social opportunities have five features:

- prevalence;
- relevance;
- urgency;
- accessibility; and
- radicalness.[63]

Social entrepreneurial opportunities are pursued to maximize *social utility*. This refers to the benefits accrued to society or a community by the exploitation of a particular opportunity. There is an abundance of social opportunities because of the existence of a variety of social needs and the inability of governments to address them.

Like business opportunities, social opportunities tend to have a "window of opportunity"—the period during which the entrepreneur can provide maximum value to the customer before circumstances change or reduce that value. This concept was introduced by Timmons and Spinelli, who contend that opportunities exist or are created in real time.[64] For an entrepreneur to seize an opportunity, the window must first be open and then remain open long enough to achieve market-required returns.[65] In social entrepreneurship, the window of opportunity may include a period during which the social venture will have maximum impact. Although competition in the social sector is not as fierce as in the commercial one, it is possible that being the first to start a social venture in a particular community may yield first-mover advantage. It is also true that circumstances may evolve and render some social problems more pressing than others. Social opportunities are also like business opportunities insofar as they must be financially sustainable.

Opportunities for social ventures abound everywhere and are not confined to specific countries or geographic clusters. Entrepreneurship empowers people to explore opportunities in distant locations, transforming their energies into worldwide movements to improve social conditions and enhance the quality of human existence.[66]

3.2   Understanding Social Entrepreneurial Opportunities

Social entrepreneurial opportunities are normally based on the need to create some type of social value—that is, to benefit the local community by solving a social problem or providing assistance in an area/sector of need or disadvantage.[67] Some may argue that opportunity recognition in social entrepreneurship is no different from opportunity recognition in commercial entrepreneurship insofar as the desire to exploit an opportunity as a result of market failure is apparent in both forms. As explained in Chapter 1, however, opportunities in social entrepreneurship are focused on addressing social needs, whereas opportunities in commercial entrepreneurship are geared toward adding economic value for the entrepreneur and his/her investors. Indeed, some authors argue that the key difference between opportunities in commercial and social entrepreneurship is that the primary focus is on economic returns in the former, whereas the focus is on social returns in the latter.[68] In addition, others contend that there are more opportunities in social than commercial entrepreneurship. Specifically, the demand for social entrepreneurship programs and services usually far exceeds the capacity of a social enterprise to meet these needs.[69]

One may argue that social opportunities, like business opportunities, may come from both imprinting and reflexivity. Imprinting refers to the profound influence of social and historical context in constraining the perceptual apparatus of entrepreneurs and delimiting the range of opportunities for innovation that are available to them. Reflexivity operates at both the individual and the collective level of analysis to generate the ability of entrepreneurs to overcome the constraints of imprinting.[70] Social opportunities are also like business opportunities insofar as they must be financially sustainable. Thus, social entrepreneurs should assess how and whether their social venture will sustain itself over time and ask themselves whether their idea will satisfy needs of their target communities. To fail to do so is to invite a lack of demand and difficulty in stimulating it.[71] This implies that social entrepreneurs should start by conducting a needs assessment when thinking about social venture opportunities. For example, they should consider following questions:

•   Is there a social need in the community that is not served by current market forces or government policies?
•   Will the social venture effectively meet those needs?
•   Will the community effectively benefit from the social venture's services?

Answering these questions correctly is important when starting a new social venture because not every idea will lead to a viable social opportunity.

The two major theories of opportunity recognition—the discovery theory and the creation theory—could prove useful in understanding social opportunities. Opportunity creation theory asserts that opportunities do not exist independently of the entrepreneur but are created by the actions, reactions, and behaviors of entrepreneurs as they explore new ways to create new products or services.[72] This view contends that entrepreneurs do not search for opportunities; rather, they create them. In the case of social value creation, effectuating social entrepreneurs would try to shape and create a solution to a social need based on resources at hand rather than try to predict what the ideal solution would be and assemble resources to facilitate it.[73] The second view of entrepreneurial opportunities contends that opportunities exist in the external environment and so can be discovered by clever entrepreneurs.[74] This perspective views entrepreneurs as different from non-entrepreneurs insofar as the former are able to identify opportunities where others do not.[75]

Summary

This chapter discussed entrepreneurial opportunities with a particular emphasis on social entrepreneurial opportunities. It began with a discussion of ideas because an idea lies at the start of every venture, be it commercial or social. However, ideas are not opportunities in themselves. They must be transformed into opportunities, which in turn must be transformed into business or social concepts.

Key Terms

Alertness; brainstorming; business concept; corridor principle; creation theory; day-in-the-life research; design thinking; discovery theory; effectuation theory; focus group; idea; opportunity recognition; signal detection theory; social utility; social venture concept; social venture opportunity; wicked problems; window of opportunity

Review Questions

1 What is the difference between a business opportunity and a social venture opportunity?
2 What is the difference between an idea and an opportunity?
3 Explain the difference between an opportunity and a business concept.
4 Explain the key assumptions of the discovery theory of entrepreneurial opportunity.
5 Explain the key assumptions of the creation theory of entrepreneurial opportunity.
6 What are the main differences between the effectuation and discovery theories of entrepreneurial opportunity?
7 Explain the differences between a business concept and a social venture (or social business) concept.
8 Explain how design thinking can help to address wicked problems.
9 How can being alert help individuals to spot social venture opportunities?
10 Discuss some of the techniques of idea generation, such as brainstorming and focus groups, and apply them to social venture opportunities.

Application Questions

1 Form groups of three to five students and brainstorm on the opportunity for a new social venture. Based on the results of the brainstorming session, transform your idea into a business concept. Is it a business opportunity or merely an idea? Explain.
2 Travel around your town and identify opportunities for a social venture. Explain why you believe that this opportunity is a viable one.
3 Entrepreneurship diary. From the beginning of this class, keep a diary of entrepreneurial ideas. You can ask your relatives, friends, and classmates for their venture ideas. You can also read entrepreneurship magazines, such as *Entrepreneur* and *Inc.*, as well as the small business sections of major newspapers, such as the *Wall Street Journal* and the *New York Times*. Generate as many ideas as possible. Write a paragraph to indicate why you think each idea is viable.
4 Apply the concept of design thinking to social entrepreneurship. Use Table 5.3 as a guideline for your project.
5 Social venture idea generation exercise. The purpose of this exercise is to help you understand and practice the process of generating ideas for social ventures. Use your personal experiences, interests, and values to list as many ideas as possible. The exercise consists of four steps.

Step 1

Generate as many ideas as possible. Use your personal experiences, interests, knowledge, life-style, personal values, and the contributions you would like to make toward your community, nation, or the world. The idea should focus on solving a societal problem that plagues your community, city, country, or the world.

Step 2

Identify five people who know you well and share your ideas with them. Write down the content of your discussion and their feedback regarding your list.

Step 3

Based on the feedback from the five people with whom you discussed your ideas, write down your observations, insights, and conclusions. Identify the main ideas that you would consider for a social venture based on their capacity to tackle societal problems that concern you deeply.

Application Case 1: Mark Juarez: What to Make of a New Product[76]

In March 1991, Mark Juarez, an American, was living in Berlin, Germany, where he worked under contract as a masseur. He had invented a product that he found helpful in his work and was considering what to do with it. The product consisted of four small wooden balls, approximately one inch in diameter, that were connected to a larger one, about two inches in diameter, with wooden dowels that angled out about one inch each from the bottom of the large ball. In use, the product was gripped by a masseur as an aid in transmitting pressure to the client, reducing the strain on the masseur's hand while applying the pressure more firmly at the same time. It had been well received by a few of Mark's colleagues, for whom he had manufactured copies, and by their customers.

Mark wondered how he should apply his time and very limited personal financial resources. Should he pursue licensing, manufacturing, or patenting, or investigate whether there were already other such products on the market, and if so, with what sequence of specific actions? Or should he simply stick to his massage work and let his simple product find its own way into whatever market might—or might not—exist? What would be involved in creating a company to produce and sell the device, and how might such things best be done, if that were his chosen path?

Background

Mark had held a number of different jobs prior to becoming a masseur. In the mid-1970s he studied marketing at Chabot Community College in California while working nine months for a wine company, followed by seven months with ARA Services, a national company providing laundry services for institutions and restaurants. In early 1977 he began working in sales for a company that marketed energy-efficient domestic air-conditioning systems. Although successful, by 1978 Mark already felt that his life was unrewarding and his lifestyle was incompatible with his ideas. After two weeks of driving up and down the West Coast, he quit his job and flew out of the county. Thereafter, he spent ten of the next fifteen years in Europe, working odd jobs during his travels. Whenever he ran out of money completely, he would return to America and work to save enough to go back to Europe. During these return visits, he started a landscaping company, sold "environmentally correct" living/work spaces, and participated in other small ventures.

Mark became interested in massage in 1987, by which time he was living in Berlin. At first he thought it would be difficult to learn locally, since he did not speak German and did not have much money to pay for classes. But a massage teacher explained that massage could be learned irrespective of the language barrier, because it was all about touch and the body—both universal subjects. To encourage Mark further, the teacher offered him a job at the massage school. By the end of the year, Mark was a certified massage therapist. Eventually, he became a massage teacher himself. He also learned that traditional massage techniques are very tiring on the hands and can even cause serious injury: many massage therapists were developing carpal tunnel syndrome at the time.

Then, one February morning in 1991, through a vision in a dream, Mark conceived of the device that might help with his work. He envisaged a wooden ball with four wooden legs and smaller wooden balls on the end of each leg. He also envisioned painting a smiley face on the big wooden ball. He told a friend about his idea and she encouraged him to visit a woodturner, who would be able to make the balls and the dowels. Some prototypes were completed, and Mark tried them on his students. The students said they loved the device and the following week they requested some of their own. Mark and the woodturner made more, and enthusiasm and demand for the new tool increased.

Because of his students' interest, Mark began to think about protecting his design by seeking a patent. He visited an American patent attorney in Berlin, who quoted a fee of $4,000 for "researching" the patent. This task was not to be confused with actually *filing* to receive a patent for the new device. The attorney would simply look through the records of prior US patents to ascertain whether the same product features had been patented previously in the United States. If they had not, then Mark could try to obtain a patent, which would cost considerably more. Should this be granted, he would be able to claim that anyone who imitated his product in the country where the patent was issued had violated his patent and he would have the right to sue. If the patent court agreed with Mark's opinion, he could prevent any further imitations. Those who obtained US patents found that the process typically took about two years. Either way, Mark had to make a decision about whether to try to launch his product on the market, and if so, how. He was not wealthy.

Discussion Questions

1   To what extent could it be said that Mark's invention is evidence of business opportunity and how would you characterize the nature of that opportunity?
2   Was the opportunity there before Mark conceived his invention, and was that opportunity either changed or superseded by his idea?
3   What will Mark require in order to exploit his idea (if it is exploitable)?
4   Is this opportunity addressing a social need?

Application Case 2: EasySport: Doing Business for Nature and against Poverty[77]

Jack has a dream. He wants to build a sustainable holiday resort in the Caribbean. It will be built and managed in a sustainable way, will not produce waste, will generate its own electricity, and will be CO_2 neutral ("zero emission"). When discussing it with Jack, you cannot miss his enthusiasm. His eyes are shining. His dream is based on ideals, but also on his frustration with how tourism is developing in the Caribbean. He sees crowds of tourists crowding onto the islands, either disembarking from enormous cruise ships or staying in one of the huge hotels. Billions of dollars are being earned, but only 3 percent of this money benefits the local communities. The rest goes to the already wealthy countries, especially the United States. The result, as Jack sees it, is a poor population, a beach where only tourists are welcome, a shortage of clean drinking water, and seriously threatened coral reefs. He wants to do it differently. Why should the local community not benefit from the returns generated by tourism and why not run a hotel that does not exhaust natural resources and damage the beautiful natural environment of the Caribbean?

Jack is a diving instructor, and diving is still his passion. On one of his many diving trips he arrived at Roatan, an island near the Honduran coast. It is small—only 40 kilometers long, 6 kilometers wide—but one of the best diving regions in the world. In fact, it is a pure and untouched paradise. Jack fell in love with this place and now he wants to realize his dream on this exact spot. It will be a luxurious, four-star holiday resort, constructed using the latest sustainable-building techniques, and comprising comfortable villas in a tropical park, a wellness center, a training center for the local people, and a congress center where knowledge can be shared with the local region. Both the carbon footprint[78] and the ecological footprint[79] will remain as small as possible. To cite two examples: the wellness center will use only locally produced oils and creams; and the restaurant will serve only organic food that has been produced locally and sustainably. Last but not least, the local community will be educated in practical, sustainable solutions, knowledge that will provide them with incomes, regardless of the resort.

Jack has thoroughly thought through his idea. He has an intricate plan of the project he wants to build and how he will fund his dream. He has explored many potential ways to shape the organization and has had to take into consideration both Dutch and Honduran law—no easy task. Moreover, most legal entities do not easily allow for the combination of doing well with doing good. After endless research, Jack finally decided that the best structural form would be a cooperative association. This association, called EasySport, will comprise an investment company, a commercial organization, and two foundations (the Profit for Change Foundation and the World Improvement Foundation). Jack describes EasySport itself as a "profit for change" organization. Hence, its slogan is: "Doing business for nature and against poverty." Members of the cooperative association will receive a fair return on their investment. All of EasySport's profits will be reinvested in education, retraining, infrastructure, knowledge dissemination, and environmental protection. Investing in the association is therefore a form of "green" investment, and so tax deductible. Of course, donating to one of the two foundations is also an option. In total, Jack will need around $12 million to start building.

In the meantime, he does not just sit around and wait for the money to materialize. On the contrary, Jack makes a virtue of his need to generate money by organizing workshops to help managers and entrepreneurs think about sustainable enterprise in a totally new way. By so doing, he also expands his own knowledge base and builds new network connections for EasySport. He is investigating how partnerships with local contributors might be shaped, and if and how carbon trade can be used to finance the initiative itself as well as the local projects.

For those who will eventually stay at the resort, "experience" will be a central term. Not only will they get to experience the beautiful island, both above and under the water, but they will experience something that might be termed "pro-poor tourism." While enjoying a fabulous holiday—with diving, biking, hiking, rafting, sailing, or just enjoying the cultural and natural beauty of the island or the resort's wellness center all on offer—the guests will help with the conservation of the island, its reefs, and its people. After all, the resort's profits will all be reinvested in idealistic projects. Jack wants EasySport to become an inspirational example for the whole region. He just needs $12 million to get started.

Discussion Questions

1   Is Jack's dream a social venture opportunity or merely a dream?
2   How would you translate his dream into a social venture concept?
3   What would be your advice with regards to the $12 million? Do you think that Jack will be able to raise such a large amount of money?
4   Do you personally subscribe to Jack's dream?
5   What (if anything) would you do (differently)?

Notes

1   Davidsson, P. (2015). Entrepreneurial opportunities and the entrepreneurial nexus: A re-conceptualization. *Journal of Business Venturing*, 30(5), 674–695; Alvarez, S. A., & Barney, J. B. (2014). Entrepreneurial opportunities and poverty alleviation. *Entrepreneurship Theory and Practice*, 38(1), 159–184; Alvarez, S. A., Barney, J. B., & Anderson, P. (2013). Forming and exploiting opportunities: The implications of discovery and creation processes for entrepreneurial and organizational research. *Organization Science*, 24(1), 301–317; Austin, J., Stevenson, H., & Wei-Skillern (2006). Social and commercial entrepreneurship: Same, different, or both? *Entrepreneurship Theory and Practice*, 30(1), 1–22.
2   Kickul, J., & Lyons, T. S. (2012). *Understanding social entrepreneurship: The relentless pursuit of mission in an ever changing world*. New York: Routledge.
3   Timmons, J. A., & Spinelli, S. (2007). *New venture creation: Entrepreneurship for the 21st century*. 7th edition. New York: McGraw-Hill.
4   Kickul, J., & Lyons, T. S. (2012). *Understanding social entrepreneurship: The relentless pursuit of mission in an ever changing world*. New York: Routledge.
5   Lichtenstein, G. A., & Lyons, T. (1996). The entrepreneurial development system: Transforming business talent and community economies. *Economic Development Quarterly*, 15(1), 3–20.
6   Longenecker, J. J. G., Moore, C. W., Petty, J. W., & Palich, L. E. (2006). *Small business management: An entrepreneurial emphasis*. 13th edition. Mason, OH: Thomson South-Western.
7   Timmons, J. A., & Spinelli, S. (2007). *New venture creation: Entrepreneurship for the 21st century*. 7th edition. New York: McGraw-Hill.
8   Shane, S. (2000). Prior knowledge and the discovery of entrepreneurial opportunities. *Organization Science*, 11(4), 448–469; Shane, S. (2003). *A general theory of entrepreneurship: The individual–opportunity nexus*. Cheltenham: Edward Elgar; Shane, S., & Vankataraman, S. (2000). The promise of entrepreneurship as a field of research. *Academy of Management Review*, 25(1), 217–226.
9   Stevenson, H. H., & Jarillo, J. C. (1990). A paradigm of entrepreneurship: Entrepreneurship management. *Strategic Management Journal*, 11, 17–27.
10   Brooks, C. A. (2009). *Social entrepreneurship: A modern approach to social value creation*. Upper Saddle River, NJ: Pearson/Prentice-Hall.

11 Schumpeter, J. A. (1934). *A theory of economic development: An inquiry into profits, capital credit, interest, and the business cycle.* Cambridge, MA: Harvard University Press.

12 Timmons, J. A., & Spinelli, S. (2007). *New venture creation: Entrepreneurship for the 21st century.* 7th edition. New York: McGraw-Hill.

13 Gartner, W. B., & Bellamy, M. G. (2010). *Enterprise.* Mason, OH: South-Western Cengage Learning.

14 Gartner, W. B., & Bellamy, M. G. (2010). *Enterprise.* Mason, OH: South-Western Cengage Learning.

15 Barringer, B. R., & Ireland, R. D. (2012). *Entrepreneurship: Successfully Launching New Ventures.* 4th edition. New York: Pearson/Prentice-Hall.

16 Gartner, W. B., & Bellamy, M. G. (2010). *Enterprise.* Mason, OH: South-Western Cengage Learning.

17 Gartner, W. B., & Bellamy, M. G. (2010). *Enterprise.* Mason, OH: South-Western Cengage Learning.

18 Shane, S., & Vankataraman, S. (2000). The promise of entrepreneurship as a field of research. *Academy of Management Review*, 25(1), 217–226; Shane, S. (2003). *A general theory of entrepreneurship: The individual–opportunity nexus.* Cheltenham: Edward Elgar.

19 Kirzner, I. (1973). *Competition and entrepreneurship.* Chicago: University of Chicago Press; Kirzner, I. (1979). *Perception, opportunity, and profit: Studies in the theory of entrepreneurship.* Chicago: University of Chicago Press; Alvarez, S. A., & Barney, J. B. (2007). Discovery and creation: alternative theories of entrepreneurial action. *Strategic Entrepreneurship Journal*, 1(1–2), 11–26.

20 Alvarez, S. A., & Barney, J. B. (2007). Discovery and creation: alternative theories of entrepreneurial action. *Strategic Entrepreneurship Journal*, 1(1–2), 11–26.

21 Sarasvathy, D. S. (2001). Causation and effectuation: Toward a theoretical shift from economic inevitability to entrepreneurial contingency. *Academy of Management Review*, 26(2), 243–263; Baker, T., & Nelson, R. (2005). Creating something from nothing: Resource construction through entrepreneurial bricolage. *Administrative Science Quarterly*, 50(3), 329–366.

22 Alvarez, S. A., & Barney, J. B. (2007). Discovery and creation: Alternative theories of entrepreneurial action. *Strategic Entrepreneurship Journal*, 1(1–2), 11–26.

23 Woods, M. S., & Williams, D. W. (2014). Opportunity evaluation as rule-based decision making. *Journal of Management Studies*, 51(4), 573–602.

24 Farmer, S. M., Yao, X., & Kung-McIntyre, K. (2010). The behavioural impact of entrepreneurial identity aspiration and prior entrepreneurial experience. *Entrepreneurship Theory and Practice*, 35(2), 245–273; Wiklund. J., & Shepherd, D. A. (2008). Portfolio entrepreneurship: Habitual and novice founders, new entry, and mode of organizing. *Entrepreneurship Theory and Practice*, 32(4), 701–725.

25 Baron, R. A. (2006). Opportunity recognition as pattern recognition: How entrepreneurs "connect the dots" to identify new business opportunities. *Academy of Management Perspectives*, 20(1), 104–119; Spinelli, Jr., S., & Adams, R. (2012). *New venture creation: Entrepreneurship in the 21st century.* New York: McGraw-Hill Irwin.

26 Ucbasaran, D., Westhead, P., & Wright, M. (2009). The extent and nature of opportunity identification by experienced entrepreneurs. *Journal of Business Venturing*, 24(2), 99–115.

27 Baron, R. A. (2004). The cognitive perspective: A valuable tool for answering entrepreneurship's basic "why" questions. *Journal of Business Venturing*, 19(2), 221–239.

28 Ucbasaran, D., Westhead, P., & Wright, M. (2009). The extent and nature of opportunity identification by experienced entrepreneurs. *Journal of Business Venturing*, 24(2), 99–115.

29 Baron, R. A. (2006). Opportunity recognition as pattern recognition: How entrepreneurs "connect the dots" to identify new business opportunities. *Academy of Management Perspectives*, 20(1), 104–119; Baron, R. A., & Ensley, M. D. (2006). Opportunity recognition as the detection of meaningful patterns: Evidence from comparisons of novice and experienced entrepreneurs. *Management Science*, 52(9), 1331–1344.

30   Baron, R. A. (2004). The cognitive perspective: A valuable tool for answering entrepreneurship's basic "why" questions. *Journal of Business Venturing*, 19(2), 221–239; Baron, R. A., & Ensley, M. D. (2006). Opportunity recognition as the detection of meaningful patterns: Evidence from comparisons of novice and experienced entrepreneurs. *Management Science*, 52(9), 1331–1344.

31   Simon, A. H. (1985). What we know about the creative process. In R. L. Kuhn (Ed.), *Frontiers in creative and innovative management* (pp. 3–20). Cambridge, MA: Ballinger.

32   Thoren, K., & Brown, T. E. (2010). The sarimner effect and three types of ever-abundant business opportunities. *International Journal of Entrepreneurial Venturing*, 2(2), 114–128; Barringer, B. R., & Ireland, R. D. (2012). *Entrepreneurship: Successfully launching new ventures*. 4th edition. New York: Pearson/Prentice-Hall.

33   Baron, R. A., & Ensley, M. D. (2006). Opportunity recognition as the detection of meaningful patterns: Evidence from comparisons of novice and experienced entrepreneurs. *Management Science*, 52(9), 1331–1344.

34   Starr, J., & Bygrave, W. (1991). The assets and liabilities of prior start-up experience: An exploratory study of multiple venture entrepreneurs. In *Frontiers of entrepreneurship research* (pp. 213–227). Wellesley, MA: Babson College.

35   Gruber, M., Kim, S. M., & Brinckmann, J. (2015). What is an attractive business opportunity? An empirical study of opportunity evaluations by technologists, managers, and entrepreneurs. *Strategic Entrepreneurship Journal*, 9(3), 205–225.

36   Venkataraman, S. (1997). The distinctive domain of entrepreneurship research: An editor's perspective. In J. Katz & R. Brockhaus (Eds.), *Advances in entrepreneurship, firm emergence, and growth* (3, pp. 119–138). Greenwich, CT: JAI Press; Shane, S. (2000). Prior knowledge and the discovery of entrepreneurial opportunities. *Organization Science*, 11(4), 448–469.

37   Shane, S. (2000). Prior knowledge and the discovery of entrepreneurial opportunities. *Organization Science*, 11(4), 448–469.

38   Busenitz, I., & Barney, J. (1997). Differences between entrepreneurs and managers in large organizations: Biases and heuristics in strategic decision making. *Journal of Business Venturing*, 21(1), 9–30; Shepherd, D. A., & DeTienne, D. R. (2005). Prior knowledge, potential financial reward, and opportunity identification. *Entrepreneurship Theory and Practice*, 29(1), 91–112.

39   Wood, M. S., McKelvie, A., & Haynie, J. M. (2014). Making it personal: Opportunity individuation and the shaping of opportunity beliefs. *Journal of Business Venturing*, 29(2), 252–272.

40   Valliere, D. (2013). Toward a schematic theory of entrepreneurial alertness. *Journal of Business Venturing*, 28(3), 430–442; Kirzner, I. (1979). *Perception, opportunity, and profit: Studies in the theory of entrepreneurship*. Chicago: University of Chicago Press.

41   Tang, J., Kacmar, K. M., & Busenitz, L. (2012). Entrepreneurial alertness in the pursuit of new opportunities. *Journal of Business Venturing*, 27(1), 77–94.

42   Kuratko, F. D., & Hodgetts, M. R. (2001). *Entrepreneurship: A contemporary approach*. Fort Worth, TX: Harcourt.

43   Tang, J., Kacmar, K. M., & Busenitz, L. (2012). Entrepreneurial alertness in the pursuit of new opportunities. *Journal of Business Venturing*, 27(1), 77–94, at p. 79.

44   Swets, A. J. (1992). The science of choosing the right decision threshold in high stakes diagnostics. *American Psychologist*, 47(4), 522–532.

45   Swets, A. J. (1992). The science of choosing the right decision threshold in high stakes diagnostics. *American Psychologist*, 47(4), 522–532; Brooks, C. A. (2009). *Social entrepreneurship: A modern approach to social value creation*. Upper Saddle River, NJ: Pearson/Prentice-Hall.

46   Brooks, C. A. (2009). *Social entrepreneurship: A modern approach to social value creation*. Upper Saddle River, NJ: Pearson/Prentice-Hall.

47   Baron, R. A., & Shane, A. S. (2005). *Entrepreneurship: A process perspective*. Mason, OH: South-Western.

48   Barringer, B. R., & Ireland, R. D. (2012). *Entrepreneurship: Successfully launching new ventures*. 4th edition. New York: Pearson/Prentice-Hall; Spinelli, Jr., S., & Adams, R. (2012). *New venture creation: Entrepreneurship in the 21st century*. New York: McGraw-Hill Irwin.

49 Barringer, B. R., & Ireland, R. D. (2012). *Entrepreneurship: Successfully launching new ventures*. 4th edition. New York: Pearson/Prentice-Hall; Barringer, B. R., & Ireland, R. D. (2016). *Entrepreneurship: Successfully launching new ventures*. 5th edition. New York: Pearson/Prentice-Hall.

50 Sarasvathy, D. S. (2001). Causation and effectuation: Toward a theoretical shift from economic inevitability to entrepreneurial contingency. *Academy of Management Review*, 26(2), 243–263.

51 Sarasvathy, D. S. (2001). Causation and effectuation: Toward a theoretical shift from economic inevitability to entrepreneurial contingency. *Academy of Management Review*, 26(2), 243–263.

52 Echardt, J. T., & Shane, S. A. (2003). Opportunities and entrepreneurship. *Journal of Management*, 29(3), 333–349; Short, J. C., Ketchen, D, J., Shook, C. L., & Ireland, R. D. (2010). The concept of opportunity in entrepreneurship research: Past accomplishments and future challenges. *Journal of Management*, 36(1), 40–65; Vaghely, I. P., & Julien, P. A. (2010). Are opportunities recognized or constructed? An information perspective on entrepreneurial opportunity identification. *Journal of Business Venturing*, 25, 73–86; Hansen, D. J., Shrader, R., & Monillor, J. (2011). Defragmenting definitions of entrepreneurial opportunity. *Journal of Small Business Management*, 49(2), 283–304.

53 Alvarez, S. A., & Barney, J. B. (2007). Discovery and creation: Alternative theories of entrepreneurial action. *Strategic Entrepreneurship Journal*, 1(1–2), 11–26.

54 Simon, A. H. (1969). *The science of the artificial*. Cambridge, MA: MIT Press; McKim, R. (1973). *Experiences in visual thinking*. Monterey, CA: Brooks/Cole Publishing Co.

55 Glen, R., Suciu, C., & Baughn, C. (2014). The need for design thinking in business schools. *Academy of Management Learning and Education*, 13(4), 653–667.

56 Kolko, J. (2015). Design thinking comes of age. *Harvard Business Review*, September, 66–71; Brown, T., & Martin, R. (2015). Design for action: How to use design thinking to make great things actually happen. *Harvard Business Review*, September, 56–64; Glen, R., Suciu, C., & Baughn, C. (2014). The need for design thinking in business schools. *Academy of Management Learning and Education*, 13(4), 653–667; Brown, T. (2008). Design thinking. *Harvard Business Review*, June, 1–9; Simon, A. H. (1969). *The science of the artificial*. Cambridge, MA: MIT Press.

57 Ignatius A. (2015). How Indra Nooyi turned design thinking into strategy. *Harvard Business Review*, September, 80–85.

58 Simon, A. H. (1969). *The science of the artificial*. Cambridge, MA: MIT Press.

59 Buchanan, R. (1992). Wicked problems in design thinking. *Design Issues*, 8(2), 5–21.

60 Buchanan, R. (1992). Wicked problems in design thinking. *Design Issues*, 8(2), 5–21; Rittel, H., & Webber, M. (1973). Dilemmas in a general theory of planning. *Policy Sciences*, 4(2), 155–169.

61 Simon, A. H. (1969). *The science of the artificial*. Cambridge, MA: MIT Press.

62 Beinecke, R. (2009). Leadership for wicked problems. *Innovation Journal*, 14(1), 1–17.

63 Zahra, S. A., Rawhouser, H. N., Bhame, N., Neubaum, D. O., & Hayton, J. C. (2008). Globalization of social entrepreneurship opportunities. *Strategic Entrepreneurship Journal*, 2(2), 117–131.

64 Timmons, J. A., & Spinelli, S. (2007). *New venture creation: Entrepreneurship for the 21st century*. 7th edition. New York: McGraw-Hill.

65 Timmons, J. A., & Spinelli, S. (2007). *New venture creation: Entrepreneurship for the 21st century*. 7th edition. New York: McGraw-Hill; Spinelli, Jr., S., & Adams, R. (2012). *New venture creation: Entrepreneurship in the 21st century*. New York: McGraw-Hill Irwin.

66 Zahra, S. A., Rawhouser, H. N., Bhame, N., Neubaum, D. O., & Hayton, J. C. (2008). Globalization of social entrepreneurship opportunities. *Strategic Entrepreneurship Journal*, 2(2), 117–131.

67 Henry, C. (2015). Doing well by doing good: Opportunity recognition and the social enterprise partnership. *Journal of Social Entrepreneurship*, 6(2), 137–160.

68 Austin, J., Stevenson, H., & Wei-Skillern (2006). Social and commercial entrepreneurship: Same, different, or both? *Entrepreneurship Theory and Practice*, 30(1), 1–22; Corner, P. D., & Huo, C. (2010). How opportunities develop in social entrepreneurship? *Entrepreneurship Theory and Practice*, 34(4), 635–659.

69   Austin, J., Stevenson, H., & Wei-Skillern (2006). Social and commercial entrepreneurship: Same, different, or both? *Entrepreneurship Theory and Practice, 30*(1), 1–22.

70   Suddaby, R., Bruton, G. D., & Steven, S. X. (2015). Entrepreneurship through a qualitative lens: Insights on the construction and/or discovery of entrepreneurial opportunity. *Journal of Business Venturing, 30*(1), 1–10.

71   Brooks, C. A. (2009). *Social entrepreneurship: A modern approach to social value creation.* Upper Saddle River, NJ: Pearson/Prentice-Hall.

72   Eckhardt, J. T., & Shane, S. A. (2003). Opportunities and entrepreneurship. *Journal of Management, 29*(3), 333–349.

73   Corner, P. D., & Huo, C. (2010). How opportunities develop in social entrepreneurship. *Entrepreneurship Theory and Practice, 34*(4), 635–659.

74   Sarason, Y., Dean, T., & Dillard, J. F. (2006). Entrepreneurship as the nexus of individual and opportunity: A structural view. *Journal of Business Venturing, 21*(3), 286–305.

75   Alvarez, S. A., & Barney, J. B. (2007). Discovery and creation: Alternative theories of entrepreneurial action. *Strategic Entrepreneurship Journal, 1*(1–2), 11–26.

76   Source for this whole section: Study drafted by Karl H. Vesper in 1998, based on a case written by Susan Devan and Michael Pisenti under the supervision of Dr. William B. Gardner at San Francisco State University's College of Business, with the support of the Corporate Design Foundation, as a basis for class discussion, rather than to illustrate either effective or ineffective handling of a business situation. Reproduced with permission.

77   Source for this whole section: Dr. Karen Verduyn, VU University, Amsterdam. Reproduced with permission

78   A carbon footprint is a measure of our activities' impact on the environment, and in particular climate change. It relates to the amount of greenhouse gases produced in our day-to-day lives through burning fossil fuels for electricity, heating, and transportation. The carbon footprint is a measurement of all the greenhouse gases we, as individuals, produce in tons (or kilograms) of carbon-dioxide equivalent (see www.carbonfootprint.com).

79   The ecological footprint is a measure of human demand on the earth's ecosystems. It compares that demand with the earth's ecological capacity to regenerate. It represents the amount of biologically productive land and sea area needed to regenerate the resources a human population consumes and to absorb and render harmless the corresponding waste (see www.ecologicalfootprint.com).

Chapter 6

Developing a Social Venture Sustainability Model

Learning Objectives

1 Explain the concept of business model.
2 Describe the components of a business model.
3 Define the sustainability model of a social venture.
4 Explain the social business model canvas.

This chapter focuses on the development of a social venture sustainability model. Instead of using the term "business model," as is common in commercial entrepreneurship, the chapter uses the construct *social venture sustainability model* or *social business model* to differentiate commercial ventures from social ventures. The chapter is divided into four sections. The first section discusses the concept of business model as defined and applied in commercial entrepreneurship. The second describes the components of a business model. The third focuses on the concept of social venture sustainability model. The fourth presents strategies for building social venture sustainability models.

1 Nature of Business Models

1.1 Defining a Business Model

Before defining the concept of business model, it is important to understand what a model is. Simply put, a model is a simplified description of a phenomenon. The *American Heritage Dictionary* defines a model as a schematic description of a system, theory or phenomenon; a small object, usually built to scale, that represents in detail another, often larger object, or it can be something or someone serving as an example to be imitated or compared to.[1] As such, a model is different from what it represents. Thus, a business model is a simplified way of explaining how a firm creates, delivers, and captures value. The business model is not the firm but is a representation of the firm.

The concept of business model is relatively new and there is currently no agreement upon its formal definition. However, some definitions tend to be more accepted than others. A business model depicts the content, structure, and governance of transactions designed so as to create value through the exploitation of business opportunities, and represents a plan that shows how all major aspects of a business work together to generate profit.[2] Specifically, the business model is a firm's plan or diagram for how it competes, uses its resources, structures its relationships, interfaces with customers, and creates value to sustain itself on the basis of the profits it earns.[3] It is the logic of a firm's value creation.[4] The business model helps to answer the question: can we make money doing this?

Generally speaking, the concept of business model describes the rationale of how a company delivers value to its customers. For entrepreneurs, building a business model entails designing the rationale of how the new firm will create, deliver, and capture value. The first part, creation, refers to the new product or service the new firm intends to offer. Is the new product really new? Does it offer something of value to the customer? The second aspect concerns how to bring the product or service to the customer and deals with processes. The third element of the definition deals with how the firm will generate profit by providing the product or service. For an entrepreneur, it addresses the question of how the new venture will generate profit by exploiting the opportunity. The business model can be conceived as the architecture of the value creation, delivery, and capturing mechanisms.

A content analysis of 30 definitions of business model has led to the identification of three general categories that are deemed important:[5] *economic, operational*, and *strategic*. The economic component of a business model concerns how the firm will generate revenue and make profits by exploiting the business opportunity. It is also known as the *revenue model*. Decisions made at this level include revenue sources, pricing methodologies, cost structures, potential margins, and expected volumes. This component reflects the conceptualization of the business model as a statement of how a firm will make money and sustain its profit stream over time.[6] It focuses on the revenue-generating aspect of the venture. As such, revenue is used as a metric to gauge the effectiveness of the business model. Hence, a successful business model will generate revenue, whereas a failing business model will not generate revenue.

The operational component of the business model focuses on the internal processes and design of infrastructure that enable the firm to create value. At this level, the entrepreneur is concerned with decisions related to production and delivery methods, administrative processes, logistical streams, and resource flows. This component includes the operationalization of the business model as a system of activities and reflects the design of key interdependent systems that create and sustain a competitive business.[7] An activity in a focal firm's business model can be viewed as the engagement of human, physical, and/or capital resources of any party to the business model to serve a specific purpose toward the fulfillment of the overall objective.[8]

The strategic component emphasizes the overall direction of the firm. It includes the firm's market positioning, interactions across organizational boundaries, and growth opportunities. This component is included in the conceptualization of the business model as a concise representation of how an interrelated set of decision variables in the areas of venture strategy, architecture, and economics is addressed to create sustainable competitive advantage in defined markets.[9] Here, the business model represents the totality of how a company selects its customers, defines and differentiates its offerings, identifies the tasks it will perform itself and those it will outsource, configures its resources, goes to market, creates utility for customers, and captures profit.[10]

Table 6.1 presents a selected sample of business model definitions. These definitions capture the three components discussed above. Although several authors have defined the concept of business model, this sample of definitions helps to illustrate the existence of commonalities among definitions. For management practitioners and entrepreneurs, the sample of definitions displayed in Table 6.1 represents a snapshot of what a business model entails. Of course, managers or entrepreneurs will design and refine their business

Table 6.1 Selected business model definitions[11]

Author	Year	Definition
Timmers	1998	The business model is "an architecture of the product, service and information flows, including a description of the various business actors and their roles; a description of the potential benefits for the various business actors; a description of the sources of revenues" (p. 2).
Amit & Zott	2001	The business model depicts "the content, structure, and governance of transactions designed so as to create value through the exploitation of business opportunities" (p. 511).
Zott & Amit	2010	The business model is "a system of interdependent activities that transcends the focal firm and spans its boundaries" (p. 216).
Chesbrough & Rosenbloom	2002	The business model is "the heuristic logic that connects technical potential with the realization of economic value" (p. 529).
Magretta	2002	Business models are "stories that explain how enterprises work. A good business model answers Peter Drucker's age old questions: Who is the customer? And what does the customer value? It also answers the fundamental questions every manager must ask: How do we make money in this business? What is the underlying economic logic that explains how we can deliver value to customers at an appropriate cost?" (p. 4).
Morris et al.	2005	A business model is a concise representation of how an interrelated set of decision variables in the areas of venture strategy, architecture, and economics is addressed to create sustainable competitive advantage in defined markets" (p. 727).
Johnson et al.	2008	Business models "consist of four interlocking elements that taken together, create and deliver value" (p. 52).
Casadesus-Masanell & Ricart	2010	"A business model is a reflection of the firm's realized strategy" (p. 195).
Teece	2010	"A business model articulates the logic, the data and other evidence that support a value proposition for the customer, and a viable structure of revenues and costs for the enterprise delivering that value" (p. 179).

models based on the internalities as well as externalities that their ventures encounter. In fact, there is no standard business model, no hard-and-fast rules that dictate how a firm in a particular industry should compete. A firm's business model is inherently dependent on the collection of resources it controls and the capabilities it possesses[12] as well as the technological and regulatory shocks it faces.[13] In fact, business models represent concrete choices that management makes about how an organization must operate and the consequences of these choices.[14]

1.2 Importance of a Business Model

When discussing the importance of business models, it is worth asking the following three questions:

- Why does an entrepreneur need to build a business model?
- What is the purpose of a business model?
- Does having a business model enhance the efficiency and effectiveness of the firm?

Some researchers have suggested that business models provide a benefit to companies by operationalizing how they add value to the customer's experience and achieve the bottom line for the company. Specifically, they contend that business models help companies focus their energy on what matters most. A good business model yields value propositions that are compelling to customers, achieves advantageous cost and risk structures, and enables significant value captured by the business that generates and delivers products and services.[15] For Barringer and Ireland, having a clearly articulated business model is important because it does the following:[16]

1 Serves as an ongoing extension of feasibility analysis (a business model continuously asks the question: does the business make sense?).
2 Focuses attention on how all the elements of a business fit together and how they constitute a working whole.
3 Describes why the network of participants needed to make a business idea viable is willing to work together.
4 Articulates a company's core logic to all stakeholders, including its employees.

Other authors have underscored the importance of the business model in slightly different ways, although the core elements remain similar. For example, McGrath contends that:[17]

1 Focusing on business models reinvigorates a view of firms as continuously engaged with and adapting to changing customer values. Business models that do not create value for customers do not create value for the firms that seek to serve those customers either.
2 Business models often cannot be fully anticipated in advance. Rather, they must be learned over time, which emphasizes the critical role of experimentation in the discovery and development of new business models.
3 The business model construct encourages conversations which might identify early warning signs of model weakness and prompt the search for new ones.
4 As business models themselves evolve and mature, adopting the notion suggests a developing understanding that strategy itself is quite frequently discovery-driven rather than planning-orientated.

A business model works as both a calculative and a narrative device. It allows entrepreneurs to explore a market and to bring their innovation, a new product, a new venture and the network that supports it into existence.[18] The business model encourages the entrepreneur to:

- conceptualize the venture as an interrelated set of strategic choices;
- seek complementary relationships among elements through unique combinations;
- develop activity sets around a logical framework; and
- ensure consistency between elements of strategy, architecture, economics, growth, and exit intentions.[19]

Thus, a business model is important because it helps a venture to determine the configuration of activities necessary to add value to the customer's experience while keeping the venture profitable. Understanding such configuration will help the entrepreneur to assess which activities are necessary to increase value and which are peripheral. Without a well-developed business model, innovators will fail to deliver or capture value from their innovations.[20]

Despite its importance, a business model is not a panacea. Moreover, technology can affect the delivery component and the cost side of the business model. A business model can also be context-dependent. A business model that works perfectly in a given environment may not be successful when applied in another environment. An illustrative example was Dell Computers' Dell Direct business model. This business model consisted of bypassing middle men and selling directly to the customer. Although successful in the United States, the model was ineffective in China in the 1990s and early 2000s because Chinese customers preferred to see the physical products before buying them. This led Dell to refine its business model in China by creating Dell Kiosks, where samples of its products were displayed.

1.3 Business Model and Strategy

The development of business models is closely related to strategy formulation. Thus, it is important to explore the link between the two concepts. According to Porter, strategy is mainly about performing different activities compared to the competition or performing similar activities better.[21] The concept of business model includes operational effectiveness and efficiency, which concerns the performance of several activities to create and capture. As a consequence, a business model has elements of both operational effectiveness and strategy.[22] Porter suggests the construct of activity sets, implying that organizations configure activities in unique ways to build a competitive advantage.[23] Such configuration of activities leading to activity sets includes core activities, elaborating elements, and interactions.[24] Whereas business models refer to the logic of the firm—that is, how it operates, creates, and captures value for stakeholders in a competitive marketplace—strategy is the plan to create a unique and valuable position involving a distinctive set of activities.[25]

Table 6.2 illustrates a comparison between business model and strategy, particularly product market strategy. It shows that a product market strategy differs from a business model mainly through its focus on the positioning of the firm vis-à-vis its rivals, whereas a business model is a structural construct that centers on the pattern of the firm's economic exchanges with external parties in its addressable factor and product markets.[26] This distinction is echoed by scholars who argue that while a business model does facilitate analysis, testing, and validation of a firm's strategic choices, it is not in itself a strategy.[27] Although the concepts of business model and strategy are related, they represent different levels of information that are useful for different purposes. For example, some authors see the business model as an interface between business strategy and business processes.[28] Business strategy explains how companies hope to do better than their rivals, while business model describes how the pieces of a business all fit together.[29]

2 Components of a Business Model

As is true for the *definition* of business model, there is scant agreement on the *components* of a business model. However, entrepreneurship authors have provided some hints about what should be included in one, especially for new ventures. In their textbook, Gartner and Bellamy[30] suggest the following four components of a business model:

- revenue sources;
- cost structure and drivers;
- investment size; and
- critical success factors.

Table 6.2 Business model and product market strategy[31]

	Business model	*Product market strategy*
Definition	A structural template of how a focal firm transacts with customers, partners, and vendors. It captures the pattern of the firm's boundary-spanning connections with factor and product markets.	Pattern of managerial actions that explains how a firm achieves and maintains competitive advantage through positioning in product markets.
Main questions addressed	How to connect with factor and product markets? Which parties to bring together to exploit a business opportunity, and how to link them to the focal firm to enable transactions (what exchange mechanisms to adopt)? What information or goods to exchange among the parties, and what resources and capabilities to deploy to enable the exchanges? How to control the transactions between the parties, and what incentives to adopt for the parties?	What positioning to adopt against rivals? What kind of generic strategy to adopt (cost leadership and/or differentiation)? When to enter the market? What products to sell? Which customers to serve? Which geographic markets to address?
Unit of analysis	Focal firm and its exchange partners.	Firm.
Focus	Externally oriented: focus on firm's exchanges with others.	Internally/externally oriented: focus on firm's activities and actions in light of competition.

Revenue sources involve the different revenue streams. For instance, how will a venture generate revenue? What are the activities or products that will generate revenue for the venture? The venture may generate revenue by selling certain products or delivering certain services and not others. A case in point is the business model of Dignified Mobile Toilets of Nigeria, discussed in Chapter 3. The company generates revenue by charging a fee for use of one of the toilets. It also generates revenue by allowing companies to place their advertisements on the doors. Thus, the company has two revenue streams—fees charged to customers and revenue from advertisers. Cost structure and cost drivers help the company identify the costs of each activity. Identifying cost drivers helps a company apply activity-based costing and keep its costs under control. Investment size relates to the amount required to generate the revenues identified. At this level, the company must have a clear idea of what is needed to fund its operations. Finally, critical success factors refer to what it takes to succeed in a specific industry. This is a particularly important consideration for nascent firms. The company can use the critical success factors as an element of both internal and external benchmarking. As internal benchmarking, the company can compare itself against these critical success factors. For instance, if speed is a critical success factor, the company could assess how rapidly it serves its customers. Improvement in this critical success factor could enhance the firm's position. As external benchmarking, the firm could compare itself to its competitors.

Table 6.3 The four components of a business model[32]

Revenue sources	Cost structure drivers	Investment size	Critical success factors
All revenue streams a particular business model will produce, and the source, size, significance, and growth potential of each.	The cost structure of a business model (fixed, variable, recurring, etc.), relative importance, and how it may change over time.	Amount and timing of investment to produce positive cash flow, including cash required for startup and working capital.	Elements that have the greatest impact on the firm becoming profitable.

Morris and colleagues propose a conceptualization of a business model as a five-stage process.[33] In the process, a business model can take on a life of its own. At the start of a venture, the entrepreneur may design and implement a specific business model. This may be unique and take into account the resources the new firm can control as well as the environment in which it operates. This stage of the business model is the specification stage. The business model can be modified and refined as it is implemented. This is the refinement stage. Some aspects of the business model may work perfectly, while others may need readjustment. Sometimes, the business model may need to adapt to some external factors. It may also need major revisions. At the revision stage, the entrepreneur may completely modify the business model to adapt to environmental contingencies. In fact, business model change represents a search for new optimal design that repositions the firm in response to changing interdependencies caused by exogenous environmental changes.[34] Finally, if the business model is obsolete and no longer viable, it may have to be abandoned and replaced with a new one. This is the reformulation stage. Figure 6.1 depicts the five phases of the evolution of a business model.

According to Morris and colleagues, the specification stage corresponds to an initial period during which the model is fairly informal or implicit. It is followed by a process of trial and error, and a number of core decisions are made that set the directions in which the firm can evolve. At some point in the future, a fairly definitive, formal business model emerges. Adjustments are made and experiments are undertaken depending on the

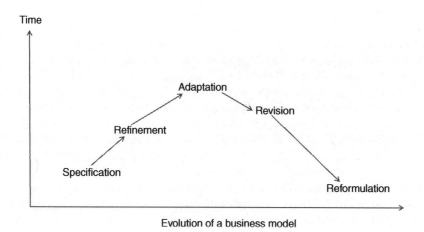

Evolution of a business model

Figure 6.1 A business model's life cycle.

contingencies that the firm faces.[35] Such adjustments are expressed in terms of *augmentation*, *reinforcement*, and *deletion*.[36] In this regard, business model development is an initial experiment based on trial-and- error learning.[37] In fact, companies that manage to create value over extended periods of time successfully shape, adapt, and renew their business models to fuel such value creation.[38] If social ventures are a new breed, then they need different business models. It is obvious that the business models that are used in for-profit ventures may not be successful when applied to social ventures. Thus, building business models geared toward social ventures is of paramount importance. The following section discusses the social venture sustainability model (or social business model) construct.

3   Social Venture Sustainability Models

When discussing business models for social ventures, it could be more appropriate to use the construct of sustainability model (or social business model). The idea is to determine how a social venture will create value for the beneficiaries and sustain itself over time to accomplish its social mission. Thus, it is important to address the following questions.

* How will the social venture sustain itself over time?
* Why does the social entrepreneur need to build his/her social venture sustainability model?

A simple answer to these questions is that social entrepreneurs need to build sustainability models to ensure that they understand what needs to be done to make the venture sustainable over time. Because social needs are often enduring, they cannot be solved in one, two, or even five years. The social venture must continue to address the same social needs—or similar ones—over a long period of time.

3.1   Defining Social Venture Sustainability Models

As we learned in the discussion of commercial entrepreneurship, the concept of business model refers to the set of activities that is used to create, deliver, and capture value. In other words, making money by doing what the company intends to do to please the customer. A similar concept is used in social entrepreneurship. However, it is appropriate in this context to refer to it as a sustainability model. This construct of social venture sustainability model (SVSM) is similar to the concept of social business model used by several writers on social entrepreneurship.[39] The social venture sustainability model helps answer the following question: how will the social venture remain sustainable while successfully addressing a particular social need? The social value proposition is the bundle of services that the social enterprise proposes to its customers or beneficiaries as well as its sponsors.

In switching from a commercial business model to a social venture sustainability model (or social business model), the first element is the specification of targeted stakeholders, and the provision that the value proposition and constellation are not focused solely on the customer, but are expanded to encompass all stakeholders. The second element is the definition of desired social profits through a comprehensive ecosystem view, resulting in a social profit equation. The third element is that the economic profit equation targets only full recovery of costs and capital, not financial profit maximization.[40] Thus, a social venture sustainability model can be defined as *the process of creating, delivering, and capturing value for all stakeholders involved in the social venture*. This definition is an extension of the definition of the business model as applied in commercial entrepreneurship to social entrepreneurship. The following sub-section contrasts business models and social venture sustainability models.

3.2 Comparing Business Models and Social Venture Sustainability Models

As discussed earlier, a business model helps to answer the question: how do I make money doing this? The social venture sustainability model poses a different question in a different context: how do I sustain this venture while solving a social problem? The pioneer in social entrepreneurship and poverty reduction initiatives, Muhammad Yunus and his colleagues, suggested in a 2010 article that social business models should challenge conventional wisdom. The social business models of the three social ventures that they studied in the article—Grameen Phone, Grameen Veolia, and Grameen Danone—are good examples of this.[41] Grameen Phone is a partnership between the Grameen Bank and Telenor, a Norwegian telecommunications giant. To establish such a venture in an impoverished country, such as Bangladesh, a basic assumption had to be changed: instead of owning a telephone handset, the new assumption was to rent it and use it when needed. Similar revisions of basic assumptions occurred with Grameen Veolia and Grameen Danone. In the case of Grameen Veolia, the basic assumption prevailing in developed countries is that water is made safe to drink in high-tech facilities and then distributed to people's homes. In a developing country, however, a new assumption could be that water merely has to meet minimal World Health Organization standards; and once it does, it can be distributed at public fountains. Finally, for Grameen Danone, the traditional assumption that a yogurt product is affordable only if produced in large quantities and distributed through retail outlets was modified for impoverished areas. In such areas, local production and door-to-door distribution can lead to an easily available and affordable dairy product.

These three examples illustrate the dynamic and iterative nature of business models as well as social venture sustainability models. The social ventures not only have to address social needs but also have to sustain themselves over time. Yunus and his colleagues identify five lessons that one can learn from social business models. The first is that social business models should challenge the prevailing conventional wisdom. An interesting example is the Grameen Bank, which challenged the conventional wisdom in the banking industry relating to the role of collateral in securing a bank loan. Grameen Bank loans are awarded to people without collateral. But challenging the conventional wisdom is not limited to social ventures. For example, Dell Computers challenged the conventional wisdom by bypassing middle men when it first introduced the Dell Direct business model. Prior to this business model innovation, computer manufacturers had relied on traditional distribution channels to sell their products. Dell's business model has now been copied by all of its competitors.

The second lesson consists of finding complementary partners. Because of the complexity of social problems, building partnerships is an important aspect of leveraging resources and expertise to create social value. Here, the competitive paradigm that prevails in commercial entrepreneurship should give way to the cooperative paradigm. The main advantage of collaborative agreement lies in the pooling of resources and knowledge leveraged by the partners.[42]

The third lesson to learn is the necessity to undertake continuous experimentation. This also holds true for business models for commercial ventures. Neither a business model nor a social venture sustainability model is immutable. Rather, they should be dynamic and involve constant experimentation. Just as for conventional business model innovation, social business models can start small, undergo refinement, and then be rolled out.[43] However, experimentation does not mean intuition; rather, it involves the ability and intention to make changes if the path first chosen turns out to be incorrect.

The fourth lesson consists of favoring social profit-oriented shareholders. In commercial ventures, the revenue model is a key aspect of the business model. It includes generating profit for the firm's owners. In social ventures, the primary focus is on addressing a social issue. Thus, the notion of profit for shareholders is not the primary focus, although the social venture must sustain itself. In building social venture sustainability models, the value proposition should include all stakeholders.

The fifth lesson is to specify social profit objectives clearly. This is important because the social profits will be the yardsticks against which to measure the social venture's performance.

Table 6.4 illustrates the comparison between business models and social venture sustainability models.

Table 6.4 Conventional social business model versus social business model for Telenor, Veolia, and Danone[44]

Grameen partner and sector	Conventional business model (predominantly in developed countries)		Social business model	
	Value proposition	*Value constellation*	*Value proposition*	*Value constellation*
Telenor, telecoms	Sale of a monthly package (phone plus air time) to individual customers	Construction of a wireless network Sale of package through retail outlets	Caller borrows a phone when needed and pays per minute	Construction of a wireless network Grameen ladies own the phones, buy discounted air time in bulk and sell minutes to users as needed
Veolia, water services	Maximum water quality Distribution of water through taps located inside people's homes	Water treatment factories with a high level of technology, recycling and purifying water	Water quality that meets WHO standards (rather than European or US standards) Village water fountains Prepaid card payments system	Construction of a simplified water plant to recycle surface water Construction of the water supply network towards the fountains New distribution channel for isolated locations: rickshaws driven by Grameen boys
Danone, dairy products	High-end products Emphasis on lifestyle Strong brand name through advertisements	Centralized purchasing and production (economies of scale) Logistics towards distribution platforms Sales through food retailers Storage by end consumers	Low price Fulfillment of basic nutritional needs Grameen brand image	Local supply of raw materials Local production Direct door-to-door sales by Grameen ladies Limited storage by end consumers

4   Building Social Venture Sustainability Models

Before we discuss the design of social venture sustainability models, it is important to learn from business model design. Such understanding should pave the way for developing better social venture sustainability models.

4.1   Designing a Business Model

Developing a business model consists of creating the content, structure, and governance of transactions designed to create value through the exploitation of business opportunities. Beyond specifying a realistic revenue architecture, designing a business model involves determining the set of lateral and vertical activities that must be performed, assessing whether and how they can be performed sufficiently economically to enable a profit to be earned, and deciding who is to perform them.[45] Designing good business models is part art and part science. As an art, it involves coordinating the different activities to add value for all stakeholders. As a science, it requires a deep understanding of customer needs, which can be acquired only through experience, learning, and listening. Management scholars, such as Zott and Amit, have proposed two sets of parameters that business model designers must consider: *design elements* and *design themes*.[46] The design elements of a business model include:

- content (what activities should be performed);
- structure (how they should be linked and sequenced); and
- governance (who should perform them and where).

The design elements refer to the conceptualization and configuration of the business model. They describe an activity's system architecture and correspond to the conceptualization of a business model as how an organization is linked to external stakeholders, and how it engages in economic exchanges with them to create value for all exchange partners.[47]

Design themes include:

- novelty;
- lock-in;
- complementarities; and
- efficiency.

Novelty consists of adopting new activities or new ways of linking the activities or new ways of governing the activities. It implies that the business model should be relatively new compared to previous ones as well as those that are used by competitors. Novelty-centered business models refer to new ways of conducting economic exchanges among various participants. Lock-in refers to the power of a business model to keep third parties attracted as business model participants. It derives from the design element. An illustrative example is the social media platform Facebook. This website's members invest considerable time and effort in personalizing their profiles, and these investments form strong impediments to switching to other providers.[48] Complementarities occur whenever bundling activities within a system provides more value than running activities separately. Finally, efficiency-centered design refers to how firms use their activity system design in order to achieve greater efficiency through reduction of transaction costs. Design themes describe the sources of the model's value creation and the holistic gestalt of a firm's

Table 6.5 An activity system design framework[49]

Framework Provides Insight By:
- Giving business model design *a language, concepts,* and *tools*
- I lighlighting business model design as a *key managerial/entrepreneurial task*
- Emphasizing *system-level design* over partial optimization

Design Elements
- Content: *What* activities should be performed?
- Structure: *How* should they be linked and sequenced?
- Governance: *Who* should perform them and *where?*

Design Themes
- Novelty: Adopt *innovative* content, structure or governance
- Lock-in: Building in elements to *retain business model stakeholders*
- Complementarities: *Bundle activities* to generate more value
- Efficiency: Reorganize activities to *reduce transaction costs*

---

business model, and they facilitate its conceptualization and measurement.[50] They are configurations of design elements or the degree to which the activities are orchestrated and connected by distinct themes.[51] Table 6.5 illustrates an activity design framework of business model design.

Some entrepreneurs start their ventures with a well-formulated business model. However, many others start without a clearly defined model. For these entrepreneurs, building the business model is done through trial and error. As explained earlier, building a business model is a dynamic and iterative process. A firm's business model evolves over time. For example, it is argued that the observable sign of the evolution of a business model is a substantial change in the structure of its costs and/or revenues, from using a new kind of resource, developing a new source of revenues, reengineering an organizational process, or externalizing a value chain activity, whether triggered internally or externally.[52]

Business models that are crafted by entrepreneurs are prospective and envisage a future venture and the value creation logic that it will entail.[53] They are part of a planning activity that relies mainly on the writing of business plans. The business model of a new venture describes how the new venture plans to make money and sustain itself over the long term.[54] It is worth noting that the effectiveness of a particular business model depends not only on its design but, more importantly, on its implementation.[55] For example, Walmart's business model is oriented toward selling more goods by reducing prices.[56] This model is effectively implemented, making the company the best discount retailer not only in the United States but around the world.

4.2   Designing a Social Venture's Sustainability Model

An interesting question raised by attempts to develop a social venture sustainability model is: how do social enterprises generate income? Regardless of the form they take, social enterprises generate income from:

- those who receive the service;
- third parties with vested interests; and
- others who pay indirectly.

Before discussing the development of social business models, it is important to revisit the development of business models as applied in the case of commercial ventures. In this regard, the framework proposed by Clayton Christensen, a Harvard business professor, and his colleagues can be useful.[57] These authors proposed a framework for successful business models that comprises four elements:

- customer value proposition (CVP);
- profit formula;
- key resources; and
- key processes.

This framework is illustrated in Table 6.6. It can easily apply to the design of social business models. The customer value proposition is the extent to which the social venture adds value to the lives of the beneficiaries. Here, the profit formula encompasses social profits. It deals with the social objective accomplished by the social venture. The key resources and key processes can be similar to those of a commercial venture. However, the specific nature of the social venture would require that the social business model be adapted to the contingencies it faces.

Table 6.6 Designing an effective business model[58]

Customer value proposition	Profit formula	Key resources	Key processes
Target customer Job to be done to solve an important problem or fulfill an important need for the target customer. *Offering* Which satisfies the problem or fulfills the need. This is defined not only by what is sold but also by how it is sold.	*Revenue model* How much money can be made price × volume. Volume can be thought of in terms of market size, purchase frequency, ancillary sales, etc. *Cost structure* How costs are allocated: includes cost of key assets, direct costs, indirect costs, economies of scale. *Marginal model* How much each transaction should net to achieve desired profit levels. *Resource velocity* How quickly resources need to be used to support target volume. Includes lead times, throughput, inventory turns, asset utilization, and so on.	Needed to deliver the customer value proposition profitability. Might include: • People • Technology/products • Equipment • Information • Channels • Partnerships, alliances • Brand	In addition to rules, metrics, and norms, which make the profitable delivery of the customer value proposition repeatable and scalable. Might include: • *Processes*: design, product development, sourcing, manufacturing, marketing, hiring and training, information technology • *Rules and metrics*: margin requirements for investment, credit terms, lead times, supplier terms • *Norms*: opportunity size needed for investment, approach to customers and channels

Research is currently under way to apply the concept of business model to the social sector. One such example is the Wharton Societal Wealth Program (WSWP).[59] Launched in 2001, this is a field action research program intended to examine how to use business models to develop projects as "weapons" to "attack" societal problems. It has launched several projects around the world. Of these projects, one concerning animal feed in Zambia is particularly illustrative of the successful application of the concept of business model to ensure the sustainability of a social venture. This project aimed to produce high-quality, lower-cost animal feed in northwest Zambia. The region was characterized by huge unemployment levels among former miners after the mines shut down when copper prices collapsed, leading to rampant malnutrition, which put thousands close to starvation. The concept was to use modern linear programming from the United States to calculate optimal feed mixes and sell this cheaper but higher-quality feed to expand local chicken production. The project started as an intrapreneurial venture, launched with six men mixing feed with shovels in a concrete-floored shed. The emergent business model was designed for local cash markets via a regionally distributed network of small producers, as opposed to a more conventional large-scale, high-volume system designed for large producers and large retail customers.[60]

Mair and Schoen analyzed the social business models of three widely known social ventures: the Grameen Bank in Bangladesh (discussed above), Sekem in Egypt, and Mondragon in Spain.[61] Each of these has been successful in addressing a particular social need and creating social value: Grameen Bank alleviated poverty for women in Bangladesh; Sekem introduced organic farming in Egypt; and Mondragon created jobs, opportunities, and community empowerment in post-Civil War Spain. All three social ventures combined social and economic value creation in a sustainable manner. The analysis of these three organizations also showed that they were similar in the creation of value networks, the procurement of strategic resources, and the management of customer interface—three elements that are essential in the implementation of a business model or a social venture sustainability model. For example, value networks are fundamental elements of business models. This is particularly important for social business models to the extent that social ventures must rely on a vast array of stakeholders who can support them with resources, expertise, and knowledge. Thus, a social venture sustainability model could also be referred to as the description of the position of a social business in the social value system and its relationships with different stakeholders who are interested in the social mission.

The above examples indicate that new business models can be used to tackle societal problems. For example, one of the goals of WSWP is to probe for opportunities by unfolding new business models and, in so doing, create new markets. New social venture sustainability models are needed because social ventures operate in environments where infrastructure, governance, politics, and technology in themselves are often problems to overcome. Even within social ventures, the concept of social business model may be different. Purely social ventures that rely on donations and grants would have sustainability models different from hybrid forms of social ventures. The latter pursue a double bottom line combining both financial and social performance.[62]

These different elements can be illustrated in the social venture sustainability canvas (or the social business canvas; see Figure 6.2). This is derived from the business model canvas and includes nine key elements:

- partners;
- activities;
- value proposition;

- beneficiary or customer relationships;
- beneficiary or customer segments;
- resources;
- channels;
- cost structure; and
- revenue stream.

For example, the social entrepreneur must be able to identify the different stakeholders who might be affected by his/her social venture and who might provide some form of assistance. Examples of stakeholders could include government agencies, public or private foundations, or even wealthy individuals who may provide financial support as well as potential suppliers and/or partners. The social entrepreneur must also identify the key activities that must be performed to start the social venture as well as the value proposition. It is similarly important to identify the specific benefit that the social venture will provide to the potential beneficiaries.

Questions such as "What problem is the social venture solving?" and "How will solving this problem have an impact?" must be explored at this stage. The social entrepreneur must also define the type of relationships to build with the beneficiaries and delineate the "target beneficiary" segment. One social venture cannot solve all of the social problems in a community. Thus, it is important to specify the type of beneficiaries who are targeted clearly. In addition, the social entrepreneur must identify all of the critical resources that are required to accomplish the social mission. The same is true for the different channels that will be used to bring the product or service to the beneficiaries. The social entrepreneur must also identify the cost structure of the social venture as well as the revenue streams. Identifying the cost structure allows the social entrepreneur to instill financial discipline in identifying the activities that are costly and determine ways of being more efficient. Finally, setting the revenue streams allows the social entrepreneur to understand the sources of revenue clearly. Revenue may come from grants, donations or earned-income activities. Generating revenue and keeping costs down will allow the social venture to generate a surplus that can contribute to its financial sustainability.

Key Stakeholders	Key Activities	Value Proposition	Customer/Beneficiary Relationships	Customer/Beneficiary Segments
Who will help the social venture implement its business model? • Governments • Foundations • Other companies	Identify the key activities to perform to accomplish the social mission.	What problem is the social venture solving? How will solving this problem have an impact?	What types of relationships should be developed with beneficiaries who do not pay for the service and with those who pay for the service?	Who are the beneficiaries or customers of the social venture? Which beneficiaries will receive the service for free? Which beneficiaries will pay?
	Key Resources What resources are needed to perform the different activities? How will these resources be acquired?		**Channels** How will the beneficiaries and/or customers be reached?	

Cost Structure	Revenue Streams
Identify cost areas. Which activities will cost the most?	How will revenue be generated? • Grants • Donations • Earned income • Surplus

Figure 6.2 Social business model canvas.

Summary

This chapter discussed business models and social venture sustainability models. In so doing, it took the view that the concept of business model is more appropriate for commercial ventures, whereas the construct of social venture sustainability model is more relevant for social enterprises. After a thorough review and discussion of the extant literature on business models, the chapter introduced the construct of social venture sustainability models and provided strategies for developing social venture sustainability models.

Key Terms

Business model; business model design; design elements; design themes; revenue model; social business model; social value proposition; social venture sustainability model

Review Questions

1 Explain the key components of a business model.
2 Identify potential differences between a business model and a social venture sustainability model as defined in the chapter.
3 Explain the difference between business model and business concept.
4 Identify the reasons why social ventures need different sustainability models compared to purely commercial ventures.
5 What are the two parameters of a business model design? Discuss their key elements.
6 Identify some of the reasons why it is important for social entrepreneurs to develop sutainability models for their social ventures.
7 Discuss the relationship between the design elements and the design themes in using an activity system design framework for designing a business model.
8 Why do you think entrepreneurs need to formulate business models at the start of their new ventures?
9 Discuss each of the phases of the life cycle of a business model.
10 Is the location of a firm an important aspect of its business model (yes or no)? Explain.

Application Questions

1 Watch the video at www.youtube.com/watch?v=QoAOzMTLP5s, then identify the key elements of a business model.
2 Identify Dell's business model. Discuss it on the basis of the information you learn in class and in your textbook. Would this business model work effectively in the developing countries of Africa, Latin America, and East Asia? Explain.
3 Twitter (http://twitter.com) is a free networking and microblogging service that allows users to send and read other users' updates (known as tweets). How does the company make money? Does it have a viable long-term business model? If so, describe it.
4 Do some research on Zipcar, the car-sharing company. Identify the company's business model. Is this business model innovative? Explain why some car rental companies, such as Enterprise, Avis, and Hertz, were unable to develop the concept of car sharing.
5 Do some research on Muhammad Yunus and the Grameen Bank. Identify the social business model of the bank. How does its social business model differ from the business models of traditional banks? Explain.

Application Case 1: One World Play Project

What power does play hold? Should kids and youth living in the world's impoverished areas be deprived of opportunities, such as playing with their peers? What could be done to make their lives a little joyful by incorporating play into their regular activities? One person decided to address these questions after seeing kids in the Darfur region in 2006 play soccer on dirt using a ball they had made by tying trash together with twine.[1] Tim Jahnigen and his wife, Lisa Tarver, created One World Play Project (http://www.oneworldplayproject.com) in 2010 with a mission to bring the transformative power of play to youth living in disadvantaged regions of the world. Very often in these regions, kids do not have play grounds appropriate for regular soccer balls. Usually, they play using makeshift soccer balls and even when they are lucky enough to get regular soccer balls, these balls are not resistant to the rough terrain and are broken within days. Jahnigen decided to tackle this problem by designing a soccer ball that could be unwearable and durable when played in harsh conditions.

However, the road to transform this vision into a reality was not an easy one. Jahnigen was looking for ways of making a ball that could never wear out, go flat or need a pump. He contacted several engineers to help him accomplish his goals but they were skeptical about the project of creating a durable and unwearable soccer ball. Nevertheless, he ended up finding a type of hard foam made of ethylene-vinyl acetate, a class of material similar to that used in Crocs, the popular and durable sandals.[2] Another challenge was to shape the PopFoam into a sphere, which was not only a technical challenge but also a financial one. According to Jahnigen's estimation, making and testing the durability of the ball would cost $300,000, which he did not have. He contacted an old friend, the singer Sting, who decided to fund the production and testing of the ball. As an act of gratitude, Jahnigen named the venture One World in homage to a song 'One World' that Sting sang.[3]

One Word Play Project is headquartered in Berkeley, California with regional offices in Africa, Asia and South America. It also has distribution centers in Fremont, California and Voerde, Germany. One World Play Project's donations are geared toward groups that utilize sport as a vehicle for teaching conflict resolution, health awareness, gender equality and other valuable skills.[4] It uses the concept of 'Buy One Give One' which consists of donating one soccer ball to organizations supporting youth for one ball bought by a customer.

One World Play Project collaborates with sponsors, individuals and organizations that support youth in disadvantaged areas. It believes in the transformational power of play. Indeed, the belief at One World Play Project is that play has a healing power and contributes to kids' and youths' psychological and emotional development. One of the major sponsors of One World Play Project is Chevrolet, a division of General Motors that joined the project in 2012 as a founding sponsor and had pledged to buy and donate over 1.5 million balls. One World Play Project has reached 175 countries and territories, supported over 45 million youth, and distributed more than 1 million balls worldwide. Recently, One World Play Project has rebranded itself, using the slogan *Everywhere, Anywhere* to emphasize the durability of its ball that can be played on any surface and in every country. In addition to distributing the balls, One World Health also provides educational materials and school supplies.

Discussion Questions

1 Identify and describe the social venture sustainability model of One World Play Project.
2 What is the revenue model of One World Play Project?
3 Would you consider the recent rebranding of One World Play Project a refinement of its business model? Yes? No? Explain.
4 Watch the YouTube video, "We Are Now a One World Play Project" at https://www.youtube.com/watch?v=ctQHOizknhc. What is your assessment of the reason for creating this social venture and its future prospects?

References

1   *https:www.oneworldplayproject.com/benefits-of-play/power-of-play-story.* [Retrieved on April 11, 2016].
2   The New York Times (November 8, 2012). Joy that lasts, on the poorest of playgrounds. *http://www.nytimes.com/2012/11/09/giving/the-one-world-futbol-promises-a-lasting-source-of-fun-in-poor-countries.html?_r=0* [Retrieved on April 11, 2016].
3   The New York Times (November 8, 2012). Joy that lasts, on the poorest of playgrounds. *http://www.nytimes.com/2012/11/09/giving/the-one-world-futbol-promises-a-lasting-source-of-fun-in-poor-countries.html?_r=0* [Retrieved on April 11, 2016].
4   Play anywhere, everywhere: One world play project rebrands as Chevrolet continues sponsorship. *http://www.forbes.com/sites/markjburns/2014/12/02/play-anywhere-everywhere-one-world-play-project-rebrands-as-chevrolet-continues-sponsorship/#7544087a6eca* [Retrieved on April 12, 2016].

Application Case 2: Grameen Phone[63]

In 1996, in partnership with three foreign companies, Grameen Bank created a mobile phone company, Grameen Phone, to extend telephone services across Bangladesh, where it is one of four companies licensed by the government to provide mobile phone services. With no landline service in most of the 80,000 villages in Bangladesh, mobile phone technology was essential to bring the country into the age of electronic communication. A UK-based consultant estimated the market in 2005 would be 250,000 mobile phones. In fact, it turned out to be about 8 million, and grew to 40 million subscribers by 2008. By challenging conventional wisdom and rules of the game, Grameen Phone had created a new market.

In developed countries, individuals contract for a monthly package including the handset and air time: this engagement ensures the profitability of the operator which, in turn, enables it to build the telecoms infrastructure required. But poor people simply cannot afford this type of commitment. So, relying on the shared know-how of its two partner companies, Grameen Phone developed another business model, based on both a non-conventional value proposition and value constellation, which turned out to be profitable even in rural areas, after having been tested in denser urban settings. People who need to make connections with a friend, family member, or business associate can borrow a phone and buy just a couple of minutes from the "Grameen Bank ladies" who provide the phone service to their villages. They, in turn, use Grameen Bank loans to buy the mobile phones and bulk air time.

By mid-2007, Grameen Phone, now owned by Telenor (62 percent), the Norwegian telecommunications giant, which had a total turnover of $4.8 billion, and Grameen Telecom (38 percent), a nonprofit company created specifically for this purpose, and run by experienced Telenor managers, had become the largest tax-generating company in Bangladesh, with over 20 million subscribers.

Discussion Questions

1   Identify Grameen Phone's social business model.
2   Do you think that this social business model could be transferred to other developing markets (yes or no)? Explain.
3   Is Grameen Phone's social business model completely in tune with the market it serves or does it need some refinement?
4   Identify the value proposition of Grameen Phone's business model.

Notes

1 *American Heritage Dictionary.* (1986). Boston: Houghton Mifflin.
2 Amit, R., & Zott, C. (2001). Value creation in e-business. *Strategic Management Journal,* 22(6/7), 493–520.
3 Amit, R., & Zott, C. (2001). Value creation in e-business. *Strategic Management Journal,* 22(6/7), 493–520; Afuah, A., & Tucci, C. L. (2001). *Internet business models.* Boston: McGraw-Hill; Afuah, A. (2004). *Business models: A strategic management approach.* New York: McGraw-Hill; Heldman, J., & Kalling, T. (2003). The business model concept: Theoretical underpinnings and empirical illustrations. *European Journal of Information Systems,* 12(1), 49–59; Al-Debei, M. M., & Avison, D. (2010). Developing a unified framework of the business model concept. *European Journal of Information Systems,* 19(3), 359–376.
4 Martins, L. L., Rindova, V. P., & Greenbaum, B. E. (2015). Unlocking the hidden value of concepts: A cognitive approach to business model innovation. *Strategic Entrepreneurship Journal,* 9(1), 99–117; Kim, S. K., & Min, S. (2015). Business model innovation performance: When does adding a new business model benefit an incumbent? *Strategic Entrepreneurship Journal,* 9(1), 34–57; DaSilva, C. M., & Trkman, P. (2014). Business model. What it is and what it is not. *Long Range Planning,* 47(6), 379–389.
5 Morris, M., Schindehutte, M., & Allen, J. (2005). The entrepreneur's business model: Toward a unified perspective. *Journal of Business Research,* 58(6), 726–735.
6 Stewart, D. W., & Zhao, Q. (2000). Internet marketing, business models, and public policy. *Journal of Public Policy Marketing,* 19(2), 287–296.
7 Mayo, M. C., & Brown, G. S. (1999). Building a competitive business model. *Ivey Business Journal,* 63(3), 18–23.
8 Zott, C., & Amit, R. (2010). Business model design: An activity system perspective. *Long Range Planning,* 43(2/3), 216–226.
9 Morris, M., Schindehutte, M., & Allen, J. (2005). The entrepreneur's business model: Toward a unified perspective. *Journal of Business Research,* 58(6), 726–735.
10 Slywotsky, A. J. (1996). *Value migration.* Boston: Harvard Business School Press.
11 Zott, C., Amit, & Mass, L. (2011). The business model: Recent development and future research. *Journal of Management,* 37(4), 1019–1042.
12 Barringer, B. R., & Ireland, R. D. (2012). *Entrepreneurship: Successfully launching new ventures.* 4th edition. New York: Pearson/Prentice-Hall.
13 Teece, D. J. (2010). Business models, business strategy and innovation. *Long Range Planning,* 43, 172–194; Amit, R., & Zott, C. (2001). Value creation in e-business. *Strategic Management Journal,* 22(6/7), 493–520.
14 Casadesus-Masanell, R., & Ricart, J. E. (2010). From strategy to business models and onto tactics. *Long Range Planning,* 43(2), 354–363.
15 Teece, D. J. (2010). Business models, business strategy and innovation. *Long Range Planning,* 43, 172–194.
16 Barringer, B. R., & Ireland, R. D. (2012). *Entrepreneurship: Successfully launching new ventures.* 4th edition. New York: Pearson/Prentice-Hall.
17 McGrath, R. G. (2010). Business models: A discovery driven approach. *Long Range Planning,* 43, 247–261.
18 Doganova, L., & Eyquem-Renault, M. (2009). What do business models do? Innovation devices in technology entrepreneurship. *Research Policy,* 38, 1559–1570.
19 Morris, M., Schindehutte, M., & Allen, J. (2005). The entrepreneur's business model: Toward a unified perspective. *Journal of Business Research,* 58, 726–735.
20 Teece, D. J. (2010). Business models, business strategy and innovation. *Long Range Planning,* 43, 172–194.
21 Porter, M. E. (1996). What is strategy? *Harvard Business Review,* 74(6), 61–78; Porter, M. (2001). Strategy and the internet. *Harvard Business Review,* 79, 62–78.
22 Siggelkow, N. (2002). Evolution toward fit. *Administrative Science Quarterly,* 47(1), 125–159.

23 Porter, M. E. (1996). What is strategy? *Harvard Business Review*, 74(6), 61–78; Porter, M. (2001). Strategy and the internet. *Harvard Business Review*, 79, 62–78.

24 Casadesus-Masanell, R., & Ricart, J. E. (2011). How to design a winning business model. *Harvard Business Review*, January–February, 101–107.

25 Zott, C., & Amit, R. (2008). The fit between product market strategy and business model: Implications for firm performance. *Strategic Management Journal*, 29, 1–26.

26 Shafer, S. M., Smith, H. J., & Linder, J. (2005). The power of business models. *Business Horizons*, 48, 199–207.

27 Morris, M., Schindehutte, M., & Allen, J. (2005). The entrepreneur's business model: Toward a unified perspective. *Journal of Business Research*, 58, 726–735.

28 Magretta, J. (2002). Why business models matter. *Harvard Business Review*, 80(5), 86–92.

29 Zott, C., & Amit, R. (2008). The fit between product market strategy and business model: Implications for firm performance. *Strategic Management Journal*, 29, 1–26.

30 Gartner, W. B., & Bellamy, M. G. (2010). *Enterprise*. Mason, OH: South-Western Cengage Learning.

31 Zott, C., & Amit, R. (2008). The fit between product market strategy and business model: Implications for firm performance. *Strategic Management Journal*, 29, 1–26, at p. 5.

32 Gartner, W. B., & Bellamy, M. G. (2010). *Enterprise*. Mason, OH: South-Western Cengage Learning.

33 Morris, M., Schindehutte, M., & Allen, J. (2005). The entrepreneur's business model: Toward a unified perspective. *Journal of Business Research*, 58, 726–735.

34 Martins, L. L., Rindova, V. P., & Greenbaum, B. E. (2015). Unlocking the hidden value of concepts: A cognitive approach to business model innovation. *Strategic Entrepreneurship Journal*, 9(1), 99–117.

35 Morris, M., Schindehutte, M., & Allen, J. (2005). The entrepreneur's business model: Toward a unified perspective. *Journal of Business Research*, 58, 726–735.

36 Siggelkow, N. (2002). Evolution toward fit. *Administrative Science Quarterly*, 47(1), 125–159.

37 Sosna, M., Trevinyo-Rodriguez, R. N., & Velamuri, S. R. (2010). Business model innovation through trial-and-error learning: The Naturhouse case. *Long Range Planning*, 43(2), 383–407.

38 Achtenhagen, L., Melin, L., & Naldi, L. (2013). Dynamics of business models: Strategizing, critical capabilities and activities for sustained value creation. *Long Range Planning*, 46(6), 427–442.

39 Seelos, C., & Mair, J. (2005). Social entrepreneurship: Creating new business models to serve the poor. *Business Horizons*, 48(3), 241–246; Yunus, M. (2007). *Creating a world without poverty: Social business and the future of capitalism*. New York: Public Affairs; Wilson, F., & Post, J. E. (2013). Business models for people, planet (& profits): Exploring the phenomena of social business, a market-based approach to social value creation. *Small Business Economics*, 40, 715–737.

40 Yunus, M., Moingeon, B., & Lehmann-Ortega, L. (2010). Building social business models: Lessons from the Grameen experience. *Long Range Planning*, 43, 308–325.

41 Yunus, M., Moingeon, B., & Lehmann-Ortega, L. (2010). Building social business models: Lessons from the Grameen experience. *Long Range Planning*, 43, 308–325.

42 Gulati, R. (1998). Alliances and networks. *Strategic Management Journal*, 19(4), 293–318.

43 Yunus, M., Moingeon, B., & Lehmann-Ortega, L. (2010). Building social business models: Lessons from the Grameen experience. *Long Range Planning*, 43, 308–325.

44 Yunus, M., Moingeon, B., & Lehmann-Ortega, L. (2010). Building social business models: Lessons from the Grameen experience. *Long Range Planning*, 43, 308–325, at p. 313.

45 Teece, D. J. (2010). Business models, business strategy and innovation. *Long Range Planning*, 43, 172–194.

46 Zott, C., & Amit, R. (2010). Business model design: An activity system perspective. *Long Range Planning*, 43, 216–226.

47 Zott, C., & Amit, R. (2007). Business model design and the performance of entrepreneurial firms. *Organization Science, 18*(2), 181–199.

48 Zott, C., & Amit, R. (2010). Business model design: An activity system perspective. *Long Range Planning, 43*, 216–226.

49 Zott, C., & Amit, R. (2010). Business model design: An activity system perspective. *Long Range Planning, 43*, 216–226.

50 Zott, C., & Amit, R. (2008). The fit between product market strategy and business model: Implications for firm performance. *Strategic Management Journal, 29*, 1–26.

51 Zott, C., & Amit, R. (2010). Business model design: An activity system perspective. *Long Range Planning, 43*, 216–226.

52 Morris, M., Schindehutte, M., & Allen, J. (2005). The entrepreneur's business model: Toward a unified perspective. *Journal of Business Research, 58*, 726–735.

53 Demil, B., & Lecocq, X. (2010). Business model evolution: In search of dynamic consistency. *Long Range Planning, 43*, 227–246.

54 Doganova, L., & Eyquem-Renault, M. (2009). What do business models do? Innovation devices in technology entrepreneurship. *Research Policy, 38*, 1559–1570.

55 Afuah, A., & Tucci, C. L. (2001). *Internet business models*. Boston: McGraw-Hill; Afuah, A. (2004). *Business models: A strategic management approach*. New York: McGraw-Hill.

56 Brea-Solis, H., Casadesus-Masanell, C., & Grifell-Tatje, E. (2015). Business model evaluation: Quantifying Walmart's sources of advantage. *Strategic Entrepreneurship Journal, 9*(1), 12–33.

57 Johnson, M. W., Christensen, C. M., & Kagermann, H. (2008). Reinventing your business model. *Harvard Business Review, 86*(12), 59–67.

58 Johnson, M. W., Christensen, C. M., & Kagermann, H. (2008). Reinventing your business model. *Harvard Business Review, 86*(12), 59–67.

59 Thompson, J. D., & MacMillan, I. C. (2010). Business models: Creating new markets and societal wealth. *Long Range Planning, 43*, 291–307.

60 Thompson, J. D., & MacMillan, I. C. (2010). Business models: Creating new markets and societal wealth. *Long Range Planning, 43*, 291–307.

61 Mair, J., & Schoen, O. (2007). Successful social entrepreneurial business models in the context of developing economies: An exploratory study. *International Journal of Emerging Markets, 2*(1), 54–68.

62 Emerson, J. (2003). The blended value proposition: Integrating social and financial returns. *California Management Review, 45*(4), 35–51; Seelos, C., & Mair, J. (2005). Social entrepreneurship: Creating new business models to serve the poor. *Business Horizons, 48*(3), 241–246; Seelos, C., & Mair, J. (2007). Profitable business models and market creation in the context of deep poverty: A strategic view. *Academy of Management Perspectives, 21*(4), 49–63; Wilson, F., & Post, J. E. (2013). Business models for people, planet (& profits): Exploring the phenomena of social business, a market-based approach to social value creation. *Small Business Economics, 40*, 715–737.

63 Source for this whole section: Yunus, M., Moingeon, B., & Lehmann-Ortega, L. (2010). Building social business models: Lessons from the Grameen experience. *Long Range Planning, 43*, 308–325.

Chapter 7

Feasibility Analysis for Social Ventures

Learning Objectives

1 Explain the nature of feasibility analysis.
2 Explain the importance of feasibility analysis in social entrepreneurship.
3 Describe the tools of feasibility analysis in social entrepreneurship.

In Chapter 5, we learned a great deal about how social venture opportunities come into being. In Chapter 6, we discussed the concept of business model. Now, in this chapter, we focus on the evaluation of social venture opportunities. Once opportunities have been discovered or created, they must be assessed to determine whether they could be translated into viable social ventures. The chapter is organized into four main sections. The first section discusses the nature of feasibility analysis. The second describes the tools used to evaluate business opportunities. The third focuses specifically on tools developed to evaluate social venture opportunities. The fourth highlights the importance of feasibility analysis for social ventures. This chapter intends to be hands-on. In addition to learning what a feasibility analysis is, students will be provided with the tools to conduct one.

In entrepreneurship, evaluation implies deciding whether the opportunity is worth pursuing. It is the key to differentiating an idea from an opportunity, and it involves risk and uncertainty. To reduce the risk and uncertainty inherent in opportunity evaluation, entrepreneurs use tools such as feasibility analysis. Opportunities are evaluated at each stage of their development, although the evaluation may be informal or even unarticulated.[1] A feasibility analysis will likely assess whether the value that a particular combination of resources can deliver will translate into economic success. A useful feasibility analysis for prospective stakeholders implies the existence of a business concept, even one that is rudimentary in form. If a business concept has yet to be developed, a feasibility analysis based on either market needs (value sought) or resources (value creation capability) can specify the business concept(s) that will be feasible.

Entrepreneurs think about the opportunity they have discovered or created and determine whether it is worth pursuing. Nascent entrepreneurs can choose to abandon the opportunities that lack promise and to continue to pursue the ones that hold promise.[2] They are more likely to decide to exploit opportunities when they assess that they are feasible—that is, when they believe that the opportunities have the potential to yield positive returns. As social psychology tells us, the feasibility of an action is an important predictor of intentions to engage in that action.[3] People are motivated to engage in actions that they consider doable. In entrepreneurship, once the venturing efforts are initiated, the ongoing evaluation of the feasibility of the opportunity is a key factor in sustaining the nascent entrepreneur's intention to pursue the opportunity, which can ultimately affect the successful commencement of the venture.[4] As we have learned, entrepreneurs systematically analyze whether to pursue an opportunity or not. They do this through a process known as feasibility analysis or feasibility study. The following section assesses the nature of feasibility analysis.

1   The Nature of Feasibility Analysis

1.1   Defining Feasibility Analysis

Feasibility refers to an opportunity's perceived practicability or difficulty.[5] A feasibility analysis is a pre-startup strategic planning tool, utilized in the pre-business plan phase of the development of a new venture. It entails collecting and analyzing data prior to the new business startup, and then using the knowledge gained to formulate the business plan.[6] Feasibility analysis allows for an informed go/no-go decision on a proposed new venture before considerable time and resources have been invested.[7] The intention is to test whether the business concept is worth pursuing and, if so, under which conditions. In a feasibility analysis, the focus is on the idea. The questions to ask in a feasibility analysis might include the following:

- What do you have to know about your customers, their needs, and this business?
- Might this concept be viable in other markets?
- What is the potential for this business?
- How much money do you think such a business might make?

The answers to such questions will provide the necessary information to assess the viability of the business opportunity. As such, a feasibility study could be used by social entrepreneurs to evaluate their social venture opportunities. It could also be used to decide whether to scale an existing social venture.

Feasibility analysis generally includes four components that are discussed below and summarized in Table 7.1. It is part of opportunity evaluation and exploitation, which is central to the entrepreneurial process.

Table 7.1 Components of a feasibility analysis

Product/service feasibility	Industry/target market feasibility	Organizational feasibility	Financial feasibility
Product/service desirability Product/service demand	Industry attractiveness Target market attractiveness	New venture team effectiveness Sufficiency of non-financial organizational resources	Total startup cash needed Financial performance of similar firms Overall financial attractiveness of the new venture

1.2   Components of Feasibility Analysis

Although there is no universal set of criteria for every feasibility analysis, it is generally accepted that the following four components should be considered:

- product/service feasibility;
- industry/target market feasibility;
- organizational feasibility; and
- financial feasibility.

1.2.1   Product/Service Feasibility

Analyzing the feasibility of a product or service implies that the entrepreneur is able to produce and deliver the product to customers. Of course, this demands possessing the ability to manufacture it. Product or service feasibility analysis refers to an assessment of the overall appeal of the product or service being proposed.[8] In evaluating the feasibility of the product, the entrepreneur should consider two main issues: *product/service desirability* and *product/service demand*. The first refers to the extent to which the product will fill a particular gap in the market, whereas the second focuses on how much of the product or service customers will want.

Desirability means that the product or service serves a particular need or problem for the customer. For instance, does the product have an appeal in the particular market? For social entrepreneurship, it is important to know whether the product or service will make a difference in the lives of the potential beneficiaries. For example, the social entrepreneur must determine whether the social need is truly important and pervasive so that the social venture may attract the support of potential stakeholders, such as donors and/or government agencies.

The best way for an entrepreneur to discover whether a product or service is desired in the market is to complete a proof-of-concept test. This involves a preliminary description of a product or service idea. To do this, the entrepreneur may write a concept statement, which describes in detail the product or service, its principal features, and its functions. It is then shown to individuals who are familiar with the industry the entrepreneur intends to enter. Any feedback will help the entrepreneur to refine the product or service or better position it in the market.

Assessing the product's desirability is generally followed by a product or service demand analysis. The entrepreneur must determine whether there is significant demand for the product or service. They can determine this by relying on primary or secondary data. To collect primary data, the entrepreneur can use a buying-intentions survey or another type of survey that could generate data about the demand for the product or service. The purpose of a buying-intentions survey is to determine whether customers would wish to buy a particular product or use a particular service, should it become available.

Figure 7.1 provides an example of a buying-intentions survey. Responses to the survey could provide an indication to the entrepreneur as to whether there is a demand for the product/service. However, the entrepreneur should bear in mind that there is not always a direct correlation between *intention* to buy and *actual* buying behavior. People may say that they will buy a product and not follow through.

Social entrepreneurs may twist the buying-intentions survey to develop a *beneficiary-intentions* survey that will provide information about the potential interest potential beneficiaries may have in a social venture's proposed product or service. Results from such

---

Product/Service Description

_____

_____

_____

_____

How likely would you be to buy the product or service described above, if we make it?

_____Definitely would buy

_____Probably would buy

_____Might or might not buy

_____Probably would not buy

_____Definitely would not buy

Figure 7.1 Buying-intentions survey.[9]

a survey will help social entrepreneurs assess the degree to which the social venture will address specific social needs.

Entrepreneurs may also use secondary data, such as library and internet research, and/or existing databases. Trade and industry magazines are good sources that can provide information about the viability of business ideas. Of course, library research and a buying-intentions survey can be pursued simultaneously.

1.2.2   Industry/Target Market Feasibility

This component requires analysis of the external environment should the opportunity be transformed into a new venture. First, entrepreneurs must determine whether the industry in which they are planning to operate is attractive. To decide this, they must consider several characteristics of the industry. Several scholars in entrepreneurship and strategic management have identified different factors that help in deciding whether an industry is attractive or unattractive.[10] (Tools for analyzing the external environment of a social venture were discussed in Chapter 5.) An analysis of the industry will reveal whether it is growing or shrinking, emerging and young or old and mature, and whether it has low or high operating margins. Such analysis will help the entrepreneur assess the attractiveness of the industry. It is better for a new venture to enter an industry that is attractive rather than one that is not. In social entrepreneurship, gaining an understanding of the social landscape will provide useful information about the severity of the social problem, and whether potential stakeholders might be sufficiently interested in the social venture to provide support.

Once the entrepreneur has analyzed the industry in which the new venture will operate, he/she must also understand the target market—the term for a narrower segment of customers with similar wants or needs. The extent to which the entrepreneur is able to satisfy those needs or wants will be crucial in their success or failure. A target market is generally attractive when it is sufficiently large at present and has the potential to expand over time.

This will facilitate scalability of the venture in the future. A target market that is small and narrow will probably mean the new venture will fail over the long term.

1.2.3   Organizational Feasibility

Organizational feasibility refers to the extent to which the new firm has the necessary human capital to exploit the opportunity successfully. For instance, does the new venture have a strong management team? Does it have enough resources in addition to financial resources? Related to the new venture management team, it is important to assemble a group of skilled and dedicated individuals. Because the startup phase is uncertain and sometimes chaotic, the new venture team should have the expertise and dedication to tackle early and unanticipated problems. It is also important to ensure that the new venture has the employees it needs to start operations. For example, a startup may need employees with particular skills, so it should ensure that they are part of the team from the outset. The startup should also protect its intellectual property rights if it has invented a new product. In addition to the new venture team, the key employees, and the protection of intellectual property, organizational feasibility includes partnerships, government support, and key equipment that will be needed for the venture.

1.2.4   Financial Feasibility

For this component of the feasibility analysis, the focus is on determining whether the venture has or will acquire the financial resources needed to start its operations. Three elements are important to consider at this stage:

- the total startup cash needed;
- the financial performance of similar businesses; and
- the overall financial attractiveness of the venture.

The entrepreneur should be able to develop a budget including all items that need to be purchased to start the venture. It is also important to determine whether friends and family members will be contacted as sources of financial support or investors will be brought on board. For example, in the United States, two online sources—SCORE (www.score.org) and the Small Business Administration (www.sba.gov)—are particularly helpful. They provide data and information on initial startup costs. Of course, each venture is unique and its needs may depend on the particular product or service, industry, and target market.

The entrepreneur may also benchmark existing firms to assess their financial performance. For example, if similar existing firms are profitable, that may convince the entrepreneur that with hard work and dedication, the new venture will be financially sound. Entrepreneurs should also assess the overall financial attractiveness of the new venture. Such an assessment should be based on financial projections. A particularly important element is the projected rate of return. It should be evident that there is a substantial rate of return for the new venture.

The four components can be combined to assess the overall feasibility of the opportunity. Table 7.2 presents a scoring of the components along three modalities: low (1), medium (2), and high (3). Assuming that an opportunity scores 1 for all four components, it will receive an overall score of 4, which will make it unfeasible. Everything else being equal, such an opportunity should not be pursued. An opportunity that ranks 2

Table 7.2 Opportunity assessment test

Feasibility components	Low	Medium	High
Product/market feasibility	1	2	3
Industry/market feasibility	1	2	3
Organizational feasibility	1	2	3
Financial feasibility	1	2	3
Overall assessment	4	8	12

on all four components will receive an overall score of 8. Such an opportunity should be refined to make it more attractive. Finally, an opportunity that scores 3 on each of the four components will receive an overall score of 12, making it an attractive opportunity to pursue.

Of course, there could be a combination of scores for the four components. An opportunity may receive the maximum score on one component and the minimum score on other components. Hence, based on this grid, the following suggestions could be made for potential social entrepreneurs. An opportunity that receives a score of 4 should always be disregarded, while one that receives a score of 12 must be given the go-ahead. In between, however, may lie opportunities in which any low-scoring components need to be refined before proceeding. The entrepreneur should develop strategies to improve the feasibility of these specific component(s).

A feasibility analysis is a first step to determining whether the venture idea is worth pursuing. Done properly, it can help an entrepreneur save time and resources. In the following section, tools for conducting a feasibility analysis are discussed.

2 Tools for Analyzing Business Opportunities

This section focuses on the different tools that can be used to test social venture opportunities. Such tools include:

- SWOT analysis;
- the Outside-in/Inside-out analysis model;
- Bygrave and Zacharakis's model;[11] and
- the Quick Screen model.[12]

2.1 SWOT Analysis as an Opportunity Evaluation Tool

SWOT analysis is commonly used in strategic management and marketing to assess the strengths and weaknesses of a firm as well as the opportunities and threats presented by the external environment in which the firm operates. This technique is also used in entrepreneurship to evaluate the soundness of entrepreneurial opportunities. It can be expanded to the evaluation of social venture opportunities. In social entrepreneurship, the focus of a SWOT analysis will be to assess the strengths and weaknesses of a social opportunity. The following questions are important to address:

- What social problem does this opportunity address?
- Will this opportunity make a difference in the lives of people and the community?

- Is the opportunity scalable?
- Will the venture be sustainable over time?
- Does the social entrepreneur have the resources or can he/she accumulate them?
- What are the opportunities and threats in the external environment?

Answering such questions will help the social entrepreneur assess the viability of the opportunity. The social entrepreneur must also identify any potential weaknesses of the opportunity. Doing so will help determine how to resolve such weaknesses. It may well be that the opportunity is not worth pursuing.

The social entrepreneur must also identify the advantages presented by the external environment in which the social venture will operate. Are there external stakeholders who might be interested in the opportunity? How will the community perceive the social venture? Addressing such questions is important for the social entrepreneur to determine whether the environment is appropriate for the type of social venture envisioned. Threats must also be identified. For example, are there external circumstances that might prevent the implementation of the social opportunity? The SWOT analysis should not be limited just to identifying elements of the four quadrants. It is important for the social entrepreneur to understand how the components are related to one another and to determine whether sufficient resources are available to take advantage of viable opportunities.

2.2   Outside-in/Inside-out Analysis Model

Proposed by Longenecker and colleagues, this tool draws heavily on the SWOT analysis.[13] Like the latter, it considers factors that are both inside and outside the firm. External factors include the general environment (economic, political/legal, social, global, and technological) and the industry environment (competition). The industry environment is analyzed using Porter's five forces model (see Chapter 4). Internal factors include the firm's resources, expertise, and the skills of managers and employees. Although this model is applied to existing companies, it can also be used to assess the soundness of new venture opportunities. For example, in evaluating a new venture opportunity, the model can be used to determine its potential to add value to the customer's experience and whether the entrepreneur has the resources that will be required to exploit the opportunity successfully. The Outside-in/Inside-out model can also be used in conjunction with a SWOT analysis.

Although it is used predominantly to analyze commercial venture opportunities, this model can also be applied to the evaluation of new social venture opportunities. Because the model helps to assess the impact of the general external environment and the immediate external environment on the opportunity, it can provide valuable information for different environments. By understanding the external environment, the entrepreneur can shape the opportunity. The model can also help entrepreneurs assess the internal resources, core competencies, and skills required to pursue an opportunity successfully.

2.3   Bygrave and Zacharakis's Model

Bygrave and Zacharakis proposed a model of opportunity evaluation that is more comprehensive than either the SWOT analysis or the Outside-in/Inside out model.[14] Their model established a set of criteria used to determine the attractiveness of a business opportunity and includes seven major assessment areas:

- industry and markets;
- economics;

- harvest issues;
- competitive advantage issues;
- management team;
- personal criteria; and
- strategic differentiation.

Although this model is primarily used to evaluate opportunities in commercial entrepreneurship, with some adaptations it can be applied to social venture opportunities, too.

Social enterprises operate in industries or markets, although the nature of these industries and markets may be different. A social venture may operate in a particular industry, such as healthcare or education. In this industry, the social venture may target a particular market. For example, a social venture may provide affordable books for inner-city kids in Western countries, while another may address children's healthcare issues in rural areas in the developing world. The area of economics described by the model is relevant for social ventures because they have to be sustainable by generating a surplus. Thus, a sound social venture sustainability model (discussed in Chapter 6) should be developed and implemented by the social entrepreneur. Harvest issues may be addressed by the social entrepreneur in assessing whether the opportunity can generate a surplus while making a difference in the lives of the intended beneficiaries. The benefits for stakeholders consist of whether this social venture accomplishes its social mission. For a hybrid social venture, harvest issues may include both addressing the social issues and generating profits for the social entrepreneur and others who invested in the venture (double bottom line).

Although competition in social entrepreneurship is not as stiff as it is in commercial entrepreneurship, social ventures do compete for government grants, philanthropic donations, and social recognition. Thus, the social entrepreneur must address the issue of whether the social opportunity is not only unique but addresses the social issue in a novel way when compared to other social ventures that address similar social issues. This could also include some form of differentiation, particularly for hybrid social ventures. Of course, no venture can succeed without a strong management team. Thus, the social entrepreneur must build such a team. Instead of attempting to "go solo," a savvy social entrepreneur should think about building a strong and complementary entrepreneurial team at the start of their new social venture.

2.4 The Quick Screen Model

Another model that is used to evaluate business opportunities is the Quick Screen model.[15] This model can be considered as a simplified version of the Bygrave and Zacharakis model insofar as it includes only three criteria:

- market and margin related issues;
- competitive advantage; and
- value creation and realization issues.

Using the model, the entrepreneur can measure the opportunity on the specific criteria identified under each category and decide whether to pursue the opportunity, abandon it, or refine it. This model has been adapted by several entrepreneurship scholars. For example, Barringer and Ireland called it "First Screen" because it is the initial step that helps to determine whether a given opportunity has the potential to become a viable business.[16] It is used in a feasibility analysis along the four dimensions described in the first section of this chapter. The final part of the First Screen is "Overall Potential," which helps the entrepreneur assess whether the opportunity should be pursued as it is or refined. The First Screen can be used as a tool for social ventures with some modifications. For instance, a social venture's market should be identified. This can comprise customers or beneficiaries. Can the social venture effectively serve this market? Do the customers or beneficiaries really need the service? Is it possible to scale the venture and expand the market? Such questions will guide the social entrepreneur to evaluate the market potential of the social venture.

Table 7.3 illustrates the key elements that should be considered when using the Quick Screen model to evaluate social venture opportunities. The four elements can be

Table 7.3 Adaptation of the Quick Screen model to social ventures

I. Market and social Impact			
Criterion	*Higher potential*	*Low potential*	
Social need/problem	Clearly identified	Unfocused	
Customers/beneficiaries	Reachable and receptive	Unreachable/not interested	
Social impact	Clearly measurable	Difficult to measure	
Value added	Significant	Insignificant	
Overall potential			
1. Market	Higher_____	Average_____	Lower
2. Social impact	Higher_____	Average_____	Lower

II. Competition and cooperation networks		
Criterion	*High Potential*	*Low Potential*
Social ventures providing similar services	Small number	Large number
Barriers to entry	Low	High
Timing	Right	Not so right
Costs	Low	High

III. Value creation and realization issues		
Criterion	*High potential*	*Low potential*
Social benefits	High	Low
Earned income	High	Low
SROI potential	High	Low

IV. Overall Potential		
Go	*No go*	*Go if …*

1. Earned income
2. Sustainability
3. Social impact
4. SROI
5. Timing
6. Other important issues

streamed down to fit social ventures. For example, for the element "Market and social impact," the social entrepreneur could consider the customers or beneficiaries of the social venture and assess whether the social venture will be likely to serve a pressing and lasting social need. If it is decided that it will, the social venture will have high potential. The beneficiaries should also be reachable and the social venture should have a clearly measurable social impact. Assessing the other three elements will help the social entrepreneur reach a firm conclusion based on an overall evaluation of the social opportunity.

The four models discussed above are often used to evaluate opportunities for commercial ventures. However, they can easily be applied to the assessment of social venture opportunities, too. This is even more true now than it was in the past, because social ventures have evolved. For instance, for-profit social ventures could easily use these tools. For social ventures that are purely philanthropic, some assessment tools are more appropriate than others. One must acknowledge, however, that while business entrepreneurs have several opportunity assessment tools from which to choose, social entrepreneurs have substantially less guidance in this area.[17] Nevertheless, two tools have recently been proposed to aid in the evaluation of social venture opportunities, and these are described in the next section.

3   Tools for Analyzing Social Venture Opportunities

This section describes Kitzi's model for evaluating social opportunities and Kickul and Lyons's model.

3.1   Kitzi's Model for Evaluating Social Opportunities[18]

While drawing heavily on Bygrave and Zacharakis's model,[19] Kitzi's assessment tool has been adapted specifically for social entrepreneurship and includes three major areas:

- social value potential;
- market potential; and
- sustainability potential.

Each of these criteria is ranked from high to low. The first area consists of assessing whether the social venture will serve a particular need. If it will, then it will add value to the potential beneficiaries. And if the opportunity adds social value, it will probably have market potential, too. Market potential implies that a group of customers or beneficiaries will need the product or service provided by the social venture. The final area concerns the sustainability of the social venture. Will the social venture be able to sustain itself over time? A social venture opportunity that passes the test in all three of these areas should be considered viable.

This model is simple and easy to apply. However, it is most suited to purely philanthropic social ventures and does not take into account the changing nature of the social venture landscape with the growth of hybrid and for-profit social ventures.

3.2   The Social Opportunity Assessment Tool[20]

Developed by Kickul and Lyons, the social opportunity assessment tool includes four major categories:

- social value potential,
- market potential;
- competitive advantage potential; and
- sustainability potential.

The authors also added an overall category—"overall potential"—which combines the first four categories. Within each of the first four categories, the authors identified five criteria by which to evaluate each social venture idea. The area "social value potential" is similar to the one described in Kitzi's model. A social opportunity must address a genuine social need. A social entrepreneur can assess whether the social opportunity has social value potential by conducting a survey of potential beneficiaries or by relying on secondary data. Information garnered from these sources can help determine whether the opportunity has the potential to make a difference in people's lives.

The opportunity must also have market potential, meaning that there should be a clearly identified market. Without a market, the opportunity cannot be considered viable. Kickul and Lyons also consider investors as customers for a social opportunity.[21] Thus, a social opportunity has market potential if it will attract investors. So social entrepreneurs must be able to convince investors of their product's or service's ability to meet the needs and desires of its intended customers.[22] The model also includes issues of competitive advantage that are discussed in Bygrave and Zacharakis's model and the concept of sustainability that is included in Kitzi's model.

As mentioned earlier, competition in the social venture landscape is not as fierce as it is in commercial ventures. However, some forms of competition do exist in the social sector, especially regarding the acquisition of resources. If one applies Porter's five forces model to social entrepreneurship (see Chapter 4), it is obvious that some barriers to entry do exist, even for social ventures. For example, Robinson identified several institutional barriers to entry (economic, social, institutional, formal, and cultural) that may prevent new social ventures from entering certain markets.[23] The economic barriers include difficulties accessing much-needed financial resources to start a venture. This is a particularly pertinent issue in developing countries, where both commercial and social entrepreneurs often have trouble raising capital. Social barriers are found within labor markets, civic organizations, business organizations, and political networks, and among other business owners.[24] The inability to access these social organizations and networks can prevent a social entrepreneur from exploiting a social opportunity. The social entrepreneur may also not fully understand the institutional environment, such as the norms, rules, and traditions of the country in which he/she wants to operate. Most developing countries do not have strong formal institutions that can facilitate the creation of social ventures, so this could represent a hindrance for social entrepreneurs.

The fourth component of the model considers the potential for the social venture to sustain itself over time. Again, this category is similar to one in Kitzi's model. Sustainability is a key aspect of social ventures, be they purely philanthropic, hybrid, or for-profit. For instance, does the social venture have the potential to generate earned income and support itself over time? Can the venture continue to attract grants and other investors over time? Does it have the resource capabilities to sustain itself over time? Such questions should be addressed to ensure that the social venture will be financially viable over the long term.

Finally, the "overall potential" category represents a composite assessment for the opportunity, ranked from low to high. A high composite rating indicates that the opportunity is worth pursuing, whereas a very low rating indicates that it should probably be abandoned. A medium potential rating suggests that the opportunity would benefit from further refinement.

A social entrepreneur can use this tool to develop composite ratings for each assessment category and for the four categories combined. Doing so will provide guidance on whether to pursue the opportunity or not. Kickul and Lyons consider this assessment tool as a pre-launch test *before* the social entrepreneur commits resources to the venture. Specifically, they contend that their model is intended to force entrepreneurs to think through an idea carefully before investing significant time and money in it. If the assessment yields a positive result, they can pursue what is clearly a genuine opportunity with relative confidence. On the other hand, if the results of the assessment are negative, they can abandon the project before incurring significant losses.[25] The four categories and their respective criteria are presented in Table 7.4.

Table 7.4 The social opportunity assessment tool[26]

Social Value Potential

Criterion	Strong opportunity	Weak opportunity
Social need	Service or product directly addresses an identified need	Service or product addresses needs only indirectly
Mission alignment	Service or product is in direct alignment with mission	Service or product is only indirectly aligned or is misaligned with mission
Achievable impact	Service or product can fulfil identified social need in a measurable way	Service or product will only minimally address the need
Social return on investment (SROI)	A strong effectiveness-to-cost ratio	A weak effectiveness-to-cost ratio, or costs exceed impact
Community support	Service or product will be positively perceived and endorsed by the community	Service or product will not be well accepted by the community

Market Potential

Criterion	Strong opportunity	Weak opportunity
Customer need or want	Target beneficiary both needs and wants the service or product	Target beneficiary is indifferent to the service or product
Window of opportunity	Timing is good	Timing is poor
Investor interest	Evidence of philanthropic, government, or private sector financial interest	Evidence of little or no interest among philanthropic, government, or private investors
Market size	Large	Small
Market share attainable	An open market, with little or no competition	Very competitive market, with several alternatives

(Continued)

Competitive Advantage Potential

Criterion	Strong opportunity	Weak opportunity
Barriers to entry	High, many	Low or non existent
Prospective partnerships or alliances	Many potential partners	Few potential partners
Control over costs	Substantial control	Little or no control
Compelling mission	Highly compelling; widespread sympathy	Less compelling; little understanding or sympathy
Management team	Strong, complete skill set	Incomplete skill set

Sustainability Potential

Criterion	Strong opportunity	Weak opportunity
Venture capacity	Sufficient physical resources to start and maintain the venture	Insufficient physical resources to start and maintain the venture
Venture capability	Sufficiently skilled entrepreneur(s), staff, and board	Insufficiently skilled entrepreneur(s), staff, and board
Investor interest	Evidence of philanthropic, government, or private sector financial interest	Evidence of little or no interest among philanthropic, government, or private investors
Ability to generate earned income	High potential for charging user fees and/or selling goods or services	Low potential for charging user fees and/or selling goods or services
Compelling mission	Highly compelling; widespread sympathy	Less compelling; little understanding or sympathy

Overall Potential

Social Value Potential			
	High	Medium	Low
Market Potential			
	High	Medium	Low
Competitive Advantage Potential			
	High	Medium	Low
Sustainability Potential			
	High	Medium	Low
Composite Potential			
	High	Medium	Low

4   The Importance of Feasibility Studies for Social Ventures

The previous three sections have explained feasibility analyses and the tools that may be used to conduct one. This section focuses on the reasons why social entrepreneurs need to conduct a feasibility study as one of their pre-startup activities. Why is it important? What advantage does it bring to the social entrepreneur and his/her social venture? Addressing these questions will help the social entrepreneur save time and resources. A feasibility analysis has an internal audience and helps the entrepreneur to focus on the opportunity and the potential to realize it. Not every social venture idea has the potential to be transformed into a viable and sustainable social venture. Thus, it is important for the social entrepreneur to conduct a preliminary study to evaluate the feasibility of the proposed venture. This analysis should help the social entrepreneur decide whether to:

- pursue the current idea;
- refine the current idea to improve its potential for success;
- abandon the current idea; or
- search for a more suitable idea.

4.1   Pursue the Current Idea

The results of a well-conducted feasibility analysis will provide useful data and information to the social entrepreneur that will help him/her decide whether to pursue the current opportunity. If they decide to go ahead, this implies that the venture has passed the feasibility test and the social entrepreneur can move to the planning stage by developing a full social venture plan. Although there is no guarantee that the social venture will succeed, at least the feasibility study will have provided solid evidence that the idea is worth pursuing.

4.2   Refine the Idea to Improve its Potential for Success

The feasibility study may reveal that the opportunity needs to be modified in order to improve its feasibility. This information will allow the social entrepreneur to take action that could prove beneficial. For example, a buying-intentions survey may reveal that potential customers or beneficiaries prefer certain other services, rather than the one proposed by the potential venture. The social entrepreneur may integrate such information in refining the opportunity. They may also learn that they need to recruit more skilled talent.

4.3   Abandon the Current Idea

A social venture proposal that fails the feasibility test should be abandoned to avoid wasting valuable time and resources. However, even though the idea may be unviable, the results of the feasibility analysis can provide useful information for the social entrepreneur with respect to future projects. It is better to abandon an idea that does not have the potential to lead to the creation of a sustainable social enterprise than to waste valuable time writing a social venture plan for it.

4.4   Search for a New Idea

A social entrepreneur whose initial opportunity is not suitable should not give up. As is commonly acknowledged, giving up is not in the DNA of entrepreneurs. Using the information from the feasibility study could help the social entrepreneur to explore new ideas if the current one is not feasible. Thus, the feasibility study can serve as an exploratory phase when ideas are refined and reconfigured to fit the type of venture that may address a particular social need.

Despite its importance, feasibility analysis is not a panacea. Very often, the preplanning phase of a new venture, including feasibility analysis and business plan writing, is unnecessary and does not always improve the new venture's performance. It is possible that social entrepreneurs may not see any need to conduct a feasibility analysis because they think that the social needs are so obvious and pervasive that people will surely benefit from the products or services that the new venture provides. The Mercy Project application case at the end of this chapter is one such project. No feasibility study was conducted prior to writing the formal business plan and launching the project.

4.5   Stakeholder Analysis in the Feasibility Study of Social Ventures

An important aspect of feasibility studies that social entrepreneurship scholars have often overlooked is the analysis of potential stakeholders who may be interested in the mission of the social venture. A stakeholder is defined as any group or individual who can affect or is affected by the achievement of the organization's objectives.[27] In fact, stakeholder analysis should be a vital part of the pre-planning phase of a social venture. For example, social entrepreneurs must ask such questions as:

- Who might be interested in the mission of the social venture?
- How might such parties be attracted to the venture?
- What benefits can these parties bring to the venture?
- What are the stakeholders' expectations?
- Would the venture make a social impact to satisfy the expectations of these stakeholders?

Answering these questions will prepare the social entrepreneur to gauge the feasibility and impact of the new venture. Yet, the literature in social entrepreneurship has not discussed this issue, especially during the pre-planning phase. However, it is important for social entrepreneurs to identify potential stakeholders when evaluating the feasibility of their social ventures. This is important because it helps to address the question of who or what really counts.[28]

When analyzing a social venture's stakeholders, the social entrepreneur should differentiate between primary and secondary stakeholders.[29] He or she must also understand what Mitchell and colleagues refer to as the "identification" and "salience" of stakeholders.[30] The first of these entails the social entrepreneur establishing who the stakeholders are, whereas the second refers to the extent to which these identified stakeholders will play a critical role in the venture's success or survival. Understanding both identification and salience will help improve stakeholder relationships.

Summary

This chapter discussed feasibility analysis as a technique that is used to evaluate social opportunities. The chapter described the feasibility analysis with particular emphasis on its four components and the tools that may be used to conduct one. Although most of the tools used in a commercial feasibility analysis could also be applied to social venture opportunities, the chapter selected two that are essential for social entrepreneurs. It also highlighted the importance of feasibility analysis for social ventures.

Key Terms

Feasibility analysis; Outside-in/Inside out model; Quick Screen model; social opportunity assessment tool

Review Questions

1 What is feasibility analysis? What is it designed to achieve and how is it different from a business plan?
2 Identify and describe the four components of a feasibility analysis.
3 Describe the elements that would make a social venture opportunity attractive.
4 Discuss the importance of using primary data in feasibility analysis.
5 Discuss the importance of using secondary data in feasibility analysis.
6 Discuss how a feasibility analysis could help anticipate the sustainability of a social venture.
7 Describe a buyer-intentions survey and explain its importance for social ventures.
8 Must a social entrepreneur conduct a feasibility analysis to determine whether to go ahead with his/her social venture idea (yes or no)? Explain.
9 Explain the difference between a buyer-intentions survey and a concept statement.
10 One of the limitations of buyer-intentions surveys is that buyer intentions do not always translate into actual buying behavior. How would you overcome this limitation in a proof-of-concept study?

Application Questions

1 Identify a social venture opportunity and conduct a feasibility study using the social opportunity assessment tool. Use this study to answer the question of whether your social venture concept is feasible or not.
2 Your former college classmate approached you with a social venture idea. He is thinking of starting a social venture to address the problems facing street children in Lagos, the largest city in Nigeria, a developing country in sub-Saharan Africa. He has traveled to Lagos on several occasions and lived there for a year as a Peace Corps agent. He believes that this social venture would make a significant difference in the lives of the children. He comes to you for advice. Based on your understanding of social entrepreneurship and particularly feasibility analysis, what issues would you like your friend to address before going ahead with his idea?
3 Identify a social venture opportunity and write a one-page concept statement. Show the concept statement to ten people. Based on the feedback received, determine whether your concept should be refined or remain in its current state.
4 Identify a social venture opportunity and conduct a buyer-intentions survey using the elements contained in Table 7.1. Show your survey to at least ten people. What would you say about your social venture concept based on the results of the buyer-intentions survey?
5 Identify a social venture opportunity and conduct a feasibility analysis using Kickul and Lyons's model. What lessons can you draw from this feasibility analysis related to the viability of your social venture opportunity?

Application Case 1: Mercy Project, Ghana[31]

The Mercy Project began when Chris Field visited Ghana in August 2009. During this trip, Field met Tomas, then a child slave. Tomas's story was not unique but part of a more systemic and societal problem—that of enslaved children in the Volta Region of Ghana. However, it was the driving force behind the decision to create the Mercy Project, which is a faith-based project. The mission of the Mercy Project is not limited to helping enslaved children but rather aims to eradicate the root problems that led to their use in the first place. As Field, now the project's executive director, put it: "We want to be creative and innovative in our economic development projects. We don't just want to rescue a few kids, we want to remove the structures that cause these children to work like this in the first place. Our ultimate goal is to work ourselves out of a job." The purpose of the Mercy Project is to seek long-term, sustainable solutions that empower and equip the Ghanaians who put the children to work.

Ghana is a poor country in West Africa and some of the families are too poor to provide decent education for their children. Some families are so poor that they sell their children to those who can take care of them. This problem is very acute in the Volta Region. Lake Volta is the largest artificial lake in the world by surface area. It was created by the construction of the Akosombo Dam on the Volta River in the 1960s, to provide hydroelectricity to the region. Over 80,000 Ghanaians were displaced as a result of the flooding. The region is now primarily home to a large fishing industry, in which an estimated 7,000 children are forced to work as child slaves.

The Mercy Project uses a process-centered approach based on four pillars:

- establish relationships;
- replace the need for child labor;
- rescue the children; and
- monitor and evaluate.

Because Volta's fishermen are key stakeholders to the extent that they feel they require the children's labor, it is important to gain their trust. To do so, the Mercy Project engages them in addressing this social problem. It establishes partnerships with them.

The second pillar consists of finding means of economic development and empowerment in the local communities that do not require the use of child slaves. Doing so will contribute to solving the problem. Thus, the Mercy Project works in tandem with local communities to identify their needs and then address them. For example, the Mercy Project realized that aquaculture is one of the most natural fits and one of the most sustainable practices for Ghana's fishermen. Thus, its focus is on developing this activity.

By investing in a village economically and helping teach new means of making a living, the Mercy Project has gained compliance from the villagers to release the enslaved children from labor, so they can go to school. At this point, social workers begin to look for each child's real family. Upon rescue, each child spends time in an established facility which provides physical and emotional rehabilitation and some basic schooling. After this process, the children are reintegrated back into their true families. But that is not the end of the Mercy Project's involvement, as thereafter it maintains a presence within and a relationship with the villages. It monitors the economic development projects that have already been implemented and encourages each village to make wise decisions as a community. It also invests in the rescued children and their families by making sure they are provided for in a way that prevents future trafficking.

The Mercy Project has helped several villages in the Volta Region. For example, the village of Awudzakorpe released all fifty of its enslaved children. In July 2011, a team of Mercy Project supporters established a field of sustainable cassava for the village to expand its farming capacity. They also provided tools to help speed up the processing of the cassava. There is a documentary on the Mercy Project at www.youtube.com/watch?v=b4Dwv5KbMYI.

Discussion Questions

1 How could a feasibility study have helped the decision to launch the Mercy Project?
2 How would you assess the social value potential of the Mercy Project?
3 Identify the key stakeholders of the Mercy Project.
4 Why was it important to establish a partnership with the fishermen?

Application Case 2: Martha's Table[32]

Martha's Table is a community-based nonprofit organization in based in northwest Washington, D.C. In 1980, Veronica Maz started Martha's Table with $93 and the support of Father Horace B. McKenna, a Jesuit Catholic priest, as a place for poor children to receive food after school. Since then, it has expanded to diversify its activities and become a sustainable social venture with a strong reputation and name recognition in the Washington area and beyond. For example, by 1994, the annual cash budget of Martha's Table was $1.4 million, and in 2004 the project received total financial and in-kind support of more than $5.7 million. Today, Martha's Table addresses the immediate and long-term effects of poverty through its food, education, and opportunity programs, which serve over 18,000 residents each year.

The project is driven by compassion, dedication, and self-reliance. In the words of Veronica Maz, "life is not a handout. Although people are poor, they must be given the chance and opportunity to break the cycle of poverty." Martha's Table's mission is to build a better future for Washington's poorest residents by providing healthy food, affordable clothing, and high-quality education. It fulfills this mission in three areas of service:

- children and youth programs;
- family services; and
- food services.

It provides food for the homeless at numerous sites throughout Washington via its mobile soup kitchen, McKenna's Wagon, 365 days a year; meals for senior citizens; and food supplies from its headquarters on 14th Street. It also provides educational and recreational programs throughout the year for approximately 300 at-risk children (ranging in age from 3 months to 18 years) from the Shaw and Columbia Heights neighborhoods. Finally, it offers family support services, including a laundromat, a health education office, a clothing distribution center, a day-care center, and information and referrals about other community and government services.

Through these programs for vulnerable children and families, Martha's Table has helped over 20,000 families since its launch. In 2014, it added a "Success Center" to its range of operations, which is designed to engage parents in their children's successes. Patty Stonesifer, a former CEO of the Bill and Melinda Gates Foundation, is now the CEO of Martha's Table. Her vision is to deepen and expand the organization and turn it into a national model for service-based nonprofits, with the goals of reaching more than 15 locations around the city, helping kids succeed in school, helping parents contribute to their children's success, and ending childhood hunger.

Martha's Table relies on help from volunteers as well as paid employees. It coordinates more than 10,000 volunteer shifts annually. Several political and business luminaries have volunteered, including former presidents George H. W. Bush and George W. Bush and former first ladies Barbara Bush and Laura Bush. President Barack Obama and his family also volunteered to serve at Martha's Table the day before Thanksgiving in 2013 (see www.youtube.com/watch?v=5PGvzWsASks).

Discussion Questions

1   Martha's Table did not conduct a formal feasibility study before launching in 1980. Do you think that today's social entrepreneurs should always conduct a feasibility analysis before launching their social ventures? Identify some of the advantages and disadvantages of conducting one.
2   How do you think a feasibility study would have helped the founder of Martha's Table, Veronica Maz?
3   Martha's Table launched its Success Center in 2014. How would conducting a feasibility study help it scale this center?
4   How would a feasibility study help determine whether there is market potential for new versions of Martha's Table in other large cities in the United States and around the world?

Notes

1   Timmons, J. A., Muzyka, D. F., Stevenson, H. H., & Bygrave, W.D. (1987). Opportunity recognition: The core of entrepreneurship. In N. C. Churchill *et al.* (Eds.), *Frontiers of Entrepreneurship Research* (pp. 109–123). Wellesley, MA: Babson College.
2   Dimov, D. (2010). Nascent entrepreneurs and venture emergence: Opportunity confidence, human capital, and early planning. *Journal of Management Studies*, 47(6), 1123–1153.
3   Ajzen, I. (1991). The theory of planned behavior. *Organizational Behavior and Human Decision Processes*, 50(2), 179–211.
4   Dimov, D. (2010). Nascent entrepreneurs and venture emergence: Opportunity confidence, human capital, and early planning. *Journal of Management Studies*, 47(6), 1123–1153.
5   Justis, R. T., & Kreigsmann, B. (1979). The feasibility study as a tool for venture analysis. *Business Journal of Small Business Management* 17(1), 35–42; Tumashja, A., Welpe, I., & Sporrle, M. (2013). Easy now, desirable later: The moderating role of temporal distance in opportunity evaluation and exploitation. *Entrepreneurship Theory and Practice*, 37(4), 859–888.
6   Castrogiovanni, J. G. (1996). Pre-start up planning and the survival of new small businesses: Theoretical linkages. *Journal of Management*, 22(6), 801–822.
7   Justis, R. T., & Kreigsmann, B. (1979). The feasibility study as a tool for venture analysis. *Business Journal of Small Business Management* 17(1), 35–42; Currie, R. R., Seaton, S., & Wesley, F. (2009). Determining stakeholders for feasibility analysis. *Annals of Tourism Research*, 36(1), 43–61.
8   Barringer R. B., & Ireland, R. D. (2012). *Entrepreneurship: Successfully launching new ventures.* 4th edition. New York: Pearson.
9   Adapted from Barringer R. B., & Ireland, R. D. (2012). *Entrepreneurship: Successfully launching new ventures.* 4th edition. New York: Pearson, at p. 84.
10 Porter, M. E. (1985). *Competitive advantage.* New York: Free Press; Porter, M. E. (2008). The five competitive forces that shape strategy. *Harvard Business Review*, January, 25–40.
11 Bygrave, W. D., & Zacharakis, A. (2004). *The portable MBA in entrepreneurship.* 3rd edition. New York: Wiley; Bygrave, W. D., & Zacharakis, A. (2008). *Entrepreneurship.* New York: Wiley.
12 Timmons, J. A., & Spinelli, S. (2007). *New venture creation: Entrepreneurship for the 21st century.* 7th edition. New York: McGraw-Hill/Irwin.

13 Longenecker, J. J.G., Moore, C. W., Petty, J. W., & Palich, L. E. (2006). *Small business management: An entrepreneurial emphasis*. 13th edition. Mason, OH: Thomson South-Western.

14 Bygrave, W. D., & Zacharakis, A. (2004). *The portable MBA in entrepreneurship*. 3rd edition. New York: Wiley; Bygrave, W. D., & Zacharakis, A. (2008). *Entrepreneurship*. New York: Wiley.

15 Timmons, J. A., & Spinelli, S. (2007). *New venture creation: Entrepreneurship for the 21st century*. 7th edition. New York: McGraw-Hill/Irwin.

16 Barringer R. B., & Ireland, R. D. (2012). *Entrepreneurship: Successfully launching new ventures*. 4th edition. New York: Pearson.

17 Kickul, J., & Lyons, S. T. (2012). *Understanding social entrepreneurship: The Relentless pursuit of mission in an ever changing world*. New York: Routledge.

18 Kitzi, J. (2001). Recognizing and assessing new opportunities. In J. D. Dees, J. Emerson, & P. Economy (Eds.), *Enterprising nonprofits: A toolkit for social entrepreneurs* (pp. 43–62). New York: Wiley.

19 Bygrave, W. D., & Zacharakis, A. (2004). *The portable MBA in entrepreneurship*. 3rd edition. New York: Wiley; Bygrave, W. D., & Zacharakis, A. (2008). *Entrepreneurship*. New York: Wiley.

20 Kickul, J., & Lyons, S. T. (2012). *Understanding social entrepreneurship: The relentless pursuit of mission in an ever changing world*. New York: Routledge.

21 Kickul, J., & Lyons, S. T. (2012). *Understanding social entrepreneurship: The relentless pursuit of mission in an ever changing world*. New York: Routledge.

22 Kickul, J., & Lyons, S. T. (2012). *Understanding social entrepreneurship: The relentless pursuit of mission in an ever changing world*. New York: Routledge.

23 Robinson, J. (2006). Navigating social and institutional barriers to markets: How social entrepreneurs identify and evaluate opportunities. In J. Mair, J. Robinson, & K. Hockerts (Eds.), *Social entrepreneurship* (pp. 95–120). New York: Palgrave Macmillan.

24 Robinson, J. (2006). Navigating social and institutional barriers to markets: How social entrepreneurs identify and evaluate opportunities. In J. Mair, J. Robinson, & K. Hockerts (Eds.), *Social entrepreneurship* (pp. 95–120). New York: Palgrave Macmillan

25 Kickul, J., & Lyons, S. T. (2012). *Understanding social entrepreneurship: The relentless pursuit of mission in an ever changing world*. New York: Routledge.

26 Kickul, J., & Lyons, S. T. (2012). *Understanding social entrepreneurship: The relentless pursuit of mission in an ever changing world*. New York: Routledge, at pp. 52–53.

27 Freeman R. E. (1984). *Strategic management: A stakeholder approach*. Boston: Pitman.

28 Freeman R. E. (1984). *Strategic management: A stakeholder approach*. Boston: Pitman.

29 Mitchell, R. K., Bradley, R. A., & Wood, J. D. (1997). Toward a theory of stakeholder identification and salience: Defining the principle of who and what really counts. *Academy of Management Review*, 22(4), 853–886; Laplume, O. A., Sonpar, K., & Litz, A. R. (2008). Stakeholder theory: Reviewing a theory that moves us. *Journal of Management*, 34(6), 853–886.

30 Mitchell, R. K., Robinson, R. E., Marin, A., Lee, J. H., & Randolph, A. F. (2013). Spiritual identity, stakeholder attributes, and family business workplace spirituality stakeholder salience. *Journal of Management, Spirituality & Religion*, 10(3), 215–252; Mitchell, R. K., Agle, B. R., Chrisman, J. J., & Spence, L. J. (2011). Toward a theory of stakeholder salience in family firms. *Business Ethics Quarterly*, 21(2), 235–255; Mitchell, R. K., Bradley, R. A., & Wood, J. D. (1997). Toward a theory of stakeholder identification and salience: Defining the principle of who and what really counts. *Academy of Management Review*, 22(4), 853–886.

31 Sources for this whole setion: www.mercyproject.net/our-story; http://mercyproject.net/their-story/general-ghana-info, both retrieved March 25, 2016.

32 Sources for this whole section: http://en.wikipedia.org/wiki/Martha's_Table; http://marthastable.org, both retrieved March 25, 2016.

Chapter 8

Planning for Social Ventures

Learning Objectives

1 Understand the importance of writing a business plan.
2 Understand the importance of social venture planning.
3 Identify the components of a social venture plan.
4 Describe the process of writing a social venture plan.

Chapter 7 discussed feasibility analysis. This chapter focuses on writing a social venture plan. Both the feasibility analysis and the social venture plan are parts of the pre-planning stage of a new social venture. This chapter is organized into four sections. The first section presents a brief overview of business plans as commonly understood in commercial entrepreneurship. The second discusses the wisdom of writing a business plan. In so doing, it presents the two sides of the argument on business plan writing. One side advocates the benefits of business plan writing, whereas the other suggests the process is almost worthless. The third section focuses on the development of a social venture plan. Although similar to a regular business plan, the social venture plan has some particularities insofar as it focuses on addressing social needs. The fourth section provides guidelines for presenting a social venture plan to an external audience.

1 What Is a Business Plan?

1.1 Defining a Business Plan

A business plan is a written document that describes the current state and the supposed future of an organization.[1] It summarizes how an entrepreneur will create an organization to exploit a business opportunity,[2] and usually outlines the markets to be served, the products or services to be provided, the resources required, including money, and the expected growth and profit.[3] It helps the entrepreneur spell out how the new venture will be run. The business plan has a dual purpose and serves both an external and internal audience. It serves the former by helping to convince others to become engaged in the business, giving investors something to react to and representing somehow a selling document. It indicates that the entrepreneur has thought deeply about the venture and how it should be run. Meanwhile, the business plan serves an internal audience by representing a roadmap for the entrepreneur as well as future employees. It provides a game plan for the business and shows how the game of winning in the market will be played by the entrepreneur. The business plan also provides an opportunity to practice operating the business. It acts as a communication and marketing tool that informs and sells the venture's vision and strategy to financiers.[4]

Business plans can make a positive impact in two ways: by improving the venture's entrepreneurial capability; and by increasing the resources available to the venture.

1.2   Comparing Business Plans and Feasibility Studies

A business plan has primarily an external audience, whereas a feasibility study has a largely internal audience. In doing a feasibility analysis, the focus is on the idea and whether the entrepreneur should pursue it or not. In writing a business plan, the focus is on how the new venture will operate. Writing a business plan implies that the venture is feasible and the entrepreneur should now organize how it will be run. Table 8.1 illustrates the key points of comparison between a feasibility study and a business plan. As indicated in Chapter 7, the focus of the feasibility study is internal to the extent that the entrepreneur assesses whether the opportunity should be pursued or not. The focus of the business plan, however, is external. The approach used in a feasibility study is that of testing and discovery. The entrepreneur intends to test the business concept to see whether it works or needs refinement or should be abandoned.

The approach in a business plan is to convince and prove to others that the concept works and therefore deserves their attention—and often their resources. A business plan is therefore a *persuasion tool*. The purpose of the feasibility study is to answer the question of whether the opportunity is worth pursuing, whereas the purpose of the business plan is to convince others that the opportunity is worth pursuing. The feasibility study addresses the question of the resources at hand, whereas the business plan addresses the issue of the resources that will be needed to start and run the venture. Profit expectations tend to be realistic and conservative in a feasibility study, whereas they tend to be exaggerated in a business plan. The feasibility study and the business plan have different impacts on student learning experiences. For example, doing a feasibility study helps students reshape the opportunity and move on, whereas students who write a business plan find themselves stuck with a bad idea. Finally, a feasibility study relies on primary data, whereas a business plan often uses secondary data.

Table 8.1 Comparison between feasibility study and business plan

	Feasibility study	Business plan
Focus	Internal (entrepreneur)	External (stakeholders)
Approach	Testing/discovery	Convince/proving
Opportunity	Is it worth pursuing?	Convince others it is worth pursuing
Resources	What do I have?	Here is what I need
Profits	More conservative	Exaggerated
Student experience	Reshape or move on	Stuck with bad idea
Data collection	Primary	Secondary

1.3   Format of a Business Plan

A business plan has three main components:

- the executive summary;
- the core; and
- the supporting documents.

The following sub-sections describe the key elements of each of these components, each which must be well crafted.

1.3.1   Executive Summary

The executive summary is the first part of a business plan. It summarizes the content of the business plan. Its usefulness rests on the fact that it is succinct and must be on target. It is the first part that a potential investor will read. If it tells a compelling story, the reader will be motivated to read the rest of the business plan. Thus, the executive summary must be well crafted. It will generally include the following:

- name of company;
- mission;
- brief description of product/service;
- profitability issues;
- financial needs; and
- vision.

These six elements should comprise a total of between one and two pages. The executive summary's aim is to help entrepreneurs make their "elevator speeches" and explain their business plans in no more than a couple of minutes.

1.3.2   Core of the Business Plan

The core of the business plan presents the various aspects of the plan in detail. It includes:

- a description of the business;
- its mission and vision;
- the venture team;
- the marketing strategy;
- the industry analysis;
- the schedule of operations; and
- the financial statements.

1.3.3   Supporting Documents

Also known as the appendix, this section includes résumés of the founder(s), board members, and key personnel. It can also include product templates and relevant data as well as letters of support from interested parties. For instance, if a foundation has pledged support for helping a social venture accomplish its social mission, this should be included in the supporting documents. If data are cited in the social venture plan, the sources must be provided.

Table 8.2 Components of a business plan

Executive summary	Core of the business plan	Supporting documents
Brief summary of the business plan that generally includes: name of company, mission, brief description of product/service, profitability issues, financial needs, and vision.	Includes the different aspects of the business plan: description of the business, mission and vision, industry analysis, marketing strategy, schedule of operations, financial analysis, and risk assessment.	Also known as the appendix, includes: supporting documents, such as résumés of founders and key managers, letters of support, product templates, relevant data, etc.

2 The Wisdom (or Otherwise) of Writing a Business Plan

Before discussing the writing of a social venture plan, it is important to explain the benefits of writing a business plan as well as the potential drawbacks. There is an ongoing debate among entrepreneurship scholars on the wisdom of writing a business plan. This invites the following two questions:

- Does writing a business plan improve the odds of a new venture launching?
- Does it lead to success for the new venture?

Such questions have been addressed by entrepreneurship scholars, but the research on planning in general, and on pre-startup planning in particular, has yielded mixed results.[5] Some studies have found a positive relationship between writing a business plan and new venture performance, whereas others have found no significant relationship. The following sub-sections present the two views concerning business plans and their potential effects on the success of new ventures.

2.1   Drawbacks of Writing a Business Plan

Some entrepreneurship scholars consider business plan writing as a worthless activity that has no impact on improving a new venture's performance.[6] For instance, in a study conducted on a sample of 396 nascent organizations, Honig and Karlsson examined the factors that led nascent entrepreneurs to write business plans. They examined both the production and the outcomes of these plans and found that institutional forces, such as coercion and mimetic forces, influence the propensity for entrepreneurs starting new ventures to write business plans. However, they found no evidence to support the contention that writing business plans improves the performance of the new ventures.[7] These results indicate that writing a business plan is not always a rational process, as one might think. In fact, entrepreneurs may write business plans merely because others are doing it or because external stakeholders, such as investors and other financiers, expect it of them.[8] It is safe to say that business plans are a prevalent feature of new venture management and are encouraged by government agencies, educational institutions, and consultants.[9] Therefore, the process of writing a business plan is undertaken by nascent entrepreneurs to gain legitimacy. After all, writing a business plan is one of the most widely regarded aspects of the pre-startup planning.[10]

Other scholars argue that writing a business plan interferes with the efforts of time-constrained entrepreneurs to undertake more valuable firm-organizing actions, such as marketing and promotion, gives them the potentially harmful illusion of control over information, and leads to decision-making errors in estimating customer needs.[11] As a consequence, writing a business plan imposes an opportunity cost on the time of entrepreneurs.[12] In a study conducted on a sample of 116 new ventures started by Babson College alumni who graduated between 1985 and 2003, Lange and colleagues found no significant difference between the performance of new businesses launched with or without formal written business plans. Based on these findings, the authors suggest that unless a would-be entrepreneur needs to raise substantial startup capital from institutional investors or business angels, there is no compelling reason to write a detailed business plan before launching a new business. Rather, the entrepreneur should limit his/her efforts to making financial projections, especially cash flow projections.[13] This suggestion is consistent with the "just do it" school of thought, which advocates that when an emerging venture does not need outside resources, and/or when nascent entrepreneurs understand the competitive situation, the process of writing a business plan should commence only *after* other startup activities have been completed.[14]

Another aspect of business plan writing is that different audiences look at different parts of the business plan. For example, bankers stress the financial aspects of the business plan and give little emphasis to the market, the entrepreneur, or other issues. As equity investors, venture capital fund managers and business angels have very different approaches, emphasizing both market and financial issues. Business angels give more emphasis than venture capital fund managers to the entrepreneur and "investor fit" considerations.[15] Writing business plans has now become ubiquitous in business schools and training centers. For example, most schools around the world have courses focusing specifically on business plan writing and some even organize business plan contests.

Several entrepreneurship scholars argue that written business plans fail to communicate realistic goals or anticipate problems, lack evidence of commitment to the venture, do not demonstrate that the entrepreneur has sufficient experience to launch and run the venture, and do not identify a market niche.[16] Others contend that business plans merely present dry facts and do not convey enthusiasm or commitment. Such criticism has led some scholars to advise making business plans more personal.[17] In such personalized business plans, entrepreneurs describe their backgrounds, personal and professional experiences, and how they relate to the new venture. Still other entrepreneurship scholars argue that entrepreneurs rarely follow their written business plans anyway. Therefore, writing one is a futile exercise.

Other potential drawbacks include the physical appearance of the business plan itself, lack of clarity, inaccurate financial projections, and a tendency to exaggerate the level of development and the qualifications of the team.[18]

2.2 The Benefits of Writing a Business Plan

Notwithstanding the limitations described above, some entrepreneurship authors argue that writing a business plan prior to starting a new venture is beneficial because it improves performance and helps survival.[19] For example, Delmar and Shane argue that business planning offers the following three advantages:

- it facilitates faster decision-making by identifying missing information without first requiring the commitment of resources;
- it provides tools for managing the supply and demand of resources in a manner that avoids time-consuming bottlenecks; and
- it identifies action steps to achieve broader goals in a timely manner.

The authors emphasize the positive role of business plans by noting that completing one and establishing a legal entity in the life of a new venture are advantageous because these activities facilitate the transition to other firm-organizing activities.[20]

Delmar and Shane empirically examined 223 new ventures in Sweden and found that business plans helped entrepreneurs to make decisions to balance supply and demand and to turn abstract goals into concrete operational steps. They also helped to reduce the likelihood of a venture failing and accelerated product development and venture activity.[21] In another study, Shane and Delmar found that entrepreneurs who drafted business plans before talking to customers and beginning marketing and promotional activities had a lower risk of termination than other organizing efforts.[22]

Entrepreneurship scholars who emphasize the necessity of writing business plans have noted a positive relationship between business plans and post-startup performance. For example, a study of 468 small businesses found that the existence of a business plan generally led to new venture success. Moreover, prior planning led to subsequent planning, thereby increasing success and efficiency.[23] Thus, these studies conclude that having a business plan can be an important indicator of a venture's potential for success.[24]

Writing a business plan also facilitates the decision to start the new venture effectively. Entrepreneurs who go through the process of writing business plans tend to stick with it and start their ventures. Using data from the US Panel of Entrepreneurial Dynamics (USPED), Liao and Gartner found that nascent entrepreneurs who completed a business plan were 2.6 times more likely to persist in the process of business startup than those who did not complete a business plan.[25]

Business plans also provide evidence to potential investors that the entrepreneur has thought through the process of starting the new venture. A business plan represents the primary source of information for the investment-screening decision.[26] Timmons emphasized the importance of business plans by stating that they serve as much more than fundraising tools. He specifically suggested that a business plan articulates what the opportunity conditions are, why the opportunity exists, the entry and growth strategy to seize that opportunity, and why the entrepreneur and his/her team have what it takes to succeed.[27] This clearly indicates the benefit of writing a business plan for a new venture.

When writing a business plan, entrepreneurs must consider who their audiences are and why they might read the business plan. As Gartner and Bellamy put it, a business plan is like an invitation to a dance, but it is not the dance itself.[28] Thus, the business plan should be written in a language that the intended audience can easily understand. Potential investors read many business plans and they are not keen on wasting valuable time trying to decode the message a potential entrepreneur is trying to convey. So a poorly written business plan will surely fail to convince them to invest. Of course, this does not mean that a well-crafted one will always obtain funding, but at least it will stand a better chance.

If the scholars who advocate business planning are correct, clearly social entrepreneurs could benefit from writing their own plans (known as social venture plans), especially when they are trying to enlist the support of external stakeholders. It is to this process that we now turn.

3   Understanding and Writing a Social Venture Plan

3.1   What Is a Social Venture Plan?

A social venture plan can be defined as a written document that details how a venture addressing a social need will be launched and run. It is to a social venture what a business plan is to a commercial venture. As discussed in Chapter 1, a social venture may assume one of several forms: purely philanthropic and relying exclusively on grants and/or donations; hybrid; or for-profit. The form could have a significant influence on the contents of the social venture plan.

But first we should consider whether it is important for a social entrepreneur to write a social venture plan at all. Some authors have argued that this process is often overlooked by social entrepreneurs because they tend to believe that they can best express the venture in person, utilizing all of the enthusiasm and optimism that stimulated the enterprise in the first place.[29] This assumption is echoed by research evidence. For example, a qualitative analysis of 23 social ventures found that developing a business plan was not central to their launch.[30] However, some social entrepreneurs certainly do draft business plans. An illustrative example is Global Health Corps (see Chapter 4), co-founded by Barbara Bush, daughter of the former US president George W. Bush. She and the other founders met over a weekend in Baltimore, Maryland, to craft the business plan of their new social venture.[31]

3.2   Writing a Social Venture Plan

Although there are countless books on writing business plans, there are very few on writing social venture plans. This may be due to two factors. First, social entrepreneurs may consider the existing literature on writing business plans as adequate to guide them toward writing social venture plans. After all, the construct of "social venture plan" does not really exist because most social entrepreneurs call their venture plans business plans anyway. Second, social entrepreneurship scholars have not empirically expressed the need to study social venture plans as a specific topic of academic inquiry compared to business plans in commercial entrepreneurship.

The following sub-sections present a detailed analysis of how to write a social venture plan. Although there are close similarities with what might be included within a business plan, there are also some differences, to the extent that the social venture plan focuses more on addressing a social issue. In addition, the marketing plan and the financial projections are different from those of a commercial venture's business plan.

3.2.1   Description of the Social Venture

This section presents the social venture to the reader. Thus, the social entrepreneur should describe his/her venture in detail. Here, the mission and vision of the social venture should be stated. This implies that the entrepreneur should write a mission statement for the new venture. This spells out the reason why the organization should exist. The mission of the social venture should be compelling enough to attract potential donors. The location and legal form of the social venture should also be indicated. The social entrepreneur may provide a historical perspective of the idea. What prompted the social entrepreneur to consider pursuing this idea? Where did the idea originate?

This section should be thoroughly developed to attract the attention of potential external stakeholders. After the description, the social entrepreneur should move on to an analysis of the external environment in which the social venture will operate.

3.2.2   Analysis of the Social Landscape

In commercial entrepreneurship, it is important for entrepreneurs to understand the industry that the new venture will enter. The industry's size, its growth rate, and the sales projections should all be indicated. Such data can be obtained through secondary sources regarding the particular industry. For instance, if an entrepreneur intends to create a small firm to resell computers, an estimation of the growth and sales of desktop computers, laptops, and computer tablets could be obtained through publications such as *PC Computer*. The entrepreneur must also understand the structure of the industry. Is it dominated by a few large players or is it fragmented?

Obtaining such knowledge is also important for social ventures because every social venture operates in a particular environment. To differentiate this analysis from a classical industry analysis, the construct of "social venture landscape" is used to describe the external environment of social ventures. This environment includes the set of social ventures addressing similar social needs as well as economic, cultural, and social factors. For example, there are several social ventures fighting poverty around the world. This is also true for social ventures combating endemic illnesses and health issues among the poor.

The social entrepreneur should also identify the critical success factors in the industry as well as the basis on which the different social ventures compete. Although competition in social entrepreneurship is not as stiff as in commercial entrepreneurship, it is important to understand the competitive landscape of social ventures. Social ventures do not always compete to outgun others and drive them out of the market.

This section should also include the trends affecting the social landscape. Such trends could include economic, social, environmental, technological, and demographic factors. Analyzing the social venture landscape could help the social entrepreneur to develop a better understanding of the social problem as well as the other social ventures that are attempting to address similar social issues.

3.2.3   Market Analysis

Generally, in a commercial business plan, the section on marketing analysis follows the industry analysis and focuses on a particular segment of the industry. In fact, the market analysis breaks the industry into segments and zeroes in on the specific target market to which the new venture will try to appeal.[32] The marketing analysis consists of two main elements: market segmentation and competitor analysis. The market segmentation consists of targeting a particular segment of the industry. No venture can satisfy all customers. Thus, it is important for the entrepreneur to target a particular segment. A market can be segmented by geography (region, state, city), gender (male, female), income, or any other criterion that is deemed useful. The business plan should describe in detail the chosen segment of the market. For example, this section should clearly describe the behaviors of the customers in this particular segment. This is important because knowledge of customers can help tailor products and/or services to their specific needs.

The second aspect of the market analysis—competitor analysis—is a detailed assessment of the participants in the industry. A new venture may have direct competitors, indirect competitors, and future competitors (firms that may enter the industry at a later date). The purpose of a competitor analysis for social ventures is to understand the social landscape of social ventures that address similar social needs.

3.2.4   Social Venture Marketing Strategy

The social venture's marketing strategy will consist of three main parts:

- identification of the beneficiary or customer segment;
- formulation of the social value proposition; and
- strategies to reach the beneficiaries or customers.

3.2.4.1   IDENTIFICATION OF THE BENEFICIARY OR CUSTOMER SEGMENT

The first part of the marketing analysis identifies the potential customers or beneficiaries. At this level, it is important to answer the question: who are the beneficiaries or customers? The social entrepreneur may explore the extent to which the beneficiaries or customers will buy the products or services themselves or whether a third party will buy them. In the case of third parties paying for the products or services, it is important to identify them.

- How will you identify specific customers?
- How will you target these customers?
- How will you attract these customers?
- Will these customers purchase the products or services or will third parties pay for these services?

For example, in the case of the social venture TechWadi, described at the end of this chapter, the young entrepreneurs who are the beneficiaries of the programs do not pay for the services. The same is true for TOMS, the second case discussed at the end of this chapter. Indeed, the shoes are donated to those who need them.

3.2.4.2   THE SOCIAL VALUE PROPOSITION

The social entrepreneur must clearly indicate how the social venture will deliver value to the beneficiary or customer. This section should be well crafted to entice potential stakeholders who may be willing to support the social venture. In doing so, the entrepreneur must address the following questions:

- What is the product or service providing to the customer?
- Will this product or service make a difference in the life of the beneficiary or customer?
- What impact will it have on the community?

At this level, the social entrepreneur may decide to develop metrics to measure potential impact or include a section on impact measurement.

This section should also include a description of the product or service. The social entrepreneur may also include a product or service prototype. A product prototype will be a physical representation of the product the firm intends to sell to specific customers. Pictures of it should be included in the "Supporting Documents" section.

If the social venture is providing a service, a service prototype should be included. This is a representation of the service and the potential reactions of customers or beneficiaries who will experience it.

Describing the product or service clearly will help explain its use and the resources that will be needed to provide it, and will help readers anticipate the reactions of potential customers.

3.2.4.3 CONNECTING TO THE BENEFICIARY OR CUSTOMER

In this section, the social entrepreneur should explain how the product or service will reach its targets by asking: how will the product or service get to the beneficiary or customer? This section must include a description of sales activities, advertising, promotion strategies, as well as the purchase process and channel(s) of distribution. Internal and external sales forces and tasks must be described, and sales goals must be set. This is particularly important for hybrid or for-profit ventures that have commercial activities. The social entrepreneur must also determine the pricing structure, the expected margins, merchandising, and beneficiary or customer support policies in the case where the social venture is involved in earned-income activities.

3.2.5 Management Team and Social Venture Structure

Describing the social venture management team and its ability to execute is an important aspect to consider when writing a social venture plan. It is important to indicate the people who will manage the social venture and what activities they will perform. It is also necessary to identify key managerial and organizational skills that are requirements for various positions within the social enterprise. This section should have three parts:

- the social venture team;
- the board of directors or advisers; and
- the organizational chart.

The new social venture team includes the founder(s) and key personnel. A profile for each team member should be provided. Particularly, this section should indicate the duties and responsibilities of each team member as well as their experience and background. It is also important to show how their skills will help the social venture succeed.

If the social venture has a board of directors or advisers, this should be indicated, and their names and qualifications provided. A board of directors is a group of individuals elected by the shareholders of a company. Their duties and responsibilities are to oversee the operations of the corporation. Although they are not actively involved in the day-to-day operations of the corporation, they will be involved in key decisions, such as approving the strategic direction of the company and hiring top managers, such as the CEO and other senior executives. A board of advisers is a panel of experts whom a firm's management asks to provide counsel and advice on an ongoing basis.[33] It is useful to indicate the responsibilities of board members and what value they will add to the social venture.

The best way to indicate how a social venture is structured and will be run is to provide an organizational chart. This is a graphical representation of the connections between the various departments within an organization. Although there is no single best way of structuring a social venture, some guidelines that are used by for-profit ventures might prove useful. A social venture may adopt a simple organizational structure or a more complex structure, depending on the number of paid workers and volunteers and its geographic coverage.

3.2.6   Operations of the Social Venture

This section should focus on the activities that must be performed to generate value for the customer or beneficiary. Issues such as what activities will be performed and who will perform them must be addressed. This section is all about implementation and execution. The entrepreneur should provide a detailed description of the activities necessary to run the day-to-day operations of the social venture. It may be important for the social entrepreneur to differentiate between front-line activities and backstage activities as well as set priorities. For example, some activities are of primary importance and represent the core activities of a social venture. A social venture that focuses on distributing food in homeless shelters will have the distribution of meals as its front-line activity. However, the food must be sourced and cooked before it is distributed. Thus, buying the ingredients and cooking the meals are backstage activities. The social venture will need volunteers and/or paid employees both to cook and to distribute the food.

This section should also include the geographic location of the social venture. This is important because, as in commercial entrepreneurship, location can help build a competitive advantage. For instance, a social venture that addresses the needs of AIDS orphans in a developing country like Uganda will operate in that country, because this will allow it to maintain close contact with the beneficiaries.

The operations plan should also describe the social venture's facilities and equipment. If the social venture already has some facilities and equipment, this should be stated. The social entrepreneur should also indicate how these facilities and equipment were acquired. If the social venture does not yet have any facilities or equipment, this should also be stated. In this case, the social entrepreneur must indicate how the facilities and equipment will be acquired.

The social entrepreneur should also indicate the timeline of critical operations. For instance, the plan should include the dates when certain activities, such as incorporating the social venture, writing grants, hiring key personnel, and buying equipment, will commence. It is advisable to draft a table of activities.

3.2.7   Financials of the Social Venture

This section should usually start with the economics of the social venture—that is, a description of how the venture will generate revenue and a comparison of this revenue with costs. The revenue stream of a social venture may include donations, grants, or earned income. Purely philanthropic social ventures may rely only on donations and grants, whereas hybrid social ventures may combine earned income with donations and grants. If earning income is part of the social venture's activities, then this must be stated in the social venture plan. Social entrepreneurs must explain how engaging in earned-income activities relates to the social mission, and why it will not distract from that mission.[34] For instance, a social venture may generate revenue through grants. However, applying for a grant would incur some costs related to paying whoever drafts the grant application. The same is true for soliciting donations and generating earned income.

In commercial entrepreneurship, costs associated with generating revenues are often described as costs of goods sold (COGS). In social entrepreneurship, such costs could be described as costs associated with revenue generation to the extent that the purpose of social ventures is to address social issues. The principal purpose is not to generate revenues through sales, although the social venture may do so to improve its ability to deliver the social services. In addition to the costs associated with generating revenue, the social venture plan should identify any fixed costs. These are incurred whether revenue is generated or not.

As in a commercial business plan, the social venture plan must include financial projections. Three types of financial statements are useful and should be included:

- income statements;
- balance sheet; and
- cash-flow statements.

Making projections about financial statements should start with an assumption sheet. This indicates the basic assumptions underlying the projections made in the financial statements. For instance, if a social venture intends to raise $1 million in revenue through donations, grants, and earned income, it must indicate how this will be done. Financial projections should be made on the basis of the specific financing needs of the business. The cash-flow statement serves as the fundamental operating document for the day-to-day management of the social venture. The social entrepreneur should compare the performance estimates of his/her proposed venture to standards related to other social ventures that address similar needs. It may also be important to perform some ratio analysis to indicate whether the social venture will be financially viable in the long run. Projections should generally cover a three-to-five-year period, as in commercial venture plans. Although financial projections are products of the imagination, they should always be realistic, plausible, and as accurate as possible.

3.2.8 Social Impact Measurement

The social entrepreneur must identify the potential impact of the social venture. This comprises the consequences of the social venture on the entire community. This section should also include a measurement of social return on investment (SROI). The two concepts of social impact measurement and social return on investment are discussed in detail in Chapter 14. By indicating the potential social impact of the social venture, the social entrepreneur will demonstrate the social benefit of the venture to potential stakeholders. When measuring social impact, the social entrepreneur must show that the venture meets both financial performance and social objectives. A social venture that demonstrates a clear social impact and a social return on investment is far more likely to attract potential stakeholders than one that does not. Measuring social impact represents an opportunity to convince stakeholders that the social venture will fulfill an important social mission. The tools for measuring social impact are also described in Chapter 14. For example, social return on investment is a powerful tool for measuring the impact of a social venture.

3.2.9 Risk Assessment

Entrepreneurship is a risky business. This is true in both commercial and social entrepreneurship. Thus, the social venture plan should contain a section on risk assessment and strategies to mitigate the effects of such risks. The social entrepreneur must identify the potential risks that the social venture may face, including political risks, financial risks, economic risks, talent risks, and any other factors that might prevent the social venture from accomplishing its mission. For example, some social ventures operate in developing countries where corruption and political instability are endemic. A good example of this is Dignified Mobile Toilets (see Chapter 3), which operates in Nigeria, a country where corruption is rampant and where the Boko Haram insurgency has led to safety concerns. DMT has to take such factors into account when operating in certain parts of the country. Similarly, the organization had to overcome a major talent risk when its founder, Isaac Durojaiye, died in 2012.

If the social venture relies on donations and grants, it is always useful to determine alternative sources of funding should a particular grant run out. It is well known that people donate more to charities in periods of economic prosperity and less in periods of economic difficulty. Such economic risks should therefore be considered in the social venture plan.

Although risks cannot be eliminated, actions should be undertaken to mitigate their negative impact. It is important for the social entrepreneur to show potential investors that he or she understands the risks involved in starting and running the social venture. Sahlman's advice to entrepreneurs—to assess the risks and rewards of any commercial venture carefully—could equally be applied to social ventures.[35] The entrepreneur should provide an assessment of everything that *might* go wrong and a discussion of how the venture's team will respond.

3.2.10   *Supporting Documents*

This section, which is generally the final one, includes the founder's or founders' résumés, the résumés of key employees, and copies of contracts or templates of products if needed. The entrepreneur may also include:

- market analysis data and market research studies;
- action plans for sales and distribution;
- product specifications and photos;
- action plans for production, operations, and service;
- letters of reference;
- census and demographic data;
- contracts;
- letters of commitment from customers, suppliers, and lenders; and
- buy/sell agreements among partners.

They might also include letters of support from potential stakeholders, such as donors and/or government agencies.

Although the process of writing a business plan obliges a commercial entrepreneur to invest significant time and energy into thinking about the business and doing his/her homework,[36] it is not a panacea. Hence, the social venture plan should not be considered as a panacea, either. Rather, it should be viewed as a work-in-progress that can be iterated based on the contingencies the social entrepreneur faces. Recently, some entrepreneurship scholars have advocated the lean startup approach, which contends that entrepreneurs should focus on experimentation and iteration instead of formal planning when starting their new ventures.[37]

Table 8.3 Outline of a social venture plan

1 Executive Summary
2 Social Venture Description
   • Mission statement
   • Vision
   • Type of social venture
3 Social Landscape Analysis
4 Social Venture Marketing Strategy
   • Beneficiary/customer segment
   • Social value proposition
   • Promotion
5 Social Venture Management Team
   • Background of team members
   • Board of directors
   • Board of advisers
   • Employees
6 Social Venture Operations
   • Key activities
   • Physical location
   • Timeline of activities
7 Financial Projections
   • Capital requirements
   • Assumptions sheet
   • Beginning balance sheet
   • Years 2, 3, comments on financial statements
   • 3-year projected income statements
   • 3-year projected balance sheets
   • 3-year projected cash-flow statements
   • Break-even analysis
8 Social Impact
   • Social return on investment
   • Scaling of the social venture
9 Critical Risks
   • Additional risks
   • Proactive management
   • Insurance provisions
10 Supporting Documents/Appendix
   • Founder's and partners' résumés
   • Employees' résumés
   • Additional materials

4   Presenting a Social Venture Plan

Presenting a social venture plan is both an art and a science. As an art, the presentation depends on the communication skills and personality of the social entrepreneur or the social venture team. The presentation represents an opportunity for the social entrepreneur to make a good first impression and attempt to persuade potential donors and/or investors of the quality of the social venture. For example, some scholars argue that entrepreneurs should not hesitate to signal some degree of confidence in their ventures while also acknowledging their weaknesses because doing so may increase their trustworthiness and the likelihood of securing funds. However, they should not engage in excessive organizational promotion or criticize their competition. Such actions may result in potential investors perceiving them as dishonest, opportunistic, or simply misinformed or unrealistic about the actual risks their ventures will face.[38]

Possessing good communication skills and a positive personality can lead to a good presentation. However, the content of the social venture plan and the value of the social idea are of paramount importance. The social venture should address an important social need which should be clearly and succinctly explained to the audience. It is worth acknowledging that no matter the quality of the presentation, if the need addressed by the social venture seems trivial, the chances are that the audience will not share the enthusiasm of the presenter or the presenting team.

4.1 Preparing the Presentation

The presentation for the social venture plan is an important step that should not be neglected by the social entrepreneur. For instance, they should prepare some PowerPoint slides as visual display helps to capture an audience's attention. However, it is usually better to keep to a limited number of slides, rather than bombard the audience with dozens of them. Generally, between 12 and 14 slides should be acceptable. The first slide should contain the name of the social venture and logo (if there is one) as well as the name(s) and contact details of the founder(s). The second should include an outline of the presentation.

If there is a team of social entrepreneurs, they should present the social venture plan together. It is important to share this task equally among all members as this avoids the appearance of dysfunction or slacking. The team should also rehearse the presentation and anticipate any potential questions from the audience. It is advisable to make a mock-presentation and seek feedback prior to the actual presentation.

Finally, the team should arrive at least 15 minutes before the presentation to set up, check that all equipment is in working order, and prepare themselves.

Table 8.4 illustrates the key elements to include in the presentation of a social venture plan.

4.2 Tips for Making a Convincing Presentation

There is no universal format for successful presentation of a social venture plan. However, some guidelines might give entrepreneurs an edge in presenting their plans to an audience. Generally, as a rule of thumb, presenters should maintain eye contact and avoid reading too much of the text on their slides. If the rehearsal is done well, presenters should not have a problem conveying their message to the audience. Questions from the audience should be answered clearly and succinctly. If the presenter does not have a ready answer to a particular question, it is better to acknowledge that fact rather than guess or lie. Honesty and integrity are important in persuading people to invest in a venture and generating interest for an idea. Appearance is also important—it is always better to dress professionally rather than casually.

Summary

This chapter described how to write a social venture plan, and the pros and cons of doing so. It used the concept of social venture plan to differentiate planning for a social venture from planning for a commercial venture. The chapter argued that planning for a social venture is important because it helps the entrepreneur to focus. A social venture plan is also important because it represents a selling document that the social entrepreneur can

Table 8.4 Guidelines for social venture plan presentation

Topic	Explanation
1. Title slide	Introduce the presentation with your social venture's name and the name of the founder(s).
2. Problem	State the social problem to address.
3. Solution	Explain how your social venture will successfully address this social problem.
4. Beneficiary or customer	Identify the beneficiary or customer segment.
5. Social landscape	Explain the social environment of the social venture, including other social ventures that address similar social issues. Explain how the social venture will cooperate with or compete against existing social ventures.
6. Marketing and sales	Explain the social venture's marketing strategy. Explain whether beneficiaries or third parties will pay. Identify advertising strategies and pricing issues.
7. Management team	Describe the social venture's management team. Explain the backgrounds of the team members and the skills they possess to run the social venture successfully. Explain the management structure and explain whether the social venture will employ workers or recruit volunteers.
8. Financials	Briefly discuss the financials. Stress when the firm will achieve profitability, how much capital it will take to get there, and when its cash flow will break even. Use additional slides if needed to display your information properly, but don't go overboard.
9. Social impact	Explain the social impact of the social venture. Issues of impact on the community and social return on investment should be discussed.
10. Financing sought	Determine how much financing you will need for the social venture and how you will use it.
11. Conclusion/summary	Conclude by highlighting the key points of the social venture.

use to persuade potential stakeholders to provide assistance. It can also serve as a marketing tool to communicate the details of the social venture to investors and donors. Finally, the chapter provided useful guidelines for presenting a social venture plan to an audience.

Key Terms

Assumption sheet; board of advisers; board of directors; executive summary; market analysis; market segmentation; marketing strategy; mission statement; social venture landscape; social venture plan; timeline

Review Questions

1 Identify and discuss the differences between a business plan and a feasibility analysis.
2 Identify the components of a business plan.
3 Explain the importance of an executive summary in a social venture plan.
4 What is the purpose of writing a social venture plan?
5 What are some of the criticisms geared toward writing business plans? Do you think these criticisms are justified?

6 Some entrepreneurship authors argue that writing a business plan is a futile exercise. Do you agree with this assumption (yes or no)? Explain.
7 Is there a difference between writing a business plan and writing a social venture plan? Explain.
8 What are the advantages of preparing a social venture plan for a new social venture? Explain.
9 Why should the executive summary, which is one of the first things to appear in a business plan, be written last?
10 Explain why a social venture plan should contain a section on risk assessment.

Application Questions

1 Your friend, Michael, has recently approached you about an idea for a social venture to address the problem of street kids in Lagos, the largest city of Nigeria. He has set aside the next few weeks to write a social venture plan and then travel to Lagos. Do you think your friend is proceeding in the right way (yes or no)? Explain.
2 John recently decided to quit his job to start a social venture. As he puts it, "I am pretty much interested in helping to make the world a better place." His social venture intends to improve literacy in a developing country. He comes to you for advice because he is wondering whether writing a social venture plan is important. What advice will you give him concerning the benefits and drawbacks of writing a social venture plan?
3 Suppose you have been asked by your local chamber of commerce to conduct a two-hour workshop on how to write an effective social venture plan. The workshop will be attended by people who are thinking about starting their own social ventures but do not currently have written social venture plans. Write a one-page outline detailing what you would cover in the two-hour session.
4 You and two of your friends have decided to start a new social venture. To this end, you have the task of writing the social venture plan. Describe how you will go about this. Indicate the critical information that you must include.
5 Your team of three social entrepreneurs is scheduled to present its social venture plan to a group of potential donors. You are the team leader. Describe the preparation for this presentation and the key points you will highlight during the presentation.

Application Case 1: TechWadi: Building Bridges for Entrepreneurship in the Middle East[39]

Although the "Arab Spring" that started in 2011 was mostly political, there have been other social changes in the Arab world that have not gained such wide publicity. One such change concerns the efforts made by Arab entrepreneurs and professionals based in Silicon Valley to connect with young entrepreneurs in the Middle East and North Africa (MENA) region. To this end, TechWadi was created as a social venture to connect Silicon Valley to the Arab world. As a nonprofit organization, its mission is to transfer entrepreneurial knowledge and skills to the MENA region. In so doing, it aims to support emerging entrepreneurs in the region. It is a way for some successful Arab entrepreneurs and professionals in the United States to engage with the region of their ancestors through the use of an e-mentoring program, called

MentorCloud. Today, it is the leading nonprofit organization building bridges between Silicon Valley and the Arab world.

From its beginnings as a community of top Arab-American technology professionals in Silicon Valley, TechWadi has evolved into a powerful platform for collaboration with members and events around the world. It brings together technology movers and shakers via conferences, networking events, seminars, and workshops in addition to MentorCloud. In the MENA region, TechWadi works with leading regional and international organizations to empower high-impact entrepreneurs and build a sustainable infrastructure to help entrepreneurship thrive and succeed.

In addition to connecting mentors to young entrepreneurs in the MENA region, TechWadi has recently launched an accelerator program, called the Sprint Accelerator Program. This initiative is intended to provide valuable entrepreneurial skills, networking opportunities, and startup finances to young entrepreneurs in the region. It could also help address one of the endemic problems in the region—youth unemployment—which can foment into social unrest and political agitation.

TechWadi has a board of directors and an executive team. The chairman at the time of writing was Ossama Hassanein. There is a video on YouTube that explains the organization's goals and activities (www.youtube.com/watch?v=ofbA22L5Vhc).

Discussion Questions

1 How would writing a formal business plan have helped TechWadi?
2 What do you think about the formal structure of TechWadi?
3 Do some research on TechWadi and identify the Arab countries where it has helped young entrepreneurs.
4 Visit the TechWadi website and do additional research on the organization. How does it sustain itself?

Application Case 2: TOMS: A For-Profit Social Venture[40]

The story of TOMS illustrates how for-profit social ventures can work. The company was created with both an economic motive and a social purpose: the intention was to channel the company's profits into providing shoes for barefoot children in the developing world.

While doing volunteer work in Buenos Aires, the capital of Argentina, Blake Mycoskie, the founder of TOMS, noticed that many of the children were running barefoot. He soon realized that the lack of shoes was a problem not only in this community but in other parts of Argentina and other developing countries. Back in the United States, he decided to create TOMS in 2006 to address the problem. However, instead of starting a charity or a social venture, Mycoskie decided to create a for-profit business that would donate one pair of shoes for every pair of shoes sold— a business model known as "one-for-one." This model eventually became an integral part of what is now known as "caring capitalism" or "creative capitalism."[41]

By the time of writing, TOMS had given away more than 10 million pairs of shoes in 56 countries, including Argentina, Ethiopia, Guatemala, Rwanda, South Africa, and even the United States. TOMS's distribution system is quite complex. The company relies on "giving partners"—organizations that receive the shoes from TOMS and then donate them to the kids in need. There are more than 100 of these giving partners spread across the 56 countries where

TOMS operates. The company has recently started selling and donating eyewear in addition to footwear. As Mycoskie has stated, "TOMS is not a company, it is a movement."

Despite its success, some critics argue that TOMS is treating the symptoms rather than the disease. For example, Scott Gilmore, CEO of Building Markets, a nonprofit, argues that the problem of persistent poverty is "not a lack of shoes, but a lack of opportunity and a lack of jobs." While the critics may be right, it is worth mentioning that TOMS's business model has been replicated by other companies and it certainly provides some much-needed relief to the world's poor. For example, Figs Scrubs, Dog for Dog, and One World Futbol have all adopted the "one-for-one" model. For every set of scrubs sold, Figs Scrubs donates a set to a healthcare professional in the developing world. So far, it has donated 1,500 sets in Botswana, Ecuador, Haiti, Honduras, Kenya, and South Sudan. For every dog treat sold, Dog for Dog donates a Dogsbar to a shelter in the country of sale. So far, more than 54,000 dogs have had a treat. For every soccer ball sold, One World Futbol donates another to organizations working with disadvantaged communities. So far, more than 325,000 soccer balls have been distributed across more than 160 countries.

Discussion Questions

1   How would have a formal business plan help TOMS?
2   What is your assessment of TOMS's business model? For which products might it be applicable? For which will it be inapplicable? Explain.
3   Which products should TOMS add to its product line?
4   Do you agree with TOMS's critics that it is treating the symptoms rather than the disease (yes or no)? Explain.

Notes

1   Van Werven, R., Bouwmeester, O., Joep P., & Cornelissen, J. P. (2015). The power of arguments: How entrepreneurs convince stakeholders of the legitimate distinctiveness of their ventures. *Journal of Business Venturing*, 30(4), 616–631; Sutton, G. (2012). *Writing winning business plans: How to prepare a business plan that investors will want to read and invest in*. Scottsdale, AZ: BZK Press. Honig, B., & Karlsson, T. (2004). Institutional forces and the written business plan. *Journal of Management*, 30(1), 29–48.
2   Stevenson, H., & Van Slyke, J. (1985). Pre-start analysis: A framework for thinking about business ventures. Harvard Business School Case Study Number 9–386-075.
3   Cassar, G. (2010). Are individuals entering self-employment overly optimistic? An empirical test of plans and projections on nascent entrepreneur expectations. *Strategic Management Journal*, 31(8), 822–840.
4   Brinckmann, J., & Kim, S. S. (2015). Why we plan: The impact of nascent entrepreneurs' cognitive characteristics and human capital on business planning. *Strategic Entrepreneurship Journal*, 9(2), 153–166; Gartner, W. B., & Bellamy, M. G. (2010). *Enterprise*. Mason, OH: South-Western Cengage Learning.
5   Castrogiovanni, G. J. (1996). Pre-startup planning and the survival of new small businesses: Theoretical linkages. *Journal of Management*, 22(6), 801–822.
6   Carter, N., Gartner, W., & Reynolds, P. (1996). Exploring start-up event sequences. *Journal of Business Venturing*, 11, 151–166; Bhide, A. V. (2000). *The origin and evolution of new businesses*. New York: Oxford University Press; Honig, B., & Karlsson, T. (2004). Institutional forces and the written business plan. *Journal of Management*, 30(1), 29–48; Karlsson, T., & Honig, B. (2009). Judging a business by its cover: An institutional perspective on new ventures and the business plan. *Journal of Business Venturing*, 24(1), 27–45; Honig, B., & Samuelsson,

M. (2012). Planning and the entrepreneur: A longitudinal examination of nascent entrepreneurs in Sweden. *Journal of Small Business Management, 50*(3), 365–388.

7   Honig, B., & Karlsson, T. (2004). Institutional forces and the written business plan. *Journal of Management, 30*(1), 29–48.

8   Castrogiovanni, G. J. (1996). Pre-startup planning and the survival of new small businesses: Theoretical linkages. *Journal of Management, 22*(6), 801–822; Honig, B., & Karlsson, T. (2004). Institutional forces and the written business plan. *Journal of Management, 30*(1), 29–48.

9   Perry, S. C. (2001). The relationship between written business plans and the failure of small businesses in the US. *Journal of Small Business Management, 39*(3), 201–218; Delmar, F., & Shane, S. (2003). Does business planning facilitate the development of new ventures? *Strategic Management Journal, 24*(12), 1165–1185; Gruber, M. (2007). Uncovering the value of planning in new venture creation: A process and contingency perspective. *Journal of Business Venturing, 22*(6), 782–807; Lange, J. E., Mollov, A., Pearlmutter, M., & Singh, S. (2007). Pre-start-up formal business plans and post-start-up performance: A study of 116 new ventures. *Venture Capital: An International Journal of Entrepreneurial Finance, 9*(4), 237–256; Burke, A., Fraser, S., & Greene, F. J. (2010). The multiple effects of business planning on new venture performance. *Journal of Management Studies, 47*(3), 391–415.

10   Honig, B., & Karlsson, T. (2004). Institutional forces and the written business plan. *Journal of Management, 30*(1), 29–48.

11   Carter, N., Gartner, W., & Reynolds, P. (1996). Exploring start-up event sequences. *Journal of Business Venturing, 11*(3), 151–166; Bhide, A. V. (2000). *The origin and evolution of new businesses.* New York: Oxford University Press.

12   Gifford, S. (1992). Allocation of entrepreneurial attention. *Journal of Economic Behavior and Organization, 19*(3), 265–284.

13   Lange, J. E., Mollov, A., Pearlmutter, M., & Singh, S. (2007). Pre-start-up formal business plans and post-start-up performance: A study of 116 new ventures. *Venture Capital: An International Journal of Entrepreneurial Finance, 9*(4), 237–256.

14   Bhide, A. (2000). *The origin and evolution of new business.* New York: Oxford University Press.

15   Mason, C., & Start, M. (2004). What do investors look for in a business plan? A comparison of the investment criteria of bankers, venture capitalists and business angels. *International Small Business Journal, 22*(3), 227–248.

16   Kuratko, D., & Hodgetts, R. M. (2001). *Entrepreneurship: A contemporary approach.* Orlando, FL: Harcourt.

17   Sahlman, W. (1995). How to write a great business plan. *Harvard Business Review, 75*(4), 98–108.

18   Baron, R., & Shane, S. A. (2005). *Entrepreneurship: A process perspective.* Mason, OH: Thomson South-Western.

19   Timmons, J. A. (1980). A business plan is more than a financing device. *Harvard Business Review,* March–April, 53–59; Timmons, J. A., Smollen, L. E., & Dingee, A. L. M., Jr. (1985). *New venture creation: A guide to entrepreneurship.* 2nd edition. Homewood, IL: Richard D. Irwin; Delmar, F., & Shane, S. (2004). Legitimizing first: Organizing activities and survival of new ventures. *Journal of Business Venturing, 19*(3), 385–410; Delmar, F., & Shane, S. (2004). Planning for the market: Business planning before marketing and the continuation of organizing efforts. *Journal of Business Venturing, 19*(6), 767–785; Brinckmann, J., Grichnick, D., & Kapsa, D. (2010). Should entrepreneurs plan or just storm the castle? A meta-analysis on contextual factors impacting the business planning–performance relationship in small firms. *Entrepreneurship Theory and Practice, 25*(1), 24–40; Chwolka, A., & Raith, G. M. (2012). The value of business planning before start-up: A decision theory perspective. *Journal of Business Venturing, 27*(3), 385–399.

20   Delmar, F., & Shane, S. (2004). Legitimizing first: Organizing activities and survival of new ventures. *Journal of Business Venturing, 19*(3), 385–410.

21 Delmar, F., & Shane, S. (2003). Does business planning facilitate the development of new ventures? *Strategic Management Journal*, 24(12), 1165–1185.

22 Delmar, F., & Shane, S. (2004). Planning for the market: Business planning before marketing and the continuation of organizing efforts. *Journal of Business Venturing*, 19(6), 767–785.

23 Kraust, S., & Schwatz, E. (2007). The role of pre-start-up planning in new small business. *International Journal of Management and Enterprise Development*, 4(1), 1–17.

24 Chen, X. P., Yao, X., & Kotha, S. (2009). Entrepreneur passion and preparedness in business plan presentations: A persuasion analysis of venture capitalists' funding decisions. *Academy of Management Journal*, 52(1), 199–214.

25 Liao, J., & Gartner, W. (2008). The influence of pre-venture planning on new venture creation. *Journal of Small Business Strategy*, 18(2), 21–30.

26 Zacharakis, A. L., & Meyer, G. D. (2000). The potential of actuarial decision models. *Journal of Business Venturing*, 15(4), 323–346.

27 Timmons, J. A. (1980). A business plan is more than a financing device. *Harvard Business Review*, March–April, 53–59; Timmons, J. A., Smollen, L. E., & Dingee, A. L. M., Jr. (1985). *New venture creation: A guide to entrepreneurship*. 2nd edition. Homewood, IL: Richard D. Irwin.

28 Gartner, W. B., & Bellamy, M. G. (2010). *Enterprise*. Mason, OH: South-Western Cengage Learning.

29 Brooks, A. C. (2009). *Social entrepreneurship: A modern approach to social value creation*. Upper Saddle River, NJ: Pearson/Prentice-Hall.

30 Katre, A., & Salipante, P. (2012). Start-up social ventures: Blending fine-grained behaviors from two institutions for entrepreneurial success. *Entrepreneurship Theory and Practice*, 36(5), 967–994.

31 www.youtube.com/watch?v=JVYhPhmfTQ4, retrieved on March 26, 2016.

32 Barringer R. B., & Ireland, R. D. (2012). *Entrepreneurship: Successfully launching new ventures*. 4th edition. New York: Pearson; Spinelli, S., & Adams, R. (2012). *New venture creation: Entrepreneurship for the 21st century*. 9th edition. New York: McGraw-Hill Irwin.

33 Barringer R. B., & Ireland, R. D. (2012). *Entrepreneurship: Successfully launching new ventures*. 4th edition. New York: Pearson.

34 Brooks, A. C. (2009). *Social entrepreneurship: A modern approach to social value creation*. Upper Saddle River, NJ: Pearson/Prentice-Hall.

35 Sahlman, W. (1995). How to write a great business plan. *Harvard Business Review*, 75(4), 98–108.

36 Sutton, G. (2012). *Writing winning business plans: How to prepare a business plan that investors will want to read and invest in*. Scottsdale, AZ: BZK Press, LLC.

37 Blank, S. (2013). Why the lean start-up changes everything? *Harvard Business Review*, 91(5), 110–112.

38 Parhankangas, A., & Ehrlich, M. (2014). How entrepreneurs seduce business angels: An impression management approach. *Journal of Business Venturing*, 29(3), 543–564.

39 Sources for this whole section: http://techwadi.org/about/who-is-techwadi; www.techwadi.org, both retrieved on January 15, 2015.

40 Sources for this whole section: Chu, J. (2013). TOMS sets out to sell a lifestyle, not just shoes. *Fast Company*, June 17. www.fastcompany.com/3012568/blake-mycoskie-toms; www.toms.com, both retrieved on February 22, 2015.

41 Mackey, J., & Sisodia, R. (2013). *Conscious capitalism: Liberating the heroic spirit of business*. Boston: Harvard Business Review Press.

Chapter 9

Marketing Challenges for Social Ventures

Learning Objectives

1 Understanding the importance of marketing for entrepreneurial social ventures.
2 Applying market tools to entrepreneurial social ventures.
3 Developing skills to engage social venture customers.
4 Developing a social venture marketing plan.

The purpose of this chapter is to help students develop an understanding of the marketing tools needed by startups and early-stage social ventures to engage customers or beneficiaries and other stakeholders. Social entrepreneurs must also consider how their social ventures will leverage the limited marketing resources available to meet their social objectives. The chapter is divided into four main sections. The first section describes the fundamentals of marketing for social ventures. The second discusses the relevance of the four elements of the marketing mix (product, promotion, price, and place) for social ventures. The third focuses on social marketing, the use of marketing tools, and techniques for social causes. The fourth provides guidelines for developing social venture marketing plans.

I Fundamentals of Marketing for Social Ventures

Marketing is generally defined as the process of planning and executing the conception, pricing, promotion, and distribution of goods and services to satisfy customers and accomplish organizational objectives.[1] As a process, marketing involves the completion of several activities to satisfy customers and permeates every facet of an organization. For example, a manufacturing department that designs and makes products with the consumer in mind is practicing marketing, as is the management of a company that decides to introduce new products or services.

The marketing activities alluded to in most definitions are generally organized into four categories that constitute the four Ps of marketing: product, price, place, and promotion. In fact, the management of marketing can be characterized as a careful planning process which is informed by market research to guide the selection of target markets, and the composition of a marketing mix with which to position products competitively in the marketplace.

Although the conventional marketing approach may be helpful to new ventures, and especially social ventures, it lacks some flexibility and entrepreneurial flavor. For example, Hills and colleagues argue that marketing in SMEs deviates from mainstream marketing.[2]

This deviation is captured in the term "entrepreneurial marketing." To some extent, marketing in social ventures deviates from mainstream marketing as described in conventional marketing textbooks. Social ventures face opportunities and challenges that large for-profit organizations do not necessarily encounter. They can target their marketing efforts toward beneficiaries or customers as well as potential stakeholders who might provide some form of support. The following sub-section explains the field of entrepreneurial marketing and its importance for social ventures.

1.1   Entrepreneurial Marketing for Social Ventures

The umbrella term "entrepreneurial marketing" is used to capture conceptualizations of marketing as an innovative, risk-taking, proactive area of managerial responsibility.[3] Some authors have defined entrepreneurial marketing as a spirit, an orientation, as well as a process of pursuing opportunities and launching and growing ventures that create perceived customer value through relationships, especially by employing innovativeness, creativity, selling, market immersion, networking, or flexibility.[4] The process of managing entrepreneurial marketing is different from that of managing conventional approaches to marketing. Three reasons may explain these differences. First, entrepreneurial firms operate in unstable environments, so much so that not too much planning of marketing activities takes place.

Second, entrepreneurial firms often do not have a full-time staff or department devoted to marketing activities. Rather, they have a market orientation, which allows them to engage in marketing activities spontaneously. The concept of market orientation could assume a different meaning in social entrepreneurship, where it may mean focusing on beneficiaries and customers but also on the stakeholders who provide several forms of support. It means listening to the various constituencies. For example, a study conducted on 258 nonprofit community centers in South Korean found that learning orientation and market orientation were both positively related to innovation. Commitment to learning fosters innovation and efforts to fulfill customer needs.[5]

Third, in entrepreneurial firms, an informal rather than a formal approach is often adopted with respect to the management of marketing activities.[6] Within such an organizational context, the need to manage the process of marketing becomes less necessary as marketing becomes an activity owned and managed by the whole organization.[7] The competencies required for conventional marketing include planning, rigor, and familiarity with statistics and figures. In contrast, the management of entrepreneurial marketing is characterized by intuition, informality, and speedy decision-making.[8]

Entrepreneurial marketing can be applied to social ventures. In a study aimed at assessing the use of entrepreneurial marketing in social enterprises in the United Kingdom, Shaw found that social enterprises use marketing informally and on an ad hoc basis like their for-profit counterparts. She also noticed that marketing came as second nature to social enterprises.[9] The lesson is that marketing activities occur within social ventures even though they may not be performed in a systematic way. To some extent, the flexibility afforded by such an informal approach is appropriate, given the fluctuating and challenging environments within which many social enterprises operate.[10] Marketing scholars often consider three types of entrepreneurial marketing techniques that can prove useful for social ventures:

- guerrilla marketing;
- buzz marketing; and
- viral marketing.[11]

1.1.1   Guerrilla Marketing

Jay Conrad Levinson coined the term "guerrilla marketing" to describe an approach to marketing that differs from traditional marketing by relying on bootstrapping, the creative use of available resources, and a highly targeted mix of innovative communication techniques.[12] As an illustration, in nascent firms, marketing efforts are often limited by resources. Resource scarcity demands a high degree of effectiveness and efficiency in the marketing efforts of young companies. Therefore, small firms must develop imaginative forms of marketing that are low cost but produce a strong impact in the marketplace.[13] However, some authors have argued that Levinson's approach is more tactical than strategic, concentrates more on promotional tools than other marketing variables, and is useful only for those starting and running small businesses.[14]

Guerrilla marketing could be appropriate in the context of social entrepreneurship, where social enterprises often face limited resources. Social ventures could use their limited resources to market the services they provide. Such a guerrilla marketing tactic could help them attract beneficiaries and potential investors and/or donors. For example, in their book, *Guerrilla Marketing for Nonprofits*, Levinson and colleagues identified several techniques that nonprofit organizations can use to promote, motivate, and raise more money.[15] This indicates that social ventures can use guerrilla marketing to engage their multiple stakeholders. The same could also be true for using buzz marketing.

1.1.2   Buzz Marketing

Buzz marketing is a form of word-of-mouth communication which emerged as a reaction to the fact that ever more consumers were becoming critical of traditional advertising. It is an attempt to stimulate recipients through the use of spectacular actions so that the product becomes the subject of discussion or gossip.[16] Buzz marketing uses the recipients' internet, email, or cellphone networks to generate a buzz about a product or a brand, thereby leaving the advertising to the customers themselves. This can be done via an event or an activity which causes a ruckus and thereby generates publicity, enthusiasm, and information for the customers and leads to brand-building.[17] Buzz is not only initiated by media campaigns; media coverage itself is part of the buzz. Buzz marketing's target people are often opinion leaders with central hub positions in their social networks. Therefore, they can disseminate a message in an exponential way.

In social entrepreneurship, buzz marketing could be used to facilitate the use of social services. For example, community leaders were used in some African countries, such as Nigeria and Liberia, to convince people in rural areas to use mosquito nets to prevent the spread of malaria. In such communities, people tend to trust and respect their leaders. Buzz marketing may often rely on word-of-mouth in regions where online access is limited. For instance, in rural areas of India and Africa, where people have limited access to the internet, employing community leaders to relay important messages can be a valuable medium of communication. Buzz marketing can also be combined with viral marketing.

1.1.3   Viral Marketing

The term "viral marketing" describes a form of marketing that uses social networks (family, friends, neighbors, colleagues) to draw attention to brands, products, or campaigns by spreading messages and rumors about them, mostly through word-of-mouth.[18] This dissemination is usually voluntary and entails honest communication by customers with the aim of promoting something they like.[19] Successful viral campaigns can spread in a seemingly uncontrolled fashion, mostly over the internet.

The principal advantage of viral marketing is its low cost, as the message is spread voluntarily over the internet or via emails. Social media, such as Twitter, Facebook, and YouTube, may all be used to spread a message quickly. Social ventures can use viral marketing to create awareness of and generate support for their attempts to address social issues.

1.2   The Importance of Entrepreneurial Marketing for Social Ventures

It may appear odd for a social venture whose mission is to address a social need to market its products or services. Common sense would dictate that *when you intend to help someone, you do not need to shout about it*. Yet, in a world of television, the internet, and social media, it is no longer possible or even desirable merely to produce a mousetrap. You need to inform potential beneficiaries or customers that the mousetrap exists, and that it is an excellent means to catch mice.

The application of marketing to social issues and nonprofit organizations is nothing new. Several marketing scholars have argued that marketing is not just a business function but also a vital function for nonprofit organizations, and that all organizations—both for-profit and nonprofit—have marketing problems and so all need to understand marketing.[20] As a consequence, we may conclude that marketing is a pervasive societal activity that goes beyond the selling of particular products or services.

To the extent that marketing is viewed as a technology or a tool, it could be applied to a variety of situations. For a social venture, the goal is to persuade beneficiaries to use the services or products that are offered to them. Very often, ignorance and lack of information are the main reasons why people do not use the social services that are available in their community. For example, Dignified Mobile Toilets (DMT), in Nigeria, encourages people to use its services instead of defecating in open spaces (see Chapter 3). In doing so, the venture puts an emphasis not only on hygiene but also on its beneficiaries' sense of pride and dignity as human beings. DMT uses marketing to spread awareness of its services. In so doing, it also encourages corporations to display advertisements on the toilets—for a fee—which generates much-needed income.

Effective marketing, like that employed by DMT, can boost the image of any social venture. To this end, social ventures must employ all of the tools and techniques of marketing, starting with the segmentation of the market they intend to enter. The following sub-section discusses the importance of segmenting the social venture market.

1.3   Market Segmentation for Social Ventures

Segmentation is the core of what makes the entrepreneurial firm succeed or fail. But does market segmentation make sense for social ventures? Should they even care about it? The answer to both of these questions is a resounding "yes" because social ventures cannot address every social need, nor can they operate in every geographic location. Therefore, they must focus on a particular set of needs that they are able to satisfy well. For instance, the Mercy Project, described in Chapter 7, is addressing the issue of slave children in Ghana. It deals only with slave children, and only in a particular region of the country where the need for intervention is most obvious. Ghana suffers from many other social problems—such as the plight of street children in the capital, Accra—but the Mercy Project does not overstretch itself by attempting to solve those issues, too.

A social venture can segment its market in much the same way as a commercial venture segments its market. For instance, characteristics such as age, gender, geography, and economic status can all be considered in the segmentation process. For market segmentation to be worthwhile, there should be:

- homogeneity of needs and wants within the segment;
- heterogeneity of needs and wants between segments; and
- small differences within segments when compared to differences across segments.

For social ventures, this implies that beneficiaries' needs should be significantly different between segments and largely similar within segments.

After segmenting the market, the social entrepreneur must select a target market—that is, a particular set of beneficiaries that it is targeting and able to satisfy. In social entrepreneurship, the target market is a particular population whose social needs must be addressed in such a way that the social venture remains sustainable over time. It is important for the social venture to develop a unique identity while addressing the particular social need.

1.4   Branding Social Ventures

As is commonly discussed in the literature in marketing, a brand refers to a set of attributes—positive or negative—that customers associate with a company. When customers associate positive attributes with a company, they can become very loyal to it. However, when they associate the company with negative attributes, they will be reluctant to use its products or services. Worse, they may even persuade others, such as relatives and friends, not to use the company's products or services.

One may wonder whether social ventures really need to brand themselves since the people they serve are often needy and have few alternative options. However, branding a social venture may help create a sense of pride and trust among beneficiaries.

Four questions need to be asked when an organization sets about building its brand:

- Who are you (*brand identity*)?
- What are you (*brand meaning*)?
- What do I think or feel about you (*brand responses*)?
- What kind of association and how much of a connection would I like to have with you (*brand relationships*)?

Answering these questions helps companies build their brands, and the same is true for social venture branding.

How can social ventures brand themselves? This question is relevant because a social venture must be recognized as providing valuable services to its beneficiaries. This is important for at least two reasons: beneficiaries will continue to *seek out* the social venture's products or solicit its services; and investors and donors will be attracted to the venture. If the social venture is associated with positive attributes, stakeholders, such as investors and donors, will be more likely to support it. On the other hand, if a social venture is associated with negative attributes, investors and/or donors may withhold funding. A social venture should therefore aim to brand itself by developing a set of positive attributes. Indeed, a brand can be considered as the most important asset of a social venture or some other nonprofit organization.

A good example is Médecins Sans Frontières (Doctors Without Borders), a French orga-nization that tends to the wounded and sick in conflict-ravaged regions or where pandemic illnesses prevail. This nonprofit is usually perceived as a caring organization and has a reputation for providing reliable medical services. Because of these attributes, it attracts other organizations that provide financial resources and equipment as well as volunteer physicians and nurses. Médecins Sans Frontières was particularly active during the 2014 Ebola outbreak in Guinea, Liberia, and Sierra Leone.

At present, branding is rarely perceived as important for social ventures. However, with the changing landscape of social enterprises, ranging from purely philanthropic to hybrid and for-profit, it will probably play an increasingly important role. Social ventures can build their brands in much the same way as commercial ventures do—through advertising, public relations, support for social causes, social media, and other means. This allows them to develop strong relationships with key stakeholders and attract paid employees as well as volunteers. A recent study extended the concept of branding—and particularly internal branding—to social ventures with a sample of 301 nonprofit organizations in the United Kingdom. ("Internal branding" refers to an organization's attempts to persuade employees to buy into the brand value of the organization.) The study found that internal branding helped social ventures to attract both donations and volunteers.[21]

1.5   Relationship Marketing: A Necessity for Social Ventures

"Relationship marketing" refers to all marketing activities directed toward establishing, developing, and maintaining successful relational exchanges.[22] It goes beyond attracting new customers and focuses on maintaining continuous relationships with all customers. If marketing is important for social ventures, then every social venture should have a *marketing orientation* that consists of establishing long-term relationships with beneficiaries and other key stakeholders. A marketing orientation is a marketing method based on an understanding of the needs and desires of the market. A social venture should clearly understand the needs and desires of the people whose needs it addresses. By doing so it could benefit from relationship marketing. By interacting with its multiple stakeholders, a social venture should be able to develop trust and loyalty.

Social ventures interact with at least three key groups of stakeholders:

- beneficiaries (or customers);
- sponsors; and
- the general public.

Establishing good relations with these stakeholders may prove valuable in securing much-needed funds as well as establishing a good reputation. Thus, stakeholder analysis could be an important element of the marketing plan of social ventures.

2   Marketing Mix for Social Ventures

"Marketing mix" refers to the set of tools a firm uses to produce the response it wants in its target market.[23] The four elements of the marketing mix are: product, price, promotion, and place. Each of these four elements is equally important, although some may receive more attention than others, depending on the market situation and strategies. For instance, a social venture whose mission is to provide medicine to the poor, such as OneWorld

Health (see Chapter 1), will focus primarily on price, because ensuring that the medicine is affordable to the recipients is of paramount importance. However, another social venture may focus on place, such as Dignified Mobile Toilets (see Chapter 3), which ensures that its toilets are positioned where they are most needed and then promotes their availability.

At first glance, it may seem odd to expect social entrepreneurs to concern themselves with the four Ps of marketing, because any competition they face will be minimal when compared with that faced by their commercial counterparts. In addition, one may argue that the beneficiaries of a social venture's products or services may be happy just to receive them. So why bother to employ sophisticated marketing techniques? As mentioned earlier, though, using marketing tools can generate two main advantages for social ventures: it can create awareness and loyalty among beneficiaries; and it can attract potential investors and donors. For these reasons, it is important to draft a marketing strategy including the four elements of the marketing mix. The following sub-sections explain how the four elements of the marketing mix may be combined to produce a powerful marketing strategy for a social venture.

2.1   Product

In describing the elements of the marketing mix, "product" can refer to any physical product that a company manufactures and sells or to a service that it provides. A social venture may offer a physical product, as in the case of the BRCK discussed in Chapter 4, or a service, as in the case of Ascovime discussed at the end of this chapter. The social venture should clearly describe the product or service offered to the customer or beneficiary by explaining its distinctive features and the value it will add. For example, it could use referent accounts to establish credibility. A reference account is an early user of a firm's product or service who is willing to provide a testimony regarding his or her experience.[24]

2.2   Price

Pricing is important in hybrid or for-profit social ventures. In philanthropic social ventures, beneficiaries often do not pay for the services they receive because they are too poor to do so. In such cases, third parties pay for the services. It is interesting to determine how social ventures whose primary missions are to address social needs price their products or services. Research in marketing generally considers two types of pricing: *cost-based* and *value-based pricing*. In cost-based pricing, the price of a product (or service) is set as a function of the costs that are incurred to make it, plus a markup. The markup percentage can be determined by the vendor or may be an industry standard. This pricing method mostly focuses on the producer rather than the customer and how much that customer is willing to pay. Value-based pricing, by contrast, focuses on how much the customer is willing to pay for the product or service based on his or her perception of its attributes. For instance, if the customer associates positive attributes with the product, he or she may be willing to pay a premium price.

How should social ventures navigate these two pricing methods? The basic rule in pricing a "social service good" is that the price should not be perceived as so high as to be considered a rip-off. How, then, might social ventures determine the right price for their products or services? They should charge a price that allows the beneficiaries to afford the product or service. For instance, the mission of OneWorld Health is to provide cheap medicines to poor people who otherwise could not afford them. The organization therefore tries to set its prices not on the basis of perceived value or even costs but on the ability of the beneficiaries to pay. This is also true for organizations that help distribute AIDS drugs to patients in Africa. Some of these medicines are subsidized to reduce their costs and therefore the price per treatment.

2.3   Promotion

"Promotion" refers to the set of activities a firm undertakes to communicate its products or services to customers with the goal of generating sales. There are several promotional activities that commercial enterprises undertake to promote their products or services. However, for social ventures, the landscape may be different because of limited resources. Thus, it would be better for social ventures to focus on just three promotional activities that all have the potential to create awareness and attract interest for relatively little outlay:

- advertising;
- social media; and
- public relations.

2.3.1   Advertising for Social Ventures

Advertising is commonly defined as any activity whose goal is to create awareness of a product or service with the goal of persuading people to buy it. Social entrepreneurs may use it to create awareness of their products or services with the intention of attracting beneficiaries, investors, and/or donors. Advertising could be a means of disseminating information, because one of the problems in delivering social services is that the beneficiaries often do not know about these services. It may also be used to solicit donations. An illustrative example is St. Jude Hospital, which uses direct mailing to solicit donations and explain its social mission. As a token of appreciation, it offers small notepads and self-sticking address labels to potential contributors.

Hybrid and for-profit social ventures can use advertising much as commercial ventures do. Commercial advertising is used for the following reasons:

- to raise customers' awareness of a product or service;
- to explain a product's or service's comparative features and benefits; and
- to create associations between a product or service and a certain lifestyle.

Just as companies advertise their products or services through a variety of means, including direct mail, radio, television, newspapers, magazines, the internet, and social media, social ventures could use the same means to advertise their services or to solicit donations. For example, Childfund International (www.childfund.org)—a nonprofit organization devoted to helping children in poor countries—uses TV commercials to solicit donations and create awareness of the organization's program. The commercials ask viewers to sponsor a needy child for less than a dollar a day and conclude with the slogan "Say yes to a child." These days, such messages are often delivered via social media, which is discussed next.

2.3.2   Social Media

Many companies now use social media—including social networking sites and blogs—to promote their products and services. For example, blogs familiarize potential customers with a business and help build an emotional bond between the business and its customers. Similarly, social ventures can use them to create a community of stakeholders, including beneficiaries, donors, and members of the public, and to inform those stakeholders about new developments and future prospects. Ever more social ventures are also now using the likes of Twitter, LinkedIn, YouTube, and Facebook to facilitate relationship-building and stakeholder engagement.[25] For example, most of the social ventures discussed in this book have posted YouTube videos, and several have a presence on Care2 (www.care2.com), a website that promotes healthy and green lifestyles and often takes action on social causes.

Any social venture that plans to use social media to promote its products or services must have an integrated plan. First, it should select which social media to use. Second, it should designate a person to coordinate and update the organization's messages on the social media site. As social media are all about sharing and interaction, the social venture must update its information constantly. Some industry gurus claim that an organization that does not participate in Facebook, YouTube, and even Second Life is not part of cyberspace any more.[26] Social media is a good way for a firm to interact with its customers. For example, Starbucks has a social media platform—My Starbucks Idea—where customers submit their ideas for the company. Social media can also help with the co-creation of brand. By interacting with key stakeholders on social media, social ventures can build strong brands.

2.3.3 Public Relations

Another means of promoting a company and its products or services is through public relations. A public relations campaign is generally less expensive than a comparable advertising campaign. The only costs that the company incurs in public relations relate to the time and effort devoted to contacting journalists, bloggers, radio hosts and so forth.

Good public relations can help social ventures build credibility. To do so, social ventures should develop press kits to distribute to members of the media. A press kit generally comprises a statement on the venture's activities and accomplishments to date.[27] Social ventures must inform the public about their activities and can do so through printed media outlets as well as via social media, as discussed in the section above. For example, the local Ghanaian press has published information from the Mercy Project's press kit which outlines the organization's mission of compassion and care. Similarly, participating in CNN's "Heroes of the Year" event can provide free publicity for a social venture; and persuading key government officials or celebrities to endorse a social venture can help it gain legitimacy.

2.4 Place

The fourth element of the marketing mix—place—includes all activities that help to move the product or service from the firm to the customer. Also known as distribution, this includes the network of intermediary organizations that work together to facilitate the movement of goods from producer to end-user. The distribution system may include a *direct channel* (producer to consumer) or an *indirect channel* (producer through middlemen to consumer). A firm must decide whether to sell directly to its customers (direct channel) or through intermediaries (indirect channel). Its choice will depend on what the company considers the best way to reach its customers—there are no hard and fast rules. Companies may rely on direct selling through websites or distribution channels, or on indirect selling through wholesalers and retailers. Similarly, social ventures that make physical products, such as the BRCK (see Chapter 4), might decide to use either direct or indirect channels. The BRCK could be distributed by selling the device on Ushahidi's website. However, in most developing countries, those who need the product may not be able to purchase it online. Therefore, the BRCK would benefit from a combination of direct and indirect selling.

In discussing the distribution network, the entrepreneur must understand the product's supply chain. This is the complete network of businesses involved in obtaining inputs, making goods, and delivering products to customers. The logistics include a system to manage and coordinate the many steps of the supply chain to achieve an efficient flow of materials and exchange of information across the channel. Social ventures that make physical products should therefore develop an understanding of their supply chains. In such cases the distribution systems are closely related to those used in commercial ventures, so any knowledge gleaned from the current literature on commercial supply chains would be useful for social ventures.

Understanding the 4Ps should allow social ventures to develop their marketing capabilities. A marketing capability refers to the integrative process of applying collective organizational knowledge, skills, and resources to market-related needs.[28] A recent study conducted on hybrid social enterprises in the United Kingdom and Japan showed that in the case of British social ventures the marketing capabilities of pricing, product, and market information management were positively associated with social performance, whereas pricing, product, and channel management were positively associated with economic performance. In the case of Japanese social ventures, however, none of the marketing capabilities was associated with either social or economic performance.[29] The study therefore concluded that not all marketing capabilities are positively associated with social enterprise performance. Hence, social ventures must be selective in their choice of marketing capabilities. This is particularly important because of the unique context in which each social venture operates.

Social entrepreneurs can improve their marketing capabilities by being cognizant of the tools and techniques of social marketing. The next section discusses this and explains how social entrepreneurs can use it as an effective marketing tool.

3   Social Marketing: A Tool for Social Ventures

3.1   Definition and Nature of Social Marketing

The history of social marketing can be traced back to the early 1950s, when the American sociologist G. D. Wiebe posed the question: "Why can't you sell brotherhood as you sell soap?"[30] This question implies that businesses are more effective than social causes at marketing themselves, so the latter should learn from the commercial world's example. Wiebe concluded that the more a social change campaign mimics a commercial marketing campaign, the more likely it is to succeed.[31] Almost two decades later, Kotler and Levy coined the term "social marketing" when describing marketing activities in the nonprofit sector in their seminal 1969 article, "Broadening the concept of marketing."[32] Then, in 1971, Kotler and Zaltman defined social marketing as the design, implementation, and control of programs calculated to influence the acceptability of social ideas and involving considerations of product planning, pricing, communication, and marketing research.[33] This definition was subsequently echoed and refined by several scholars, who argued that social marketing is the application of marketing knowledge, concepts, and techniques to enhance social as well as economic issues.[34] Social marketing is also considered as the application of commercial marketing technologies to the analysis, planning, execution, and evaluation of programs designed to influence the voluntary behavior of target audiences in order to improve their personal welfare and that of wider society.[35] Defined as such, social marketing is not limited to social advertising or social communication.[36] It can be applied to a wide variety of social problems. It is used in nonprofit organizations, such as hospitals, colleges, social service agencies, cultural organizations, and organizations that combat poverty and disease in the developing world.[37]

These various definitions of social marketing all imply that there is more to it than the mere communication to the public of a social cause through an advertising campaign, however carefully crafted. Rather, social marketing can be construed as a "package" that helps market a particular product or service that addresses a specific social problem. It coordinates product, price, place, and promotion factors (the four Ps) to motivate and facilitate desired forms of behavior,[38] then enacts social change via:

- market research;
- product or service development;
- use of incentives; and
- facilitation.

With social marketing, it is important to understand the needs of the market, just as a company would with its marketing. While it may seem appropriate to take the tradition of the four Ps as gospel, doing so might blind a social entrepreneur to important differences at the heart of the entrepreneurial experience. For example, some marketing scholars argue that strict adherence to the four Ps misses the fundamental point of marketing, which is adaptability, flexibility, and responsiveness,[39] and that it is both wasteful and inappropriate, and consequently ineffective.[40]

3.2   Importance of Social Marketing for Social Entrepreneurs

When applying social marketing techniques to their ventures, social entrepreneurs must clearly understand the needs of the population they want to help. This implies that a needs assessment must be performed. This can be done through sound market research. Once the market is understood, social entrepreneurs should design their product or service accordingly. Surprisingly, social entrepreneurs sometimes do not understand what their own product or service actually is. In social marketing, a seller must package the social idea in such a manner that the target audience finds it appealing and is willing to acquire or use it.[41] Often, this entails offering incentives to convince the potential beneficiaries to use the product or service. For example, a social venture that promotes healthy lifestyles may provide some incentives to potential beneficiaries to change their diet. The facilitation activity in social marketing includes social advertising and communication to create not only awareness but also opportunities for behavioral change. In fact, social marketing is concerned not only with persuading people to adopt new behaviors but also with facilitating the maintenance of those behaviors.[42]

Social marketing was used to introduce a project aimed at reducing destructive fishing practices in southwest Madagascar, an African island nation in the Indian Ocean. The campaign resulted in a reduction in such practices in the targeted communities.[43] A more recent example is the use of social marketing to create awareness and encourage people to protect themselves against Ebola in Guinea, Liberia, and Sierra Leone, the three countries worst affected by the epidemic in 2014.

For-profit organizations may also employ social marketing.[44] As an example, insurance companies were instrumental in the campaign to promote the use of car seat belts. Of course, they had a vested interest in this because people are more likely to avoid serious injury during crashes if they use seat belts.

4   Developing a Social Venture Marketing Plan

This section focuses on developing marketing plans for social ventures. However, before discussing the various steps in detail, it is important to revisit the key elements of a traditional marketing plan.

4.1   Understanding the Key Components of a Marketing Plan

A marketing plan is a written document that outlines a company's entire marketing strategy and tactical actions. It is the main tool for organizing and managing a marketing effort. It invariably starts with an executive summary, which provides a short overview that will help marketing managers to grasp the key elements of the plan. This should contain all of the critical information that a busy marketing manager will need in order to decide whether to continue reading the whole plan. The section on the analysis of the current marketing situation must provide information relating to the four elements of the marketing mix as well as any competitors. The section on the opportunity or opportunities to be exploited should basically comprise a SWOT analysis. In other words, it is important to include a clear assessment of the product's or service's strengths, weaknesses, opportunities, and threats.

The objectives of the marketing plan must be clearly specified because these will serve as the yardsticks against which to measure the plan's success. In addition, the overall marketing strategy should be defined and explained. The social entrepreneur must also detail exactly how the marketing plan will be executed, including financial projections and anticipated costs. Finally, a control mechanism—comprising a set of monitoring mechanisms—must be designed to assess the marketing plan's effectiveness. This will keep the implementation of the plan in line with the organization's objectives by monitoring action programs, analyzing performance results, and, if necessary, taking corrective action.[45]

These elements should all prove useful when devising a marketing plan for a social venture, as should those that are detailed in the next sub-section.

4.2   Elements of a Social Venture Marketing Plan

It will be remembered that the social venture plan discussed in Chapter 8 included a section on marketing strategy. Now we explore the steps involved in building the marketing plan of a social venture. Table 9.1 illustrates the key components of such a plan. As it indicates, each plan should start with an executive summary as in the case of a traditional marketing plan. However, the social entrepreneur must perform a needs assessment before starting his or her social venture. Indeed, the needs assessment should occur at the beginning of a social venture. After all, the mission of a social venture is to address a particular social need. The social entrepreneur should also perform a stakeholder analysis, which consists of identifying potential stakeholders who might be interested in the social venture and its products or services. The following questions are important at this stage:

- Who are the social venture's stakeholders?
- What are their expectations?
- How will those expectations be met?
- What type of support can they provide?
- How will the stakeholders be enlisted?

Table 9.1 Steps in building a social venture marketing plan

Steps	Actions
1. Executive summary	Define the plan's goals in terms of sales, market share, and profit.
2. Needs assessment	Identify the social needs the venture is addressing. Determine how the needs are addressed.
3. Stakeholder analysis	Who are the social venture's stakeholders? What are their expectations? How will their expectations be met? What type of support can they provide? How will their support be enlisted?
4. Social venture landscape analysis	Who are the social venture's competitors? What is the social venture's position? How does the social venture intend to differentiate itself from its competitors? With whom can the social venture cooperate?
5. Social marketing mix (product/service, price, place, promotion)	How will the product or service be designed to meet the social need? Should the product or service be given away for free or bought by beneficiaries? If the product or service is to be bought, how much should it cost and who should pay? How should the social venture communicate with beneficiaries and other stakeholders? Which form of media should be used? Where should the product or service be distributed?
6. Objectives	Define the plan's goals in terms of number of beneficiaries to reach, sustainability of the venture, and social profit.
7. Plan of action	Detail the concrete steps and actions that will be taken to execute the plan.
8. Financial projections	Explain the financial implications of the plan. Are the costs bearable, based on the financial resources available?
9. Control mechanisms	Explain how the success of the plan will be measured? Anticipate potential corrective actions in case of failure.

All of these questions should be thoroughly addressed. Doing so should help the social venture to focus on its mission and attract potential donors and other stakeholders.

When developing the marketing plan for a social venture, the social entrepreneur must also analyze the competitive landscape, even though competition in social entrepreneurship is generally not as fierce as it is in the commercial world. The following questions should be addressed:

- Who are the social venture's competitors?
- What is the social venture's position?
- With whom might the social venture cooperate?
- Are other social ventures already addressing similar needs?
- If yes, how will the new social venture differentiate itself from them?
- Should it compete against or cooperate with them?

The fifth element of the social marketing plan is the social marketing mix. As in a regular marketing plan, the social marketing mix comprises the four Ps that must be clearly addressed.

When the social entrepreneur has determined that a particular social need exists and must be addressed, he or she should design the best product or service to address it. This product or service should be tailored to the needs of the potential beneficiaries. Some products do not need to be sophisticated for use in some areas. For example, the BRCK device described in Chapter 4 is simple enough to be used by customers in African villages, and it is affordable. The social entrepreneur must also decide whether the product or service will be given away for free to the beneficiaries or purchased. If it is to be given away, then the social entrepreneur must determine how the venture will make the product or deliver the service and how it will remain sustainable over time. If the product or service is to be purchased, it is important to set a price that allows the venture to fulfill its social mission. Then it must be decided whether the beneficiaries will pay for the product or service themselves or whether a third party will purchase it on their behalf.

Next, the social entrepreneur should develop strategies to promote the social venture. The following questions must be carefully addressed:

- How should the social entrepreneur communicate with beneficiaries and other stakeholders?
- Which form of media should be used?

An effective promotional campaign can help a social venture reach its customers and brand itself. A poor promotional campaign can prevent a social venture from accomplishing its social mission. The social venture must also determine where to deliver the product or service. This is a particularly important consideration in poor countries, where roads and other components of the physical infrastructure are often deficient. An illustrative example is the mobile hospital provided by Ascovime in rural Cameroon (see below). Reaching the village populations who need this free healthcare service is challenging because of the lack of paved roads in remote parts of the country.

The sixth element of the social marketing plan entails defining its objectives.

- Why is the social venture developing a marketing plan?
- What objectives must the plan accomplish?
- How will the success of the plan be gauged?

There are two reasons for setting clear objectives: it keeps the social entrepreneur focused on the most important aspects of the plan; and it establishes internal benchmarks against which to measure the plan's success.

The seventh element involves describing the concrete steps that will be taken to implement the plan.

The eighth element entails outlining the financial implications of the plan clearly. Since most social ventures are resource-limited, it is important to understand whether the costs of developing and implementing a social marketing plan are bearable for the social venture.

Finally, as in a traditional marketing plan, the social marketing plan should include control mechanisms that are designed to monitor the success of the plan and implement corrective actions, if necessary.

The marketing plan for social ventures can be integrated within the social venture plan (see Chapter 8) or developed as a standalone document. The latter is probably more appropriate if an established social venture is developing a marketing strategy to improve its connections with beneficiaries and stakeholders. However, if a social entrepreneur is working on a startup, the marketing strategy would usually form part of the overall social venture plan.

A marketing plan should always focus on understanding how the use of marketing tools and techniques will allow the venture to serve its customers and, if necessary, compete with other ventures. The same is true for a social venture marketing plan, which allows the social entrepreneur to develop a beneficiary and stakeholder orientation.

Summary

This chapter presented the marketing challenges that social ventures face. The marketing tools a social enterprise uses to address these challenges may depend on the form the venture takes. Marketing in a purely philanthropic social venture will probably differ from that employed by a hybrid or for-profit social venture. Whatever the form, though, the chapter emphasized the important role of marketing in establishing connections between the social venture and its stakeholders—mainly beneficiaries, investors and donors, and the general public. The chapter also explained that the basic elements of marketing—such as market segmentation, target markets, and the elements of the marketing mix—could be applied to social entrepreneurship. Finally, the chapter provided guidelines on how to develop a marketing plan for a social venture.

Key Terms

Brand; branding; buzz marketing; entrepreneurial marketing; guerrilla marketing; marketing; marketing control system; marketing mix; marketing plan; market segment; place; price; product; promotion; public relations; relational marketing; social marketing; viral marketing

Review Questions

1 Do you think social ventures should market their products or services (yes or no)? Explain.
2 Should social ventures segment their markets?
3 Explain the difference between marketing for social ventures and cause-related marketing.
4 Is social marketing different from marketing for social ventures (yes or no)? Explain.

5   Discuss the importance of social media for social ventures.
6   Identify the difference(s) between social marketing and commercial marketing.
7   Explain why social ventures should integrate the four Ps in their marketing campaigns.
8   Explain how understanding marketing concepts and techniques could help social ventures design more effective products or services.
9   Explain the differences and similarities between selling a product or service in a commercial venture and selling a product or service in a social venture.
10 Explain each of the four components of a social marketing campaign.

Application Questions

1   Watch the video at www.youtube.com/watch?v=33si-6BkkMk\ and answer the following questions. What do you think about texting while driving? Texting while driving is prohibited in some parts of the United States and in other countries. Do you agree with such laws (yes or no)? Explain.
2   Suppose that you have been asked to design a social media strategy for a social venture. How would you proceed and what social media would you choose? Explain.
3   You have been asked to develop a social marketing plan for a purely philanthropic social venture. Describe the key components of your social marketing plan. Also describe how you would implement the plan and assess its effectiveness.
4   Suppose you and two of your friends have recently started a social venture aimed at reducing the incidence of malaria in an African country. Select the country that the social venture will target. How will you package your service(s) in this particular country? What do you need to know about the country? How will you measure the success of your social venture?
5   You have been asked to develop a public relations campaign for a recently launched social venture that helps street children in São Paulo, Brazil. Describe how you would develop and implement such a campaign.

Application Case 1: Ascovime: The Mobile Hospital in Cameroon

In 2008, Dr. Georges Bwelle, a surgeon at the hospital in Yaounde, launched Ascovime to provide free healthcare to Cameroon's rural populations. In addition to addressing healthcare, Ascovime offers free books to schoolchildren and teachers. Most rural populations in Cameroon and elsewhere in sub-Saharan Africa do not have access to healthcare facilities because of the poor infrastructure, such as roads, electricity, and running water. Moreover, the lack of physicians, endemic corruption, and mismanagement make matters worse. It was in this context that Dr. Bwelle decided to launch his mobile clinic.

The mobile clinic concept did not originate in Cameroon—by 2008, several were already operating in other sub-Saharan African countries and elsewhere around the world. However, Ascovime is different because it is organized as a social venture that does not rely on the government but rather on the vision of Dr. Bwelle. Moreover, it is staffed entirely by volunteers from several countries, including Belgium, France, Spain, and the United States, and funded by a combination of donations and a proportion of Dr. Bwelle's private salary.

Since 2008, Ascovime has provided free medical care to more than 32,000 patients. Although Dr. Bwelle does not formally advertise his social venture or the services it offers, his media appearances have generated significant visibility and name recognition. For instance, several YouTube videos provide details of the venture and its services. However, its principal marketing tool remains word-of-mouth, since those who have received free healthcare through the mobile clinic inform others about it.

In 2010, Dick Gordon of North Carolina Public Radio interviewed Dr. Bwelle on his radio show, which generated several positive tweets on Twitter and a degree of free publicity for Ascovime. Three years later, Dr. Bwelle was nominated as one of the ten "CNN Heroes" for 2013. The nomination ceremony—held in the United States in December of that year—allowed him to raise Ascovime's profile still further by relating the clinic's story to a large, supportive audience.

Discussion Questions

1 How are social media helping Ascovime and Dr. Bwelle gain visibility?
2 Watch the video about Ascovime and Dr. Bwelle at www.youtube.com/watch?v=SEQ1B34mOLc and describe your reactions to the story and the organization's work.
3 Based on your understanding of the work of Ascovime, would you volunteer to provide any service you could to the organization (yes or no)? Explain.
4 If you were asked to develop a marketing plan for Ascovime, how would you proceed? How would you implement such a plan? How would you measure its success?

References

1 Trekking through mud, rivers, and jungle to provide free medical care. *http://www.cnn.com/2013/08/01/world/africa/cnnheroes-bwelle-cameroon-doctor/index.html*. [Retrieved, September 30, 2015].
2 The doctor who travels through every snag to deliver free medical care in all corners of Cameroon. *http://achhikhabre.com/georges-bwelle-cnn-hero-cameroon-free-medical-care*. [Retrieved, September 30, 2015]. Website: www.ascovime.org

Application Case 2: BlinkNow Foundation

It is often said that one person can make a difference. Indeed, Maggie Doyne, once a high school student and a part-time babysitter in New Jersey, is making a difference in the lives of children and women in Nepal. After a trip in Nepal during which she had the opportunity to witness poverty first-hand, she decided to take action. Doyne was born in Mendham Borough, New Jersey. After graduating from high school in 2005, she took a gap year to travel to India and Nepal before deciding whether to attend college. It is during this trip that she discovered her true passion—caring for children. She took $5,000 from her own savings and bought a piece of land in Surkhet, in the western district of Nepal.[1] In addition to her personal savings, she raised $60,000 with the help of friends and benefactors. She then completed the first facility, the Kopila Valley Children's Home, which opened its doors in 2008 with 44 students. Today, it houses more than 50 children who are orphaned. Two years later, she opened the Kopila Valley Primary School with 220 students in 2010.[2] The school enrollment now is more than 370 students. She also built a women's center.

She started the BlinkNow Foundation (http://www.blinknow.org) to support her activities. BlinkNow Foundation's mission is to empower young people to become pioneers in developing their own solutions to world poverty.[3] It accomplishes its mission by providing an education and a loving, caring home for orphaned, impoverished and at-risk children as well as women. By so doing, BlinkNow contributes to the reduction of poverty, the empowerment of women, the improvement of health, sustainability and social justice in Nepal. The project started in successive steps. She started first with a home to take care of orphaned children and then added a school. She then created a center for women and later added a small clinic and a counseling center. To be sustainable, the project decided to grow its own food. Recently, BlinkNow Foundation bought a new property and is moving toward using solar energy and has plans to build a high school. The place functions like a community where people are caring for one another.

BlinkNow Foundation has a heavy social media presence on Facebook, Twitter, and Instagram. It relies on individual contributions, grants and donations to sustain itself and fund its activities. For example, on its website (http://www.blinknow.org) it solicits donations. To be self-sufficient, it grows its own food. Doyne won numerous awards for her efforts including the 2013 Forbes Excellence in Education Award, the 2014 Unsung Hero of Compassion, awarded by the Dalai Lama, and the 2015 CNN Hero of the Year Award. During her 2015 CNN Hero of the Year's Award ceremony she empathetically indicated that people have the power to create the world that they want to live in, just as they want it.[4]

Discussion Questions

1 Suppose you have been hired as a consultant to increase awareness about BlinkNow and its activities. How would you use social media to market its activities?

2 If you were in charge of designing a media campaign for BlinkNow, what would you like the public to know about it? How would you create a social brand for BlinkNow?

3 Explain to what extent winning awards, such as the CNN Hero of the Year Award or the Forbes Excellence in Education Award, represents a form of publicity.

4 Watch the YouTube video at https://www.youtube.com/watch?v=xDqypdBkQHM. What is your impression of the work done by BlinkNow? Would you donate money or other resources such as books and school supplies to this social venture? Yes? No? Explain.

References

1 How babysitting money planted a seed to help Nepali kids blossom. *http://www.cnn.com/2015/04/09/living/cnnheroes-doyne*.

2 How babysitting money planted a seed to help Nepali kids blossom. *http://www.cnn.com/2015/04/09/living/cnnheroes-doyne*.

3 Huffpost greatest person of the day: Maggie Doyne builds orphanage and school for kids in Nepal. *http://www.huffingtonpost.com/2011/06/01/maggie-doyne-blinknow-nepal_n_869906.html*. [Retrieved on April 15, 2016].

4 How babysitting money planted a seed to help Nepali kids blossom. *http://www.cnn.com/2015/04/09/living/cnnheroes-doyne*.

Notes

1 Kotler, P. T., & Armstrong, G. (2015). *Principles of marketing*. Upper Saddle River, NJ: Pearson/ Prentice-Hall.

2 Hills, G. E., Hultman, C. M., & Miles, M. P. (2008). The evolution and development of entrepreneurial marketing. *Journal of Small Business Management*, 46(1), 99–113.

3 Morris, M. H., Berthon, P. R., Pitt, L. F., Murgolo-poore, M. E., & Ramshaw, W. F. (2001). An entrepreneurial perspective on the marketing of charities. *Journal of Nonprofit and Public Sector Marketing*, 9(3), 75–87.

4 Hills, G., C. Hultman, C., Kraus, S., & Schulte, R. (2010). History, theory and evidence of entrepreneurial marketing: An overview. *International Journal of Entrepreneurship and Innovation Management*, 11(1), 3–18.

5 Choi, S. (2014). Learning organization and market orientation as catalyst for innovation in nonprofit organizations. *Nonprofit and Voluntary Sector Quarterly*, 43(2), 393–413.

6 Hills, G. E., & Hultman, C. (2013). Entrepreneurial marketing: Conceptual and empirical research opportunities. *Entrepreneurship Research Journal*, 3(4), 437–448; Hills, G. E., Hultman, C., Kraus, S., & Schulte, R. (2010). History, theory and evidence of entrepreneurial marketing: An overview. *International Journal of Entrepreneurship and Innovation Management*, 11(1), 3–18; Bjerke, B., & Hultman, C. L. (2002). *Entrepreneurial marketing: The growth of small firms in the new economy era*. Aldershot: Edward Elgar; Collison, E. M., & Shaw, E. (2001). Entrepreneurial marketing: A historical perspective on development and practice. *Management Decision*, 39(2), 761–767; Stokes, D. (1995). *Small business management: An active learning approach*. London: D. P. Publications.

7 Miles, M., Gilmore, A., Harrigan, P., Lewis, G., & Sethna, Z. (2015). Exploring entrepreneurial marketing. *Journal of Strategic Marketing*, 23(2), 94–111; Hills, G. E., & Hultman, C. (2013). Entrepreneurial marketing: Conceptual and empirical research opportunities. *Entrepreneurship Research Journal*, 3(4), 437–448; Hills, G. E., Hultman, C., Kraus, S., & Schulte, R. (2010). History, theory and evidence of entrepreneurial marketing: An overview. *International Journal of Entrepreneurship and Innovation Management*, 11(1), 3–18; Stokes, D. (1995). *Small business management: An active learning approach*. London: D. P. Publications, Ltd.

8 Shaw, E. (2004). Marketing in the social enterprise context: Is it entrepreneurial? *Qualitative Market Research: An International Journal*, 7(3), 194–205.

9 Shaw, E. (2004). Marketing in the social enterprise context: Is it entrepreneurial? *Qualitative Market Research: An International Journal*, 7(3), 194–205.

10 Shaw, E. (2004). Marketing in the social enterprise context: Is it entrepreneurial? *Qualitative Market Research: An International Journal*, 7(3), 194–205.

11 Morris, M. H., Schindehutte, M., & LaForge, R.W. (2002). Entrepreneurial marketing: A construct for integrating emerging entrepreneurship and marketing perspectives. *Journal of Marketing Theory and Practice*, 10(4), 1–19.

12 Levinson, J. C. (1984). *Guerrilla marketing: Secrets for making big profits from your small business*. Boston: Houghton Mifflin.

13 Gruber, M. (2004). Marketing in new ventures: Theory and empirical evidence. *Schmalenbach Business Review*, 56, 164–199.

14 Morris, M. H., Berthon, P. R., Pitt, L. F., Murgolo-poore, M. E., & Ramshaw, W. F. (2001). An entrepreneurial perspective on the marketing of charities. *Journal of Nonprofit and Public Sector Marketing*, 9(3), 75–87.

15 Levinson, C. J., Adkins, F., & Forbes, C. (2010). *Guerrilla marketing for nonprofits: 250 tactics to promote, motivate, and raise more money*. Irvine, CA: Entrepreneur Press.

16 Groeger, L., & Buttle, F. (2014). Word-of-mouth marketing influence on offline and online communications: Evidence from case study research. *Journal of Marketing Communications*, 20(1/2), 21–41; Rosenbloom, R. S. (2000). Leadership, capabilities, and technological change: The transformation of NCR in the electronic era. *Strategic Management Journal*, 21(10/11), 1083–1103.

17 Ahuja, R. D., Michels, T. A., Walker, M. M., & Weissbuch, M. (2007). Ten perceptions of disclosure in buzz marketing. *Journal of Consumer Marketing*, 24(3), 151–159.

18 Schulze, C., Schöler, L., & Skiera, B. (2014). Not all fun and games: Viral marketing for utilitarian products. *Journal of Marketing*, 78(1), 1–19; Camarero, C., & San Jose, R. (2011). Social and attitudinal determinants of viral marketing dynamics. *Computers in Human Behavior*, 27(6), 2292–2300; Scott, M. D. (2010). *The new rules of marketing and PR: How to use social media, blogs and news releases, online video, viral marketing to reach buyers directly*. Hoboken, NJ: Wiley & Sons; Phelps, J. E., Lewis, R., Mobilio, L., Perry, D., & Raman, N. (2004). Viral marketing or electronic word-of-mouth advertising: Examining consumer responses and motivations to pass along email. *Journal of Advertising Research*, 44(4), 333–348; Godin, S., & Gladwell, M. (2001). *Unleashing the idea virus*. San Francisco: Do You Zoom Inc.

19 Rosenbloom, R. S. (2000). Leadership, capabilities, and technological change: The transformation of NCR in the electronic era. *Strategic Management Journal*, 21(10/11), 1083–1103.

20 Kotler, P., & Levy, S. (1969). Broadening the concept of marketing. *Journal of Marketing*, 33(1), 10–15; Morris, M. H., & Joyce, M. (1998). On the measurement of entrepreneurial behavior in not-for-profit organizations: Implications for social marketing. *Social Marketing Quarterly*, 4(4), 1–23.

21 Liu, G., Chapleo, C., Ko, W. W., & Ngugi, I. K. (2015). The role of internal branding in nonprofit brand management: An empirical investigation. *Nonprofit and Voluntary Sector Quarterly*, 44(2), 319–339.

22 Morgan, R. M., & Hunt, S. D. (1994). The commitment-trust theory of relationship marketing. *Journal of Marketing*, 58(3), 20–38.

23 Kotler, P. T., & Armstrong, G. (2015). *Principles of marketing*. Upper Saddle River, NJ: Pearson/Prentice-Hall;Boone, L. E., & Kurtz, D. L. (2012). *Contemporary marketing*. 15th edition. Cincinnati, OH: Cengage Learning.

24 Barringer, R. B., & Ireland, R. D. (2016). *Entrepreneurship: Successfully launching new ventures*. 5th edition. New York: Pearson; Barringer, R. B., & Ireland, R. D. (2012). *Entrepreneurship: Successfully launching new ventures*. 4th edition. New York: Pearson.

25 Svensson, P. G., Mahoney, T. Q., & Hambrick, M. E. (2015). Twitter as a communication tool for nonprofits: A study of sport-for-development organizations. *Nonprofit and Voluntary Sector Quarterly*, 44(6), 1086–1106; Guo, C., & Saxton, G. D. (2014). Tweeting social change: How social media are changing nonprofit advocacy. *Nonprofit and Voluntary Sector Quarterly*, 43(1), 57–79; Nah, S., & Saxton, G. D. (2013). Modeling the adoption and use of social media by nonprofit organizations. *New Media & Society*, 15(2), 294–313; Lovejoy, K., & Saxton, G. D. (2012). Information, community, and action: How nonprofit organizations use social media. *Journal of Computer-Mediated Communication*, 17(3), 337–353; Lovejoy, K., Waters, R. D., & Saxton, G. D. (2012). Engaging stakeholders through Twitter: How nonprofit organizations are getting more out of 140 characters or less. *Public Relations Review*, 38(2), 313–318.

26 Kaplan, M. A., & Haenlein, M. (2010). Users of the world unite! The challenges and opportunities of social media. *Business Horizons*, 53(1), 59–68.

27 Barringer, R. B., & Ireland, R. D. (2016). *Entrepreneurship: Successfully launching new ventures*. 5th edition. New York: Pearson; Barringer, R. B., & Ireland, R. D. (2012). *Entrepreneurship: Successfully launching new ventures*. 4th edition. New York: Pearson.

28 Liu, G., Eng, T. Y., & Takeda, S. (2015). An investigation of marketing capabilities and social performance in the UK and Japan. *Entrepreneurship Theory and Practice*, 39(2), 267–298.

29 Liu, G., Eng, T. Y., & Takeda, S. (2015). An investigation of marketing capabilities and social performance in the UK and Japan. *Entrepreneurship Theory and Practice*, 39(2), 267–298.

30   Wiebe, G. D. (1951–1952). Merchandising commodities and citizenship on television. *Public Opinion Quarterly, 15*(4), 679–691.
31   Wiebe, G. D. (1951–1952). Merchandising commodities and citizenship on television. *Public Opinion Quarterly, 15*(4), 679–691.
32   Kotler, P., & Levy, S. (1969). Broadening the concept of marketing. *Journal of Marketing, 33*(1), 10–15.
33   Kotler, P., & Zaltman, G. (1971). Social marketing: An approach to plan social change. *Journal of Marketing, 35*(3), 3–12.
34   Lazer, W., & Kelley, E. J. (Eds.) (1973). *Social marketing: Perspectives and viewpoints.* Homewood, IL: Richard D. Irwin.
35   Andreasen, R. A. (1994). Social marketing: Definition and domain. *Journal of Public Policy & Marketing, 13*(1), 108–114; Andreasen, R. A. (2003). The life trajectory of social marketing: Some implications. *Marketing Theory, 3*(3), 293–303; Andreasen, R. A. (2006). *Social marketing in the 21st century.* Thousands Oak, CA: Sage Publications.
36   Fox, K. F. A., & Kotler, P. (1980). The marketing of social causes: The first ten years. *Journal of Marketing, 44*(4), 24–33.
37   Fox, K. F. A., & Kotler, P. (1980). The marketing of social causes: The first ten years. *Journal of Marketing, 44*(4), 24–33.
38   Kamin, T., & Anker, T. (2014). Cultural capital and strategic social marketing orientations. *Journal of Social Marketing, 4*(2), 94–110; Burchell, K., Rettie, R., & Patel, K. (2013). Marketing social norms: Social marketing and the social norm approach. *Journal of Consumer Behavior, 12*(1), 1–9; Lee, N. R., & Kotler, P. (2011). *Social marketing: Influencing behaviors for good.* 4th edition. Thousand Oaks, CA: Sage Publications; Dann, S. (2010). Redefining social marketing with contemporary commercial marketing definitions. *Journal of Business Research, 63*(2), 147–153; Fox, K. F. A., & Kotler, P. (1980). The marketing of social causes: The first ten years. *Journal of Marketing, 44*(4), 24–33.
39   McKenna, R. (1991). *Relationship marketing: Successful strategies for the age of the customer.* Reading, MA: Addison-Wesley.
40   Carson, D. (1993). A philosophy for marketing education in small firms. *Journal of Marketing Management, 9*(2), 189–204.
41   Kotler, P., & Zaltman, G. (1971). Social marketing: An approach to plan social change. *Journal of Marketing, 35*(3), 3–12.
42   Fox, K. F. A., & Kotler, P. (1980). The marketing of social causes: The first ten years. *Journal of Marketing, 44*(4), 24–33.
43   Andriamalala, G., Peabody, S., Gardner, J. C., & Westerman, K. (2013). Using social marketing to foster sustainable behavior in traditional communities in southwest Madagascar. *Conservation Evidence, 10*, 37–41.
44   Kotler, P. (1979). Strategies for introducing marketing into nonprofit organizations. *Journal of Marketing, 43*(1), 37–44; Kotler, P., & Roberto, E. (1989). *Social marketing: Strategies for changing public behavior.* New York: The Free Press.
45   Saini, A., Krush, M., & Johnson, J. L. (2008). Anomie and the marketing of function: The role of control mechanisms. *Journal of Business Ethics, 83*(4), 845–862.

Chapter 10

Managing the Financial Side of Social Ventures

Learning Objectives

1 Describe the importance of raising capital for social ventures.
2 Identify sources for raising capital for social ventures.
3 Learn how to manage social venture finances.
4 Develop skills to assess the financial viability of a social venture.

One of the key elements of starting and running a social venture is to find capital. Without money, however small the amount, no venture can begin. But securing the financial resources to start a new venture is not always an easy task, particularly for social ventures that do not often provide positive financial returns on investment. The purpose of this chapter is to explore how social ventures raise much-needed capital and manage their financial resources. It intends to help students and would-be social entrepreneurs to address the following questions:

- How do social ventures raise the funds they need?
- Are the conventional fundraising techniques that are used by commercial ventures applicable to social ventures?
- Can other means of raising funds, such as bootstrapping, microfinancing, and crowd-funding, work for social ventures?

After all, raising the money to start a new venture, be it commercial or social, is a delicate balancing act.[1]

The chapter is divided into three main sections. The first section discusses the sources and strategies for raising capital for social ventures. The second addresses the management of the financial assets of social ventures. The third describes the means for assessing the financial vitality of a social venture.

1 Raising Capital for Social Ventures

Firm financing is a critical entrepreneurial activity[2] that is usually defined as the acquisition of funding and the management of these resources.[3] For example, a social entrepreneur may decide to keep his or her venture small and thereby maintain tight control. In such a situation, the social entrepreneur may be better off relying on personal funds, debt, or bootstrapping. However, if the social entrepreneur expects to grow the social venture regardless of maintaining control, he or she may turn to social angels or social venture capitalists. In this case, social entrepreneurs should seek investors who are interested in both social impact and financial performance. Known as *impact investors*, these investors may expect competitive returns but at least they will understand the social venture's multiple priorities and value a diversity of goals and outcomes.[4] The impact of social ventures, including such topics as social accounting and auditing, blending value accounting (BVA), and social return on investment (SROI), will be discussed in detail in Chapter 14.

All examples of social entrepreneurship and social innovation need financial resources to start, grow, and go to scale.[5] Before discussing the importance of raising money for social ventures, however, it is necessary to explain one or two of the basics of financial management. This is important because the form adopted by the social venture (purely philanthropic, hybrid, or for-profit) may affect its bottom line. Financial management deals with two activities: raising money; and managing finances in a way that yields the highest positive return on investment. The financial objectives of a firm are fourfold: profitability; liquidity; efficiency; and stability. These objectives, although generally applied to the management of for-profit organizations, are also relevant for social ventures. In fact, no social venture can accomplish its social mission if it lacks adequate financial resources. Table 10.1 compares commercial and social ventures in regard to these four financial objectives.

Capital is the fuel that powers a social venture, so success can depend on a social entrepreneur's ability to navigate diverse funding sources.[6] Before raising capital, the social entrepreneur must identify the financial needs of his or her social venture. This could be facilitated by writing a formal business plan (see Chapter 8). Although social entrepreneurs may raise capital by using personal funds or relying on friends, there are various other sources they can turn to in order to meet their financial needs. Examples of

Table 10.1 Comparing the financial objectives of commercial and social ventures

Financial objectives	Commercial ventures	Social ventures
Profitability	Ability to earn a profit. Ability to grow and prosper. Ability to remain viable and provide positive ROI.	Ability to generate a surplus. Ability to be sustainable.
Liquidity	Ability to meet short-term obligations. Carefully track inventories and accounts payable.	Ability to meet short-term obligations. Ability to generate earned income, revenue through grants, and/or donations.
Efficiency	Utilize assets effectively relative to revenue and profits.	Utilize assets effectively relative to earned income, revenues from grants, and/or donations, and surplus.
Stability	Strength of financial situation: • make profit; • remain liquid; • keep debt in check.	Strength of financial sustainability: • have resources available to meet social mission; • spend cash wisely.

Table 10.2 Potential sources of funding for social ventures[7]

Personal resources	Relationships	Grants	Fellowships	Crowdfunding	Angels/venture capitalists	Loan providers
Savings accounts	Family	Social Innovation	Acumen Fund	Kiva	Blue Ridge	Calvert Foundation
Credit cards	members	Fund	Ashoka	Cause Vox	Foundation	Shore Bank
Personal lines of	Friends	Kaufman	Echoing Green	Change.org	Calvert Group	Triodos Bank
credit	Contacts and	Foundation	Skoll Foundation	Chase Community	Good Capital	Partners for the
Home equity line	referrals	DoSomething. org	Unreasonable	Giving	Gray Ghost	Common Good
of credit		Google Grants	Institute	Pepsi Refresh	Ventures	Wainwright Bank
				Project	Investors' Circle	
				Kickstarter	Mission Markets	

such funding sources are displayed in Table 10.2. These sources include grants, fellowships, crowdfunding, angels/venture capitalists, and traditional loan providers, such as banks. Most entrepreneurship scholars agree that there are three main reasons why new firms need to raise money: cash-flow challenges; capital investment; and lengthy product development cycles.[8]

For example, the lag between spending to generate revenue and earning income from the firm's operations can generate cash-flow challenges. Because of these challenges, a social venture must track its *burn rate*. In financial management, this refers to the amount of cash a company is using during a given period (usually a set number of months). Suppose that the social venture Dignified Mobile Toilets (discussed in Chapter 3) has a burn rate of $15,000 per month and $180,000 in the bank. That will mean it can survive for only a year (12 months) on its available cash. At the end of the year, it will need an additional influx of cash; otherwise, it will face severe cash-flow problems.

Because social ventures often have difficulty attracting funding, especially from investors, it is important that their founders explore several alternative sources. A social venture may also face capital investment challenges. For example, the Global Soap Project (Application Case 2 at the end of this chapter) has recently built a factory in Las Vegas to recycle soap. This is an example of significant capital expenditure by a social venture. The new factory may help Global Soap Project to continue to recycle soap and may also allow it to add other products that could ensure its long-term viability.

1.1   *Personal Sources of Funding for Social Ventures*

Using personal funds consists of tapping into one's own financial resources. Such resources may include savings, checking accounts, credit cards, or home equity lines of credit. In commercial entrepreneurship, the vast majority of founders contribute personal funds as well as *sweat equity* to their ventures. The latter comprises the total time and effort that a founder invests in a new venture.[9] Founders of commercial ventures may also ask friends and family members to fund their new ventures.

Social entrepreneurs frequently turn to their personal funds and friends and relations for money, too. For example, Dr. Georges Bwelle used a portion of his own salary and savings to launch and run Ascovime (see Chapter 9). Although this method of financing a social venture is straightforward and it can help social entrepreneurs to start their ventures, it has some significant drawbacks. For instance, unless the social entrepreneur is extremely wealthy, relying on personal funds and close relationships can limit the scalability of the venture.

1.2 Grants

Grants are another source of funding for social ventures. Organizations such as Ashoka, the Skoll Foundation, the Social Innovation Fund, the Kaufman Foundation, DoSomething. org, and Google Grants provide grants for social ventures. A social entrepreneur who is willing to ask for grants should always consider applying to such foundations, although competition for the funding they offer can be fierce. In the United States, a number of federal agencies and state agencies offer grants to social ventures. Meanwhile, development agencies and donor organizations, such as the World Bank, the United States Agency for International Development (USAID), and the British Agency for Overseas Development, provide funding for social ventures in developing and emerging countries.

1.3 Fellowships and Social Venture Plans Competition

Fellowships are another means of securing funding for social ventures. Examples of such fellowships include those offered by the Acumen Fund, Ashoka, Echoing Green, the Skoll Foundation, and the Unreasonable Institute. The emergence of social entrepreneurship has also led to the development of social venture plan competitions. The University of California at Berkeley and Rice University run such competitions, which can be sources of seed money for starting a social venture. CNN's "Heroes of the Year" competition is another example of a fellowship that can generate considerable publicity and funding opportunities for social ventures. Several of the social entrepreneurs who are featured in this book, including Dr. Georges Bwelle (see Chapter 9) and Derreck Kayongo of the Global Soap Project (see below), have benefited from this program.

Table 10.3 provides a list of fellowship programs for social entrepreneurs. Such fellowships not only provide much-needed funds but can also help social entrepreneurs to learn valuable skills and extend their professional networks.

Table 10.3 List of social entrepreneurship fellowships

Organization	Web address
Acumen Fund	http://acumen.org/leadership/global-fellows/
Ashoka	http://usa.ashoka.org/nominate-ashoka-fellow
Aspen Institute (First Movers)	www.aspeninstitute.org/policy-work/business-society/corporate-programs/first-movers-fellowship-program
Draper Richards Kaplan Foundation	www.drkfoundation.org
Echoing Green	www.echoinggreen.org
IDEO	www.ideo.org/fellows
Kiva	www.kiva.org/fellows
Schwab Foundation	www.schwabfound.org
Skoll Foundation	http://skoll.org/
Social Venture Partners	www.socialventurepartners.org/get-involved/encore-fellows
Stanford University	www.gsb.stanford.edu/stanford-gsb-experience/academic/social-innovation/fellowships/sif
Unreasonable Institute	http://unreasonableinstitute.org
Wharton	http://whartonsocialventurefellows.org

1.4   Social Angels and the Funding of Social Ventures

Angel investors are wealthy individuals who provide funds for startups. Their primary motivation is usually a willingness to help others, but they also often want to make money and therefore look for high rates of return on their investments. The funding and close monitoring of a new venture (whether commercial or social) provide opportunities for angel investors to experience the challenge of starting and growing a project vicariously. Generally, commercial angel investors look for companies that have the potential to grow by 30 or 40 percent. The Angel Capital Association (ACA) lists 300 American groups on its database.[10]

For social ventures, it may be more appropriate to refer to angel investors as "social angels," because, unlike commercial startups that can generate profit and positive returns on investment, social ventures rarely provide such opportunities. When funding social ventures, social angels are almost always interested in fighting for a particular cause, rather than securing profits for themselves.

Unsurprisingly, not every social venture will be able to attract this sort of funding. Even in commercial entrepreneurship, only 15 percent of new ventures are funded by angels. The Investor's Circle and the Social Venture Network both facilitate connections between social entrepreneurs and social angel investors through events and other activities.[11] However, this funding source is generally more viable for hybrid and for-profit social ventures than for purely philanthropic ones.

1.5   Social Venture Capitalists and the Financing of Social Enterprises

Venture capitalists are individuals or firms that provide venture capital financing. They generally expect a hefty return on their investment. Usually, they come in some time after startup when the new venture has proven its ability to be profitable and grow. They generally expect to see a positive return on their investment within about five years, and certainly no longer than ten years. Recently, venture capitalists have started to enter the arena of social enterprises, leading to the emergence of what are now called social venture capitalists. Social venture capital is a form of venture capital that provides capital to socially driven businesses and social ventures. Such investments are not donations. Rather, they are intended to generate attractive returns on investment while at the same time using market-based solutions to address social issues. Table 10.4 provides a list of social venture capital institutions. However, this list is far from exhaustive because more of these institutions are emerging all the time.

Table 10.4 Social venture funds

Institution	Website
Aavishkaar	www.aavishkaar.in
Acumen Fund	www.acumen.org
Grassroots Business Fund	www.gbfund.org
Gray Ghost Ventures	www.grayghostventures.com
Omidyar Network	www.omidyar.com
Renewal 2	www.renewafunds.com
RSF Social Finance	www.rsfsocialfinance.org
Root Capital	www. rootcapital.org
Shell Foundation	www.shellfoundation.org
Triodos Bank	www.triodos.com
Venturesome Fund	www.cafonline.org/venturesome

Despite the increasing number of social venture capital firms, securing funding from such organizations is not always easy for social entrepreneurs, especially new ones without proven records of past performance or previous entrepreneurial experience. Hence, the issues that commercial entrepreneurs have long faced in securing funds from venture capitalists are now plaguing nascent social entrepreneurs. For example, research on venture capital funding reveals that previous experience influences entrepreneurs' likelihood of securing funding from venture capitalists.[12] In the commercial world, founders with prior startup experience tend to be favored by venture capitalists. The same seems to be true for social entrepreneurs. Venture capitalists may also view previous experience as a sign that the entrepreneur is credible and has the ability to make the new venture successful.

1.6 Loan Providers

Loan providers for social ventures include traditional banks as well as other financial institutions, such as the Calvert Foundation, Shore Bank, Triodos Bank, Partners for the Common Good, and Wainwright Bank. Securing a loan is not always easy for social ventures since they may not have any collateral with which to secure the loan. Of course, one of the main drawbacks of a loan is that the money must be paid back.

Although mainstream financial institutions and practices have tended to marginalize social entrepreneurs,[13] there are indications that some banks are now revising their policies toward lending to social ventures and taking an active role in helping social entrepreneurs. For example, microfinance institutions are tapping into conventional capital markets through securitization, arranged by banking multinationals such as Citigroup.[14] Nevertheless, because of the ongoing difficulty of securing bank loans, which still often demand collateral, social entrepreneurs would be well advised to consider other sources of funding. One such source is crowdfunding.

1.7 Crowdfunding

Crowdfunding is a new way of funding businesses and social ventures. An entrepreneur goes online and requests the external financing they need for their venture from a large audience—the crowd—so each individual member of that crowd will probably need to invest only a relatively small amount of money.[15] This allows founders of for-profit, artistic, and cultural ventures to fund their projects without the need to deal with traditional financial institutions.[16]

There are usually three essential elements in crowdfunding:

- the entrepreneur;
- the crowd (a group of people who are able and willing to donate); and
- the platform (the website that connects the entrepreneur with the crowd).

A prominent example of a crowdfunding platform is Kickstarter, where sponsors had pledged over $350 million to 30,000 creative projects by 2014.[17] Crowdfunding is particularly popular in the music industry, the movie industry, the financial sector, and the nonprofit sector. Table 10.5 provides a list of major crowdfunding platforms.

The academic literature on crowdfunding is still at an early stage.[18] None the less, some entrepreneurship scholars have explored the application of crowdfunding in social venture financing.[19] For example, Lerner studied 36 cases of social ventures that have

Table 10.5 Crowdfunding platforms[20]

Platforms	Web address	Focus
Bandstocks	www.bandstocks.com	Musicians
BKR	www.bkr.nl	Profit and nonprofit
Cameesa	www.cameesa.com	Fashion design
Catwalkgenius	www.catwalkgenius.com	Fashion design
Createfund	www.createfund.com	Nonprofit
Crowdaboutnow	www.crowdaboutnow.nl	Profit and nonprofit
IndieGoGo	www.indiegogo.com	Entrepreneurs and artists
Fundable	www.fundable.com	Nonprofit
Grow VC	www.growvc.com	Financial services
Kapipal	www.kapipal.com	Nonprofit
Kiva	www.kiva.org	Entrepreneurs and artists
Kickstarter	www.kickstarter.com	Entrepreneurs and artists
Sellaband	www.sellaband.com	Musicians
Slicethepie	www.slicethepie.com	Musicians
Tenpages	www.tenpages.com	Artists and writers

used crowdfunding. He observes that there is a constant exchange of ideas between the social entrepreneur and the crowd, leading to a co-creation of the social entrepreneurial opportunity. [21]

A successful crowdfunding campaign can send a signal that the venture is viable and improve the probability of securing more funding elsewhere.[22] For example, Ahlers and colleagues empirically examined the effectiveness of signals that entrepreneurs use to induce (small) investors to commit financial resources in an equity crowdfunding context. They studied the impact of venture quality (human capital, social capital, intellectual capital, and uncertainty) on fundraising success. Their data indicated that retaining equity and providing more detailed information about risk could be interpreted as effective signals and could therefore strongly impact the probability of funding success. Meanwhile, social capital and intellectual capital had little or no impact on funding success.[23]

The use of crowdfunding as a legitimate source of funding has led to the development of online communities of both investors and entrepreneurs. Thus, developing online social capital could help an entrepreneur in his or her crowdfunding campaign. Indeed, crowdfunding communities are becoming foci of social interaction in which members are embedded in social relationships and develop internal social capital.[24] A study using an econometric analysis of a sample of 669 Kickstarter projects found that the internal social capital that entrepreneurs may develop inside the crowdfunding community provides crucial assistance in igniting a self-reinforcing process.[25]

In the social entrepreneurship context, the framing of an opportunity could influence the success of a crowdfunding campaign. Allison and colleagues examined how framing affects fundraising outcomes in the context of prosocial lending in a sample of microloans made to over 36,000 entrepreneurs in 51 countries via the online crowdfunding platform Kiva. They found that lenders respond positively to narratives that highlight the venture as an opportunity to help others, and less positively when narratives are framed as business opportunities.[26]

Moss and colleagues suggest that microenterprises' narratives on microfinancing platforms are an important means to signal valuable characteristics and behavioral intentions to prospective lenders. Studying microenterprises that use Kiva, they found that those which signal autonomy, competitive aggressiveness, and risk-taking are more likely to receive funding—and to receive it quickly—than those which signal conscientiousness, courage, empathy, and warmth.[27]

1.7 Bootstrapping in Social Ventures

"Bootstrapping" refers to finding ways to avoid the need for external funding.[28] It is usually done through creativity, ingenuity, thrift, or cost-cutting.[29] In commercial entrepreneurship, bootstrapping usually consists of getting a business up and running quickly by looking for rapid, break-even, cash-generating projects and offering high-value products or services that are suited to direct personal selling. Bootstrapping entrepreneurs focus on cash rather than profits, market share, or indeed anything else.[30] For example, in a study of financial bootstrapping conducted in Sweden, the authors found that:

- 78 percent of the small businesses bought used rather than new equipment;
- 74 percent negotiated the best conditions with suppliers;
- 45 percent withheld managers' salaries;
- 44 percent deliberately delayed payments to suppliers and implemented routines for speeding up invoicing; and
- 42 percent borrowed equipment from other businesses.[31]

All of these measures were undertaken to reduce costs.

Social entrepreneurs may use similar bootstrapping techniques to jumpstart their social ventures. Social entrepreneurship is primarily concerned with the development of innovative solutions to society's most challenging problems. Since social ventures usually operate in resource-constrained environments, success may depend on the extent to which social entrepreneurs can combine and apply the scant resources they do have in creative and useful ways, often referred to as bricolage.[32] As bootstrapping emphasizes finance acquisition during startup and bypassing external funding sources, such as equity and debt financing, it could be viewed as a form of bricolage.[33] Thus, using bootstrapping may be a useful way for the social entrepreneur to start his or her venture.

Traditional sources of funding may be out of the question for social enterprises in developing or emerging countries. In most of these areas, the venture capital market is weak—if not nonexistent—and bank loans are invariably granted with stringent restrictions. Under such circumstances, social entrepreneurs tend to turn to international development agencies for financial assistance, but their funds are always limited. These constraints force the entrepreneurs to find innovative ways in which to use their existing resources and acquire new ones in order to achieve financial sustainability and attain their social goals.[34] Some entrepreneurs even resort to using credit cards to keep their ventures afloat.[35]

When social entrepreneurs make the most of what they have to hand, this bootstrapping or bricolage may be considered as a form of effectuation.[36] Social entrepreneurs who are confronted with institutional constraints often engage in bricolage to reconfigure the resources they have to hand.[37] For example, a study of Kenyan innovator–entrepreneurs who designed low-cost, renewable energy solutions for the rural population found that they used three forms of bricolage to generate positive outcomes: they developed a social mindset combined with resourcefulness; they made do with existing resources; and they improvised in order to carry the venture forward.[38]

1.8 Microfinance and Social Ventures

"Microfinance" refers to the provision of funding to populations that are typically ignored by traditional financial institutions and comprises a social innovation to alleviate poverty.[39] Conceived as an alternative to mainstream financing,[40] it is now a major industry in its own right, with thousands of organizations serving about 155 million clients worldwide.[41] In microlending, the loans are generally small in nature, yet they can prove beneficial if the social venture does not require much seed money. The Grameen Bank is considered as the pioneer of microfinance and microlending. Other examples include Banco Solidario, Caja de Ahorro y Prestamo,[42] and ACCION International in Latin America, and the Self-Employed Women's Association in India.

VisionSpring, another microfinance institution, has recently transformed the concept into *microfranchise* opportunities in developing countries. VisionSpring loans a "business in a bag" to aspiring entrepreneurs. The bag contains all the products and materials necessary for marketing and selling eyeglasses, in addition to some basic business tools, such as customer tracking and inventory management tools. The entrepreneurs also receive training and support from local staff, and then pay VisionSpring for the glasses they sell. On its website (www.visionspring.org), VisionSpring features a series of successful entrepreneurs who have benefited from its microfranchising concept. One such is Vicky, from El Salvador, who makes $600 a month selling VisionSpring glasses in her community, a good income in an impoverished nation.[43]

The type of financing sought by new firms varies according to where they are based. One study that analyzed data from the World Bank's Enterprise Survey, which includes more than 100,000 randomly sampled firm-level observations collected in cross-sectional surveys in 123 countries, found that younger firms rely less on bank financing and more on informal financing in all countries. However, these younger firms had greater access to bank finance, relative to older firms, in countries with a stronger rule of law and better credit information, with a consequent reduction in their reliance on informal finance.[44] As mentioned earlier, increasing numbers of microfinance institutions are tapping into conventional capital markets through securitization, and some are even launching share offerings. For instance, Compartamos Banco, a Mexican microfinance firm that became a for-profit company after starting as a charity, launched a hugely successful initial public offering in 2007.

It should be pointed out that some microfinance institutions charge very high interest and/or engage in practices such as joint-liability payments which impose significant economic burdens on already impoverished borrowers.[45] For example, a recent study in Bangladesh analyzed the selection of borrowing partners in joint-liability payments. The authors made the distinction between *risky borrowers* (those who have a history of defaulting on loans and/or are deemed likely to default on the current loan) and *safe borrowers* (those who have a history of repaying loans and are considered unlikely to default on the current loan). When partnered with risky borrowers, safe borrowers tended to spend considerable time closely monitoring the behavior of their risky partners. Of course, this placed an additional burden on the safe borrowers, who not only had to monitor their partners but also had to design enforcement mechanisms to ensure joint repayment of the loan. To address this potential weakness of microfinance institutions, some authors have advocated new social projects involving multiple stakeholders, such as microfinance institutions, borrower communities, governments, and social venture employees.[46]

1.9   Social Finance and the Funding of Social Ventures

The funding of social enterprises through nonconventional finance has led to the development of a new field—social finance.[47] This refers to the supply of capital to charities, social ventures, and businesses with social missions. More than a discipline, social finance is an approach to managing capital that yields social dividends as well as economic returns. It includes five major components:

- microfinance;
- social impact bonds;
- sustainable businesses;
- social enterprise lending; and
- grants.

Social capital ventures and social angel investors are also active in social finance. Microfinance, social enterprise lending, and grants have all been discussed above. Social impact bonds are bonds issued to undertake socially oriented projects, whereas sustainable businesses are social ventures whose financial bottom lines should help them survive over time while fulfilling their social missions.

Proponents of social finance argue that financial innovation can help the neediest in society. Recent developments have shed light on the important role that it is now playing. For instance, on September 1, 2009 a San Francisco conference was dedicated to the development of social capital markets. This event advocated the development of a social stock exchange and the creation of sustainable hedge funds. Twenty-four days later, the Clinton Global Initiative launched the Global Impact Investment Network (GIIN), whose goal is to share information, agree on a common language and measures of performance, and lobby for helpful laws and regulations. This is, in effect, a commitment to create a new asset class—impact investing—that will yield a financial return *and* a social or environmental benefit. The network's 20 or so members include several big banks (Citigroup, Deutsche Bank, JP Morgan), philanthropic institutions (the Bill and Melinda Gates Foundation and the Rockefeller Foundation), the Acumen Fund (which invests in firms that provide healthcare, clean water, and so forth in Africa and India), and Generation Investment Management, a green-tinged fund manager co-founded by former vice-president Albert Gore.[48] Other examples of social finance organizations include Root Capital and ResponseAbility in the United States, and the Calvert Foundation and Social Finance in the United Kingdom.

2   Managing the Financial Side of Social Ventures

A firm is obligated to track its financial performance to see how it is managing its financial resources. Doing so helps the firm become economically sustainable. This is particularly true for social ventures that must blend a social and an economic sustainability model. In other words, they must accomplish their social mission and at the same time generate resources that will help sustain that mission. In commercial entrepreneurship, managing the finances of a new venture normally starts with projecting how much revenue and profit (or loss) is expected. This requires the use of financial statements. Good financial planning is important for social ventures, too. For example, once pro forma financial statements are generated, they can be modified based on particular scenarios ("what if" scenarios). The social entrepreneur may envisage several contrasting scenarios, such as low revenue or high revenue, and then the effects of different assumptions on financial outcomes can be examined.

Social ventures must also report on the benefits they provide to society. Techniques such as social accounting and audits and social return on investment (SROI) are generally used to assess social value creation. As indicated at the beginning of this chapter, these techniques will be discussed in detail in Chapter 14, which focuses exclusively on social ventures' impact. As a consequence, this chapter will limit itself to discussing regular financial statements, such as balance sheet, income statement, and cash-flow statement.

The benefits of financial statements are threefold:

- they tell the firm how much money it is making or losing (income statement);
- they help the firm to track its assets and liabilities (balance sheet); and
- they help the firm to monitor the cash that is coming in and going out (statement of cash flow).

These three financial statements, which are used routinely by commercial ventures, are also relevant for social enterprises.

Table 10.6 illustrates the process of financial management, which social ventures can utilize to manage their resources effectively.

2.1   Income Statement

As is widely acknowledged in accounting and financial management, the income statement reflects the results of the operations of a firm over a specified period of time. Generally prepared on a monthly, quarterly, or annual basis, it describes revenues generated, costs associated with those revenues, and resulting net profit or loss–the difference between the firm's revenues and its expenses during the specified time period. The key numbers to track on an income statement include net sales, cost of goods sold, and operating expenses.

For a social venture, certain elements of the income statement may vary substantially from those that are found on a commercial venture's income statement. For instance, a purely philanthropic social venture generates no sales. Rather, it finances its operations through revenue

Table 10.6 The process of financial management

Historical financial statements	Forecast	Pro forma financial statements	Ongoing analysis of financial results

Income statement
Balance sheet
Statement of cash flow
	Income
	Expenses
	Capital expenditures
	Note: should be
	    preceded by an
	    assumptions sheet
		Pro forma income
		    statement
		Pro forma balance sheet
		Pro forma statement of
		    cash flow
			Ratio analysis
			Measuring results against
			    plans
			Measuring results against
			    industry norms

Table 10.7 Social Venture Partners' statement of activities (or income statement) in US dollars[49]

	2013	2012
Revenue and support:		
Contributions	2,051,669	1,982,253
Grants	585,000	28,000
Other income	75,870	19,276
Total revenue and support	**2,712,539**	**2,029,529**
Expenses:		
Program services	1,846,670	1,590,224
Management and general	225,225	201,384
Fundraising	206,800	139,346
Total expenses	**2,278,695**	**1,930,954**
Change in net assets	433,844	98,575
Net assets, beginning of year	390,323	291,748
Net assets, end of year	**824,167**	**390,323**

derived from grants, donations, or other sources. However, the costs of securing such dona-tions and grants may be included in the income statement. Commercial ventures calculate their gross profit by subtracting costs of products or services sold from revenues. However, because purely philanthropic social ventures do not aim to make profits, it is appropriate to consider the difference between revenue and the cost of obtaining that revenue as *gross surplus*. Table 10.7 presents the income statement of Social Venture Partners, a social venture that intends to drive community change by building strong relationships within communities.

2.2   Balance Sheet

The balance sheet describes what the business owns and owes at a particular moment. In a typical balance sheet, assets are listed in order of liquidity. An important aspect is that a balance sheet must always balance, so:

Assets = Liabilities + Owner's Equity

A balance sheet helps to answer two fundamental questions:

- Does the firm have sufficient short-term assets to cover its short-term debt?
- Is the firm financially sound overall?

Answering these two questions is important for both commercial and social ventures. Commonly, business scholars and managers argue that accounting is the language of busi-ness. It could also be the language of *social* business because financial viability is critical to any social venture that wishes to remain sustainable and accomplish its social mission. However, social entrepreneurs are often unfamiliar with the language of accounting and financial management.

Table 10.8 illustrates the key elements of a balance sheet. Understanding the terminol-ogy of accounting and especially the elements of a balance sheet is essential for social entrepreneurs. Table 10.9 illustrates Social Venture Partners' balance sheet.

Table 10.8 Explanation of the key elements of a balance sheet

Assets	Liabilities + Owner's Equity

Current assets:
  Cash + items that are readily convertible to cash
Fixed assets:
  Long-term assets, such as buildings,
  equipment,real estate, furniture
Other assets:
  Such as accumulated goodwill
	Current liabilities:
	  Obligations payable in a year, accounts payable,
	  accrued expenses, current portion of long-term
	  debt
	Long-term liabilities:
	  Notes or loan payable beyond one year
	Owner's equity:
	  Equity invested by owner + retained earnings

Table 10.9 Social Venture Partners' statement of financial position (or balance sheet) in US dollars[50]

	2013	2012
Assets:		
Cash and cash equivalents	697,498	367,190
Accounts receivable	8,170	9,739
Pledges receivable	69,750	21,500
Other assets	66,839	
Investments		
Property, furniture, and equipment, net	138,360	58,237
Total assets	**980,617**	**456,666**
Liabilities and net assets:		
Liabilities:		
Accounts payable and accrued expenses	73,421	46,343
Deferred rent and tenant improvement allowance	63,029	
Grants payable	20,000	20,000
Total liabilities	**156,450**	**66,343**
Net assets:		
Unrestricted net assets	416,350	364,271
Temporarily restricted net assets	407,817	26,052
Total net assets	**824,167**	**390,323**
Total liabilities and net assets	**980,617**	**456,666**

2.3   Statement of Cash Flow

The statement of cash flow summarizes the changes in a firm's cash and expenses over a specific period. There are three activities to consider:

- operating activities (net income, depreciation, and changes in current assets and liabilities);
- investing activities (purchase of, sale of, or investment in fixed assets); and
- financing activities (cash raised by borrowing money or selling stocks, or cash used to pay dividends).

Although these three components may not be reflected in social ventures' statements of cash flow, it is important for social entrepreneurs to keep track of cash in and cash out. The statement of cash flow allows the venture to do this and so helps it to determine whether it has enough cash to meet its short-term obligations and whether its activities in terms of

Table 10.10 Social Venture Partners' statement of cash flow in US dollars[51]

	2013	2012
Cash flows from operating activities:		
Change in net assets:		
Adjustments to reconcile change in net assets to net cash provided by operating activities	433,844	98,575
Depreciation	20,318	
Changes in assets and liabilities:		
Accounts receivable	1,569	(9,512)
Pledges receivable	(48,250)	(8,000)
Other assets	(66,839)	
Accounts payable and accrued expenses	27,078	17,226
Deferred rent and tenant improvement allowance	63,029	
Grants payable		20,000
Net cash provided by operating activities	**430,749**	**118,289**
Cash flows from investing activities:		
Purchase of investments	(164,429)	(244,224)
Proceeds from the sale of investments	222,666	438,152
Purchase of property and equipment	(158,678)	
Net cash (used) provided by investing activities	**(100,441)**	**193,928**
Net change in cash and cash equivalent	330,308	312,217
Cash and cash equivalents, beginning of year	367,190	54,973
Cash and cash equivalents, end of year	**697,498**	**367,190**

cash in and out are adequate to ensure smooth functioning. The statement of cash flow is usually calculated on a monthly or a quarterly basis.

A startup may not have enough cash to hand, so it may not be able to compute a statement of cash flow based on historical data. However, it is important for the social entrepreneur to be able to develop pro forma or projected cash-flow statements. Doing so will help him or her understand where the money will come from and what it may be used for. It will represent a better tracking system than a balance sheet or an income statement. Although it is important for social ventures to meet their social missions, they can do so only if they have the necessary financial resources. Table 10.10 presents Social Venture Partners' statement of cash flow.

3   Assessing the Financial Vitality of a Social Venture

Social entrepreneurship tends to focus on fulfilling social objectives. Yet, no social mission can be accomplished without adequate resources. Because most social problems are endemic and persist over time, it is necessary for those ventures that intend to address them to look at the long term. This requires the maintenance of lasting social ventures; and social ventures cannot last unless they are financially sustainable and viable.

A useful means for assessing the viability of commercial ventures is to compute several financial ratios to assess their financial health. For social enterprises, the challenge is to determine whether these traditional financial ratios also apply to them. This important question lies at the core of social venture sustainability. This section focuses on measures to determine whether a social venture is financially sound. It is divided into two parts.

The first part discusses the usefulness of ratio analysis for social ventures, whereas the second focuses on measuring the financial risk or vulnerability of social ventures.

3.1   Applying Financial Ratio Analysis to Social Ventures

There are several widely used financial ratios, but here we shall focus on profitability ratios and debt ratios, both of which might prove useful when assessing the financial sustainability of a social venture. Because of the emphasis on financial sustainability, social ventures are required to generate some surplus in order to fund their operations. In this regard, the concepts of *gross surplus*, *gross surplus margin*, and *net surplus margin* are all used.

Gross surplus represents the difference between a social venture's revenue and expenses. It is calculated in much the same way as gross profit is calculated for commercial ventures. Then the gross surplus margin is calculated by dividing gross surplus by revenue:

Gross Surplus = Revenue – Expenses
Gross Surplus Margin = Gross Surplus/Revenue

In addition to gross surplus margin, a social venture may compute its net surplus margin. This is calculated by dividing net surplus by revenue:

Net surplus margin = Net Surplus/Revenue

Both the gross surplus margin and the net surplus margin help to determine strategies to generate further income or reduce costs.

In addition to surplus margin, a social venture's *working capital* should be tracked to determine whether it has the necessary capital to continue operating. The working capital is the difference between current assets and current liabilities:

Working Capital = Current Assets – Current Liabilities

Other ratios that help in assessing the debt situation of a social venture should also be calculated. These include the *current ratio* and the *debt ratio*. The current ratio determines the venture's present debt situation by showing its ability to pay current obligations by converting assets into cash in the near term. It is therefore calculated by dividing current assets by current liabilities:

Current Ratio = Current Assets/Current Liabilities

Usually, anything above a ratio of 2:1 is considered good, as this implies that the venture has twice as many assets as liabilities.

The current ratio can be calculated along with the total debt-to-assets ratio (or debt ratio for short), which is obtained by dividing total debt by total assets:

Total Debt-to-Assets Ratio = Total Debt/Total Assets

The debt ratio measures the extent to which the funds borrowed by a venture (both short term and long term) have been used to finance its operations. Generally, a low ratio is better than a high ratio. When applied to social entrepreneurship, the debt ratio may help to measure whether the borrowed funds have been used to finance a social venture's operations—that is, whether they have been used for activities that are directly related to the social mission.

Monitoring the financial aspects of a business or a social venture is important because without adequate financial resources a business cannot grow and a social venture cannot be sustainable over time. It is therefore necessary to ensure that the venture remains financially viable regardless of its social mission and/or profit motive.

3.2   Determining the Financial Risk of Social Ventures

Assessing the financial viability of a social venture can help to mitigate the financial risks that it may face. For example, if a source of income, such as a grant or a donation, is decreasing because of economic hardship, the social venture may contemplate taking corrective actions to compensate for the potential loss of income. As a consequence, it may engage in earned-income activities. As we have seen, ratio analysis can help to determine the financial sustainability of a social venture. Alex Nicholls, a social entrepreneurship researcher, has discussed the concept of "blended value accounting," which refers to a spectrum of disclosure logics used by social entrepreneurs to access resources and realize organizational mission objectives with key stakeholders.[52]

It is important to determine whether a social venture is financially sound or vulnerable. Tuckman and Chang propose that a nonprofit is financially vulnerable if it is in the lowest quintile of at least two of the following four ratios:

- net assets;
- administrative costs;
- revenue sources; and
- operating margin.

They conclude that a nonprofit is financially vulnerable if it is "likely to cut back its service offering immediately when it experiences a financial shock."[53] For example, a deterioration of the gross surplus margin may indicate that a social venture is not generating enough revenue through grants, donations, or earned income, or that its expenses are increasing. A subsequent strategy may be to diversify sources of revenues or reduce costs. The authors proposed four measures to assess the financial vulnerability of charitable organizations:

- equity balance;
- revenue concentration;
- administrative costs; and
- operating margins.[54]

Each of these four measures is described below.

3.2.1   Equity Balance

A company's equity balance represents its total assets minus its liabilities. In general, higher equity lowers the financial vulnerability of a firm. For example, social ventures with greater amounts of equity are more flexible in the face of financial shocks than those with comparatively lower amounts of equity. The following formula is used to calculate equity balance:

Equity Balance = Assets − Liabilities/Total Revenue

A higher value indicates a lower level of financial vulnerability. For example, if a social venture has $1 million in assets and $700,000 in liabilities, and a total revenue of $1.5 million, then its equity balance is 0.2. This figure indicates that the social venture is financially vulnerable because it does not have enough cash to sustain itself over time, should it face a financial shock.

3.2.2　Revenue Concentration

Revenue concentration refers to a company's revenue streams. A nonprofit organization's revenue concentration refers to the proportion of funding it receives from its different sources of income.[55] A nonprofit may earn its revenue from a few key products or from a diversity of products. In the first case, the revenue is concentrated, whereas in the second case it is diversified. The same applies to social ventures. For example, financial vulnerability is high when a social venture receives most of its revenue from relatively few sources. Too much revenue concentration can expose a social venture to financial hardship should these sources dry up. Hence, nonprofit organizations with diversified revenues are more flexible than those with concentrated revenues.[56]

Revenue concentration is measured by summing up the square of each revenue source i, where si is a proportion of total revenue:

$$\text{Revenue Concentration} = si^2 + si^2 + si^2 \ldots$$

A lower total indicates revenue diversification. Suppose that social venture A has just two sources of revenue (government grants and donations), while social venture B has five sources of revenue (government grants, donations, earned income, investment income, and private grants). Now suppose that social venture A receives 50 percent of its revenue from government grants and 50 percent from donations, whereas social venture B receives 10 percent of its revenue from government grants, 20 percent from donations, 20 percent from earned-income activities, 25 percent from investment, and 25 percent from private grants. Clearly, social venture A's revenue concentration is higher than social venture B's, as is indicated in the following equations:

$$\text{Revenue Concentration for A} = .50^2 + .50^2 = .50$$
$$\text{Revenue Concentration for B} = .10^2 + .20^2 + .20^2 + .25^2 + .25^2 = .29$$

Social venture B therefore has more diversified revenue than social venture A. As a consequence, it will be less financially vulnerable than social venture A.

3.2.3　Administrative Costs

For a social venture, administrative costs refer to the money that is spent on managers' salaries, fundraising, and office expenses. They are usually measured as a proportion of the venture's total costs:

Administrative Costs/Total Costs

A high ratio could threaten the survival of a social venture. Donors often pay particular attention to efficiency ratios, conditioning their gifts on the basis of their effective use by nonprofit organizations. In this regard, high administrative costs may lead to reductions in donors' contributions and threaten the survival of the social venture.[57] To remedy this, it is usually advisable to inform donors upfront that overhead costs will be met by other sources. This strategy was supported by a recent study of 40,000 potential donors in which an overhead-free solution was compared with other common uses of initial donations. The authors found that informing potential donors that overhead costs would be covered by an initial donation significantly increased the donation rate by 80 percent (or 94 percent) and total donations by 75 percent (or 89 percent) compared with the seed (or matching) approach.[58]

Although high administrative costs (as a proportion of total expenses) might explain why an organization is facing financial distress in the first place, Tuckman and Chang argue that such costs can provide a buffer against financial shocks.[59] That is, they claim that organizations with high administrative costs can cut back on those expenses in lean times, rather than reduce their programs.

3.2.4   Operating Margins

A company's operating margin is the money it has to save or invest and the insurance it has against future uncertainty. It is measured as the difference between total annual revenues and costs as a percentage of annual revenues.

Operating Margin (TR − TC/TR) × 100

A higher operating margin indicates a lower level of financial vulnerability.

Several scholars, such as Max Hager, have studied Tuckman and Chang's four measures, including operating margin, to gauge the financial vulnerability of companies. The greater the operating margin, the more surplus the organization is able to save or invest. The greater the surplus, the more the organization has to draw on in the event of decline or financial shock.[60] A high operating margin is therefore a source of financial flexibility.[61]

3.3   The Financial Viability Index

Tuckman and Chang combined their four measures to compute a financial viability index (FVI),[62] which Trussel and colleagues have since refined.[63] It is now widely used to measure the financial vulnerability of social ventures. No social venture will accomplish its social mission without financial viability. In other words, financial vulnerability can imperil a social venture's mission. When Hager tested Tuckman and Chang's model, he found that low equity balance was a viable predictor of demise among art museums, theaters, and music organizations, whereas high revenue concentration was a useful predictor of the death of visual arts organizations, theaters, music organizations, and generic performing arts organizations. In addition, low administrative costs were associated with the loss of both theaters and music organizations, while a low operating margin was significantly related to the closure of theaters and generic performing arts organizations.[64]

Summary

This chapter discussed the financial challenges facing social ventures. It examined the importance of financial management for social ventures. Sources of social venture financing include social angels, social venture capitalists, bank loans, microfinance, personal sources, and creative mechanisms such as crowdfunding and bootstrapping. The chapter also explored the three main financial statements—the income statement, the balance sheet, and the statement of cash flow—and their importance for social ventures. Finally, the chapter discussed the important role played by financial ratio analysis when assessing the financial viability of social ventures.

Key Terms

Balance sheet; bootstrapping; burn rate; crowdfunding; donations; financial management; financial ratio; financial vulnerability; financial vulnerability index; grants; income statement; microfinance; revenue concentration; social angels; social finance; social venture capitalists; statement of cash flow

Review Questions

1   Discuss the purpose of the income statement for social ventures.
2   Discuss the purpose of the balance sheet for social ventures.
3   Discuss the purpose of the statement of cash flow for social ventures.
4   What is bootstrapping and how can it help a social entrepreneur start and run a social venture?
5   Do you think that it makes sense to use the terms "surplus" and "deficit" rather than "profit" and "loss" when drafting a purely philanthropic social venture's income statement?
6   Under what conditions do you think a social entrepreneur would be well advised to use his or her personal funds?
7   Why do high administrative costs rarely impede the financial sustainability of a social venture, according to Tuckman and Chang?
8   Should financial metrics be used to determine the worth of a social venture (yes or no)? Explain.
9   Discuss the process of crowdfunding and its importance in funding social ventures.
10 What types of social ventures are likely to use microfinancing?

Application Questions

1   Visit the Investors' Circle website at www.investorscircle.net and click on "Entrepreneurs," then click on "Funding Process." Identify the key issues involved in Investors' Circle's funding process. What are the benefits of using Investors' Circle as an investment source? What is the application fee? If you were a social entrepreneur looking for funding, would you use this source (yes or no)? Explain.
2   The Global Impact Investment Network (GIIN) is a nonprofit organization dedicated to improving the effectiveness of social investments. Visit its website at www.thegiin.org and discuss the benefits GIIN provides. How can a social venture leverage the services offered by this network?
3   John, a friend of yours, has asked you to help him understand the importance of financial statements for his new social venture. He wonders whether he should include pro forma financial statements on his social venture plan. Explain the importance of the three financial statements—income statement, balance sheet, and statement of cash flow—for social ventures. Be as specific as you can be. What are the key items that John should look for in these financial statements?
4   Financial ratio analysis is often performed by commercial ventures. Explain why social entrepreneurs should also utilize it when assessing the financial sustainability of their ventures.
5   Do some research on the internet to identify institutions that provide microfinance. What activities do they finance? Could microfinance be a reliable source of social venture financing?

Application Case 1: ClearlySo: Connectng Social Ventures to Impact Investors

Funding a social venture can be a daunting and challenging task. Indeed, the investment industry for social ventures and other non-profit organizations is not as well developed as that of commercial ventures. To address this issue, ClearlySo (https://www.clearlyso.com), a social impact investment venture in the United Kingdom (UK), is playing the role of intermediary between social ventures and potential social impact investors. ClearlySo was created in 2008 by Rodney Schwartz and Julia Meek in the United Kingdom. Rodney Schwartz serves as the CEO of ClearlySo. In 2016, ClearlySo raised more than 143 million dollars, with 85.8 million coming from ClearlySo's extensive network of institutional and high-net-worth individual investors.[1] This performance makes ClearlySo the market leader in the United Kingdom.

There are at least five reasons for which one would expect impact investing to have a promising future. First, social impact investing is entering the institutional mainstream because it is becoming more acceptable now than before. Second, cultural changes lead the millennial generation to focus more on joining for-purpose organizations. Third, there is a growing interest in entrepreneurship as an engine of economic and social progress. In fact, more and more people tend to believe that some of the world's intractable problems can effectively be addressed through entrepreneurial and innovative actions. Fourth, governments, everywhere, are reducing their involvement in addressing social issues because of limited resources. This form of institutional void provides opportunities for social entrepreneurs and likely-minded individuals and organizations to address social issues. Finally, national governments tend to provide an environment that is conducive to the emergence and success of social ventures.[2] These five drivers could transform social impact investing into mainstream investing. For example, it has been observed that raising capital for high-impact organizations is becoming easier with an increasing number of social impact investors. As of today, ClearlySo has helped more than 75 businesses and funds with far global reach. For example, it has helped Aduna (http://aduna.com) raise capital to create under-utilized natural products from small-scale producers in rural Africa.[2]

ClearlySo acts as an intermediary between social ventures and social impact investors. It provides financial advice and introduces businesses, charities and funds to potential institutional or individual investors that share their objectives and values. ClearlySo also operates Clearly Social Angels, an impact-focused angel network in the United Kingdom. Each year, more than 1,200 entrepreneurs pitch their ideas to ClearlySo.[3] ClearlySo praises itself on two elements that help drive the growth of social ventures. First, it helps ambitious social entrepreneurs to prepare to raise capital and then helps them to raise the capital. Second, it helps investors to invest in ambitious social businesses.[4] Its networking activities include face-to-face events, such as conferences, seminars, and office-based tea parties.[5]

ClearlySo focuses on the areas of clean energy, clean water, early childhood and primary education, financial services, health delivery and youth job skills and covers the following geographic areas: Asia, Africa and Europe. Its vision is a world where the financial system is a powerful force for good and the impacts of businesses are considered in all investment decisions. ClearlySo sees its mission as bringing impact as the third dimension into investing, where all investors consider risk, return and impact as important, thereby creating a win-win situation for entrepreneurs, businesses, and investors. Creating such an environment can help make a significant difference.

Discussion Questions

1 Explain the concept of impact investing.
2 Why do you think some investors care about the impact of their investment?

3 What does ClearlySo believe its social mission is?

4 Watch the interview of Rodney Schwartz on YouTube at: https://www.youtube.com/watch?v=IDqgEnJa470. How would you describe his view on social impact investing?

References

1 Capital raised by ClearlySo clients surpasses 100 million. *https://www.clearlyso.com/capital-raised-by-clearlyso-clients-surpasses-100-million.*

2 Rod Schwartz: The future of impact investing (December 21, 2015). *http://www.wearesalt.org/rod-schwartz-the-future-of-impact-investing* [Retrieved on April 11, 2016].

3 htpp://search.enableimpact.com/funders/clearlyso (May 28, 2013).

4 ClearlySo and raising capital for social enterprises. *http://www.reconomy.org/clearlyso-and-capital-raising-for-social-enterprises.* [Retrieved on April 11, 2016].

5 ClearlySo and raising capital for social enterprises. *http://www.reconomy.org/clearlyso-and-capital-raising-for-social-enterprises.* [Retrieved on April 11, 2016].

Application Case 2: Global Soap Project[65]

An awkward experience turned Derreck Kayongo, a native of Uganda turned refugee in Kenya, who immigrated to the United States in the 1990s, into a social entrepreneur. His Eureka moment came when he stayed at a hotel in Philadelphia upon his arrival in the United States. Kayongo noticed that his bathroom was replenished with new soap bars every day, even though they were only slightly used. At first, he tried to return the new soap to the concierge thinking that he was charged for the replacement of the soap but he was told it was just hotel policy to provide new soap every day.[1] This experience was not only surprising for Kayongo but it also sparked an idea in him. After sharing this surprising experience with his father who used to make soap in Uganda, he decided to take action. His idea was simple. "What if we took some of this soap and recycled it, made brand new soap from it and then sent it home to people who couldn't afford soap?"[2] Kayongo had the vision of recycling soap to save lives through sanitation. Soap recycling provides both health and environmental benefits. There is evidence that hand washing with soap can cut child morbidity rates by 50% in developing countries. Likewise, there are approximately 4.7 million hotel rooms in the United States alone, which collectively discard an estimated 2.6 million bars of partially used soaps each day.[3] Recycling these discarded soaps could help to remove them from the landfills where they would have undoubtedly ended up.

Kayongo started the Global Soap project in 2009 to bring his idea to fruition. The project was first located in Atlanta, Georgia, where Kayongo had settled. The project works as follows. It enlists hotels as partners that donate their used soaps that are then recycled into 'new soaps' that are donated to organizations in developing countries to distribute them to the needy free of charge. More than 300 hotels in the United States have joined the collection effort, generating more than 100 tons of soap.[4] At its start, the project relied heavily on volunteers who collect the hotel soaps and ship them to the group's warehouse in Atlanta where they are cleaned, reprocessed and packaged and ready for shipping.

Global Soap Project partners with national organizations, especially NGOs (Non-Governmental Organizations) that distribute the soaps to vulnerable populations. Global Soap Project does not charge the NGOs that receive the soaps for distribution. In addition to distributing the soaps, these NGOs also provide hygiene education. The goal of Global

Soap Project is to make sure that the populations incorporate the use of soap into their daily routines to maintain proper hygiene. Global Soap Project generally relies on donations and volunteers to keep operating costs low. Recently, the social venture relocated its factory to Las Vegas, Nevada. The factory recycles about 4 million bars of soap annually. This translates into removing more than 1 million used soaps from landfills annually.

Kayongo attributes the success of Global Soap Project to his passion for making a difference in the lives of poor people and having a positive impact on society. For his efforts, Kayongo was nominated one of the Top Ten CNN Heroes of the Year in 2011. He is also a sought-after speaker on projects addressing social issues in developing countries. Global Soap Project is partnering with several organizations, such as Clean the World, the Centers for Disease Control (CDC), CARE, Partners in Health and several hotel chains, including Hilton Worldwide. Its partnership with Clean the World allows it to focus more on the worldwide distribution of the soaps while Clean the World collects and processes the used soaps. The Global Soap Project has been accepted as a member of the PPPHW (Global Public Policy Partnership for Hand Washing) to promote the washing of hands with soap. Global Soap Project works in different regions of the world including Africa, Asia, and Central and South America. To help the beneficiaries of the soaps be self-reliant over time, Global Soap Project runs a microloan program that provides financial support to small-scale start-up soap makers.

Discussion Questions

1 Do some research on how the Global Soap Project is funded including visiting its website at www.globalsoap.org.
2 Is the strategy of Global Soap Project that consists of not charging any fees to the local NGOs that distribute the soaps to vulnerable populations financially sound?
3 If you were a consultant to Global Soap Project, what would you advise to make this project financially viable?
4 Watch the YouTube video at https://www.youtube.com/watch?v=z13P4PmYsvY. Would you donate to the Global Soap Project? Yes? No? Explain.

References

1 *http://www.cnn.com/2011/US/06/16/cnnheroes.kayongo.hotel.soap*. [Retrieved on January 10, 2015.]
2 *http://www.cnn.com/2011/US/06/16/cnnheroes.kayongo.hotel.soap*. [Retrieved on January 10, 2015.]
3 *http://www.one.org/us/2014/07/21/global-soap-project-is-helping-to-put-more-girls-back-in-school*. [Retrieved, April 16, 2016].
4 *http://www.cnn.com/2011/US/06/16/cnnheroes.kayongo.hotel.soap*. [Retrieved on January 10, 2015.]

Notes

1 Barringer, R. B., & Ireland, R. D. (2012). *Entrepreneurship: Successfully launching new ventures*. 4th edition. New York: Pearson.
2 Shane, S. (2003). *A general theory of entrepreneurship: The individual–opportunity nexus*. Cheltenham: Edward Elgar.
3 Uzzi, B., & Gillespie, J.J. (2002). Knowledge spillover in corporate financing networks: Embeddedness and the firm's debt performance. *Strategic Management Journal*, 23, 595–618;

Jonsson, S., & Lindbergh, J. (2013). The development of social capital and financing of entrepreneurial firms: From financial bootstrapping to bank funding. *Entrepreneurship Theory and Practice*, 37(4), 661–686.

4   Dean, J. T. (2014). *Sustainable venturing: Entrepreneurial opportunity in the transition to a sustainable economy*. New York: Pearson.

5   Chatterjie, K. A., & Seamans, C. R. (2012). Entrepreneurial finance, credit cards, and race. *Journal of Financial Economics*, 106(2), 182–195.

6   Kickul, J., & Lyons, S. T. (2012). *Understanding social entrepreneurship: The relentless pursuit of mission in an ever changing world*. New York: Routledge.

7   Kickul, J., & Lyons, S. T. (2012). *Understanding social entrepreneurship: The relentless pursuit of mission in an ever changing world*. New York: Routledge, at p. 143.

8   Barringer, R. B., & Ireland, R. D. (2012). *Entrepreneurship: Successfully launching new ventures*. 4th edition. New York: Pearson.

9   Barringer, R. B., & Ireland, R. D. (2012). *Entrepreneurship: Successfully launching new ventures*. 4th edition. New York: Pearson.

10 Kerr, R. W., Lerner, J., & Schoar, A. (2010). The consequences of entrepreneurial finance: A regression discontinuity analysis. Harvard Business School, Working Paper Number 10-086.

11 Dean, J. T. (2014). *Sustainable venturing: Entrepreneurial opportunity in the transition to a sustainable economy*. New York: Pearson.

12 Hsu, H. D. (2007). Experienced entrepreneurial founders, organizational capital, and venture capital funding. *Research Policy*, 36, 722–741.

13 Moore, M. L., Westley, R. F., & Nicholls, A. (2012). The social finance and social innovation nexus. *Journal of Social Entrepreneurship*, 3(2), 115–132.

14 *Economist, The* (2009). Financial innovation and the poor: A place in society. September 25. www.economist.com/node/14493098, retrieved on December 25, 2013.

15 Belleflamme, P., Lambert, T., & Schwienbacher, A. (2014). Crowdfunding: Tapping the right crowd. *Journal of Business Venturing*, 29(5), 585–609.

16 Mollick, E. (2014). The dynamics of crowdfunding: An exploratory study. *Journal of Business Venturing*, 29(1), 1–16.

17 www.kickstarter.com; Dean, J. T. (2014). *Sustainable venturing: Entrepreneurial opportunity in the transition to a sustainable economy*. New York: Pearson.

18 Colombo, M. G., Franzoni, C., & Rossi-Lamastra, C. (2015). Internal social capital and the attraction of early contributions in crowdfunding. *Entrepreneurship Theory and Practice*, 39(1), 75–100; Cholakova, M., & Clarysse, B. (2015). Does the possibility to make equity investments in crowdfunding projects crowd out reward-based investments? *Entrepreneurship Theory and Practice*, 39(1), 145–172; Belleflamme, P., Lambert, T., & Schwienbacher, A. (2014). Crowdfunding: Tapping the right crowd. *Journal of Business Venturing*, 29(5), 585–609; Mollick, E. (2014). The dynamics of crowdfunding: An exploratory study. *Journal of Business Venturing*, 29(1), 1–16.

19 Lehner, O. M. (2014). The formation and interplay of social capital in crowdfunded social ventures. *Venture Capital: An International Journal of Entrepreneurial Finance*, 15(5–6), 478–499; Lehner, M. O. (2013). Crowdfunding social ventures: a model and research agenda. *Venture Capital: An International Journal of Entrepreneurial Finance*, 15(4), 289–311.

20 Beugré, D. C. (2014). The legitimacy of crowdfunding: An institutional theory perspective. Paper presented at the Annual Meeting of the Academy of Management, Philadelphia, PA, August 1–5.

21 Lehner, O. M. (2014). The formation and interplay of social capital in crowdfunded social ventures. *Venture Capital: An International Journal of Entrepreneurial Finance*, 15(5–6), 478–499.

22 Ahlers, G. K. C., Cummings, D., Günther, C., & Schweizer, D. (2015). Signaling in equity crowdfunding. *Entrepreneurship Theory and Practice*, 39(4), 955–980; Colombo, M. G., Franzoni, C., & Rossi-Lamastra, C. (2015). Internal social capital and the attraction of early contributions in crowdfunding. *Entrepreneurship Theory and Practice*, 39(1), 75–100; Beugré, D. C. (2014). The legitimacy of crowdfunding: An institutional theory perspective. Paper presented at

the Annual Meeting of the Academy of Management, Philadelphia, PA, August 1–5; Spence, M. (2002). Signaling in retrospect and the information structure of markets. *American Economic Review, 92*, 434–459.

23 Ahlers, G. K. C., Cummings, D., Günther, C., & Schweizer, D. (2015). Signaling in equity crowd-funding. *Entrepreneurship Theory and Practice, 39*(4), 955–980.

24 Colombo, M. G., Franzoni, C., & Rossi-Lamastra, C. (2015). Internal social capital and the attraction of early contributions in crowdfunding. *Entrepreneurship Theory and Practice, 39*(1), 75–100.

25 Colombo, M. G., Franzoni, C., & Rossi-Lamastra, C. (2015). Internal social capital and the attraction of early contributions in crowdfunding. *Entrepreneurship Theory and Practice, 39*(1), 75–100.

26 Allison, T. H., Davis, B. C., Short, J. C., & Webb, J. W. (2015). Crowdfunding in a prosocial microlending environment: Examining the role of intrinsic versus extrinsic cues. *Entrepreneurship Theory and Practice, 39*(1), 53–73.

27 Moss, T. W., Neubaum, D. O., & Meyskens, M. (2015). The effect of virtuous and entrepreneurial orientations on microfinance lending and repayment: A signaling perspective. *Entrepreneurship Theory and Practice, 39*(1), 27–52.

28 Cornwall, J. (2009). *Bootstrapping*. Upple Saddle River, NJ: Prentice-Hall; Dean, J. T. (2014). *Sustainable venturing: Entrepreneurial opportunity in the transition to a sustainable economy.* New York: Pearson.

29 Cornwall, J. (2009). *Bootstrapping*. Upple Saddle River, NJ: Prentice-Hall.

30 Gartner, W. B., & Bellamy, M. G. (2010). *Enterprise*. Mason, OH: South-Western Cengage Learning.

31 Winborg, J., & Lanstrom, H. (2001). Financial bootstrapping in small businesses: Examining small business managers' resource acquisition behaviors. *Journal of Business Venturing, 16*(3), 235–254.

32 Gundry, K. L., Kickul, R. J., Griffiths, D. M., & Bacq, C. S. (2011). Creating social change out of nothing: The role of entrepreneurial bricolage in social entrepreneurs' catalytic innovations. *Advances in Entrepreneurship, Firm Emergence, and Growth Issue, 3*, 1–24.

33 Di Domenico, M. L., Haugh, H., & Tracey, P. (2010). Social bricolage: Theorizing social value creation in social enterprises. *Entrepreneurship Theory and Practice, 34*(4), 681–703.

34 Di Domenico, M. L., Haugh, H., & Tracey, P. (2010). Social bricolage: Theorizing social value creation in social enterprises. *Entrepreneurship Theory and Practice, 34*(4), 681–703.

35 Chatterjie, K. A., & Seamans, C. R. (2012). Entrepreneurial finance, credit cards, and race. *Journal of Financial Economics, 106*(2), 182–195.

36 Sarasvathy, S. D. (2001). Causation and effectuation: Toward a theoretical shift from economic inevitability to entrepreneurial contingency. *Academy of Management Review, 26*(2), 243–288.

37 Desa, G. (2012). Resource mobilization in international social entrepreneurship: Bricolage as a mechanism of institutional transformation. *Entrepreneurship Theory and Practice, 36*(4), 727–751.

38 Linna, P. (2013). Bricolage as a means of innovating in a resource-scarce environment: A study of innovator–entrepreneurs at the BOP. *Journal of Developmental Entrepreneurship, 18*(3), 1–23.

39 Sun, S. L., & Im, J. (2015). Cutting microfinance interest rates: An opportunity co-creation perspective. *Entrepreneurship Theory and Practice, 39*(1), 101–128; Kent, D., & Dacin, H. T. (2013). Bankers at the gate: Microfinance and the high cost of borrowed logics. *Journal of Business Venturing, 28*, 759–773.

40 Yunus, M. (2007). *Banker to the poor: Micro-lending and the battle against world poverty.* New York: Public Affairs.

41 Armendariz, B., & Morduch, J. (2010). *The economics of microfinance.* Cambridge, MA: MIT Press.

42 Battilana, J., & Dorado, S. (2010). Building sustainable hybrid organizations: The case of commercial microfinance organizations. *Academy of Management Journal, 53*(6), 1419–1440.

43 www.visionspring.org; Dean, J. T. (2014). *Sustainable venturing: Entrepreneurial opportunity in the transition to a sustainable economy.* New York: Pearson.

44 Chavis, L., Leora Klapper, L., & Inessa, L. (2010). International differences in entrepreneurial finance. The World Bank, Enterprise Note Number 11, pp. 1–4.

45 Sun, S. L., & Im, J. (2015). Cutting microfinance interest rates: An opportunity co-creation perspective. *Entrepreneurship Theory and Practice, 39*(1), 101–128.

46 Sun, S. L., & Im, J. (2015). Cutting microfinance interest rates: An opportunity co-creation perspective. *Entrepreneurship Theory and Practice, 39*(1), 101–128.

47 Benedikter, R. (2011). *Social banking and social finance: Answers to the economic crisis.* New York: Springer.

48 *Economist, The* (2009). Financial innovation and the poor: A place in society. September 25. www.economist.com/node/14493098, retrieved on December 25, 2013.

49 http://socialventurepartners.org.s3.amazonaws.com/www.socialventurepartners.org/sites/40/2014/03/2013-0630-Social-Venture-Partners-FS.pdf, retrieved on March 28, 2016.

50 http://socialventurepartners.org.s3.amazonaws.com/www.socialventurepartners.org/sites/40/2014/03/2013-0630-Social-Venture-Partners-FS.pdf, retrieved on March 28, 2016.

51 http://socialventurepartners.org.s3.amazonaws.com/www.socialventurepartners.org/sites/40/2014/03/2013-0630-Social-Venture-Partners-FS.pdf, retrieved on March 28, 2016.

52 Nicholls, A. (2009). "We do good things, don't we?" Blended value accounting in social entrepreneurship. *Accounting, Organizations and Society, 34*(6–7), 755–769.

53 Tuckman, H. P., & Chang, C. F. (1991). A methodology for measuring the financial vulnerability of charitable nonprofit organizations. *Nonprofit and Voluntary Sector Quarterly, 20*(4), 445–460, quote at p. 445.

54 Tuckman, H. P., & Chang, C. F. (1991). A methodology for measuring the financial vulnerability of charitable nonprofit organizations. *Nonprofit and Voluntary Sector Quarterly, 20*(4), 445–460.

55 Tuckman, H. P., & Chang, C. F. (1991). A methodology for measuring the financial vulnerability of charitable nonprofit organizations. *Nonprofit and Voluntary Sector Quarterly, 20*(4), 445–460.

56 Tuckman, H. P., & Chang, C. F. (1991). A methodology for measuring the financial vulnerability of charitable nonprofit organizations. *Nonprofit and Voluntary Sector Quarterly, 20*(4), 445–460.

57 de Andres-Alonso, P., Garcia-Rodriguez, I., & Romero-Merino, M. E. (2015). The dangers of assessing the financial vulnerability of nonprofits using traditional measures: The case of the nongovernmental development organizations in the United Kingdom *Nonprofit Management and Leadership, 25*(4), 371–382; Wellens, L., & Jegers, M. (2014). Effective governance in nonprofit organizations: A literature-based multiple stakeholder approach. *European Management Journal, 32*(2), 223–243.

58 Gneezy, U., Keenan, E. A., & Gneezy, A. (2014). Avoiding overhead aversion in charity. *Science, 346*(6209), 632–635.

59 Tuckman, H. P., & Chang, C. F. (1991). A methodology for measuring the financial vulnerability of charitable nonprofit organizations. *Nonprofit and Voluntary Sector Quarterly, 20*(4), 445–460.

60 Hager, M. A. (2001). Financial vulnerability among arts organizations: A test of the Tuckman–Chang measures. *Nonprofit and Voluntary Sector Quarterly, 30*(2), 376–392.

61 Tuckman, H. P., & Chang, C. F. (1991). A methodology for measuring the financial vulnerability of charitable nonprofit organizations. *Nonprofit and Voluntary Sector Quarterly, 20*(4), 445–460.

62 Tuckman, H. P., & Chang, C. F. (1992). Nonprofit equity: A behavioral model and its policy implications. *Journal of Policy Analysis and Management, 11*(1), 76–87.

63 Trussel, J. M., Greenlee, J. S., & Trady, T. (2002). Predicting financial vulnerability in charitable organizations. *CPA Journal*, 72(6), 66–69.

64 Hager, M. A. (2001). Financial vulnerability among arts organizations: A test of the Tuckman–Chang measures. *Nonprofit and Voluntary Sector Quarterly*, 30(2), 376–392.

65 Source for this whole section: Ruffins, E. (2011). Recycling hotel soap to save lives. CNN Heroes, June 16. www.cnn.com/2011/US/06/16/cnnheroes.kayongo.hotel.soap, retrieved on January 10, 2015.

Chapter 11

Organization and Management of Social Ventures

To accomplish its social mission, a social venture must be well organized and managed, particularly when it comes to its workforce. In fact, most entrepreneurship scholars often contend that a well-conceived business plan cannot get off the ground unless a firm has the leaders and personnel to carry it out.[1] Therefore, this chapter focuses on the importance of organizing a social venture and managing its human capital. Particularly, it focuses on the formation of a new social venture team, the establishment of a board of directors and/or advisers, and the management of paid employees and volunteers. The chapter is divided into three major sections. The first section discusses the importance of a social venture's founding team. The second analyzes the management of paid employees. The third focuses on volunteers and their role in helping social ventures accomplish their goals.

1 Building A New Venture's Top Management Team

Before discussing new venture teams and the management of human capital in social ventures, it is important to acknowledge issues of governance in such organizations. This is important because social ventures face the same governance challenges as commercial businesses.

Organizational governance in the social sector is understood as the systems and processes concerned with ensuring the overall direction, control, and accountability of an organization.[2] After all, a key task of governance is to allow a proper alignment and prioritization of diverse and sometimes conflicting interests.[3] As discussed in Chapter 1, social ventures can take several forms. They can be purely philanthropic, relying mostly on donations and subsidies; hybrid, combining donations and earned income; or for-profit ventures with a social mission. The form that a social venture takes can affect its governance structure, including the founding team, whether to form a board of directors or advisers, and how to address agency problems.

1.1   *Forming a Social Venture's Founding Management Team*

Benjamin Schneider once said that "the people make the place."[4] Hence, a new social venture will be successful if the people who work for it are dedicated and sufficiently skilled to perform the tasks required for high performance. One important element of any new venture is the founding team—that is, the group of individuals who initially form the new venture. The terms "founding team" (FT) and "new venture team" (NVT) are used interchangeably to designate the founding members of any new venture. An NVT is the group of individuals that is chiefly responsible for the strategic decision-making and ongoing operations of a new venture.[5] For example, in a social venture, the NVT creates the initial policies and procedures to hire paid employees and volunteers and shape the culture of this new organization. It provides leadership for the nascent organization. The Global Health Corps application case in Chapter 4 provides an example of an FT for a social venture. Before starting the social venture, the founding team got together in Baltimore to write a business plan.

Figure 11.1 illustrates the key components of a new social venture team. They include the founder or founders, the board of directors (mainly for hybrid or for-profit social ventures), the board of advisers, paid employees, and volunteers. The founders are at the center of the new social venture as they can select members of the board of directors and/or the board of advisers. They can also hire paid employees and/or recruit volunteers and imprint their values onto the organization.

A social venture may be started by a single individual or a group of people. Studies on the creation of commercial new ventures suggest that 50–70 percent of them are started by single individuals.[6] However, despite popular legends about individual entrepreneurs, the creation and successful management of new ventures is often a team effort, shared among individuals with a diversity of skills and experiences.[7] There are numerous examples of highly successful for-profit organizations that have been created by two or more individuals, such as Microsoft and Google. But that is not to say that individual entrepreneurs are unable to create successful organizations on their own. An illustrative example is Facebook, which Mark Zuckerberg created almost singlehandedly.

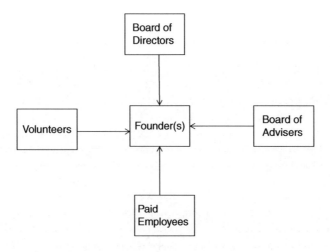

Figure 11.1 Components of a new social venture team.

In the sphere of social entrepreneurship, the decision to go it alone or to join forces with others may depend on the social entrepreneur's expectations regarding control of the venture. A social entrepreneur who intends to maintain full control of his or her social venture may decide to go it alone. For example, Dr. Georges Bwelle started Ascovime on his own (see Chapter 9). Likewise, EasySport was started by a single individual (see Chapter 5). By contrast, We Care Solar, a social venture discussed at the end of this chapter, was started by Dr. Laura Stachel with the help of her husband. Even though a social entrepreneur might have started a social venture alone, he or she may be flexible and add new partners and/or experienced advisers and even managers to the nascent social venture.

Entrepreneurial research on founding teams indicates that they bring more talent, resources, ideas, and professional network opportunities to new ventures.[8] They also have the benefit of providing psychological support to the members of the team during critical times.[9] Although there is no ideal size for a founding team, it is often suggested that anything more than four members is too large to be practical.[10] This may be due to the fact that large teams can generate conflict among the members, which may impede the new venture's performance.

1.2   Characteristics of the Founding Team

The characteristics and qualities of the founding team are important factors in the success or failure of a new venture. As is often argued, the founding team is the only asset that a new venture has at its disposal from the beginning. Thus, the skills, competencies, experience, and education of the founders can be crucial in the survival of the new enterprise.

The quality of the founding team and board members can have a *signaling effect*. Signaling is an important means through which one actor communicates their quality to others in the presence of asymmetric information.[11] In social entrepreneurship, a founding team can signal quality (or a lack of it) to potential stakeholders. For instance, entrepreneurship scholars have suggested that a venture can emit a signal to investors vis-à-vis both board structure[12] and CEO/top management team attributes.[13] Founding teams are important because organizations serve as reflections of their top executives.[14]

Some of the most important characteristics of founding team members are:

- prior entrepreneurial experience;
- industry experience (in the sector where the new venture will operate);
- networking; and
- education.

Scholars have found that prior entrepreneurial experience is one of the most consistent predictors of future entrepreneurial success.[15] Creating and running a new venture is a difficult and complex task; therefore, those who have prior experience can leverage such experience to help their new ventures succeed. The same is true for those who have relevant industry experience. If an entrepreneur has worked in a particular sector, he or she will not only understand the industry but should be able to exploit professional networks that may prove useful in providing additional resources for the nascent venture. Education is also important. The qualifications of the venture's founding team should be clearly spelled out in the social venture plan discussed in Chapter 8 because education provides the knowledge that is necessary to understand the intricacies of managing a new venture.

The founders' skills, experience, qualifications, and social/professional networks are therefore usually good indicators of whether the new venture will succeed. A nonprofit organization that has a strong base of skilled and experienced people is in the best position to raise a large sum of money and deliver the highest-quality services or products.[16]

New venture founding teams can be either homogeneous or heterogeneous. In a homogeneous founding team the members share similar backgrounds and experience, whereas in a heterogeneous team the members have dissimilar backgrounds and experience. As yet, there is no conclusive evidence as to whether homogeneous teams perform better than heterogeneous ones. For example, Klotz and colleagues contend that there is no clear relationship between new venture teams' heterogeneity and their ventures' performance.[17] While some other studies have produced mixed results,[18] most have echoed Klotz and colleagues' findings.[19] Nevertheless, some teams may have specific advantages. For instance, homogeneous teams may be able to work fast and avoid conflict since they will probably be familiar with one another's methods and share similar backgrounds. On the other hand, heterogeneous teams may have the advantage of addressing problems from a variety of perspectives (although, of course, this may lead to conflict and disagreement).

Members of the founding team must also possess strong leadership skills, because entrepreneurship is a special type of leadership that occurs in a specific setting.[20] After all, managing an organization effectively, be it a for-profit business, a social venture, a government agency, or even a country, demands sound leadership. In the case of social ventures, high-quality leadership is important for several reasons. Scholars have argued that good leadership *gets* a small business going, whereas management *keeps* it going. In other words, leaders are the architects of small businesses, while managers are the builders.[21]

When organizing the structure of the social venture, the social entrepreneur may think about establishing a board of directors.

1.3 Board of Directors

Currently, there are no universally agreed rules that govern the selection of board members for social ventures, or even whether they should appoint such a board at all. In commercial entrepreneurship, the board of directors is defined as a panel of individuals who are elected by a corporation's shareholders to oversee the management of the firm.[22] In social ventures, it is often quite different—a panel of individuals elected by key stakeholders, such as donors, and/or governments to oversee the management of the enterprise. However, when the social venture operates as a for-profit enterprise and is legally incorporated as a corporation, it may elect board members in much the same way as commercial enterprises do.

Several questions arise when a social venture considers establishing a board of directors:

- How many members will the board have?
- How and when will the board members be elected?
- What term will they serve?
- What officers and committee structure will the board have?

Addressing these questions is important in helping to build a strong board of directors. As indicated earlier, board members' qualifications and experience are important for a new venture. Possessing business and professional experience will help the board members make valuable contributions to the enterprise. Equally, if they sit on other boards, they will be able to use their professional networks to help the new venture. For instance, a board member's business connections might generate funds and donors for a social venture. Likewise, prior board experience, fundraising skills, and concern for social causes and community development can all be valuable assets for a nascent social venture.

Board members should also be committed to the social venture and its mission, as this will make them more likely to devote the necessary time and effort to fulfill their obligations. A social venture's board of directors may well perform similar functions to a commercial venture's board. Members often provide guidance, advice, and support to a venture's managers. They also lend credence to new enterprises. Entrepreneurship scholars often contend that a new firm's board is just as important as the founding team as an indicator of the likely success of the venture. Without a credible indicator, it is difficult for potential customers, investors, or employees to identify high-quality startups.[23] By contrast, when high-quality individuals join the board of a nascent firm, all of these stakeholders are likely to assume that the venture has a good chance of success.[24] The quality of the board may also add legitimacy to a new venture.

However, it should be acknowledged that, as in commercial entrepreneurship, social ventures' boards of directors may well face serious agency problems. Indeed, both for-profit and nonprofit organizations are characterized by separation of ownership and control.[25]

1.3.1   Agency Issues in Social Ventures

A principal–agent relationship is defined as a contract under which one or more people— the principal(s)—engage another person—the agent—to perform a service on their behalf which involves the delegation of some decision-making authority to the agent.[26] Agency theory assumes that the agent will not always act in the best interests of the principal because of goal conflict between the two. It therefore specifies two primary mechanisms for overseeing agents: monitoring the behavior of management and staff; and monitoring outcomes directly.[27] The first mechanism is accomplished in purely philanthropic social ventures by monitoring how the social mission is achieved. For hybrid or for-profit social ventures, the monitoring will need to include the economic mission as well as the social mission. The second mechanism is accomplished in purely philanthropic social ventures by monitoring how social results are obtained, while in hybrid and for-profit ventures it is accomplished by monitoring how social and financial results are obtained. Because the primary purpose of a social venture is to achieve a specific social mission, the board of directors must decide which control mechanism to use to maximize that mission and reduce the risk of mission drift. Mission drift is the tendency for social ventures, especially hybrid and for-profit enterprises, to lose sight of their social mission in their efforts to remain financially sustainable.[28]

In nonprofit organizations, other parties besides the owner(s), such as volunteers and donors, are involved.[29] Because of this multiplicity of ownership, several authors advocate an extended principal–agent theory for nonprofit organizations with multiple principals.[30] However, it should be acknowledged that agency theory cannot provide a clear explanation of accountability issues in nonprofit organizations. It is therefore recommended to combine it with other theories, such as stewardship theory and stakeholder theory.[31] In stewardship theory, the behavior of the steward is collective, because the steward seeks to attain the objectives of the organization.[32] For example, in nonprofit organizations, the principal can partner with the agent to accomplish the organization's objectives.[33]

1.3.2   Accountability and Stakeholder Theory in Social Ventures

Maintaining board member activity in social ventures and other nonprofit organizations is a challenging task. For example, when asked to identify board members' most important contributions to a venture, nonprofit executives listed "vitality" or "active participation" among the top five.[34] A study using data relating to 591 board members in 64 nonprofit organizations showed that gender, experience as a nonprofit board member, service on other nonprofit boards, mission attachment, and training were the most consistent predictors of confidence and active participation in board activities.[35] Some social ventures and other nonprofit organizations tend to select board members who do not have the necessary expertise in the field in which they operate. This often happens because nonprofit board members are volunteers, unpaid, and avocational, so they are frequently chosen more for their boundary-spanning attributes than for their professional knowledge of the field.[36]

In nonprofit organizations, the board of directors can be seen as an interface between the social venture and the external stakeholders.[37] Table 11.1 illustrates the various stakeholders that social ventures must interact with and manage.

In a for-profit organization, the board asks how the shareholders' value can be maximized. In a social venture, the board asks what the stakeholders want the enterprise to do. This question may be refined for social ventures that are community-based or run as cooperatives, following the Western European model. In this regard, the board must ensure that the social venture is *accountable* to its stakeholders. After receiving survey responses from 924 nonprofit board members, researchers from Stanford University found that many of these directors did not have a deep understanding of their organizations, were not engaged with their missions, and did not understand their own obligations. They also found that

Table 11.1 Stakeholders of a social venture[38]

Stakeholder type	Description
Interface stakeholders:	
Board members	The board is the governing body of the social venture. As such, it represents the social venture to the outside world and makes sure that the social mission is carried out.
Internal stakeholders:	
Managers	Management of the social venture.
Paid employees	Paid employees of the social venture.
Volunteers	Volunteers who are directly involved in the provision of the goods/ services that are delivered.
External stakeholders:	
Funders	Individuals or organizations that donate to the social venture and governments or government agencies that give subsidies to the social venture.
Beneficiaries/customers	Those who benefit from the products or services of the social venture.
Suppliers/contractors	For-profit, nonprofit, or governmental organizations that provide goods or services to the social venture.
Competitors	For-profit, nonprofit, or governmental organizations that compete with the social venture.
Organizational partners	For-profit, nonprofit, or governmental organizations that collaborate with the social venture.
Others	Other stakeholders, such as the media, community groups, and persons or groups, who are affected by externalities produced by the social venture.

most nonprofit organizations lack formal governance structures and processes.[39] To remedy these shortcomings, the researchers made several recommendations that are summarized in the box below.

Recommendations for Improving Nonprofit Boards' Performance[40]

1 Ensure your organization's mission is focused and its skills and resources are well aligned with it.
2 Ensure your mission is understood and embraced by the board, management, and other key stakeholders.
3 Establish explicit goals and strategies that are directly tied to achieving your mission.
4 Develop rigorous performance metrics that reflect those goals and strategies.
5 Hold the executive director accountable for meeting those performance metrics and evaluate his or her performance with a sound, objective process.
6 Ensure your board comprises individuals with the necessary skills, resources, generosity, diversity, and dedication to address the needs of the organization. This includes ensuring that there is a small group of committed and cohesive leaders.
7 Define the roles and responsibilities of board members explicitly to leverage their leadership, time, and resources effectively.
8 Establish well-defined board, committee, and ad hoc processes that reflect your organization's needs and context, and ensure optimal handling of key decisions and responsibilities.
9 Regularly review and assess each board member's leadership contributions as well as the board's overall performance. This includes ensuring that board members view their time as well spent.

1.4   Board of Advisers

In addition to—or in lieu of—a board of directors, a social venture may appoint a board of advisers. An advisory board is a panel of experts who are asked by a firm's managers to provide counsel and advice on an ongoing basis. It is different from a board of directors in two important ways:

- It is not elected by shareholders and does not have any legal authority over the organization.
- It has no legal responsibility and its advice is not legally binding.

Regardless of its legal form (corporation or partnership), any firm can decide to appoint a board of advisers. The principal advantage of doing so is that the board of advisers can play the same role as a board of directors without any of the legal implications. For instance, it can facilitate sound management and strategic advance, enhance a firm's network, and be instrumental in securing funding. Of course, the latter is particularly important for social ventures. There is no ideal number, but boards of advisers usually comprise between five and fifteen members.

These members are not paid, unlike members of boards of directors (at least in commercial companies), but they do receive an honorarium for their services. Social ventures may well be advised to appoint a board of advisers for several reasons. The founding team may benefit from the advisers' free counsel and guidance. Moreover, the advisers could add legitimacy to the social venture and thereby attract donors and other interested parties. For example, individuals who are well known and well connected in the nascent social venture's sector or community will automatically increase its profile.

In addition to building a founding team and assembling a board of directors or a board of advisers, a social venture must recruit and manage two types of workers—paid employees and volunteers. Managing this human capital is of paramount importance. Growing evidence suggests that founders' inability to manage their human resources successfully is an important factor in their ventures' ultimate failure.[41] This is particularly critical for social ventures, which rarely have the financial resources to recruit top talent.

It is often argued that any plan for launching a new enterprise should include a roadmap for evolving the organizational structure and the human resource system that parallels the timeline for financial and technological growth.[42] The following two sections discuss the management of paid employees and volunteers in social ventures. First, though, it is worth mentioning that social ventures must address particular human resource management issues that commercial ventures rarely have to face. For example, they usually have to recruit and manage both paid employees *and* volunteers, which can be extremely challenging.

2 Managing Paid Employees in Social Ventures

To understand the management of paid employees in social ventures, and specifically in nascent enterprises, it is important to have a grasp of human resource management in small and emerging ventures. Nonprofit organizations are increasingly applying management practices and techniques that were originally developed for the business sector, such as strategic planning, forecasting and budgeting techniques, market analysis, and performance management.[43] One of the characteristics of small and emerging enterprises is that their human resource management policies and systems tend to be informal because of the scarcity of resources. For example, recruitment in small and emerging ventures often involves the use of methods that are convenient, inexpensive, and directly controllable by the company, such as direct applicants, personal and employee referrals, and newspaper advertisements.[44]

While most of our knowledge of traditional human resource topics in large firms may also apply to small or emerging organizations, evidence suggests that new ventures are somewhat different.[45] For instance, nascent entrepreneurial firms often lack formal HR policies and systems on account of the limited resources they have at their disposal.[46] And, of course, emerging social ventures which have to rely on grants and donations are likely to possess even fewer resources. Other limiting factors are the very newness and smallness of these enterprises, which mean that they face greater challenges than their larger, more established counterparts.[47] For example, a new social venture will rarely possess the sort of high-profile reputation that will draw in top talent. Similarly, small ventures often have trouble attracting well-qualified employees.

2.1 Hiring Paid Employees in Social Ventures

Paid employees are full-time or part-time individuals who receive direct compensation for their contributions to a social venture or a nonprofit organization. They maintain contractual relations with the social ventures for which they work. For example, John, a recent MBA graduate, decided to work for a social venture as its marketing director. In this capacity, he is a paid employee.

Although most traditional, commercial human resource practices could apply to social ventures, it is worth mentioning that the economic, social, and organizational environments in which social ventures operate are quite different and merit some adjustments. For example, it is well known that social ventures generally pay less than their for-profit counterparts. Therefore, some extra characteristics should be considered when hiring paid employees. For instance, in addition to possessing the knowledge and skills required to perform a task effectively, an applicant should display commitment to the venture's social mission and a willingness to help and make a difference in the lives of others. Hence, during the interviewing process, social ventures should provide realistic job previews for the applicants, communicating both positive and negative aspects of the role. They could also stress that work is about much more than money in social ventures. Instead, it is about making an impact in the lives of others. The *psychic income* motive may be an important motivator to attract potential employees to work for social ventures. This refers to the satisfaction that accrues from performing a job that makes a difference in others' lives. In such situations, it is important to align the applicant's competencies with organizational values and culture rather than aligning basic knowledge, skills, and abilities with minimum qualifications for the job.[48]

Before making a decision to hire employees, the social venture must address the following questions:

- What type of assistance is needed?
- Why is this type of assistance needed?
- What skills and abilities should the potential employee(s) have?

The answers to these questions will determine whom to hire. They will also guide the social entrepreneur to perform a needs assessment to determine the positions to fill and the qualifications that are required to fill them. Human resource management experts often advise that hiring decisions should start with a needs assessment, which itself is the result of job analysis—a technique that is used to analyze the content of a job. A job analysis can be performed by the incumbent who is in that role at present, a supervisor, or a consultant. It generally has two outcomes: a job description and a job specification. The former is a written statement that spells out the content of a given job. The latter is a written statement that spells out the qualifications that are needed for a given job. For example, book-keeping, performing financial analysis, and raising funds could be elements in a job description; whereas possession of a bachelor's degree in accounting, knowledge of accounting software, and the ability to develop and analyze financial statements could be aspects of a job specification—what is required to do the job.

A needs assessment also helps a firm develop a skills profile. This is a chart that depicts the most important skills that are needed, and where there are any skills gaps.[49] Table 11.2 illustrates the skills profile of a potential social venture. Mark, a recent graduate from a business school's management information systems department, has recently started a social venture with two friends, John and Jane. Mark has excellent skills in management information systems and will perform all of the tasks in this area. John has excellent management and leadership skills, and Jane has excellent marketing skills. Because of the nature of the new social venture, it needs people with expertise in grant writing, accounting and finance, and administrative skills to oversee the office. From the outset, the

Table 11.2 Example of skills profile for a new social venture

	Leadership skills	Marketing skills	Management information systems skills	Accounting and finance skills	Grant writing skills	Office administration skills
Mark			X			
John	X					
Jane		X				
Gap1				O		
Gap2					O	
Gap3						O

Key: X = position filled; O = position vacant

founding team of Mark, John, and Jane decides to fill three of the six positions themselves. They will fill the rest with applicants. The skills profile depicted in Table 11.2 illustrates this situation.

2.2 Managing Paid Employees

The management of paid employees in social ventures and nonprofit organizations is a complex and difficult task. This complexity stems from the nature of these organizations and the resources that are needed to manage such a workforce. Hence, scholars studying such issues usually advocate the use of conventional management and human resource practices in social ventures. Areas such as motivation, training and development, performance appraisal, and compensation are often discussed. Indeed, for social ventures to be effective in accomplishing their social missions, the people they employ must perform at their best. This requires the use of sound human resource management practices. However, social ventures, particularly newer and smaller enterprises, often do not have the resources that are needed to manage their human capital effectively.

There are also preconceived assumptions about the workforces in social ventures that prevent a better understanding of the challenges facing the management of human resources in social ventures and other nonprofit organizations. For example, as one author pointed out when discussing remuneration, if all you knew about nonprofits came from the media, you might think that nonprofit employees were scandalously overpaid. Similarly, if you relied on nothing but academic studies of nonprofit remuneration, you might think that the employees of social ventures do not make significant sacrifices when compared with their for-profit peers. However, if you have ever worked for or with a nonprofit organization, you will know that neither of these assertions is true.[50]

Social ventures should train and develop their paid employees to help them acquire the skills and competencies that they need to improve their performance. Although they may not have formal human resources departments to run training and development programs, they can outsource such tasks or use local higher education institutions.

In addition to training and developing their paid employees, social ventures should assess the latter's work performance. Research on human resources in entrepreneurial firms suggests that their HR policies and systems often tend to be informal, especially in

Table 11.3 Motivation plan for paid employees in social ventures

Organizational factors	Job characteristics	Psychic income
Acceptable compensation	Meaningful work	Personal satisfaction
Opportunities for training and development	Work that makes a difference in the lives of others	Altruism
Performance appraisal	Enriching job	Moral engagement
Opportunities for promotion	Work that provides opportunities for personal growth	Sense of personal pride
Good supervision		

nascent firms, for the same is true for nascent social ventures. This informality may lead to a lack of opportunities to use standard HR management practices—such as performance appraisal, socialization, promotion, and other techniques—effectively.

As indicated previously, nonprofit employees often struggle to get adequate remuneration in return for their contributions. Because of their relatively limited resources, social ventures cannot use money as a motivator to attract and retain high-performing employees. Therefore, they must develop other motivational schemes. For instance, they should emphasize the values of altruism, sacrifice, and giving. Their motivational plan should focus on the content of the job and the values that can create a sense of pride and a willingness to help others and make a positive contribution to society. It should also consider the characteristics of the tasks performed to increase the level of intrinsic motivation. Focusing on altruism and meaningful tasks can compensate, at least to some extent, for the lack of adequate financial compensation.

Table 11.3 illustrates the three components of a motivational plan for social ventures: *organizational factors*; the *work itself*; and the *psychic income*. Organizational factors include compensation, relationships with supervisors, opportunities for training and development, opportunities for promotion, performance appraisal, and working conditions. The work component includes the characteristics of the job performed by a paid employee. The job should be meaningful and enriching; it should provide opportunities for personal growth and make a difference in the lives of others. The third component, psychic income, includes the personal satisfaction derived from doing the job, the sense of altruism, the moral engagement, and the sense of personal pride. The presence of these three components should provide considerable motivation to paid employees.

In addition to paid employees, social ventures usually rely on the services of volunteers. The next section discusses the hiring and management of this volunteer workforce.

3   Hiring and Managing Volunteers in a Social Venture

Before discussing the management of volunteers in social ventures and other nonprofit organizations, it is important to define the concepts of "volunteering" and "volunteer." Volunteering refers to the process of giving time freely without pay to any organization that has the aim of benefiting people in a particular cause.[51] Volunteers are often defined as people who perform activities:

- out of free will;
- without remuneration;

- in a formal organization; and
- for the benefit of others.[52]

The most obvious formal characteristic of volunteers is the absence of pay. Thus, volunteers have no monetary (or legal) reason to join or remain with an organization.[53]

Social ventures rely on volunteers to accomplish their social missions. For example, nonprofit organizations such as Médecins Sans Frontières (Doctors Without Borders), Teach for America, Big Brothers and Big Sisters all rely on volunteers. To some extent, the hiring and management of such volunteers should follow the practices that are utilized in the hiring and management of paid employees.

3.1   Hiring Volunteers

The process of attracting and selecting volunteers should be similar to the one used to attract and retain paid employees in social ventures. However, this process often uses an open call to recruit volunteers. Because volunteers perform tasks that are useful to the same degree as those performed by paid employees, social ventures must ensure that the volunteers have the skills required to complete their tasks successfully. Although volunteering is gratifying and rewarding, it can bear some risk if the volunteers are given insufficient training, support, and/or protection, and if there is a disparity of information between volunteers and managers.[54]

Certain factors lead some people to volunteer more than others. For example, employees who are satisfied with their current job tend to do more volunteering than those who are not. Moreover, such volunteers are often highly committed and tend to remain longer with nonprofit organizations. It is also possible that employees who are dissatisfied with their current jobs may volunteer in the hope that doing so will provide some compensation for their negative work experiences. In addition, personal and family factors—such as, age, not cohabiting with a partner, and the presence of older children in a household—all increase the likelihood of volunteering.[55]

An important decision the management of a social venture must make is whether or when to use volunteers rather than paid employees. Management should decide which tasks should be performed by volunteers and which should be undertaken by paid employees. It should also determine the appropriate ratio of paid employees to volunteers. Whenever volunteers are to be used, the process of recruiting them should be well planned and coordinated. Social ventures often rely on word of mouth, newspaper ads, and referrals to recruit volunteers. However, although such procedures are certainly helpful in attracting applicants, they may not always attract the *best* applicants.

Once the volunteers have been recruited, they must be managed. The following subsection analyzes volunteer management systems and their importance in retaining well-qualified volunteers.

3.2   Managing Volunteers

Social ventures that rely primarily on volunteers generally operate a volunteer management system (VMS) headed by a volunteer resource manager (VRM). The VMS is a set of policies and procedures aimed at attracting and retaining volunteers in a social business and/or a nonprofit organization. It can be computerized or manual. Without policies, a volunteer program risks undermining the professionalism of the volunteers.[56]

Volunteers bring an important benefit to a social venture—they perform tasks at no or little cost to the organization. Some scholars note that in a world that is undergoing profound and accelerated change, when volunteers agree to do unpaid work that is performed for the benefit the community they:

- contribute to the coordination and development of a more cohesive, tolerant, and democratic society;
- reproduce and consolidate the values of solidarity and public benefit; and
- promote sustainable development in its three dimensions—social, economic, and environmental—in both developed and developing countries.[57]

Managers and supervisors in social ventures and nonprofit organizations should therefore view the management of volunteers as one of their most important tasks.

The hiring and management of volunteers always incur some costs. The cycle of volunteer management comprises five phases:

- incorporation;
- development;
- assessment;
- monitoring; and
- retention.

The incorporation phase costs are incurred when drafting the job description, attracting the volunteers (both actively and passively), and selecting and inducting the successful applicants. The development stage costs relate to training, communication between the volunteer and the organization, and the expenses incurred by the volunteer in the course of his or her output-producing work. Assessment involves the application of systematic methods to gather information on the efficacy and efficiency of the volunteers' work, while monitoring—which is key to motivating and controlling the volunteers—includes such tasks as recording and evaluating their activities, and keeping track of the resources that are assigned to volunteer work.[58] The retention phase consists of developing strategies to persuade volunteers to remain active within the social venture.

The line between volunteers and paid employees is often fluid insofar as volunteers can perform many of the tasks that are performed by paid employees and vice versa. An interesting question, however, is whether there is a *psychological contract* between volunteers and the social venture. This question is important because volunteers are not compensated for their services. They do the work because they enjoy it or wish to make a contribution to society. A psychological contract refers to an individual's beliefs regarding the terms and conditions of the reciprocal exchange agreement they have negotiated with another party.[59] Indeed, there is a value-based psychological contract between volunteers and the social ventures that use their services. This is defined as a credible commitment to pursue a valued cause or principle (not limited to self-interest) that is implicitly exchanged at the nexus of the individual–organization relationship.[60] Volunteers donate their time, expertise, and commitment to help social ventures accomplish their missions.

Nonprofit organizations often employ both paid employees and volunteers. This coexistence sometimes generates problems, as several authors have indicated.[61] Hence, nonprofit managers face challenges in reconciling these internal stakeholders. Volunteers may feel that they are intrinsically motivated and express prosocial motivation. Conflict between paid employees and volunteers often stems from job threat,[62] especially when the volunteers display that they can perform certain roles just as well as paid staff.[63] One way of reducing this conflict is to create a climate of partnership and cooperation between the two groups. This demands effective leadership. Improving communication, training both paid employees and volunteers, setting clear objectives, and building a climate of mutual trust can all reduce any animosity.

Good communication between volunteers and paid staff is important because it helps with volunteer retention and can generate valuable feedback that will improve the operation of the venture.[64] Effective management of the relationship between the volunteers and the organization is always mutually beneficial, but when something goes wrong the volunteers may be less invested in addressing the problem than paid staff. In such circumstances, they may simply leave rather than work with the organization to address the issue.

Summary

This chapter discussed the importance of managing people in new social ventures. It started by exploring the role of the founding team, the board of directors or the board of advisers. The latter are particularly suited to social ventures as they can provide guidance and increase legitimacy for minimum cost. The chapter also analyzed the hiring and management of paid employees and volunteers in social ventures.

Key Terms

Agency theory; board of advisers; board of directors; legitimacy; motivational profile; needs assessment; paid employees; psychic income; signaling effect; skills profile; stakeholder theory; volunteer management system; volunteer resource manager; volunteering; volunteers

Review Questions

1 Do you think that there is an ideal number for a social venture founding team? Why do you think a large number would be detrimental?
2 Explain why selecting a well-known and highly respected board of directors is likely to add legitimacy to a nascent social venture.
3 Explain why selecting a well-known and highly respected board of advisers is likely to add legitimacy to a nascent social venture.
4 What is signaling and what role does it play in adding legitimacy to a nascent social venture?
5 Explain some of the challenges in the hiring and management of paid employees in social ventures.
6 Explain some of the challenges in the hiring and management of volunteers in social ventures.
7 Why do social ventures need paid employees?
8 Why do social ventures need volunteers?
9 Discuss the importance of psychic income as a motivating factor.
10 Explain the factors leading to potential conflict between paid employees and volunteers.

Application Questions

1   Suppose that you have recently started a new social venture with two friends. As you contemplate adding employees to your venture, one of your friends tells you that you need to develop a skills profile to establish your hiring priorities. Taking your friend's advice, develop a skills profile and explain how it will help you identify the positions you need to fill.

2   Sue recently started a social venture aimed at increasing school retention in inner-city schools in the United States. The venture employs five paid employees and 15 volunteers. Sue wonders how she might motivate her volunteers since she does not have the financial resources to pay them. She comes to you for advice. Particularly, she would like you to develop a motivational plan for the volunteers that might help instill a sense of sacrifice, generosity, and helping behavior. Describe the key components of your motivational plan and explain how it will motivate the volunteers.

3   Mark is the founder and president of a social venture in your community. He employs both paid employees and volunteers, and has recently observed conflict between these two groups. He comes to you for advice and help to identify the root causes of the conflict and propose solutions. Develop a plan of action that includes how you will identify the causes of the conflict and what remedies you propose. Also mention how you plan to assess the success of your intervention. Be as specific as you can be.

4   Your friend John has just created a new social venture which aims to tackle homelessness in his city. He is thinking about creating a board of advisers for his venture and comes to you for recommendations. What will you advise? Make your recommendations as specific as possible and consider such issues as the composition, size, characteristics, and potential responsibilities of the board.

5   Jennifer graduated from college with an MBA. After working for ten years in a large corporation, she decided to start a hybrid social venture along with her husband and a friend. She is contemplating setting up a board of directors. What advice would you offer regarding how to form an effective board?

Application Case 1: We Care Solar: Lighting UP Childbirth[65]

In the developed world, delivering a baby is a joyful and routine experience. In other parts of the world, particularly in the poorest ones, however, it is an experience that is full of risks, including postnatal complications and even maternal deaths. Often, these negative consequences are not due to the lack of qualified medical personnel or midwives. Rather, they are often due to the lack of reliable electricity in health facilities. The lack of reliable electricity implies that in developing countries, power outage is a frequent phenomenon. For example, in Africa, power outage is a common occurrence. Frequent power outage can impair medical equipment and endanger simple medical procedures. Even the most experienced doctor cannot deliver babies in the darkness. However surprising this might sound, it is an experience lived by millions of women and families in the developing world.

During a trip in Nigeria to research the causes of maternal death, Dr. Laura Stachel, an obstetrician-gynecologist in Berkeley, California, observed first-hand how darkness could complicate the work of doctors and midwives. She witnessed one day when the light went out when doctors were in the middle of a Caesarean section and she had to provide her own flashlight to help the doctors complete the surgery. She also observed on countless occasions that midwives were using all kinds of makeshift lighting, such as Kerosene lanterns, candles, and even cell phones to deliver babies.[1] This situation struck her at the core and she decided to take action. The key motivation behind her actions was to see a world where women can deliver babies safely and with dignity, and women don't have to fear an event that is considered a joy in the United States. To see birth associated with death and fear is an outrage.[2]

She contacted her husband, Dr. Al Aronson, a solar energy educator, to provide a techno-logical solution to the problem. Dr. Aronson designed a solar kit that helped solve the problem at the hospital she was in Nigeria. When she came back to the United States, she and her husband created a social venture, *We Care Solar* (www.wecaresolar.org), to provide electricity to hospitals and health clinics in the developing world. *We Care Solar*'s mission is to provide reliable electricity for human purposes. It focuses on maternal health clinics in the developing world where pregnancy complications claim the life of a mother every 90 seconds. According to estimates, there are more than 300,000 health clinics worldwide that do not have reliable electricity and therefore reliable lighting when night falls.[3]

We Care Solar developed a solar suitcase that is an easy-to-use portable power unit that provides health workers with highly efficient medical lighting and power for mobile commu-nication, laptop computers and small medical devices.[4] The system includes high-efficiency LED medical task lighting, a universal cell phone charger, a battery charger for AAA or AA batteries, and outlets for 12V DC devices. The basic system comes with 40 or 80 watts of solar panels, and a 12 amp-hour lithium ferrous phosphate battery. The maternity kit comes with a fetal doppler. An expansion kit is available for utilizing larger batteries and additional lights.[5] The solar suitcase is priced $1,500 but there are efforts to reduce the price and make it more affordable.

The solar suitcase is making a difference in the developing world. As of today, it has been used in 32 countries in Africa, South Asia, the Caribbean and Central America (see Table 1). For example, in one hospital in Nigeria, its introduction contributed to the reduction of mater-nal deaths by 70 percent and the hospital's ability to see patients increased by 16 percent.[6] For her efforts, Dr. Stachel was among the top 10 2013 CNN Heroes of the Year. *We Care Solar* was the recipient of a $1 million grant from the United Nations Department of Economic and Social Affairs (DESA).[7] *We Care Solar* partners with several organizations including the MacArthur Foundation, the Blum Center for Developing Economies, Global Health Founda-tion, Solar Energy International, STARR International Foundation, and UBS Optimus Foun-dation. In addition to selling the solar suitcase, it also solicits donations on its website. Table 1 illustrates the regions and countries where the solar suitcases have been installed and are in operation.

Table 1 Solar Suitcase Installations

Africa	Asia	Caribbean	Central America
Cameroon	Afghanistan	Haiti	Mexico
Democratic	Burma		Nicaragua
Republic of Congo	India		
Eritrea	Pakistan		
Ethiopia	Japan		
Kenya	Nepal		
Liberia	Papua New		
Malawi	Guinea		
Nigeria	Philippines		
Rwanda	Tibet		
Senegal	Vietnam		
Sierra Leone			
Somalia			
South Sudan			
Tanzania			
The Gambia			
Uganda			
Zimbabwe			

Discussion Questions

1   Visit the website of *We Care Solar* at www.wecaresolar.org and explain how you could help this organization accomplish its social mission.
2   Describe the background of the founding team of *We Care Solar*. What skills and experience were useful in launching and making this social venture successful?
3   Visit the website of *We Care Solar* at www.wecaresolar.org and discuss whether this social venture is using volunteers. For what activities are volunteers used?
4   What role did leadership play in the creation of We Care Solar? Would you consider Dr. Stachel an effective leader? Yes, No? Explain.

References

1   *http://www.cnn.com/2013/02/28/health/cnnheroes-stachel-solar-power*. [Retrieved on December 15, 2015].
2   *http://www.cnn.com/2013/02/28/health/cnnheroes-stachel-solar-power*. [Retrieved on December 15, 2015].
3   *http://www.pbs.org/newshour/rundown/delivering-in-the-dark-we-care-solar*. [Retrieved on April 22, 2016].
4   *http://wecaresolar.org/solutions/we-care-solar-suitcase*. [Retrieved on April 22, 106].
5   *http://wecaresolar.org/solutions/we-care-solar-suitcase*. [Retrieved on April 22, 106].
6   *http://www.cnn.com/2013/02/28/health/cnnheroes-stachel-solar-power*. [Retrieved on December 15, 2015].
7   *http://www.pbs.org/newshour/rundown/delivering-in-the-dark-we-care-solar*. [Retrieved on April 22, 2016].
8   *http://www.un.org/apps/news/story.asp?NewsId=51869#.Vxo8Zz_bJ9A*. [Retrieved on April 22, 2016].

Application Case 2: Sustainable Health Enterprises[66]

While interning at the World Bank's country office in Mozambique, Elizabeth Scharpf, a graduate of both Harvard Business School and the Harvard Kennedy School of Government, observed that most girls and women did not have access to affordable menstrual products because they were too expensive.[1] As a result, the girls were missing school and the women missing work during their monthly menstruation periods. She also learned that this problem was not limited to Mozambique but concerns millions of women in the developing world. The problem is not that these products do not exist in poor countries but they are often too expensive to be used by most girls and women. Hence, these women and girls use makeshift pads that are not always hygienic and can pose health risks.

Scharpf's goal was to tackle this problem by creating a social venture that could manufacture and sell affordable sanitary pads to girls and women in the developing world. In 2007, she created Sustainable Health Enterprises (SHE, http://sheinnovates.com), with the aim of providing affordable sanitary pads to women and girls in impoverished nations. Scharpf hand-picked a country, Rwanda, where she started her venture. According to Scharpf, Rwanda was selected for three main reasons: 1) the existence of organized networks of community health workers and women's groups, 2) the existence of business-friendly policies, and 3) the fact that Rwanda is a small country.[2] In addition, in Rwanda, more than eighteen

percent of girls miss, on average, 35 days of school every year due to their periods and ineffective pads.[3] SHE is partnering with networks of women to produce and sell sanitary pads
made from banana fiber.[4]

SHE has produced more than 59,000 sanitary pads.[5] The sanitary pads cost 50 percent
of the price of imported products.[6] SHE's vision is to become a viable option for the
almost five million customers in Rwanda. It has a hybrid business model that includes
health education services and micro-business linkages to distribute the sanitary pads. The
educational aspect intends to build confidence and self-esteem in the girls and women. SHE
runs an educational program on Radio Rwanda that has reached more than 2.7 million
girls and women. It also instituted a menstruation hygiene day, which is held on May 28 in
Rwanda.[7] These activities help to emphasize the importance of hygienic menstruation. The
economic aspect is to provide an opportunity for the women to be involved in economic
activities that generate income they can use to support themselves and their families. SHE
partners with organizations, such as the United Nations Children's Fund, the Segal Family
Foundation, and the Forum for African Women Educationalists, and institutions of higher
education, such as the Massachusetts Institute of Technology (MIT), North Carolina State
University in the United States, and the Kigali Institute of Science and Technology in
Rwanda.[8]

Scharpf graduated from Harvard University with an MBA (Master of Business Administration) and an MPA (Master in Public Administration). As a founder and Chief Executive
Instigator (a title she created) of Sustainable Health Enterprises, she has been recognized as a
thought leader and an effective social entrepreneur and has won numerous awards and fellowships. She was awarded the Curry Stone Design Prize in 2010. She also won the 2013 Innovation Award of the Social Ventures Network, and the 2013 Grinnel Prize (a prize honoring
social justice that is presented annually to leaders under 40 who are making creative innovations in social justice).[9] Sustainable Health Enterprises' aim is to expand its business model in
other developing countries after it has been proven successful in Rwanda.

Women processing banana leaves to make sanitary pads in Rwanda.
Sustainable Health Enterprises, Inc.

Women proud to show the sanitary pads.

Discussion Questions

1 Watch the YouTube video at https://www.youtube.com/watch?v=GfTsnBykBTE. After listening to Elizabeth Scharpf's interview, explain the source of her idea.
2 Visit the website of Sustainable Health Enterprises (http://sheinnovates.com). What can you say about its top management team?
3 Identify the different stakeholders of Sustainable Health Enterprises. How are the interests of each served?
4 Visit the website of Sustainable Health Enterprises and look at the board of directors. What signal do you think this board sends regarding the quality of management at Sustainable Health Enterprises?

References

1 *http://www.fastcompany.com/1692270/banana-based-pad-maker-elizabeth-scharpf-wants-rwandan-women-educated-period*. [Retrieved on January 28, 2015].
2 *http://www.fastcompany.com/1692270/banana-based-pad-maker-elizabeth-scharpf-wants-rwandan-women-educated-period*. [Retrieved on January 28, 2015].
3 *http://www.fastcompany.com/1692270/banana-based-pad-maker-elizabeth-scharpf-wants-rwandan-women-educated-period*. [Retrieved on January 28, 2015].
4 *http://www.fastcompany.com/1692270/banana-based-pad-maker-elizabeth-scharpf-wants-rwandan-women-educated-period*. [Retrieved on January 28, 2015].
5 http://sheinnovates.com/wp-content/uploads/2016/02/SHE-Q2-2015-Stakeholder-Report.pdf. [Retrieved on April 18, 2016].
6 *http://www.csrwire.com/blog/posts/1279-the-resilient-social-entrepreneur-an-interview-with-a-chief-instigating-officer*. [Retrieved on April 18, 2016].
7 *http://sheinnovates.com/wp-content/uploads/2016/02/SHE-Q2-2015-Stakeholder-Report.pdf*. [Retrieved on April 18, 2016].
8 *http://sheinnovates.com/about-us/#ourteam*. [Retrieved on April 18, 2016].
9 *http://sheinnovates.com/about-us/#awards*. [Retrieved on April 18, 2016].

Notes

1 Barringer, R. B., & Ireland, R. D. (2016). *Entrepreneurship: Successfully launching new ventures.* 5th edition. New York: Pearson.

2 Cornforth, C. (2012). Nonprofit governance research: Limitations of the focus on boards and suggestions for new directions. *NonProfit and Voluntary Sector Quarterly, 41*(6), 1117–1136; Cornforth, C. (2014). Nonprofit governance research: The need for innovative perspectives and approaches. In C. Cornforth & W. A. Brown (Eds.), *Nonprofit governance: Innovative perspectives and approaches* (pp. 1–14). New York: Routledge.

3 Ebrahim, A., Battilana, J., & Mair, J. (2014). The governance of social enterprises: Mission drift and accountability challenges in hybrid organizations. *Research in Organizational Behavior, 34*, 81–100.

4 Schneider, B. (1987). The people make the place. *Personnel Psychology, 40*(3), 437–453.

5 Barringer, R. B., & Ireland, R. D. (2012). *Entrepreneurship: Successfully launching new ventures.* 4th edition. New York: Pearson; Klotz, C. A., Hmieleski, M. K., Bradley, H. B., & Busenitz, W. L. (2014). New venture teams: A review of the literature and roadmap for future research. *Journal of Management, 40*(1), 226–255.

6 Miller, D., Le Breton-Miller, I., & Lester, R. H. (2011). Family and lone founder ownership and strategic behavior: Social context, identity, and institutional logics. *Journal of Management Studies, 48*(1), 1–25.

7 Ensley, D. M., Pearson, W. A., & Amason, C. A. (2002). Understanding the dynamics of new venture top management teams: Cohesion, conflict, and new venture performance. *Journal of Business Venturing, 17*(4), 365–387.

8 Iacobucci, D., & Rosa, P. (2010). The growth of business groups by habitual entrepreneurs: The role of entrepreneurial teams. *Entrepreneurship Theory and Practice, 34*(2), 351–377; Forbes, D. P., Borchert, P. S., Zellmer-Bruhn, M. E., & Sapienza, H. J. (2006). Entrepreneurial team formation: An exploration of new addition. *Entrepreneurship Theory and Practice, 30*(3), 225–248.

9 Wood, M. S., & McKinley, W. (2010). The production of entrepreneurial opportunity: A constructivist perspective. *Strategic Entrepreneurship Journal, 4*(1), 66–84.

10 Vissa, B. (2011). A matching theory of entrepreneurs' ties formation intentions and initiation of economic exchange. *Academy of Management Journal, 54*(1), 137–158.

11 Spence, M. (2002). Signaling in retrospect and the information structure of markets. *American Economic Review, 92*(3), 434–459; Spence, M. (1973). Job market signaling. *Quarterly Journal of Economics, 87*(3), 355–374.

12 Certo, S. T., Daily, C., & Dalton, D. (2001). Signaling firm value through board structure: An investigation of initial public offerings. *Entrepreneurship Theory and Practice, 26*(1), 33–50.

13 Lester, R., Certo, S. T., Dalton, C., Dalton, D., & Cannella, A. (2006). Initial public offering investor valuations: An examination of top management team prestige and environmental uncertainty. *Journal of Small Business Management, 44*(1), 1–26; Zhang, Y., & Wiersema, M. (2009). Stock market reaction to CEO certification: The signaling role of CEO background. *Strategic Management Journal, 30*(7), 693–710.

14 Hambrick, D. C., & Mason, P. A. (1984). Upper echelons: The organization as a reflection of its top managers. *Academy of Management Review, 9*(2), 193–206.

15 Audretsch, D. B., Bonte, W., & Keilbatch, M. (2008). Entrepreneurial capital and its impact on knowledge diffusion and economic performance. *Journal of Business Venturing, 23*(6), 687–698; Hoang, H., & Gimeno, J. (2010). Becoming a founder: How founder role identity affects entrepreneurial transitions and persistence in founding. *Journal of Business Venturing, 25*(1), 41–53.

16 Hudson, M. (1999). *Managing without profit: The art of managing third-sector organizations.* 2nd edition. London: Penguin.

17 Klotz, C. A., Hmieleski, M. K., Bradley, H. B., & Busenitz, W. L. (2014). New venture teams: A review of the literature and roadmap for future research. *Journal of Management, 40*(1), 226–255.

18 Ensley, M. D., & Hmieleski, K. M. (2005). A comparative study of new venture top manage-ment team composition, dynamics and performance between university-based and independent startups. *Research Policy, 34*(7), 1091–1105.

19 Chowdhury, S. (2005). Demographic diversity for building an effective entrepreneurial team: Is it important? *Journal of Business Venturing, 20*(6), 727–746.

20 Vecchio, R. P. (2003). Entrepreneurship and leadership: Common trends and common threads. *Human Resource Management Review, 13*(2), 303–327; Carland J. C., & Carland, J. W. (2012). A model of shared entrepreneurial leadership. *Academy of Entrepreneurship Journal, 18*(2), 71–81.

21 Scarborough, M. N. (2014). *Essentials of entrepreneurship and small business management.* 7th edition. New York: Pearson.

22 Lester, R. H., Hillman, A., Zardkoohi, A., & Cannella, Jr., A. A. (2008). Former government officials as outside directors: The role of human and social capital. *Academy of Management Journal, 51*(5), 999–1013. Dalziel, T., Gentry, R. J., & Bowerman, M. (2011). An integrated agency–resource dependence view of the influence of directors' human and relational capital on firms' R&D spending. *Journal of Management Studies, 48*(6), 1217–1242.

23 Barringer, R. B., & Ireland, R. D. (2016). *Entrepreneurship: Successfully launching new ventures.* 5th edition. New York: Pearson.

24 Connelly, B. L., Certo, S. T., Ireland, R. D., & Reutzel, C. R. (2011). Signaling theory: An assess-ment and review. *Journal of Management, 37*(1), 39–67.

25 Fama, E. F., & Jensen, M. C. (1983). Separation of ownership and control. *Journal of Law and Economics, 26*(2), 301–325.

26 Jensen, M. C., & Meckling, W. H. (1976). Theory of the firm: Managerial behavior, agency costs and ownership structure. *Journal of Financial Economics, 3*(4), 305–360.

27 Eisenhardt, K. M. (1989). Agency theory: An assessment and review. *Academy of Management Review, 14*(1), 57–74; Jensen, M. C., & Meckling, W. H. (1976). Theory of the firm: Mana-gerial behaviour, agency cists and ownership structure. *Journal of Financial Economics, 3*(4), 305–360; Dalton, D. R., Hitt, M. A., Certo, S. T., & Dalton, C. M. (2007). The fundamental agency problem and its mitigation: Independence, equity, and the market for corporate control. *Academy of Management Annals, 1*(1), 1–64.

28 Ebrahim, A., Battilana, J., & Mair, J. (2014). The governance of social enterprises: Mission drift and accountability challenges in hybrid organizations. *Research in Organizational Behavior, 34*, 81–100; Battilina, J., & Lee, M. (2014). Advancing research on hybrid organizing: Insights from the study of social enterprises. *Academy of Management Annals, 8*(1), 397–441.

29 Van Puyvelde, S., Caeers, R., Du Bois, C., & Jegers, M. (2012). The governance of nonprofit organizations: Integrating agency theory with stakeholder and stewardship theories. *Nonprofit and Voluntary Sector Quarterly, 41*(3), 431–451.

30 Steinberg, R. (2010). Principal–agent theory and nonprofit accountability. In K. J. Hopt & T. von Hippel (Eds.), *Comparative corporate governance of nonprofit organizations* (pp. 73–125). Cambridge: Cambridge University Press; Jegers, M. (2008). *Managerial economics of non-profit organizations.* London: Routledge.

31 Steinberg, R. (2010). Principal–agent theory and nonprofit accountability. In K. J. Hopt & T. von Hippel (Eds.), *Comparative corporate governance of nonprofit organizations* (pp. 73–125). Cambridge: Cambridge University Press.

32 Davis, J. H., Schoorman, J. D., & Donaldson, L. (1997). Toward a stewardship theory of management. *Academy of Management Review, 22*(1), 20–47.

33 Cumberland, D. M., Kerrick, S. A., D'Mello, J., & Petrosko, J. M. (2015). Nonprofit board balance and perceived performance. *Nonprofit Management & Leadership, 25*(4), 449–462.

34 Brown, W. A., & Guo, C. (2010). Exploring key roles for nonprofit boards. *Nonprofit and Voluntary Sector Quarterly, 39*(3), 536–546.

35 Brown, A. W., Hillman, J. A., & Okun, A. M. (2012). Factors that influence monitoring and resource provision among nonprofit board members. *Nonprofit and Voluntary Sector Quarterly, 41*(1), 145–156.

36   Reid, W., & Turbide, J. (2012). Board/staff relationships in a growth crisis: Implications for nonprofit governance. *Nonprofit and Voluntary Sector Quarterly, 41*(1), 82–99.

37   Mason, C., Kirkbride, J., & Bryde, D. (2006). From stakeholders to institutions: The changing face of social enterprise governance theory. *Management Decision, 45*(2), 284–301.

38   Adapted from: Van Puyvelde, S., Caeers, R., Du Bois, C., & Jegers, M. (2012). The governance of nonprofit organizations: Integrating agency theory with stakeholder and stewardship theories. *Nonprofit and Voluntary Sector Quarterly, 41*(3), 431–451.

39   Larcker, D. F., Donatiello, N., Meehan III, W. F., & Tayan, B. (2015). *2015 survey on board of directors of nonprofit organizations.* Stanford: Stanford Graduate School of Business, Rock Center for Corporate Governance.

40   Larcker, D. F., Donatiello, N., Meehan III, W. F., & Tayan, B. (2015). *2015 survey on board of directors of nonprofit organizations.* Stanford: Stanford Graduate School of Business, Rock Center for Corporate Governance.

41   Baron, R. A. (2003). Human resource management and entrepreneurship: Some reciprocal benefits of closer links. *Human Resource Management Review, 13*(2), 253–256.

42   Baron, J. N., & Hannan, M. T. (2002). Organizational blueprints for success in high-tech start-ups: Lessons from the Stanford project on emerging companies. *California Management Review, 44*(3), 8–36.

43   Dart, R. (2004). Being "business-like" in a nonprofit organization: A grounded and inductive typology. *Nonprofit and Voluntary Sector Quarterly, 23*(2), 290–310.

44   Heneman, H. G., & Berkley, R. A. (1999). Applicant attraction, practices and outcomes in small businesses. *Journal of Small Business Management, 37*(1), 53–74.

45   Cardon, S. M., & Stevens, E. C. (2004). Managing human resources in small organizations: What do we know? *Human Resource Management Review, 14*(3), 295–323.

46   Markman, G. D., & Baron, R. A. (2003). Person–entrepreneurship fit: While some people are more successful as entrepreneurs than others. *Human Resource Management Review, 13*(2), 281–301.

47   Stinchcombe, A. (1965). Social structure and organizations. In J. G. March (Ed.), *Handbook of organizations* (pp. 142–193). Chicago: Rand McNally.

48   Heneman, H. G., & Berkley, R. A. (1999). Applicant attraction, practices and outcomes in small businesses. *Journal of Small Business Management, 37*(1), 53–74.

49   Barringer, R. B. & Ireland, R. D. (2016). *Entrepreneurship: Successfully launching new ventures.* 5th edition. New York: Pearson.

50   Manzo P. (2004). The real salary scandal. *Stanford Social Innovation Review*, Winter, 65–67.

51   Gaskin, K., & Smith, J. D. (1997). *A new civil Europe? A study of the extent and role of volunteering.* London: National Volunteering Centre.

52   Cnaan, R., Handy, F., & Wadsworth, M. (1996). Defining who is a volunteer: Conceptual and empirical considerations. *Nonprofit and Voluntary Sector Quarterly, 25*(3), 364–384.

53   Kreutzer, K., & Jäger, U. (2011). Volunteering vs. managerialism: Conflict over organizational identity in voluntary associations. *Nonprofit and Voluntary Sector Quarterly, 40*(4), 634–661.

54   Dong, H. K. D. (2015). The effects of individual risk propensity on volunteering. *Nonprofit Management and Leadership, 25*(1), 5–18.

55   Ariza-Montes, A., Roldan-Salgueiro, J. L., & Leal-Rodriguez, A. (2012). Employee and volunteer: An unlikely cocktail. *Nonprofit Management and Leadership, 25*(3), 255–268.

56   Connors, T. D. (Ed.). (2012). *The volunteer management handbook: Leadership strategies for success.* 2nd edition. Hoboken, NJ: Wiley.

57   Sajardo, A., & Serra, I. (2011). The economic value of volunteer work: Methodological analysis and application to Spain. *Nonprofit and Voluntary Sector Quarterly, 40*(5), 873–895; Handy, F., Mook, L., & Quarter, J. (2008). The interchangeability of paid staff and volunteers in nonprofit organizations. *Nonprofit and Voluntary Sector Quarterly, 37*(1), 76–92.

58   Sajardo, A., & Serra, I. (2011). The economic value of volunteer work: Methodological analysis and application to Spain. *Nonprofit and Voluntary Sector Quarterly, 40*(5), 873–895.

59 Rousseau, D. M. (1989). Psychological and implied contracts in organizations. *Employee Responsibilities and Rights Journal*, 2(2), 121–139.
60 Thompson, J. A., & Bunderson, J. S. (2003). Violations of principle: Ideological currency in the psychological contract. *Academy of Management Review*, 28(4), 571–586.
61 Ariza-Montes, A., Roldan-Salgueiro, J. L., & Leal-Rodriguez, A. (2012). Employee and volunteer: An unlikely cocktail. *Nonprofit Management and Leadership*, 25(3), 255–268.
62 Pearce, J. (1993). *Volunteers: The organizational behavior of unpaid workers*. London: Routledge.
63 Pearce, J. (1993). *Volunteers: The organizational behavior of unpaid workers*. London: Routledge.
64 Garner, T. J., & Garner, T. L. (2011). Volunteering an opinion: Organizational voice and volunteer retention in nonprofit organizations. *Nonprofit and Voluntary Sector Quarterly*, 40(5), 812–828.
65 Source for this whole section: O'Reilly, C. (2013). "Solar suitcase" saving moms, babies. CNN, October 14. http://edition.cnn.com/2013/02/28/health/cnnheroes-stachel-solar-power/, retrieved on December 15, 2013.
66 Source for this whole section: Nerenberg, J. (2010). Banana-based pad maker Elizabeth Scharpf wants Rwandan women educated. Period. *Fast Company*, September 30. www.fastcompany.com/1692270/banana-based-pad-maker-elizabeth-scharpf-wants-rwandan-women-educated-period, retrieved on January 28, 2015.

Chapter 12

Social Venture Effectiveness

Learning Objectives

1 Help students understand the concept of effectiveness.
2 Help students understand the concept of efficiency in social entrepreneurship.
3 Help students identify the different models of organizational effectiveness.
4 Help students develop the skills required to measure the effectiveness of social ventures.
5 Help students develop the skills required to measure the efficiency of social ventures.

The purpose of this chapter is to introduce the concepts of effectiveness and efficiency in the context of social entrepreneurship. The chapter focuses on the internal aspects of the organization and does not deal with its social impact, as the latter will be discussed in Chapter 14. The chapter is divided into four sections. The first section defines and explains the concepts of effectiveness and efficiency following the tradition of organization theory. The second describes the tools that are used to measure organizational effectiveness. The third analyzes the concept of effectiveness in social ventures. The fourth describes the measures used to assess the efficiency of social ventures.

1 Understanding Organizational Efficiency and Effectiveness

Before discussing effectiveness in social ventures, it is important to retrace the historic roots of the concept of organizational effectiveness. This is important because recent work tends to neglect the impact of this literature on the study of the effectiveness of social ventures and other nonprofit organizations.[1] Because social enterprises play an important role in today's society, it is important to understand whether they do what they intend to do effectively. Etzioni's classic comment on the pervasiveness of organizations in our lives is relevant to our understanding of the role of social ventures:

> we are born in organizations, educated in organizations, and most of us spend much of our lives working in organizations. We spend much of our leisure time paying, playing, and praying in organizations. Most of us will die in an organization, and when the time comes for burial, the largest organization of all, the state, must grant official permission.[2]

Questions of effectiveness have become increasingly important in the world of practice, as government and philanthropic funders, clients, and the public exert increased pressure on nonprofit organizations to demonstrate their impact on complex social problems.[3]

The concept of effectiveness has been extensively studied in organizational behavior and management. However, there seems to be no agreed definitions of organizational effectiveness in the literature, so much so that some authors contend that there are as many definitions as there are organizations, because such definitions rest on individual perceptions and judgments.[4]

Despite the lack of a clear definition, one might define "organizational effectiveness" simply as the extent to which an organization accomplishes its core objectives, whereas "efficiency" refers to the extent to which an organization is able to use fewer resources and yet still accomplish its core objectives. It is argued that the attitudes and behaviors of an organization's members and the internal processes of the organization may contribute to effectiveness but should not be confused with it.[5] Organizational effectiveness evaluations compare organizational performance to existing standards and to the performance of other organizations.[6] They are generally prompted by a number of queries:

- to diagnose correlates of success and failure;
- to predict future performance; and
- to differentiate between good and poor performers.[7]

Common indicators of effectiveness include mission statements, recent needs assessments, planning documents, measurements of client satisfaction, formal appraisal processes for chief executive officers and employees, independent financial audits, and statements of organizational effectiveness criteria.[8] Effective organizations tend to use most or all of these criteria, whereas ineffective organizations generally use fewer of them.[9]

An extensive review of the literature on organizational effectiveness spanning from 1977 to 1997 reveals that effectiveness has been conceptualized in a variety of ways and that research objectives pursued by scholars have changed over time.[10] Such research has often adopted a social constructionist view, considering organizational effectiveness as a socially constructed concept that emphasizes issues of process over measurement.[11] The following sub-sections discuss two main models of organizational effectiveness that could provide insights for social entrepreneurs to understand the importance of assessing their social ventures' effectiveness.

1.1   Evolution of Organizational Effectiveness Models

Several models have been developed to identify and explain the factors that are conducive to effectiveness. The first focuses on goal attainment[12] and considers an organization as effective when it accomplishes its stated goals. Known as the purposive-rational model of organizational effectiveness, it assumes that organizations have goals that must be accomplished.[13] In this perspective, the yardstick for measuring organizational effectiveness is based either on the goals an organization *claims* to be pursuing (public or official goals) or the goals the organization *actually* pursues (private or operative goals).[14]

Despite its widespread use in early works on organizational effectiveness, the purposive-rational model had several limitations that diminished its validity. For example, organizational goals were often vague, multiple, or could change over time. These shortcomings led to the emergence of several alternative models, such as the system models of effectiveness, which focus on a broader set of variables when assessing the means that are necessary to achieve an organization's goals.[15] System models construe effectiveness as the ability of an organization to exploit its environment in the acquisition of scarce and valued resources to sustain its operations.[16] Thus, an organization's ability to maintain sufficient internal resources is the main criterion for assessing its effectiveness. More modern models of organizational effectiveness have also been developed. However, here we will focus only on the two models that are most relevant to the study and management of social ventures: the multiple-constituency model and the social constructionist perspective.

1.2   The Multiple-Constituency Model

The multiple-constituency model suggests that organizations have multiple stakeholders and so must strive to meet the expectations of each of them. In this perspective, an organization is effective only when it meets its stakeholders' expectations. In other words, effectiveness lies in the eye of the stakeholder(s). Of course, what is effective for one stakeholder may be perceived as ineffective by another. This model is relevant for social ventures because they must navigate between the expectations of multiple stakeholders. Since social ventures have multiple stakeholders, each stakeholder develops criteria with which to measure the effectiveness of the organization. Different constituents are likely to use or attach different priorities to different criteria, making the possibility of widely applicable dimensions unlikely.[17] Therefore, measuring effectiveness is a complex and daunting task because competing values are involved in its assessment. For example, a recent review of the literature on performance measures among international social ventures and a series of interviews with 12 US social entrepreneurs found some significant differences in the use of performance measures among the various types of social enterprises related to the focus on stakeholders and the emphasis on inputs, outputs, or outcomes.[18]

These findings are consistent with those of previous research that has investigated stakeholders' perceptions of effectiveness. Scholars have investigated whether the effectiveness of nonprofit organizations is judged consistently by differing constituencies and whether changes in board effectiveness and overall organizational effectiveness (judged by differing constituencies) result from changes in the use of practices regarded as the "right" way to manage. The results show that different constituencies judge the effectiveness of nonprofit organizations differently.[19] This seems obvious, because people have different values, expectations, and criteria regarding what is or what should be important for an organization. Thus, the task of the social venture and its managers is to develop the necessary skills to manage a range of stakeholder expectations. In fact, one of the main tasks of stakeholder management is to interpret the nature of stakeholders' expectations and weigh the appropriateness of those expectations against the values and mission of the organization, the executives' own professional norms, and the organization's interpretation of the public good.[20]

In this regard, effectiveness depends on the responsiveness of the social venture to stakeholders' concerns. And effectiveness is considered as an organization's ability to satisfy key strategic constituencies in its environment. Because multiple criteria are used to assess effectiveness, one may say that effectiveness is a portfolio of performance dimensions assessed by a group of evaluators.[21] A study that used the Delphi Technique to measure effectiveness found that practitioner–experts define "objective effectiveness" simply as employing correct procedures, whereas stakeholders frequently vary substantially in their judgment of the effectiveness of a single organization. Stakeholders' judgments are seldom related to objective effectiveness; and different stakeholders use different bases when making their effectiveness judgments in addition to some common measures—most notably, board effectiveness.[22]

1.3   The Social Constructionist Perspective

The social constructionist perspective is not a model of effectiveness per se because social constructionism is a more general ontological perspective that considers reality—or some parts of reality—to be created by the beliefs, knowledge, and actions of people.[23] This reality is not a thing that is independent of people, although people may also believe that what they have created exists independently of themselves.[24] In the social constructionist view, individuals do not *discover* the world and its ways but collectively *invent* them.[25] As they invent reality, people may come to agree or disagree on what this reality actually is. The social constructionist perspective therefore treats effectiveness as stakeholders' judgments that are formed in an ongoing process of sensemaking and negotiation.[26] In this regard, effectiveness is not an objective reality but a social construction, an achievement of organizational agents and other stakeholders in convincing one another that an organization is pursuing the correct objectives in the correct way.[27] This has led some authors to argue that performance and social impact measurement is socially constructed and does not represent truth to seek or discover.[28] Here, it interesting to ask who should determine what is relevant and therefore what should be taken into account when measuring the effectiveness of a social venture.

The social constructionist perspective shares with the multiple-constituency model an emphasis on effectiveness as judgments by stakeholders. They both also treat stakeholders' goals as rationally predictable and rather stable.[29] However, the social constructionist perspective conceives judgments of effectiveness as outcomes of a stream of interactions and impressions, in which the stakeholders may be unaware—or incompletely aware—of their criteria or the information they use to reach judgments on those criteria.[30] It fits well with social ventures because they often have several stakeholders with contrasting expectations. For example, the public may expect a social venture simply to fulfill its social mission, whereas investors and donors may expect it to be financially sustainable *and* fulfill its social mission. Sometimes, these expectations may come into conflict. For instance, accomplishing the social mission may necessitate depleting the organization's financial resources. Meanwhile, striving for financial stability could entail focusing on for-profit and/or earned-income activities at the expense of the core social mission. This issue has been addressed by several scholars, especially Eikenberry and Kluver, who have analyzed the dangers of third-sector marketization. According to these authors, business has its own set of values, and following these could compromise the missions of social ventures and other nonprofit organizations.[31] To remedy this potentially negative effect, managers in social ventures must strike the right balance between economic imperatives and social mission.

To complement the models described above, others focus more on the development of metrics to measure effectiveness. Some of these are discussed in the next section.

2   Measuring Organizational Effectiveness

Measuring organizational effectiveness has proved just as problematic as defining the concept of effectiveness itself, as several scholars have lamented.[32] Numerous dimensions have been suggested for inclusion in the process of assessing the effectiveness of an organization. Some of these focus on goal attainment, others on internal processes, and still others on outcomes or external factors. Understandably, several alternative models have been proposed as a result, four of which are described below.

2.1   Kushner and Poole's Model

When do we know that an organization is effective? How do we measure an organization's effectiveness? To address these questions, Kushner and Poole proposed a model for measuring organizational effectiveness that combines four dimensions:

- customer satisfaction;
- resource acquisition;
- internal processes; and
- goal attainment.[33]

The model indicates that constituent satisfaction leads to resource acquisition, which leads to effectiveness in internal processes, which leads to goal attainment, all of which contribute to increased overall effectiveness (see Figure 12.1). Each component is also considered as an antecedent of organizational effectiveness. To be effective, an organization must perform well in all four dimensions. Constituent satisfaction is based on utility received in exchange for resources offered,[34] and it can facilitate the acquisition of resources. For example, a social venture that is well run—or perceived as well run—is more likely to attract donors than one that is poorly run, or perceived as poorly run. This had led some authors to define social ventures' performance in terms of growth in resources, including financial resources, human capital, partnerships and cooperation, and expertise.[35]

However, it is one thing to acquire resources but quite another to use them wisely. Therefore, the effective use of resources is important for a social venture to accomplish its stated goals. Indeed, organizations require internal process effectiveness—that is, technical efficiency and internal social and technological systems matched to each other so they can acquire resources.[36]

The final component of the model is goal attainment, which refers to the extent to which the organization meets its stated aims.[37] This indicates that the model is recursive—the attainment of the goals could increase constituent satisfaction. The model is not specific to a particular sector. Rather, its use should match the industry in which the organization competes and the objectives of the study.[38]

In the context of social entrepreneurship (or commercial entrepreneurship), the four components of Kushner and Poole's model can be used as metrics to measure whether a social venture is effective. For example, customer satisfaction can be measured using a survey, a focus group, the number of complaints the venture receives, or a combination of these metrics. The results could be benchmarked with other social ventures or within the social venture itself at different periods. If the results meet the expected threshold, the managers may conclude that the social venture is effective on this dimension.

The resource acquisition component can be measured by assessing the critical resources the social venture is able to accumulate. For example, was the social venture able to raise

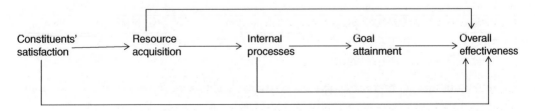

Figure 12.1 Kushner and Poole's organizational effectiveness model.

the necessary capital? Was it able to hire a sufficient number of the correct type of candidate to perform its key functions? Was it able to acquire the equipment and technology that it needs to perform efficiently? The answers to these questions will help the social venture assess its effectiveness on this dimension.

Measuring the internal processes component requires the social venture to draw up a detailed account of the key processes that are used to transform inputs into outputs. What is the cost structure of these internal processes? Is the social venture cost-effective when compared to similar social ventures? Answering these questions could help the social venture measure its effectiveness on this dimension.

Finally, goal attainment can be measured quite simply by comparing actual performance to initial targets. If the social venture is judged to have met its stated goals, it is fair to say that it has been effective on this dimension.

As mentioned above, the social venture must perform well on all four dimensions to achieve overall effectiveness. Using this tool could also help managers to take corrective actions should the social venture be ineffective on one or several dimensions.

2.2 Bhargava and Sinha's Multidimensional Model

The multidimensional model is proposed to serve as a tool for measuring organizational effectiveness. It comprises four components:

- production;
- commitment;
- leadership; and
- interpersonal conflict.[39]

In this model, production is defined as the flow of input–output of the organization, while commitment represents the degree of attachment to the organization. Leadership is defined as the degree of influence and personal ability, and interpersonal conflict refers to the degree of perceived misunderstanding between supervisors and subordinates. To be effective, an organization must perform well on all four dimensions. Bhargava and Sinha's research to validate their model shows that an organization with a heterarchical structure is perceived as having higher degrees of production, commitment, and effective leadership with less interpersonal conflict than a hierarchical structure.[40]

Although this model could be used to assess the effectiveness of social ventures, two of its components—productivity and commitment—would need some retooling and adaptation. For most social ventures, and particularly purely philanthropic enterprises, production does not often imply the transformation of inputs into outputs. Rather, social ventures provide services for beneficiaries. For instance, the Salvation Army does not produce any physical goods for its beneficiaries. Rather, it collects used items that are then distributed to the needy. Therefore, the production component could be refined to indicate how the physical good is acquired and then distributed. The same is true for a service. Understanding the process will allow managers to identify areas of inefficiency and take the appropriate corrective actions.

The commitment component could also be refined. The literature on organizational commitment identifies three components: *affective*, *calculative*, and *normative* commitment.[41] Affective commitment refers to an emotional attachment to an organization, whereas calculative commitment refers to an attachment to an organization because of tangible benefits, such as pension or salary. By contrast, normative commitment refers to an attachment to an organization on moral grounds.[42] This occurs when an employee believes that he or she has a moral obligation to stay with the organization. Because social ventures do not provide hefty tangible benefits to those who work for them, such as high salaries or bonuses, affective commitment and normative commitment probably play more important roles than calculative commitment in such organizations. Indeed, managers must ensure that paid employees and volunteers express an attachment to the social venture and feel a moral obligation to contribute to accomplishing its social mission.

In order to use this model as a tool for measuring effectiveness, managers should operationalize the components and identify instruments to measure them. For example, the production process might be measured by looking at how inputs are transformed into outputs. In doing so, managers will likely measure production costs, costs of raw materials, labor costs, and quality of outputs. Commitment, leadership, and interpersonal conflict could be measured by using scales that have been developed in the literature. A social venture that intends to use this model can also develop in-house instruments to measure commitment, interpersonal conflict, and leadership. The idea is to have reliable and valid tools to measure the social venture's performance on these dimensions. Results could then be compared to internal thresholds or benchmarked to similar social ventures.

2.3   Ridley and Mendoza's Model

This model, which was developed primarily as a tool for management consultants, integrates foundational concepts of systems theory, organizational theory, and consultation theory, and is formulated on the most basic processes of organizational effectiveness—namely, the need for organizational survival and the maximization of return on contributions.[43] The theoretical framework of the model is based on a series of assumptions, such as the availability of "organizational energy reserves," the ability to benefit from returns, the presence of resource utilization metrics, and the possession of a long-term perspective. These assumptions led the authors to develop a model that includes eleven key processes that contribute to effectiveness. The first two—organizational survival and maximization of return—are defined as "superordinate processes." The third is self-regulation, which is responsible for orchestrating a balance between the superordinate and subordinate processes. The eight remaining processes are all subordinate:

- internal–external boundary permeability;
- sensitivity to status and change;
- contribution to constituents;
- transformation;
- promoting advantageous transactions;
- flexibility;
- adaptability; and
- efficiency.

Table 12.1 presents the eleven elements of the model.

For an organization to be effective—or perceived as such—it must perform well on all eleven dimensions. In addition, it must demonstrate that it has not only the necessary resources but also the necessary resource capabilities—that is, the ability to use those resources wisely and efficiently. It is one thing to possess resources but another to use them

Table 12.1 Organizational effective processes in Ridley and Mendoza's model

Superordinate processes	Self-regulation process	Subordinate processes
Organizational survival Maximization of return	Orchestrates balance between the superordinate and the subordinate processes	Internal–external boundary permeability Sensitivity to status and change Contribution to constituents Transformation Promoting advantageous transactions Flexibility Adaptability Efficiency

efficiently to meet organizational goals. The organization should also demonstrate that it benefits from using its resources wisely.

Performing well on this model's measures should point to an organization's long-term survival. For example, a social venture that does not have the necessary resources or cannot leverage its existing resources will fail. According to this model, the social venture will survive if it meets its superordinate goals. It can operationalize all the dimensions of the model and use them as metrics to measure its overall effectiveness.

2.4   Jackson's Model of Organizational Effectiveness

This model is based on gathering perceptions of preselected effectiveness indicators. It was developed to study the differences between community- and member-based nonprofit organizations. Jackson used a survey instrument in a descriptive research study that was designed to measure perceptions of each of six indicators and the relative priority that each indicator would have within community-based and member-based nonprofits.[44] The six selected indicators of organizational effectiveness are:

- management experience;
- organizational structure;
- political impact;
- board of directors' involvement;
- volunteer involvement; and
- internal communications.[45]

Table 12.2 presents a summary of these six indicators.

For example, a management that has the experience to run a nonprofit organization is likely to manage such an organization effectively. By contrast, lack of experience may lead to mistakes and therefore compromise the social venture's performance. The model also considers the structure of an organization as an important indicator of performance. It suggests that a flexible structure is likely to facilitate good performance, whereas a more rigid and bureaucratic structure would impede performance. Therefore, organizations must design flexible structures that can facilitate change and adaptation. This is particularly true for social ventures, which must act as agents of social change and innovation.

Table 12.2 Jackson's indicators of organizational effectiveness

Indicators of organizational effectiveness	Explanation
Management experience	The extent to which management has prior experience managing similar organizations.
Organizational structure	Structure influences the performance of social ventures. Flexible structures are more likely to help increase effectiveness than rigid ones.
Political impact	Political impact influences power structure. It can improve or impede effectiveness.
Board of directors' involvement	Extent to which the board is implicated in the social venture's decision-making process on critical issues. An involved board can improve effectiveness.
Volunteer involvement	Volunteer commitment leads to a social venture's success.
Internal communications	Effective communication helps inform key stakeholders about the activities of the social venture.

Politics is used as an indicator of effectiveness because it can influence the power structure within an organization and thereby either improve or impede performance. For example, constant in-fighting among decision-makers can reduce an organization's effectiveness, whereas cooperation can improve performance and reduce the likelihood of cliques and turf wars. An effective and dynamic board of directors can stir an organization toward success. By contrast, a board that is passive and disengaged invites chaos and poor performance. (The board of directors' role in social ventures was discussed in Chapter 11.) Committed volunteers can help social ventures accomplish their missions (as was also discussed in Chapter 11), so their effective management is an important task. The final element of the model, communications, is important as well. Effective communication must occur not only within the social venture but also between the venture and its key constituents. This will help the social venture build trust and establish its reputation. By contrast, poor communication can derail a social venture's plans, generate suspicion, and reduce trust.

3 Assessing Social Ventures' Effectiveness

What does effectiveness really mean in the context of social enterprises? Does it mean that the organization is achieving its economic goals or its social mission? For social ventures that have double or triple bottom lines, effectiveness may have several meanings. How is this concept different from social impact? When do we know that a social venture is effective? There are no easy answers to these questions. As indicated earlier, most researchers agree that nonprofit organizational effectiveness remains an elusive and contested concept,[46] even though questions of effectiveness have become increasingly important in the world of practice as governments, philanthropic funders, and the public are all exerting more pressure on nonprofit organizations to demonstrate their impact on complex social problems.[47] All that can be said for sure is that effectiveness in nonprofit organizations cannot be assessed via a single indicator.

Nonprofit organizational effectiveness is a matter of comparison—with specific standards of performance and with other social ventures. Managers in social ventures should set specific objectives that can then be compared to actual performance. A social venture is effective when it attains the public's trust, defined as being able to account for the organization's implied promises to its constituencies by pursuing its stated mission in good faith and with defensible management and governance practices.[48] A recent study of 152 nonprofit organizations' leaders in the United States found that instantiation of sound principles or strategy, a grassroots approach, large organizational size and resources, a collaborative outlook, singleness of focus, campaigning abilities, funding and fundraising prowess, global scope, and quality personnel were considered as the main indicators of effectiveness.[49] Another study of leaders of international nonprofits found that most of them defined effectiveness as "outcome accountability," whereas a minority defined I as "overhead minimization."[50]

Figure 12.1, above, illustrates the process of measuring a social venture's effectiveness (if "constituents' satisfaction" is simply replaced with "customers' satisfaction"). Like commercial ventures, social ventures transform inputs into outputs. Measurements can occur at the level of the inputs or the outputs. For example, how much resource did a social venture spend to raise a certain amount of money (input)? What does the social venture produce (output)? Measurement can also occur at the transformation level (activities). Evaluation of the internal processes of a social venture can be made in three ways: continuous; rating scale; and binary scale.[51] Continuous evaluation implies that the measure used allows a counting of the outcomes. For example, we can count the number of people treated for addiction or the number of children vaccinated. A rating scale can be used when it is not possible to count the output. It can be described on a continuum from, say, very effective (5) to ineffective (1). For example, when treating patients of the Ebola outbreak in 2014, doctors used a variety of medicines. Some of these medicines were more effective than others. Finally, a binary scale can be used to measure outcomes, such as effective or ineffective, yes or no, good or bad.

Several models have been used to measure the effectiveness of nonprofit organizations. These construe effectiveness as a multidimensional concept. Measures such as social return on investment (SROI), social accounting and audit (SAA), and blended-value accounting (BVA) will be discussed in Chapter 14. The following sub-sections focus on two methods that have been used recently to assess the effectiveness of social ventures—the integrated model of nonprofit organizations' effectiveness and the balanced scorecard.

3.1   The Integrated Model of Nonprofit Organizations' Effectiveness

Sowa and colleagues developed this model, which includes two distinct dimensions—management effectiveness and program effectiveness.[52] "Management" comprises the organizational and management characteristics that are found in a social venture and the actions of its managers. Measures of management include variables that tap capacity (structure and process), as well as those that represent the outcomes of these management systems and activities. "Program" comprises the specific service or intervention that is provided by the social venture. It also has variables that relate to the capacity (structure and process) of the program, as well as the outcomes created by the intervention.

A social venture must have capable management if it is to succeed. Therefore, improving management effectiveness may lead to better program performance, as it provides a foundation for the sustainability, improvement, and growth of programs.[53] Sowa and colleagues believe that a social venture needs to operate effectively at both the management and the program levels if it is to be considered as truly effective. A social venture that is well managed and operated but delivers poor programs is not fully effective, just as a social venture that delivers well-run programs but has an unhappy workforce or poor overall organizational operations is not fully effective.

Another measure that is used to assess the effectiveness of a social venture is the balanced scorecard, which is discussed next.

3.2   Balanced Scorecard for Social Ventures

Financial considerations can play an enabling or a constraining role in social ventures, but they will rarely be the primary objective.[54] This is particularly important because it means that nonprofit organizations cannot utilize the financial measures that for-profit organizations routinely use to evaluate their performance, such as profitability or shareholder returns.[55]

One tool that is often used to measure a firm's performance is the balanced scorecard. This was developed for the private sector to overcome deficiencies in the financial accounting model, which fails to signal changes in a company's economic value as the organization makes substantial investments (or depletes past investments) in intangible assets, such as the skills, motivation, and capabilities of its employees, customer acquisition and retention, innovative products and services, and information technology.[56]

Kaplan adapted the balanced scorecard and applied it to several nonprofit organizations—such as the United Way, Duke Children's Hospital, and New Profit Inc.—and found improvements in their performance and accountability. He concluded that the balanced scorecard has enabled these nonprofit organizations to bridge the gap between vague mission and strategy statements and day-to-day operational actions.[57] In addition to the traditional financial measures of the balanced scorecard, his new system added measures from three other perspectives:

- customer;
- internal process; and
- learning and growth.[58]

It is widely accepted that financial reports measure past performance but communicate little about long-term value creation.[59] Therefore, a balanced scorecard is more likely to present an overall picture of a social venture than an evaluation which relies only on financial data. In discussing the importance of the balanced scorecard for nonprofit organizations, Kaplan notes that although these organizations must monitor their spending and comply with financial budgets, their success cannot be measured solely on the basis of how closely they keep their spending within budgeted amounts.[60] Rather, the key elements of a balanced scorecard for social ventures are customers, internal processes, financial perspective, and innovation and leadership perspective, as illustrated in Table 12.3.

Table 12.3 Key elements of a balanced scorecard for social ventures

Customers	Internal processes	Financial perspective	Innovation and leadership perspective
Beneficiaries	Management	Fundraising	Board of directors
Key stakeholders	Structure	Management of financial	Top management
	Operations	resources	

4 Assessing Social Venture Efficiency

4.1 Defining Social Venture Efficiency

Assessing the efficiency of social ventures is important because the best-performing organizations tend to be concerned with both effectiveness and efficiency.[61] Before defining social venture efficiency, it is important to understand what organizational efficiency entails. Organizational efficiency is used in reference to the extent to which an organization accomplishes its objectives by using minimum resources and also when discussing its internal functioning. Efficiency is concerned with the relationship between inputs and outputs. If an organization transforms its inputs into outputs at a lower cost than rivals in the same industry, then the organization is deemed to be efficient. In economics, a firm is efficient if it uses minimum inputs to produce a certain level of output; or if it produces maximum output from a certain level of inputs.[62] From an economics perspective, efficiency implies that organizations produce, raise funds, pay wages, or engage in any activity only up to the point that an extra dollar in expense will generate an extra dollar in revenue.[63]

This is known as the principle of equimarginality, which can be explained as follows. If the last dollar in expenses generates less than a dollar in revenues, the organization is inefficient. If, on the other hand, it generates more than a dollar, the organization is also inefficient because it is not spend enough.[64] One may extrapolate the conceptualization of efficiency to social entrepreneurship to argue that a social venture is efficient when it accomplishes its mission while using the minimum inputs. An efficient social venture minimizes its non-program expenses relative to its program expenses.[65] Being efficient therefore allows a social venture to accomplish its mission without compromising its resources.

4.2 Measuring Social Venture Efficiency

Measuring social venture efficiency is often difficult because the metrics used are often imprecise.[66] The financial ratios that are used to measure the efficiency of for-profit organizations—such as return on investment, profitability, and operating efficiencies—cannot be applied easily to social ventures. For example, in nonprofit health organizations, efficiency is often measured with a ratio of some kind—such as overhead to total costs, cash-on-hand to total revenues, non-fundraising expenses to total expenses, or donations to fundraising expenses.[67] Because social ventures constantly need to balance the search for revenue against adherence to their social missions, selecting the appropriate efficiency metrics can be tedious. According to Brooks, social ventures and other nonprofit organizations should increase their efficiency by maximizing the net revenues that are attributable to activities that are unrelated to their core programs, so as much as possible is left over to spend on those programs.[68] In other words, a social venture should spend its financial resources on fundraising and administration up to equimarginality—that is, up to the point where a dollar spent generates a dollar earned.

As indicated earlier, social ventures raise funds, pay wages, buy equipment, and engage in activities to accomplish their social missions, so efficiency should be increased in each of these activities. For example, consider two major areas where social ventures incur costs—fundraising and implementing their programs. Fundraising expenditures refer to the money that is spent to raise revenue, whereas program expenditures include all of the costs relating to the venture's core programs. Fundraising expense efficiency refers to the relationship between fundraising expenditure and fundraising revenue, whereas program expense efficiency refers to the relationship between the costs of implementing programs and the revenue that these programs generate. However, it can be difficult for some social ventures to calculate the dollar figures of a program. For instance, if a homeless shelter serves meals to homeless people, the costs can be easily quantified. But it is much more difficult to quantify the revenue that is generated. In this example, the homeless shelter is generating no revenue when it undertakes activities to accomplish its core mission. Instead, its revenue might come from donations, grants, or fundraising activities.

Measuring efficiency in social entrepreneurship is important because it can send a signal that the social venture is well managed and spending its financial resources wisely. An efficient social venture is likely to attract more potential donors and investors than one that is perceived as inefficient. Some of the financial ratios discussed in Chapter 10 can be used to measure the overall efficiency of social ventures.

Summary

This chapter discussed organizational effectiveness and efficiency and their application to social ventures. In this regard, a social venture is effective when it accomplishes its stated social mission. Meanwhile, a social venture is efficient when it accomplishes its stated goals by using the minimum amount of resources. The chapter also described several models of organizational effectiveness and presented some of the tools that are used to measure it.

Key Terms

Balanced scorecard; effectiveness; effectiveness models; efficiency; equimarginality; multiple-constituency model; operating margin; organizational efficiency; social constructionist perspective

Review Questions

1 What is organizational effectiveness?
2 What is organizational efficiency?
3 Explain the importance of efficiency for a social venture. What signal can an efficient social venture send to potential donors and investors?
4 Explain the key assumptions of the social constructionist perspective of organizational effectiveness.
5 Explain the key assumptions of Kushner and Poole's model. Indicate its relevance for measuring the effectiveness of a social venture.
6 Explain Bhargava and Sinha's multi-dimensional model and indicate its relevance for measuring the effectiveness of a social venture.
7 Explain the key assumptions of Ridley and Mendoza's model and indicate its relevance for measuring the effectiveness of a social venture.
8 Explain the key assumptions of Jackson' model of organizational effectiveness and indicate its relevance for measuring the effectiveness of a social venture.
9 Explain the importance of the balanced scorecard for social ventures.
10 Why do you think a multidimensional approach to measuring effectiveness is appropriate for social ventures?

Application Questions

1 The balanced scorecard has been considered as an appropriate measure to assess the effectiveness of social ventures and other nonprofit organizations. Select a social venture with which you are familiar and apply the balanced scorecard to measure its effectiveness. Would you conclude that the social venture you selected is effective (yes or no)? Explain.

2 Suppose you are the manager of a new social venture that aims to help reduce illiteracy rates in an African country. How would you measure the effectiveness of your social venture? What metrics would you use? When would you decide that your venture has been effective?

3 Do additional research on the multiple-constituency model and determine how it could be applied to the assessment of a social venture with which you are familiar. Identify the key stakeholders. Provide guidelines for the social venture to meet these stakeholders' expectations.

4 Watch the video at www.youtube.com/watch?v=1Oe5gws7irY. Based on your understanding of the terms "effectiveness" and "efficiency," explain when a social venture is effective and when it is efficient. Can a social venture be effective without being efficient or vice versa? Provide concrete examples.

5 Use Kushner and Poole's model to assess the effectiveness of a social venture with which you are familiar. If you are not familiar with any social ventures, do some research online or select one from the application cases in this book, then apply the model. For each of the four components of the model, describe metrics that you could use to assess the social venture's effectiveness. Would you conclude that the social venture is effective (yes or no)? Explain.

Application Case 1: FlipGive: The Online Shopping Platform

For some reasons, people do not always know how to start a fundraiser. This is particularly true when people tend to fund some causes they care about. They do not always have the ability of the information available to garner the resources they need. An organization that tries to help reduce this ignorance is FlipGive (https://www.flipgive.com), an online shopping site that connects customers, companies, and those who seek to fund social causes through online sales. It was created in 2008 by Mark Bachman, Elissa Beckett, Steve Croth, and Nicolas Lee who were enrolled at the time in the Executive MBA program at the Richard Ivey School of Business at the University of Western Ontario in Toronto, Canada. FlipGive's mission is to use the power of commerce to create positive social change.[1]

FlipGive is a free tool that allows users to shop online with popular brands and raise money. Users of FlipGIve may support an existing fundraiser, or start raising money on their own for social causes they are willing to support. Fundraisers may receive up to 50% for their cause when they get people to shop online with the selected popular retailers that are partnered with the initiative.[2] Several organizations including associations, clubs, technology and media companies, use this website. This partnership also allows FlipGive to connect retailers and customers. Hence, retailers benefit by having access to several customers that they could not reach on their own. It uses local fundraisers as an incentive to purchase merchandise and increase shopping activity.

The process works as follows. FlipGive directs the customer to a store, the customer then orders the item, FlipGive takes a percentage of the money just earned and donates it to the fundraiser of choice, the store keeps the remaining money that was not donated, and then the product is delivered to the customer. For example, FlipGive provided an easy way for parents in Canada to raise money for their kids' schools. Parents, teachers and Indogo store staff sold Indigo gift cards to their online social networks using the FlipGive platform. Every gift card sold triggered a donation to the school, drove a customer to Indigo and got the buyer a gift card that could be redeemed in-store or online.[3]

FlipGive's marketing strategy could be considered as an innovative one for addressing social issues. Buyers can give to a fundraiser of their choice or one they have created themselves while at the same time buying a product they like. Not only can users contribute to their charity of choice by purchasing brand products through FlipGive, but they can also advertise their charity, or their own brand products. This process exposes products to a whole new customer base that may be more interested in spending if it is going towards a cause. One FlipGive fundraiser causes over 3,000 new transactions, and interactions. Each year, fundraisers generate over $20 billion by selling different products. This allows people with the same goal to team up and support each other instead of competing against one another. Some brands that sell through FlipGive include Nike, Aldo, Under Armour, Buffalo Wild Wings, and Starbucks.[4]

FlipGive offers both individuals and local businesses many unique opportunities not offered anywhere else. It is a system designed to generate funds, as well as distribute those funds based upon the customer's desire. It also scales down time and confusion, decreasing the hassle and utilizing its maximum potential. FlipGive offers an opportunity to make a positive social impact. For example, it has helped the Pearson Foundation to donate more than 1 million books for global literacy.[5] As a result, taking advantage of FlipGive offers could drastically make a positive change in society.

Discussion Questions

1 How does FlipGive sustain itself?
2 Do you think people would rather purchase through FlipGive? Why, or why not? Would you personally use FlipGive?
3 What is the overall mission of FlipGive?
4 If FlipGive works towards raising money for fundraisers, why don't all companies sell products through FlipGive?

References

1 *https://www.crunchbase.com/organization/flipgive#/entity* [April 14, 2016].
2 *https://www.flipgive.com/* [retrieved on April 14, 2016].
3 FlipGive gets funded to revolutionize digital marketing while doing good. *http://www.prnewswire.com/news-releases/flipgive-gets-funded-to-revolutionize-digital-marketing-while-doing-good-171151031.html* [Retrieved on April 14, 2016].
4 *https://www.flipgive.com/* [retrieved on April 14, 2016]. Forget door-to-door, digital fundraising is all the rage. *http://www.huffingtonpost.ca/neil-parmar/better-the-world_b_1857900.html*. [Retrieved on April 14, 2016].

Application Case 2: Forex Chile, Santiago

Forex Chile (www.forexchile.cl) was founded in the financial center of Valparaiso in June 2003 to promote the advantages of online trading and investment. In late 2003, the company introduced the Education Forex Chile program to provide financial market knowledge to Chileans and potential customers. In April 2005, it opened its new headquarters in the

World Trade Center Building in Santiago, Chile's capital city. The following year, the company launched the first electronic platform in the world on which the Chilean peso could be exchanged for other currencies. During the same period, Forex Chile successfully launched the country's first Trading Championship, receiving nationwide coverage.

Forex Chile is therefore a traditional for-profit company. However, it could also be viewed as following a social value creation model because of its efforts to educate Chileans on the benefits of online investment (see below).

I visited Chile in 2013 and had the opportunity to hear a presentation by one of Forex Chile's co-founders, Erwin Andia. His first job was as a salesperson for a stockbroker in Valparaiso. One day, he received an email from a US broker inviting him to invest online, which gave him the idea for an online brokerage firm in his home country. He approached several people but was repeatedly told that his idea could not work because Chileans preferred the human touch in their economic and financial transactions. Nevertheless, he decided to go to Santiago and knocked on the doors of a number potential investors. Again, they all turned him down. Eventually, though, he pitched his idea to an old investor who said: "I don't believe you can do it, but how much do you need anyway?" The investor provided the seed money and Forex Chile was born. It was the country's first online brokerage firm.

The first few years were disastrous and almost proved the naysayers right. There were almost no sales and almost no customers. Andia came close to calling it quits. However, his self motivation kept him going. He would tell himself, "This has to work. We have to make it work because this is the future of investment." He and his partners eventually realized that Forex Chile's main problem was that Chileans had to be educated about the benefits of online investment. Thereafter, the company's mantra became "Educate the Customer." After five hard years, Forex Chile finally started to attract customers. Now, the company employs 200 people and has offices in northern and southern Chile as well as another in Lima, Peru. Forex Chile's main goal is to become the principal online brokerage player in South America with a presence in every capital city. It also hopes to provide access to the financial markets for most of Chile's population.

The company's customers are mainly well-educated Chilean professionals—architects, engineers, lawyers, physicians, and teachers. Forex Chile educates them about investment risks and how to manage such risks. It employs a young and dynamic workforce. At 37, Andia is the company's oldest employee. He says, "We enjoy what we do. We are a family. This is who we are. We care." Although this young workforce lacks experience and sometimes makes mistakes, as Andia acknowledges, it is energetic, innovative, respectful, and inspiring. The company would like to be recognized as a specialist in electronic investment in South America. Second, it wants to be known as an online investment bank. Third, it would like to democratize access to the stock market not only in Chile but throughout South America. However, it faces significant competition from the big investment banks that already have a presence in Chile and throughout the rest of South America, such as Chase and JP Morgan.

Discussion Questions

1   How would you apply the balanced scorecard to assess the effectiveness of Forex Chile?
2   Would you consider Forex Chile as an effective organization when considering its efforts to educate Chileans about online investing?
3   How would the multiple-constituency model apply to Forex Chile?
4   How would Ridley and Mendoza's model apply to Forex Chile?

Notes

1   Lecy, J. D., Schmitz, H. P., & Swedlund, H. (2012). Non-governmental and not-for-profit orga-
    nizational effectiveness: A structured literature review. *Voluntas: International Journal of
    Voluntary Nonprofit Organizations*, 23(2), 434–457.
2   Etzioni, A. (1964). *Modern organization*. Englewood Cliffs, NJ: Prentice-Hall, at p. 1.
3   Sowa, J. E., Selden, S. C., & Sandfort, J. R. (2004). No longer unmeasurable? A multidimen-
    sional integrated model of nonprofit organizational effectiveness. *Nonprofit and Voluntary
    Sector Quarterly*, 33(4), 711–728.
4   Leitcher, D. P. (1968). A study of judgments of organizational effectiveness. In *Proceedings of the
    Executive Study Conferences*. Princeton, NJ: Educational Testing Service.
5   Coulter, P. B. (1979). Organizational effectiveness in the public sector: The example of municipal
    fire protection. *Administrative Science Quarterly*, 24(1), 65–81.
6   Kushner, R. J., & Poole, P. P. (1996). Exploring structure effectiveness relationships in nonprofit
    arts organizations. *Nonprofit Management and Leadership*, 6(2), 171–180.
7   Kushner, R. J., & Poole, P. P. (1996). Exploring structure effectiveness relationships in nonprofit
    arts organizations. *Nonprofit Management and Leadership*, 6(2), 171–180.
8   Herman, R. D., & Renz, D. O. (2008). Advancing nonprofit organizational effectiveness research
    and theory: Nine theses. *Nonprofit Management and Leadership*, 18(4), 399–415.
9   Herman, R. D., & Renz, D. O. (2008). Advancing nonprofit organizational effectiveness research
    and theory: Nine theses. *Nonprofit Management and Leadership*, 18(4), 399–415.
10 Forbes, D. P. (1998). Measuring the unmeasurable: Empirical studies of nonprofit organization
    effectiveness from 1977 to 1997. *Nonprofit and Voluntary Sector Quarterly*, 27(2), 183–202.
11 Chmelik, E., Musteen, M., & Ahsan, M. (2015). Measures of performance in the context of
    international social ventures: An exploratory study. *Journal of Social Entrepreneurship*, 7(1).
    www.tandfonline.com/doi/abs/10.1080/19420676.2014.997781, retrieved March 29, 2016;
    Diochon, M. (2013). Social entrepreneurship and effectiveness: A case study of a Canadian first
    nations community. *Journal of Social Entrepreneurship*, 4(3), 302–330; Nicholls, A. (2013).
    It's more fun to compute. *Journal of Social Entrepreneurship*, 4(1), 1–3; Bagnoli, L., & Megali, C.
    (2011). Measuring performance in social enterprises. *Nonprofit and Voluntary Sector Quar-
    terly*, 40(1), 149–165; Diochon, M., & Anderson, A. (2009). Social enterprise and effectiveness:
    A process typology. *Social Enterprise Journal*, 5(1), 7–29; Forbes, D. P. (1998). Measuring the
    unmeasurable: Empirical studies of nonprofit organization effectiveness from 1977 to 1997.
    Nonprofit and Voluntary Sector Quarterly, 27(2), 183–202.
12 Etzioni, A. (1964). *Modern organization*. Englewood Cliffs, NJ: Prentice-Hall.
13 Etzioni, A. (1964). *Modern organization*. Englewood Cliffs, NJ: Prentice-Hall; Pfeffer, J. (1982).
    Organizations and organization theory. Boston: Pittman.
14 Webb, R. J. (1974). Organizational effectiveness and the voluntary organization. *Academy of
    Management Journal*, 17(4), 663–677.
15 Miles, R. H. (1980). *Macro-organizational behavior*. Glenview, IL: Scott, Foresman.
16 Mano, R. S. (2014). Networking modes and performance in Israel's nonprofit organizations.
    Nonprofit Management and Leadership, 24(4), 429–443; Seashore, S. E., & Yuchtman, E.
    (1967). Factorial analysis of organizational performance. *Administrative Science Quarterly*,
    12(3), 377–395.
17 Jun, K. N., & Shiau, E. (2012). How are we doing? A multiple constituency approach to civic
    association effectiveness. *Nonprofit and Voluntary Sector Quarterly*, 41(4), 632–655; Herman,
    R. D., & Renz, D. O. (1999). Theses on non-profit organizational effectiveness. *Nonprofit and
    Voluntary Sector Quarterly*, 28(2), 107–126.
18 Chmelik, E., Musteen, M., & Ahsan, M. (2015). Measures of performance in the context
    of international social ventures: An exploratory study. *Journal of Social Entrepreneurship*,
    7(1). www.tandfonline.com/doi/abs/10.1080/19420676.2014.997781, retrieved on March
    29, 2016.

19   Herman, R. D., & Renz, D. O. (2004). Doing things right: Effectiveness in local nonprofit organizations: A panel study. *Public Administration Review*, 64(6), 694–704.
20   Balser, D., & McClusk, J. (2005). Managing stakeholder relationships and nonprofit organization effectiveness. *Nonprofit Management and Leadership*, 15(3), 295–315.
21   Balser, D., & McClusk, J. (2005). Managing stakeholder relationships and nonprofit organization effectiveness. *Nonprofit Management and Leadership*, 15(3), 295–315.
22   Herman, R. D., & Renz, D. O. (1997). Multiple constituencies and the social construction of nonprofit organization effectiveness. *Nonprofit and Voluntary Sector Quarterly*, 26(2), 185–206.
23   Herman, R. D., & Renz, D. O. (1997). Multiple constituencies and the social construction of nonprofit organization effectiveness. *Nonprofit and Voluntary Sector Quarterly*, 26(2), 185–206.
24   Herman, R. D., & Renz, D. O. (1997). Multiple constituencies and the social construction of nonprofit organization effectiveness. *Nonprofit and Voluntary Sector Quarterly*, 26(2), 185–206.
25   Scott, W. R. (1995). *Institutions and organizations*. Thousand Oaks, CA: Sage Publications.
26   Herman, R. D., & Renz, D. O. (1997). Multiple constituencies and the social construction of nonprofit organization effectiveness. *Nonprofit and Voluntary Sector Quarterly*, 26(2), 185–206.
27   Herman, R. D., & Renz, D. O. (1999). Theses on nonprofit organizational effectiveness. *Nonprofit and Voluntary Sector Quarterly*, 28(2), 107–126.
28   Nicholls, A. (2013). It's more fun to compute. *Journal of Social Entrepreneurship*, 4(1), 1–3.
29   Herman, R. D., & Renz, D. O. (1997). Multiple constituencies and the social construction of nonprofit organization effectiveness. *Nonprofit and Voluntary Sector Quarterly*, 26(2), 185–206.
30   Herman, R. D., & Renz, D. O. (1997). Multiple constituencies and the social construction of nonprofit organization effectiveness. *Nonprofit and Voluntary Sector Quarterly*, 26(2), 185–206.
31   Eikenberry, A. M., & Kluver, J. D. (2004). The marketization of the nonprofit sector: Civil society at risk? *Public Administration Review*, 64(2), 132–140.
32   Diochon, M. (2013). Social entrepreneurship and effectiveness: A case study of a Canadian first nations community. *Journal of Social Entrepreneurship*, 4(3), 302–330; Lecy, J. D., Schmitz, H. P., & Swedlund, H. (2012). Non-governmental and not-for-profit organizational effectiveness: A structured literature review. *Voluntas: International Journal of Voluntary Nonprofit Organizations*, 23(2), 434–457; Herman, R. D., & Renz, D. O. (2008). Advancing nonprofit organizational effectiveness research and theory: Nine theses. *Nonprofit Management and Leadership*, 18(4), 399–415; Rojas, R. R. (2000). A review of models for measuring organizational effectiveness among for-profit and non-profit organizations. *Nonprofit Management and Leadership*, 11(1), 97–104.
33   Kushner, R. J., & Poole, P. P. (1996). Exploring structure effectiveness relationships in nonprofit arts organizations. *Nonprofit Management and Leadership*, 6(2), 171–180.
34   Kushner, R. J., & Poole, P. P. (1996). Exploring structure effectiveness relationships in nonprofit arts organizations. *Nonprofit Management and Leadership*, 6(2), 171–180.
35   Mano, R. S. (2014). Networking modes and performance in Israel's nonprofit organizations. *Nonprofit Management and Leadership*, 24(4), 429–443.
36   Kushner, R. J., & Poole, P. P. (1996). Exploring structure effectiveness relationships in nonprofit arts organizations. *Nonprofit Management and Leadership*, 6(2), 171–180.
37   Etzioni, A. (1964). *Modern organization*. Englewood Cliffs, NJ: Prentice-Hall.
38   Kushner, R. J., & Poole, P. P. (1996). Exploring structure effectiveness relationships in nonprofit arts organizations. *Nonprofit Management and Leadership*, 6(2), 171–180.
39   Bhargava, S., & Sinha, B. (1992). Predictions of organizational effectiveness as a function of type of organizational structure. *Journal of Social Psychology*, 132(2), 223–232.
40   Bhargava, S., & Sinha, B. (1992). Predictions of organizational effectiveness as a function of type of organizational structure. *Journal of Social Psychology*, 132(2), 223–232.
41   Allen, N. J., & Meyer, J. P. (1990). The measurement and antecedents of affective, continuance and normative commitment to the organization. *Journal of Occupational Psychology*, 63(1), 1–18; Meyer, J. R., & Allen, N. J. (1991). A three-component conceptualization of organizational commitment: Some methodological considerations. *Human Resource Management Review*, 1(1), 61–98.

42   Allen, N. J., & Meyer, J. P. (1990). The measurement and antecedents of affective, continuance and normative commitment to the organization. *Journal of Occupational Psychology*, *63*(2), 1–18; Meyer, J. R., & Allen, N. J. (1991). A three-component conceptualization of organizational commitment: Some methodological considerations. *Human Resource Management Review*, *1*(1), 61–98.

43   Ridley, C. R., & Mendoza, D. W. (1993). Putting organizational effectiveness into practice: The preeminent consultation task. *Journal of Counseling and Development*, *72*(2), 168–178.

44   Jackson, B. (1999). Perceptions of organizational effectiveness in community and member based nonprofit organizations. Doctoral dissertation, University of La Verne.

45   Jackson, B. (1999). Perceptions of organizational effectiveness in community and member based nonprofit organizations. Doctoral dissertation, University of La Verne.

46   Diochon, M. (2013). Social entrepreneurship and effectiveness: A case study of a Canadian first nations community. *Journal of Social Entrepreneurship*, *4*(3), 302–330; Nicholls, A. (2013). It's more fun to compute. *Journal of Social Entrepreneurship*, *4*(1), 1–3; Lecy, J. D., Schmitz, H. P., & Swedlund, H. (2012). Non-governmental and not-for-profit organizational effectiveness: A structured literature review. *Voluntas: International Journal of Voluntary Nonprofit Organizations*, *23*(2), 434–457; Rojas, R. R. (2011). A review of models for measuring organizational effectiveness among for-profit and nonprofit organizations. *Nonprofit Management and Leadership*, *11*(1), 97–104.

47   Sowa, J. E., Selden, S. C., & Sandfort, J. R. (2004). No longer unmeasurable? A multidimensional integrated model of nonprofit organizational effectiveness. *Nonprofit and Voluntary Sector Quarterly*, *33*(4), 711–728.

48   Kearns, K. P. (1996). *Managing for accountability*. San Francisco: Jossey-Bass.

49   Mitchell, G. E. (2015). The attributes of effective NGOs and the leadership values associated with a reputation for organizational effectiveness. *Nonprofit Management and Leadership*, *26*(1), 39–57.

50   Mitchell, G. E. (2013). The construct of organizational effectiveness: Perspectives from leaders of international nonprofits in the United States. *Nonprofit and Voluntary Sector Quarterly*, *42*(2), 322–343.

51   Brooks, C. A. (2009). *Social entrepreneurship: A modern approach to social value creation*. Upper Saddle River, NJ: Pearson/Prentice-Hall.

52   Sowa, J. E., Selden, S. C., & Sandfort, J. R. (2004). No longer unmeasurable? A multidimensional integrated model of nonprofit organizational effectiveness. *Nonprofit and Voluntary Sector Quarterly*, *33*(4), 711–728.

53   Letts, C. W., Ryan, W. P., & Grossman, A. (1999). *High performance nonprofit organizations: Managing upstream for greater impact*. New York: John Wiley.

54   Kaplan, R. S. (2001). Strategic performance measurement and management in nonprofit organizations. *Nonprofit Management and Leadership*, *11*(3), 353–370.

55   Forbes, D. P. (1998). Measuring the unmeasurable: Empirical studies of nonprofit organization effectiveness from 1977 to 1997. *Nonprofit and Voluntary Sector Quarterly*, *27*(2), 183–202.

56   Kaplan, R. S., & Norton, D. P. (1992). The balanced scorecard: Measures that drive performance. *Harvard Business Review*, January–February, 71–79; Kaplan, R. S., & Norton, D. P. (1996). *The balanced scorecard: Translating strategy into action*. Boston: Harvard Business School Press.

57   Kaplan, R. S. (2001). Strategic performance measurement and management in nonprofit organizations. *Nonprofit Management and Leadership*, *11*(3), 353–370.

58   Kaplan, R. S. (2001). Strategic performance measurement and management in nonprofit organizations. *Nonprofit Management and Leadership*, *11*(3), 353–370.

59   Kaplan, R. S. (2001). Strategic performance measurement and management in nonprofit organizations. *Nonprofit Management and Leadership*, *11*(3), 353–370.

60   Kaplan, R. S. (2001). Strategic performance measurement and management in nonprofit organizations. *Nonprofit Management and Leadership*, *11*(3), 353–370.

61   Katz, D., & Kahn, R. L. (1978). *The social psychology of organizations*. New York: Wiley & Sons.

62   Brooks, A. C. (2006). Efficient nonprofit. *Policy Studies Journal*, 34(3), 303–312.

63   Brooks, A. C. (2002). Can nonprofit management help answer public management's big question? *Public Administration Review*, 62(3), 259–266; Brooks, A. C. (2004). Evaluating the effectiveness of nonprofit fundraising. *Policy Studies Journal*, 32(3), 363–374; Brooks, A. C. (2006). Efficient nonprofit. *Policy Studies Journal*, 34(3), 303–312.

64   Brooks, A. C. (2006). Efficient nonprofit. *Policy Studies Journal*, 34(3), 303–312, at p. 305.

65   Callen, J. L., Klein, A., & Tinkelman, D. (2003). Board composition, committees, and organizational efficiency: The case of nonprofits. *Nonprofit and Voluntary Sector Quarterly*, 32(4), 493–520.

66   Keating, E., & Frumkin, P. (2003). Reengineering non-profit financial accountability. *Public Administration Review*, 63(1), 3–15.

67   Hager, M. A. (2001). Financial vulnerability among arts organizations: A test of the Tuckman–Chang measures. *Nonprofit and Voluntary Sector Quarterly*, 30(2), 376–392; Tuckman, H. P., & Chang, C. F. (1991). A methodology for measuring the financial vulnerability of charitable nonprofit organizations. *Nonprofit and Voluntary Sector Quarterly*, 20(4), 445–460.

68   Brooks, A. C. (2006). Efficient nonprofit. *Policy Studies Journal*, 34(3), 303–312, at p. 306.

Chapter 13

Scaling Social Ventures

Learning Objectives

1 Students should be able to understand the importance of scaling a social venture.
2 Students should be able to define social venture scaling.
3 Students should be able to identify growth strategies for social ventures.
4 Students should be able to acquire the skills required to formulate and implement social venture growth strategies.

The previous chapter discussed the concepts of effectiveness and efficiency in social ventures. Building on this knowledge, this chapter explains the importance of scaling social ventures. The chapter is organized into three main sections. The first section explores the importance of scaling a social venture. Specifically, it explains what scaling is and why social ventures might need to scale their activities to accomplish their social mission effectively. The second section discusses the strategies social entrepreneurs can use to scale their social ventures. The third section provides guidelines for scaling social ventures.

1 Understanding Social Venture Scaling

This section begins with the (fictitious) story of Mark, who started a social venture that has been successful in accomplishing its stated objectives. Mark has been acclaimed for the success of his venture and has garnered increasing attention and recognition in the local media. As a result, he has received recognition from policy-makers, elected officials, and community leaders. The next logical step is to build on this success and scale up his social venture—that is, expand it to new geographic locations or add new services to what he is already offering. A social venture can scale only when there is evidence of demonstrated success. It must also be able to show that its theory of change is strong, that its initial outcomes are encouraging, and that it has systems in place to track key performance data going forward.[1]

1.1 Defining Scaling

Dees defines "scaling" as increasing the impact that a social-purpose organization produces so that it better matches the magnitude of the social need or problem it seeks to address.[2] Other expressions, such as "scaling up" and "going to scale," are also sometimes used when discussing scaling. Both of these mean creating new service sites in other geographic locations that operate under a common name, use common approaches, and are either branches of the parent organization or very closely tied affiliates of that parent organization.[3]

Dees and colleagues have identified two types of scaling: *scaling up* and *scaling deep*. The former refers to the expansion of services or extension to other geographic locations. The latter implies that the social venture deepens its knowledge of the market and focuses on developing and becoming expert in providing the required services.[4] So scaling up corresponds to breadth scale, while scaling deep corresponds to depth scale. Similarly, a recent study assessing the scaling strategies of Naandi and Drishtee, two social ventures operating in rural India, indicates two distinct modes of scaling social impact—breadth and depth scale. Each venture dynamically balances a minimum critical specification of social innovation, affordability, and market penetration while scaling social impact.[5]

In their research on social venture scaling, Dees and colleagues have identified three common forms for scaling social innovations. They suggest that some innovations spread as an *organizational model*—an overarching structure for mobilizing people and resources to serve a common purpose. Others spread in the form of a *program*—an integrated set of actions that serves a specific purpose. While still others are framed in terms of *principles*—general guidelines and values about how to serve a given purpose.[6] These three forms are not always mutually exclusive and the distinctions between them are often blurred. For example, a program can entail some guiding principles and occur under a particular organizational model. Likewise, a particular organizational model can facilitate the development of certain programs.

Growth is a natural evolution of both for-profit and nonprofit organizations. In expanding, organizations enlarge the scope of their activities or their geographic reach. Organizations may also decide to focus on improving what they currently do. Social entrepreneurs face similar decisions. They must decide whether to scale their social ventures by adding more activities, expanding geographically, or simply improving what they do at present. For example, Walske and Tyson describe the challenges faced by Paul Rice, the founder and CEO of Fair Trade USA (the leading third-party certifier of fair-trade products in North America), in trying to scale his organization to make his label more prevalent and build a viable, long-term business model. After tremendous early success, Free Trade USA is now contemplating various growth strategies in order to compete with other organizations, such as the Rainforest Alliance and Utz.[7]

To some extent, scaling is comparable to undertaking a change process. Therefore, it is appropriate to advise social entrepreneurs that they could benefit from performing a *force-field analysis* as soon as they start contemplating expanding their activities. Developed by Kurt Lewin in the 1940s, a force-field analysis is used to identify the driving forces that positively influence a movement toward change as well as the restraining forces that will prevent movement.[8] It is used extensively today in organizational development and change. For a social venture, forces that could affect the decision to scale may include both internal and external stakeholders. For example, some internal stakeholders, such as paid employees and volunteers, may favor scaling, whereas others may oppose it. Likewise, some external stakeholders may favor scaling, whereas others may oppose it. The knowledge gleaned from a field-force analysis could help social entrepreneurs to develop the most appropriate scaling strategies.

Whereas in commercial entrepreneurship sustained growth means growth in both revenue and profit over an extended period of time, in social entrepreneurship sustained growth means growth in funding as well as sustainability (the ability of the social venture to fulfill its mission while remaining financially viable over time). This can be accomplished in several ways, depending on the type of social venture. For example, for purely philanthropic social ventures, sustained growth could mean fulfilling the social mission while attracting more funding. For hybrid social ventures, sustained growth could mean fulfilling the social mission, raising sufficient money from donors, and increasing the level of earned income. For for-profit social ventures, sustained growth means fulfilling the social mission while generating sufficient income through commercial activities.

A social venture can grow by expanding its products or services or by extending its geographic coverage. For example, the social venture Ascovime started by offering health-care services in rural Cameroon (see Chapter 9). It then added the provision of books and school materials to its services. This is an example of expansion by increasing activities. An example of extending geographic coverage is provided by We Care Solar, which initially distributed its solar suitcases only in Nigeria but now operates in 27 countries (see Chapter 11).

Scaling is an important step for any social venture that intends to remain successful over time, but it should always be carefully planned. In planning for scaling, social ventures should consider the following three issues:

- appreciate the nature of scaling the social venture;
- stay committed to the scaling strategy; and
- plan for scaling.[9]

When contemplating growth, the managers of a social venture must always ask themselves whether growing will help the enterprise to fulfill its social mission. Not all social ventures need to grow or have the potential to grow. Under some conditions, growth may even reduce a social venture's ability to fulfil its social mission. The social venture must also remain focused on its core mission and strategy while growing. The main idea here is that the social venture should anticipate events and carefully manage the rate of growth. Scaling is often a difficult process.[10] The approaches that work well for one organization in one situation will not necessarily work well for another organization in even a slightly different situation.[11]

1.2   Reasons for Scaling a Social Venture

Social entrepreneurship scholars have identified at least five underlying reasons for scaling social ventures:

- moral imperative;
- demand-side pressures;
- organizational needs;
- funders' expectations; and
- the personal ambition of the social entrepreneur.[12]

These five reasons for scaling are summarized in Table 13.1.

Table 13.1 Reasons for scaling a social venture

Reason	Explanation
Moral imperative	Moral obligation to make service available for more people may lead to scaling.
Demand-side pressures	Communities that are aware of the existence and benefits of a social venture may request such services. In this case, it is difficult for the social entrepreneur to resist such demands.
Organizational needs	Under some conditions, scaling could be the best way for a social venture to improve its services. Therefore, scaling becomes a need for the social venture itself.
Funders' expectations	Funders may expect the social venture to grow in order to accomplish its social mission to the best of its ability.
Personal ambition of social entrepreneur	The social entrepreneur's personal ambition may be the driving force behind scaling.

A moral imperative could lead social entrepreneurs to scale their ventures when they feel an obligation to make their services available to as many people as possible. In addition, some communities that have been made aware of a successful social program may request that the program is implemented in their communities. Under these conditions, it is very difficult for the social entrepreneur to resist the demands for such a program. It may also be that the best way for the social venture to offer its services is to grow. Thus, scaling becomes an organizational need to offer the services that are required. Such growth can enhance career opportunities for the social venture's employees and volunteers. Funders may also expect the social venture to grow in order to increase its capacity to accomplish its social mission. Finally, a social venture may grow because of the personal ambition of the founder. This can be a good thing because, after all, ambition is the "root of all achievement."[13]

Clearly, then, there are several potential reasons for scaling a social venture. However, one must always carefully consider whether scaling is a good idea. What benefits will it bring to the social venture and its stakeholders? The next section explores some of the advantages of scaling, but it is worth noting that these benefits do not accrue *during* the scaling process. Rather, they are obtained only once the social venture has been scaled.

1.3   Benefits of Scaling a Social Venture

The benefits that result from scaling a social venture can be divided into three main categories:

* increased chance of survival;
* improved efficiency; and
* enhanced effectiveness.

Scaling a social venture helps to spread the risk and create new stakeholders. Spreading the risk increases the likelihood of the social venture surviving. For example, if an organization operates in several geographic locations, a setback or downturn in one of those locations can be offset by growth in the others. Similarly, a large organization is likely to build a wide network of stakeholders and institutions on which it can rely. Scaling also increases organizational efficiency. For example, scaling a social venture can help to capture economies of scale and economies of scope[14] and may also generate learning-curve effects. Economies of scale tend to be captured when a social venture reduces the costs of the units it produces. For example, We Care Solar captures economies of scale by making more solar suitcases as a result of its geographic expansion. Economies of scope can be captured when a social venture launches a larger range of operations. The benefits of cumulative experience also usually lead to productivity improvements, because, as the members of an organization learn how to do their work more efficiently, they tend to make fewer mistakes.

In addition, scaling enhances effectiveness insofar as it allows the organization to promote innovation through local experimentation, use specialization to develop greater expertise, capitalize on name recognition, and reach the people who will benefit most from its services. It can help an enterprise to attract resources and recruit partners, serve as an advocate on relevant issues, and find systematic solutions to systemic problems.[15] Finally, it enables social ventures to attract talented employees and volunteers and usually results in an increase in the number of interested stakeholders.

1.4   Challenges of Scaling a Social Venture

Several social entrepreneurship scholars have suggested that scaling is not for everyone;[16] and social ventures invariably face a number of challenges when they choose to scale. These challenges can be significant, as is explained below, but they should not dissuade social entrepreneurs from attempting to scale their enterprises.

Scaling can pull a social venture away from its original mission, strain scarce financial and human resources, and impact effectiveness if the organization's focus turns to growth at the expense of quality. Scaling can also harm a social venture's reputation if performance becomes poor and too much bureaucracy and red tape are introduced.[17] In addition, the scaling of a social venture sometimes results in cash-flow problems. If a for-profit or hybrid social venture does not generate enough earned income, it may be difficult for it to finance diverse activities or expand into new geographic areas. Despite these challenges, the benefits of scaling far outweigh the drawbacks. In a study conducted on the transfer of social innovations in rural India which used Gram Vikas as a case study, Chowdhury and Santos found that the scaling process was fraught with difficulties. However, the authors concluded that these could be managed by focusing on the core of elements which enable a social innovation's success.[18]

2   Strategies for Scaling a Social Venture

There are several growth strategies that social ventures can use to expand their activities. To some extent, these are similar to those that are used by commercial ventures. Six of the most important strategies are summarized in Table 13.2:

- capacity building;
- dissemination;
- branching;
- affiliation;
- social franchising; and
- strategic alliances.

These are reviewed in detail below.

Table 13.2 Growth strategies for social ventures

Capacity building	Dissemination	Branching	Affiliation	Social franchising	Strategic alliances
Development of internal capabilities Strengthening of key skills Elements: • mission • structure • model • culture • data • resources; and • leadership and governance.	Diffusion of innovation Diffusion of products or services	Establishment of branches in different geographic locations Final decisions rest with headquarters Branches have less autonomy	Embedded in local communities Less control from home office Less expensive than branching	Social franchisor Extension of services by having social franchisees Allows scaling at a faster rate and at lower costs than branching	Form alliances with other social ventures or for-profit organizations to address social issues Extension of services by building partnerships

2.1   Capacity Building

Capacity building refers to the process by which an organization strengthens its internal capabilities. It may include revising the mission to acquire better equipment and more skillful employees. LaFrance and colleagues identified seven elements of capacity building for any social venture:

- mission;
- structure;
- model;
- culture;
- data;
- resources; and
- leadership and governance.[19]

Explanations of these elements are presented in Table 13.3. The first element—mission—is especially important because the social venture must never lose sight of its core mission. Everything the social venture does, including its growth, should be tied to its mission. The second element—structure—should fit within the mission and should not impede growth. The structure should be flexible enough to facilitate adaptation and change. A rigid structure may prevent an organization from changing. According to LaFrance and colleagues, the issue of structure lies between flexibility and control. "Flexibility" refers to the degree of adaptability and looseness of the structure, whereas "control" refers to the degree to which management oversees critical decisions. The balance between control and flexibility is achieved through good management skills, effective communication, building and maintaining a robust technology infrastructure, and holding branch offices accountable for outcomes as opposed to rigid performance standards.[20]

Table 13.3 The seven elements of capacity building

Element	Explanation
Mission	The reason why the social venture exists. It should never lose sight of this social mission while scaling.
Structure	How internal activities and responsibilities are organized and relate to one another. A flexible structure is better suited for change while a rigid structure can impede change.
Model	Documentation and replication of best practices. This can be done by benchmarking the leaders in the social venture's landscape.
Culture	The system of beliefs within the social venture that can facilitate or impede change.
Data	Good analytics can help a social venture build the case for scaling.
Resources	Financial and non-financial resources are essential for a social venture to scale its activities.
Leadership and governance	The effectiveness of top management and board members and their alignment with the social mission are key to providing leadership and direction for a social venture.

The third element—model—involves documenting best practices and replicating them. The fourth element—culture—refers to the system of beliefs and values within the social venture that could facilitate or impede change. When the culture is strong and unified behind the social mission, the social venture is more likely to be able to scale successfully without damaging either the mission or the organization itself.[21] The fifth element is data. Good analytics—as it is now known, which entails data-gathering, analysis, interpretation, and use for decision-making—allows a social venture to build a strong rationale for growth. Sound data can help build a compelling case for scaling. There have been some calls to integrate big data and analytics in social entrepreneurship.[22] This is particularly important because growth entails expanding products or services to more beneficiaries or covering a larger geographic area. The sixth element—resources—is an essential component of capacity building because any effort to scale a social venture will be futile without access to adequate resources. The seventh and final element—leadership and governance—refers to the effectiveness of top management and board members and their alignment to the social venture's mission. Chapter 11 discussed the roles of founders and board members in providing leadership and direction for a social venture. They are equally critical when it comes to growth and the selection of the most appropriate growth strategy.

2.2 Dissemination

Social ventures can disseminate their products or services. As conceived here, the term "dissemination" is similar to diffusion of innovation. It entails actively providing information, and sometimes technical assistance, to others who wish to bring an innovation to their community.[23] The way a social venture disseminates its products or services may depend on its resources. For instance, We Care Solar disseminates the use of its solar suitcase by training locals who then serve as consultants and field operators to install and troubleshoot the solar panel systems. By using this growth strategy, We Care Solar does not have to establish branches or subsidiaries to expand its services in those areas.

As a growth strategy, dissemination is relatively inexpensive because it does not necessarily involve acquiring additional facilities, equipment, or human capital.[24] However, one of its drawbacks is that it limits management's control over the quality of the product or service by allowing others to implement it.

2.3   Branching and Affiliation

Social entrepreneurs can scale their social ventures by using branching as a growth strategy. Before discussing this growth strategy in the context of social entrepreneurship, it is useful to explore its use in the banking industry. Generally, commercial banks have branches scattered around a country and/or the world. These branches do not have much autonomy since key decisions are always made at the headquarters.[25] Branch structures are particularly appealing when successful implementation of an innovation depends on tight quality control, specific practices, knowledge that is not explicitly documented or readily communicated, and strong organizational cultures.[26] However, branching could be expensive for social ventures and therefore may not be an efficient growth strategy. Thus, social entrepreneurs may use affiliation instead.[27]

Affiliation is similar to branching insofar as the social venture establishes units in other locations. However, the connection between the home office and the affiliates is usually more relaxed.[28] In this sense, affiliates are not so tightly controlled from the headquarters; they have more autonomy and they are embedded in the communities where they operate. An example of a social venture that has used affiliation to expand is Habitat for Humanity. This enterprise has affiliates that help with its house-building projects in each country where it operates. Affiliation is less threatening to local communities than branching because the degree of external control is reduced.[29] It is also generally less expensive than branching.

2.4   Social Franchising

Social franchising is a hybrid growth strategy that combines elements of branching and affiliation.[30] It is similar to commercial franchising and involves a parent social venture—the *franchisor*—and the *franchisee*. The franchisor's products or services are franchised by the franchisee, with the latter paying royalties and fees to the former. However, these fees are usually modest, and sometimes they are waived altogether. The social franchising model of growth is attractive because it allows scaling at a faster rate and at a lower cost than branching.[31] Some of the factors that lead to the success of social franchises are similar to those that lead to the success of commercial business franchises, but others are different.[32]

As with business franchising, access to resources, including capital, managerial expertise, and local knowledge, constitutes a key motivation for social venture franchising.[33] Franchising is also a means to increase impact.[34] Dialogue Social Enterprise (www.dialogue-se.com) and Wellcome (www.wellcome-online.de) are two examples of social ventures that use franchising to scale.[35] Dialogue Social Enterprise offers social awareness exhibitions and workshops, and it creates jobs for marginalized and disadvantaged people around the world. At the time of writing it had franchisees in 25 countries. Wellcome is a German social venture founded in 2002 by Rose Volz-Schmidt. Its main objective is to offer young mothers help with coping with the emotional and logistical stress of motherhood. It has expanded its operations rapidly through franchising and now boasts over 200 franchisees.

To some extent, social franchising provides a strategy to replicate a social venture's small-scale initial success, to mobilize much-needed resources, and to reduce agency costs through mechanisms of self-selection and self-monitoring.[36]

2.5   Strategic Alliances

Some social ventures use strategic alliances to scale their operations. Such partnerships can take several forms. They can occur between social ventures, between social ventures and for-profit organizations, and/or between social ventures and government agencies. For example, collaborative relationships between businesses and nonprofits have grown tremendously over the last few years.[37] Social ventures partner with other social ventures or for-profit organizations to create better social value for their beneficiaries. As one scholar puts it, we are living at a time when no organization can succeed on its own.[38] Austin identifies three stages in a typical partnership between a nonprofit and a for-profit organization:

- purely philanthropic—when the engagement is limited to the provision of financial and other resources;
- transactional—when there are explicit resource exchanges focused on specific activities, such as cause-related marketing, event sponsorships, and contractual service arrangements; and
- integrative—when the two partners' missions, personnel, and activities begin to merge into more collective action and organizational integration.[39]

Alliance building is considered as one of the key elements for social venture scaling in the SCALERS model, described later in this chapter. Such partnerships are now known as *social alliances*.[40] These are generally defined as voluntary collaborations between businesses and social enterprises that aim to address social problems that are too complex to be solved by unilateral organizational action.[41] One type of collaborative engagement is partnership among business, government, and civil society.[42] Outcomes of business–nonprofit partnerships have been measured at three levels:

- direct impact on the issue and its stakeholders;
- impact on building capacity, knowledge, or reputational capital that can attract new resources; and
- influence on social policy or system change.[43]

Regardless of the scaling strategy used, growth must be carefully managed because it could imply the use of several resources, including human, technological, and financial. A social venture cannot grow if it does not have sufficient resources. Growth could require hiring additional employees and/or volunteers. For example, a study assessing the factors influencing the scalability of two social ventures, Uganda's Solar Sister and India's E-Health Point, indicates the importance of the productive engagement of human assets (human capital acquisition, development, and retention) for their long-term viability and the extent to which they are able to accomplish their objectives on broader social scales.[44] Likewise, the use of technology, such as information technology, can positively influence scaling. Information technology can increase the value proposition of a program or action (depth scaling) by providing accurate and rapid needs recognition, adapting products and services. It can also increase the number of people who are reached by the organization (breadth scaling) by accessing new resources, creating synergies and networks, improving organizational efficiency, increasing the venture's visibility, and designing new access channels to beneficiaries.[45] Finally, if a social venture lacks financial resources, it will be unable to grow. And if it does not grow, it may not be able to scale its social impact and thereby attract additional resources from donors and/or investors.

In discussing the importance of crafting an appropriate scaling strategy, Dees and colleagues described what they called the five Rs of scaling:

- readiness;
- receptivity;
- resources;
- risks; and
- returns.[46]

Social entrepreneurs must address the following five questions related to the five Rs:

- Is the innovation ready to be spread (readiness)?
- Will the innovation be well received in target communities (receptivity)?
- What resources, financial or otherwise, are required to get the job done right (resources)?
- What is the likelihood that the innovation will be implemented incorrectly, or will fail to have an impact (risk)?
- What is the bottom line (returns)?[47]

Addressing these five Rs is crucial in the development of a successful scaling strategy.

3   Guidelines for Scaling a Social Venture

Taylor and colleagues have proposed a guideline for social entrepreneurs contemplating the scaling of their venture.[48] This guideline includes four steps:

1 Define specifically what the social venture wants to scale and determine its replicability.
2 Conduct an honest assessment of the opportunity.
3 Evaluate the social venture's readiness to take on the challenges of scaling.
4 Formulate a scaling strategy that fits.

Each of these four steps is discussed in detail below.

3.1   Define What to Scale and Determine Its Replicability

The first step indicates that the social entrepreneur should clearly identify what the social venture offers. This implies making sure that the value proposition offered to the beneficiaries is well defined and articulated and can be transferred to other communities. This step requires a clear understanding of the social venture's products and/or services. For example, if a social venture offers free healthcare to the poor in a particular neighborhood, it must know precisely what this comprises. Is what is provided in one community replicable to another community? Will the beneficiaries perceive the value of the social good that they are offered? Such questions must be addressed at this stage, as failure to understand this process clearly could impede the social venture's ability to scale. Often, what works well in one setting may fail in another.

3.2 Assess the Opportunity

In this step, the social entrepreneur must size up the opportunity. Is the opportunity to scale sufficiently large to be replicated elsewhere? If the answer is "no," then scaling is probably not a good idea. However, if the answer is "yes," the social venture should contemplate scaling its services. Although social needs are rarely confined to a single community, their intensity may vary across communities. Therefore, the social venture must estimate the minimum critical mass of need to justify scaling. This implies an assessment of the opportunity in terms of value offered and size. A social venture can scale in a given environment when there is a critical mass of people who will benefit from its services, although this is not to suggest that social ventures must not engage in areas where there is only a small group of needy people.[49]

3.3 Evaluate the Readiness to Scale

The social venture must assess whether it is ready to scale. This implies that it already has the desire and the resources to scale. As several social entrepreneurship scholars have pointed out, scaling is a developmental turning point.[50] The initial exploration of scaling options begins and ends with considerations of readiness.[51] Although there is no magical formula to determine whether a social venture is ready to scale, the following assumption provides some indication: a social venture is usually ready to scale when it has adequate financial, human, and other resources deemed necessary to exploit a scaling opportunity. If the social venture does not have the necessary resources, any attempt to scale is likely to fail.

3.4 Formulate a Scaling Strategy that Fits

According to Taylor and colleagues, when deciding to scale, a social venture must address four critical questions:

- How quickly will the social venture roll out, and what are the key milestones or checkpoints?
- How will the social venture be structured as it scales?
- How will sites be selected?
- How will the necessary capabilities be built and how will resources be acquired?[52]

The first question relates to the speed and rate at which the social venture must scale. When scaling, a social venture should always identify some key milestones, such as the number of geographic areas it intends to cover within a certain time period. Scaling also requires that the social venture restructures itself. It may add new people, including extra managers. Such additions could make the existing organizational structure obsolete or inadequate, and therefore unsuitable during scaling or even after scaling. Prior to scaling, the social venture must select the most appropriate sites, especially when it plans to expand in additional geographic locations. A clear understanding of these sites, along with the challenges they are likely to present, is essential to achieving successful geographic coverage. Finally, social entrepreneurs must determine how capabilities will be built and identify how resources will be acquired to implement the scaling strategy.

3.5 The SCALERS Model

Bloom and Chatterji proposed the SCALERS model to explain the conditions under which social ventures may scale their activities. The model includes seven components:

- staffing;
- communication;
- alliance building;
- lobbying;
- earnings generation;
- replication; and
- stimulating market forces.[53]

These components—or capabilities (as the authors also label them)—are known by the acronym SCALERS (see Figure 13.1). Bloom and Chatterji identified contingency factors that could lead some scaling drivers to be more successful than others. Under some

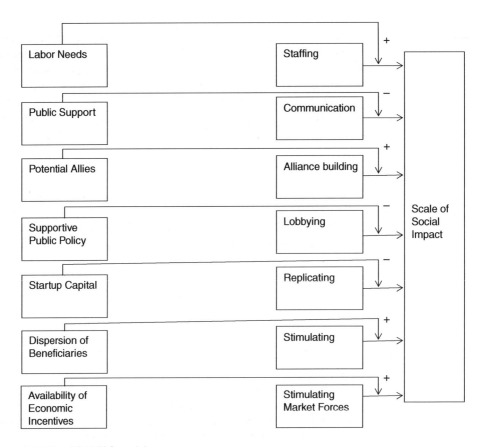

Figure 13.1 The SCALERS model.

conditions, all SCALERS are needed for a successful scaling of social impact. In other situations, only a few SCALERS may be needed for successful scaling. The authors propose that the "scale of social impact" achieved by a social venture is influenced by how effective it has been at developing some combination of the seven capabilities. Each of them is discussed in detail below.

3.5.1   Staffing

Staffing refers to the extent to which the social venture is able to fill positions with skilled and capable people, including managers, employees, and/or volunteers. It therefore relates to the ability of the social venture to acquire, develop, and maintain the necessary human capital.[54] When the social venture is able to hire talented people effectively, this can increase its ability to scale its activities. According to Bloom and Chatterji, staffing can also reinforce the other SCALERS.[55] In fact, all seven elements of the SCALERS model are related to one another. As mentioned above, the seven elements are also influenced by contingencies. For example, staffing's ability to act as an effective element in scaling a social venture depends on various contingencies, such as labor needs. Some social ventures are labor intensive, whereas others are not.

3.5.2   Communication

The second capability—communication—refers to the effectiveness with which the organization is able to persuade key stakeholders that its change strategy is worth adopting and/or supporting.[56] Good communication can convince key stakeholders of the value of the products or services that the social venture is providing. It can also act as a motivator to persuade stakeholders to support the social venture's scaling efforts. If you build it, the people will not necessarily come, *unless* they are clearly informed, frequently reminded, and convincingly persuaded that what the organization is doing benefits them.[57]

3.5.3   Alliance building

This refers to the effectiveness with which an organization has forged partnerships, coalitions, joint ventures, and other linkages to bring about social change.[58] Organizations that score highly here do not try to do things by themselves; instead, they seek and exploit the benefits of unified efforts.[59] Successful social entrepreneurs have the ability to build alliances and strong relationships with organizations and individuals that share their goals. Building alliances requires a good understanding of the social venture ecosystem. Such understanding allows the social venture to search for and collaborate with other groups.

3.5.4   Lobbying

Lobbying relates to the effectiveness with which an organization is able to advocate for government actions that may work in its favor.[60] The SCALERS model can help social entrepreneurs identify the strengths and weaknesses in their own organizations and use these insights to scale their social impact.[61] The authors define lobbying loosely to incorporate all of a social venture's efforts to gain acceptance from policy-makers. Lobbying does not only refer to commissioning registered lobbyists to advocate a cause to government officials, legislators, and policy-makers. Some situational contingencies can moderate the effect of lobbying. One such contingency factor is a set of supportive public policies, or the extent to which laws, regulations, and policies that support the organization's social change efforts are already in place.[62]

3.5.5   Earnings generation

This refers to the effectiveness with which the organization generates a stream of revenue that exceeds its expenses. Any organization that is successful in this regard will have little trouble paying its bills and funding its activities.[63] Earnings generation can be enhanced by adopting a systematic, business-like approach toward generating revenue. Unfortunately, few social entrepreneurs are willing to focus on this.[64] But they should, because earnings generation can have a large impact on other SCALERS. For example, a social venture that is able to generate significant earnings will be able to hire more qualified staff, which will have a positive impact on the staffing capability. Extra revenue will also facilitate scaling in lobbying and alliance building, which in turn should generate even more revenue, creating a virtuous circle.

3.5.6   Replication

Replication refers to the effectiveness with which a social venture can reproduce the programs and initiatives that it has originated.[65] Replication can be achieved through chapters, franchising, or affiliates. A social venture should always aim to replicate its activities and programs without any reduction in quality. It can usually do this without necessarily dictating what chapters or franchisees must do. Rather, it should establish trustful relationships with such entities. Replication results in the social venture reaching more beneficiaries.

3.5.7   Stimulating Market Forces

This relates to the extent to which an organization is able to generate incentives that encourage people or institutions to pursue private interests while also serving the public good. Organizations that score highly on this measure are adept at creating markets for their products and services, micro-loans, inexpensive health remedies, inexpensive farming equipment, or carbon credits.[66] The organization's development of such markets allows other social ventures to enter them, thereby expanding the products or services that may be offered to beneficiaries.

Among the examples given by Bloom and Chatterji to illustrate the use of their model is a US nonprofit organization, Girls on the Run, which scaled from helping 13 girls in 1996 to serving more than 40,000 in 2008 at more than 160 affiliates throughout the United States.[67] Girls between the ages of 8 and 12 now go through a 12-week after-school program designed to build their self-esteem and appreciation for healthy living, with games involving running used as a teaching modality. They cover topics like peer pressure, bullying, and healthy eating.

One year after it was devised, Bloom and Smith empirically tested the SCALERS model and found that all seven components are important predictors of scaling social impact.[68] However, they also found that alliance-building and lobbying were no longer significant when all of the SCALERS capabilities were entered into their regression analysis. They explained these findings by alluding to the nature of the organizations they studied.

Specifically, they pointed out that these organizations may have operated in situations where there were few opportunities for recruiting allies and/or supportive public policy did not leave much room for additional lobbying success.

The SCALERS model remains an important tool that social entrepreneurs use to assess the scalability of their ventures. However, an interesting question that social entrepreneurship scholars must start to ask is why some social enterprises scale while others do not.[69]

Summary

This chapter discussed the scaling of social ventures. Social ventures can scale up or scale deep. They can also use several strategies, such as affiliation, branching, capacity building, dissemination, social franchising, and strategic alliances, to scale their activities. Scaling must be carefully planned. In this regard, the SCALERS model is a useful tool for social ventures that are contemplating scaling their activities.

Key Words

Affiliation; branching; capacity building; dissemination; readiness to scale; replicability; scaling; scaling deep; scaling up; social alliances; social franchising

Review Questions

1 Explain the difference between scaling deep and scaling up.
2 Under what conditions should a social venture scale up? Under what conditions should a social venture scale deep?
3 What are the benefits of scaling a social venture?
4 What are the potential drawbacks of scaling a social venture?
5 What are the main differences between branching and affiliation as strategies for growing a social venture?
6 What are the benefits and limitations of social franchising?
7 Describe the key elements of the SCALERS model.
8 Explain why social ventures must assess their readiness to scale.
9 What are the benefits of branching and affiliation?
10 Identify some of the key benefits for a social venture that is planning to scale.

Application Questions

1 Sue owns a social venture that focuses on providing free books to disadvantaged children in her city. The social venture has been successful in donating books to high school students in the poor areas of the city. Based on this success, Sue wants to expand into other cities. What are some of the challenges that she could face as she contemplates scaling? What advice would you give her?
2 Watch the video at www.youtube.com/watch?v=tPZ9tiDEuG0 and answer the following questions. Why is it important for social ventures to scale their activities? What are the challenges of social entrepreneurship? How could social ventures gain credibility?

3   Describe a social venture with which you are familiar and explain how the SCALERS model could help scale its activities. Should the model be applied as it is or should it be refined? Explain.

4   Catherine owns a small social venture that helps disadvantaged kids in her neighborhood. The venture has been doing pretty well and Catherine is contemplating scaling it to other neighborhoods in the city. Using the guidelines for scaling, what advice would you give her?

5   Scaling a social venture is often viewed as a difficult task. Which steps and strategies do you think could help facilitate the scaling of social ventures?

Application Case 1: Twaweza: Empowering Citizens in East Africa[70]

Democracy can only be effective when citizens are well informed and elected officials are held accountable for their actions. To empower citizens through information and communication, Rakesh Rajani, a citizen of Tanzania of Indian heritage, started Twaweza (www.twaweza.org), which translates into 'we can make it happen' in the local Swahili language in 2009 in his native Tanzania.[1] Twaweza's mission is to empower people through information and help them build an ecosystem of change for themselves. Rajani believes in a form of cooperation between governments and the people to learn from each other and accomplish economic development goals. As he explained it in an interview with CNN in 2014, 'I could see a whole new modeling practice where a government says, in order for us to succeed we need your help, we need your collaboration, we need your ideas, we need your critique. The old idea that government knows everything and shuts everybody out is now so, so old thinking, it doesn't work that way.'[2]

To accomplish its mission, Twaweza uses means such as television, radios, cell phones, and newspapers to educate and inform citizens in Tanzania about government policies and decisions. Using these means of communication has allowed citizens of Tanzania and others in East Africa to have access to government information. Cell phones are a particularly useful means of accessing government information because many people in Tanzania and East Africa have access to cell phones except in the very remote areas. In Tanzania alone, there are probably over 14 million cell phone users.[3]

Access to information contributes to transparency. One of the key issues in most African countries, is the lack of transparency. This lack of transparency is a hindrance to empower citizens and give them the opportunity to hold their governments accountable. Lack of transparency facilitates corruption and other misdeeds that prevent economic development. Rajani notes that in East Africa, the lack of transparency is a real problem. If there is transparency, elected officials would make sure that budgets are earmarked properly.[4]

With the use of technology to access information, government leaders can no longer get away with lying to the public because the public has different ways of getting information; as a result, the level of control that local officials can exert over populations is much more limited.[5]

Twaweza received much of its funding from international donor agencies. It works in relationship with other organizations and institutions, such as the Center for Global Development at Harvard University, the MIT Governance Lab in the United States and Aberdeen University in the United Kingdom. In Tanzania, Twaweza has convinced cell phone providers to donate millions of SMS messages, which the venture uses to disseminate information on school funding and other government services. It is also helping radio stations to expand their ability to do investigating reporting and assisting them to broaden their reach in rural areas.[6] Indeed, Twaweza's slogan is *information for everyone*.

Rajani graduated from Harvard University with a Master's degree in Theological Studies and from Brandeis University with a bachelor's degree in philosophy and American literature. He participated in several forums around the world focusing on open governance. He was a speaker at the Open Governance Partnership in Bali, Indonesia in 2014. After heading Twaweza since its founding in 2009, Rajani joined the Ford Foundation in 2015 as Director of Civic Engagement and Government. Meanwhile, Twaweza continues its work with new leadership and is expanding its reach in other countries in East Africa. It is heavily involved in Kenya and Uganda and is planning to expand its model in other African countries.

Discussion Questions

1   What do you think of Rakesh Rajani's decision to leave Twaweza for the Ford Foundation? Was it a good move to contribute to open governance? Yes? No? Explain.
2   If you were a consultant to Twaweza, how would you help it build its capacities before thinking about scaling its operations in other African countries?
3   How could the SCALERS model help this social venture scale its activities throughout Africa?
4   How would you apply the five Rs in helping this social venture to scale its activities?

References

1   *http://edition.cnn.com/2014/05/09/world/africa/want-to-change-africa-lets-do-it/index. html?hpt=hp_bn1.* [Retrieved on May 9, 2014].
2   *http://edition.cnn.com/2014/05/09/world/africa/want-to-change-africa-lets-do-it/index. html?hpt=hp_bn1.* [Retrieved on May 9, 2014].
3   *http://www.cgdev.org/blog/connecting-citizens-twaweza%E2%80%99s-rakesh-rajani-public-accountability-east-africa.* [Retrieved on April 18, 2016].
4   *http://edition.cnn.com/2014/05/09/world/africa/want-to-change-africa-lets-do-it/index. html?hpt=hp_bn1.* [Retrieved on May 9, 2014].
5   *http://www.cgdev.org/blog/connecting-citizens-twaweza%E2%80%99s-rakesh-rajani-public-accountability-east-africa.* [Retrieved on April 18, 2016].
6   *http://www.cgdev.org/blog/connecting-citizens-twaweza%E2%80%99s-rakesh-rajani-public-accountability-east-africa.* [Retrieved on April 18, 2016].

Application Case 2: Eniware Sterile[71]

It is well known in medical practice and public health policy circles that complete sterilization for surgeries is elusive in most developing countries. Other than the deaths and complications caused by non-sterile environments, Dr. H. Mahler, a former Director-General of the World Health Organization, has expressed concerns over the citizens in developing countries who no longer trust their healthcare services because of these problems. To address these issues, Dr. James Bernstein—a physician trained in thoracic, vascular, and transplantation surgery, a former CEO of several large healthcare companies, and one-time chairman of President Carter's health policy advisory group—has recently invented a new device. Known as the Eniware Portable Sterilizer (EPS), it is manufactured and sold by Eniware Sterile, a for-profit company with a social mission, according to Dr. Bernstein, the firm's co-founder and CEO since its launch in 2008.

Eniware's sterilization system is convenient, cost-effective, portable, and does not require electricity. Thus, it can be easily used in areas where people do not have access to electricity or heating. The EPS consists of a sealed case containing a gas cartridge/ampoule of nitrogen

The Eniware Portable Sterilizer (EPS)

"Portable, Power-Free Medical Instrument Sterilization Facilitates Essential Surgery for East African Health Systems." Eniware, 2014. http://www. theessentialsurgerycompany.com/wp-content/uploads/2014/02/EAHF-poster.pdf

dioxide, a scrubber to absorb the gas, a chemical indicator, and a variety of wraps, including cellophane to preserve sterility. The unit costs approximately $500. Watch the video at www.youtube.com/watch?v=dCkd4Yv1zQ4 for a demonstration of it in action.

Eniware has partnered with the Essential Surgery Company (ESC) in Uganda to improve access to safe surgery in East Africa. Eniware is not only saving lives but also improving the quality of people's lives. In fact, simple surgical procedures can be performed effectively in several parts of Africa and elsewhere in the developing world without sophisticated equipment. According to Dr. Bernstein, reliable, effective surgical care for all can deliver extremely high social and economic returns. He explains that post-operative infections in the developing world run at three to four times the rate observed in the industrialized world, meaning that millions of people suffer and die needlessly every year.

Discussion Questions

1 Watch the interview with Dr. James Bernstein at www.youtube.com/watch?v=S62siLeYaP0 and identify the reasons behind the invention and commercialization of the EPS.
2 How might the EPS be scaled in the developing world using the SCALERS model?
3 How might building strategic alliances contribute to the scaling of the EPS?
4 According to Dr. Bernstein, Eniware Sterile is a for-profit venture with a social mission. Do you believe that for-profit businesses can pursue both an economic motive and a social impact mission (yes or no)? Explain your answer.

Notes

1 Bradach, J. L. (2003). Going to scale: The challenge of replicating social programs. *Stanford Social Innovation Review*, 1, 19–25.

2 Dees, J. G. (2008). Developing the field of social entrepreneurship. Report from the Center for the Advancement of Social Entrepreneurship, Duke University.

3 Taylor, M. A., Dees, J. G., & Emerson, J. (2002). The question of scale: Finding an appropriate strategy for building on your success. In J. G. Dees, J. Emerson, & P. Economy (Eds.), *Social entrepreneurs: Enhancing the performance of your enterprising nonprofit* (pp. 235–266). New York: John Wiley & Sons, Inc.

4 Dees, J. G., & Emerson, J., & Economy, P. (2001). *Enterprising nonprofits: A toolkit for social entrepreneurs.* New York: John Wiley & Sons, Inc.

5 Desa, G., & Koch, J. L. (2014). Scaling social impact: Building sustainable social ventures at the base of the pyramid. *Journal of Social Entrepreneurship*, 5(2), 146–174.

6 Dees, J. G., Anderson, B. B., & Wei-Skillern, J. (2004). Scaling social impact: Strategies of spreading social innovations. *Stanford Social Innovation Review*, 1, 24–32.

7 Walske, J., & Tyson, D. L. (2015). Fair trade USA: Scaling for impact. *California Management Review*, 58(1), 123–143.

8 Lewin K. (1943). Defining the field at a given time. *Psychological Review*, 50(3), 292–310.

9 Taylor, M. A., Dees, J. G., & Emerson, J. (2002). The question of scale: Finding an appropriate strategy for building on your success. In J. G. Dees, J. Emerson, & P. Economy (Eds.), *Social entrepreneurs: Enhancing the performance of your enterprising nonprofit* (pp. 235–266). New York: John Wiley & Sons, Inc.

10 Casasnovas, G., & Bruno, A. V. (2013). Scaling social ventures: An exploratory study of social incubators and accelerators. *Journal of Management for Global Sustainability*, 1(2), 173–197; Shelton, L. (2005). Scale barriers and growth opportunities: A resource-based model of new venture expansion. *Journal of Enterprising Culture*, 13(4) 333–357; Bloom, P. N. (2012). *Scaling your social venture: Becoming an impact entrepreneur.* New York: Palgrave Macmillan.

11 Bloom, P. N. (2012). *Scaling your social venture: Becoming an impact entrepreneur.* New York: Palgrave Macmillan.

12 Taylor, M. A., Dees, J. G., & Emerson, J. (2002). The question of scale: Finding an appropriate strategy for building on your success. In J. G. Dees, J. Emerson, & P. Economy (Eds.), *Social entrepreneurs: Enhancing the performance of your enterprising nonprofit* (pp. 235–266). New York: John Wiley & Sons, Inc.

13 Champy, J., & Nohria, N. (2000). *The arc of ambition.* Cambridge, MA: Perseus Books.

14 Blundel, R. K., & Lyon, F. (2015). Towards a long view: Historical perspectives on the scaling and replication of social ventures. *Journal of Social Entrepreneurship*, 6(1), 80–102; Desa, G., & Koch, J. L. (2014). Scaling social impact: Building sustainable social ventures at the base of the pyramid. *Journal of Social Entrepreneurship*, 5(2), 146–174; Weber, C., Kroger, A., & Lambrich, K. (2012). Scaling social enterprises: A theoretically grounded framework. *Frontiers of Entrepreneurship Research*, 32(19), 752–766.

15 Taylor, M. A., Dees, J. G., & Emerson, J. (2002). The question of scale: Finding an appropriate strategy for building on your success. In J. G. Dees, J. Emerson, & P. Economy (Eds.), *Social entrepreneurs: Enhancing the performance of your enterprising nonprofit* (pp. 235–266). New York: John Wiley & Sons, Inc.

16 Dees, J. G., & Emerson, J., & Economy, P. (2001). *Enterprising nonprofits: A toolkit for social entrepreneurs.* New York: John Wiley & Sons, Inc.

17 Taylor, M. A., Dees, J. G., & Emerson, J. (2002). The question of scale: Finding an appropriate strategy for building on your success. In J. G. Dees, J. Emerson, & P. Economy (Eds.), *Social entrepreneurs: Enhancing the performance of your enterprising nonprofit* (pp. 235–266). New York: John Wiley & Sons, Inc.

18 Chowdhury, I., & Santos, F. M. (2010). INSEAD Working Paper Number 2010/10/EFE/INSEAD, Social Innovation Center/ICE.

19 LaFrance, S., Lee, M., Green, R., Kaveternik, J., Robinson, A., & Alarcon, I. (2006). Scaling capacities: Supports for growing impact. Working paper, LaFrance Associates.

20 LaFrance, S., Lee, M., Green, R., Kaveternik, J., Robinson, A., & Alarcon, I. (2006). Scaling capacities: Supports for growing impact. Working paper, LaFrance Associates.

21 Kickul, J., & Lyons, T. (2012). *Understanding social entrepreneurship: The relentless pursuit of mission in an ever-changing world*. New York: Routledge.

22 Desousa, K. C., & Smith K. L. (2014). Big data for social innovation. *Stanford Social Innovations Review*, Summer, 39–43.

23 Dees, J. G., Anderson, B. B., & Wei-Skillern, J. (2004). Scaling social impact: Strategies of spreading social innovations. *Stanford Social Innovation Review*, 1, 24–32.

24 Kickul, J., & Lyons, T. (2012). *Understanding social entrepreneurship: The relentless pursuit of mission in an ever-changing world*. New York: Routledge.

25 Kickul, J., & Lyons, T. (2012). *Understanding social entrepreneurship: The relentless pursuit of mission in an ever-changing world*. New York: Routledge.

26 Dees, J. G., Anderson, B. B., & Wei-Skillern, J. (2004). Scaling social impact: Strategies of spreading social innovations. *Stanford Social Innovation Review*, 1, 24–32.

27 Kickul, J., & Lyons, T. (2012). *Understanding social entrepreneurship: The relentless pursuit of mission in an ever-changing world*. New York: Routledge.

28 Kickul, J., & Lyons, T. (2012). *Understanding social entrepreneurship: The relentless pursuit of mission in an ever-changing world*. New York: Routledge.

29 Kickul, J., & Lyons, T. (2012). *Understanding social entrepreneurship: The relentless pursuit of mission in an ever-changing world*. New York: Routledge.

30 Wei-Skillern, J., Austin, J. E., Leonard, H., & Stevenson, H. (2007). *Entrepreneurship in the social sector*. Thousand Oaks, CA: Sage Publications; Volery, T., & Hackl, V. (2010). The promise of social franchising as a model to achieve social goals. In A. Fayolle & H. Matlay (Eds.), *Handbook of research on social entrepreneurship* (pp. 155–179). Cheltenham: Edward Elgar.

31 Wei-Skillern, J., Austin, J. E., Leonard, H., & Stevenson, H. (2007). *Entrepreneurship in the social sector*. Thousand Oaks, CA: Sage Publications.

32 Tracey, P., & Jarvens, O. (2007). Toward a theory of social venture franchising. *Entrepreneurship: Theory and Practice*, 31(5), 667–685.

33 Tracey, P., & Jarvens, O. (2007). Toward a theory of social venture franchising. *Entrepreneurship: Theory and Practice*, 31(5), 667–685.

34 Mueller, S., Nazarkina, L., Volkmann, C., & Blank, C. (2011). Social entrepreneurship research as a means of transformation: A vision for the year 2028. *Journal of Social Entrepreneurship*, 2(1), 112–120.

35 Beckmann, M., & Zeyen, A. (2014). Advantages (logics) in social entrepreneurship: A Hayekian perspective franchising as a strategy for combining small and large groups. *Nonprofit and Voluntary Sector Quarterly*, 43(3), 502–522.

36 Beckmann, M., & Zeyen, A. (2014). Advantages (logics) in social entrepreneurship: A Hayekian perspective franchising as a strategy for combining small and large groups. *Nonprofit and Voluntary Sector Quarterly*, 43(3), 502–522.

37 Austin, J. E. (2000). Strategic collaboration between nonprofit and business. *Nonprofit and Voluntary Sector Quarterly*, 29(1), 69–97; Wymer, W. W. Jr., & Samu, S. (2003). Dimensions of business and nonprofit collaborative relationships. *Journal of Nonprofit and Public Sector Marketing*, 11(1), 3–22; Selsky, J. W., & Parker, R. (2005). Cross-sector partnerships to address social issues: Challenges to theory and practice. *Journal of Management*, 31(6), 849–873.

38 Austin, J. E. (2000). Strategic collaboration between nonprofit and business. *Nonprofit and Voluntary Sector Quarterly*, 29(1), 69–97.

39 Austin, J. E. (2000). Strategic collaboration between nonprofit and business. *Nonprofit and Voluntary Sector Quarterly*, 29(1), 69–97.

40 Berger, I., Cunningham, P., & Drumwright, M. (2004). Social alliances: Company/nonprofit collaboration. *California Management Review*, 47(1), 58–90; Sakaryia, S., Bodur, M., Yildirim-

Oktem, O., & Selekler-Goksen, N. (2012). Social alliances: Business and social enterprise collaboration for social transformation. *Journal of Business Research*, 65(12), 1710–1720.

41 Waddock, S. (1991).A typology of social partnership organizations. *Administration and Society*, 22(4), 480–516; Sakaryia, S., Bodur, M., Yildirim-Oktem, O., & Selekler-Goksen, N. (2012). Social alliances: Business and social enterprise collaboration for social transformation. *Journal of Business Research*, 65(12), 1710–1720.

42 Selsky, J. W., & Parker, R. (2005). Cross-sector partnerships to address social issues: Challenges to theory and practice. *Journal of Management*, 31(6), 849–873.

43 Selsky, J. W., & Parker, R. (2005). Cross-sector partnerships to address social issues: Challenges to theory and practice. *Journal of Management*, 31(6), 849–873.

44 Harris, D., & Kor, Y. (2013). The role of human capital in scaling social entrepreneurship. *Journal of Management for Global Sustainability*, 1(2), 163–172.

45 Fisac-Garcia, R., Acevedo-Ruiz, M., Moreno-Romero, A. & Thane Kreiner, T (2013). The role of ICT in scaling the impact of social enterprises. *Journal of Management for Global Sustainability*, 1(2), 83–105.

46 Dees, J. G., Anderson, B. B., & Wei-Skillern, J. (2004). Scaling social impact: Strategies of spreading social innovations. *Stanford Social Innovation Review*, 1, 24–32.

47 Dees, J. G., Anderson, B. B., & Wei-Skillern, J. (2004). Scaling social impact: Strategies of spreading social innovations. *Stanford Social Innovation Review*, 1, 24–32.

48 Taylor, M. A., Dees, J. G., & Emerson, J. (2002). The question of scale: Finding an appropriate strategy for building on your success. In J. G. Dees, J. Emerson, & P. Economy (Eds.), *Social entrepreneurs: Enhancing the performance of your enterprising nonprofit* (pp. 235–266). New York: John Wiley & Sons, Inc.

49 Taylor, M. A., Dees, J. G., & Emerson, J. (2002). The question of scale: Finding an appropriate strategy for building on your success. In J. G. Dees, J. Emerson, & P. Economy (Eds.), *Social entrepreneurs: Enhancing the performance of your enterprising nonprofit* (pp. 235–266). New York: John Wiley & Sons, Inc.

50 Taylor, M. A., Dees, J. G., & Emerson, J. (2002). The question of scale: Finding an appropriate strategy for building on your success. In J. G. Dees, J. Emerson, & P. Economy (Eds.), *Social entrepreneurs: Enhancing the performance of your enterprising nonprofit* (pp. 235–266). New York: John Wiley & Sons, Inc.

51 Dees, J. G., Anderson, B. B., & Wei-Skillern, J. (2004). Scaling social impact: Strategies of spreading social innovations. *Stanford Social Innovation Review*, 1, 24–32.

52 Taylor, M. A., Dees, J. G., & Emerson, J. (2002). The question of scale: Finding an appropriate strategy for building on your success. In J. G. Dees, J. Emerson, & P. Economy (Eds.), *Social entrepreneurs: Enhancing the performance of your enterprising nonprofit* (pp. 235–266). New York: John Wiley & Sons, Inc.

53 Bloom, P. N., & Chatterji, A. K. (2009). Scaling social entrepreneurial impact. *California Management Review*, 51(3), 114–133.

54 Becker, G. S. (1964). *Human capital: A theoretical and empirical analysis with special reference to education*. Chicago: University of Chicago Press.

55 Bloom, P. N., & Chatterji, A. K. (2009). Scaling social entrepreneurial impact. *California Management Review*, 51(3), 114–133.

56 Bloom, P. N., & Chatterji, A. K. (2009). Scaling social entrepreneurial impact. *California Management Review*, 51(3), 114–133.

57 Bloom, P. N., & Chatterji, A. K. (2009). Scaling social entrepreneurial impact. *California Management Review*, 51(3), 114–133.

58 Bloom, P. N., & Chatterji, A. K. (2009). Scaling social entrepreneurial impact. *California Management Review*, 51(3), 114–133.

59 Bloom, P. N., & Chatterji, A. K. (2009). Scaling social entrepreneurial impact. *California Management Review*, 51(3), 114–133.

60 Bloom, P. N., & Chatterji, A. K. (2009). Scaling social entrepreneurial impact. *California Management Review*, 51(3), 114–133.

61 Bloom, P. N., & Chatterji, A. K. (2009). Scaling social entrepreneurial impact. *California Management Review*, *51*(3), 114–133.
62 Bloom, P. N., & Chatterji, A. K. (2009). Scaling social entrepreneurial impact. *California Management Review*, *51*(3), 114–133.
63 Bloom, P. N., & Chatterji, A. K. (2009). Scaling social entrepreneurial impact. *California Management Review*, *51*(3), 114–133.
64 Bloom, P. N., & Chatterji, A. K. (2009). Scaling social entrepreneurial impact. *California Management Review*, *51*(3), 114–133.
65 Bloom, P. N., & Chatterji, A. K. (2009). Scaling social entrepreneurial impact. *California Management Review*, *51*(3), 114–133.
66 Bloom, P. N., & Chatterji, A. K. (2009). Scaling social entrepreneurial impact. *California Management Review*, *51*(3), 114–133.
67 Bloom, P. N., & Chatterji, A. K. (2009). Scaling social entrepreneurial impact. *California Management Review*, *51*(3), 114–133.
68 Bloom, P. N., & Smith, B. R. (2010). Identifying the drivers of social entrepreneurial impact: Theoretical development and an exploratory empirical test of SCALERS. *Journal of Social Entrepreneurship*, *1*(1), 126–145; Bloom, P. N., & Skloot, E. (2010). *Scaling social impact: New thinking*. New York: Palgrave Macmillan.
69 Walske, J., & Tyson, D. L. (2015). Built to scale: A comparative case analysis, assessing how social enterprises scale. *International Journal of Entrepreneurship*, *16*(4), 260–281.
70 Source for this whole section: Nurse, E. (2014). Want to change Africa? Let's do it ourselves! CNN, May 9. http://edition.cnn.com/2014/05/09/world/africa/want-to-change-africa-lets-do-it/index.html?hpt=hp_bn1, retrieved on May 9, 2014.
71 Sources for this whole section: Irons, K. S. (2013). New technology enables portable pre-surgery sterilization. *Echo*, September 5. http://theechonews.com/new-technology-enables-portable-pre-surgery-sterilization, retrieved on January 20, 2015; Thorpe, D. (2013). Will James Bernstein's portable sterilization technology save millions of lives? He thinks so. *Forbes*, June 11. www.forbes.com/sites/devinthorpe/2013/06/11/will-james-bernsteins-portable-sterilization-technology-save-millions-of-lives-he-thinks-so/#37315c8875c9, retrieved on January 20, 2015; www.eniwaresterile.com, retrieved on March 30, 2016.

Chapter 14

Measuring the Impact of Social Ventures

Learning Objectives

1 Assess the impact of social ventures.
2 Develop the skills required to measure social impact.
3 Be able to use the tools and techniques for measuring social impact effectively.
4 Describe and explain social return on investment and measure it.
5 Develop the skills required to manage social impact.

Social ventures intend to make a difference in the lives of others by addressing social needs. But how do we know that what they do actually helps the beneficiaries? Measuring the impact of social ventures and other nonprofit organizations has proven difficult for both social entrepreneurs and social entrepreneurship scholars. Recently, however, there have been notable efforts to address this issue. This chapter focuses on explaining how to measure the impact of social ventures and why such measurement is important. It is divided into three sections. The first section defines and explains social impact. The second describes the tools that are used to measure social impact. The third discusses the management of social impact.

1 The Nature of Social Impact

A social impact is the explicit social benefit that a social venture provides to its intended beneficiaries. It is an indication of the difference the social venture makes in the lives of the target population. For example, the mission of the social venture We Care Solar, which distributes solar suitcases in developing countries, is to improve maternal care (see Chapter 11). The social impact of this social venture can be measured in terms of the reduction in the number of maternal deaths during birth as a result of using the solar suitcases. A positive impact would indicate a drastic reduction in maternal deaths. We Care Solar's social impact could also be measured in terms of regions covered or improvements in maternal care in the countries served.

To underline the importance of measuring social impact, every social venture should write an impact report. This is a written document that includes the benefits a social venture provides for its intended beneficiaries. Such a report could form part of the social venture plan or be included in the organization's annual report. Organizations such as the TRASI Foundation Center (http://trasi.foundationcenter.org) and the IRIS-Global Impact Investing Network (https://iris.thegiin.org) offer resources and databases that social entrepreneurs can use to measure social impact.

1.1   *Understanding the Basics of Social Impact Measurement*

Affecting social change is, of course, the ultimate goal for nonprofit organizations. But you can't get to any destination without a road map and some signposts along the way. Measurement is your map, and metrics are your signposts.[1] As mentioned earlier, measuring social impact is a relatively recent practice; and it has been difficult for social entrepreneurs to measure and report the true impact of their ventures for at least three reasons.[2] First, there is a widespread perceived difficulty in establishing the relationship between complex input factors—such as grants, volunteers, market income, and social capital—and the social impact of a social venture.[3] Second, measuring what is to be reported has been problematic because there are no standardized calculative mechanisms for social value creation, nor any comparative unit of measurement.[4] The third reason relates to the purpose of measurement and reporting. In the past, social enterprises were accorded significant levels of trust purely on the basis of their stated objectives, not in consequence of their performance reporting.[5] In other words, it was assumed that these organizations were having a social impact simply because they stated that they had public missions.[6]

Before discussing social impact, it is important to understand the process by which social ventures transform inputs into outputs. To do so, we must understand the four elements of inputs, outputs, outcomes, and impacts. They are illustrated in Figure 14.1. Inputs are the resources that contribute to the activities undertaken; outputs are both activities that are undertaken to achieve the mission and direct countable goods or services obtained by means of the activities that are undertaken; outcomes are the benefits for the intended beneficiaries; and impact comprises the consequences for the wider community.

Some social entrepreneurship scholars use the construct of *blended value accounting* (BVA) to refer to accounting principles that measure both the financial performance and social impact of a social venture.[7] Blended value implies that companies achieve economic success and maximize social benefits at the same time.[8] In today's world, where corporate social responsibility (CSR) is on the rise and even demanded by the public, both for-profit and nonprofit organizations must take blended value into account.

Social entrepreneurship scholars generally agree that there are four aspects to measuring social impact:

- accountability;
- evaluation;
- outcomes; and
- effectiveness.

Accountability refers to an organization's responsibility to accomplish the mission. For example, the social venture Dignified Mobile Toilets aims to install mobile toilets in poor urban parts of Nigeria (see Chapter 3). As providing such services is the core mission of this social venture, DMT must deliver on its promise. Failure to do so would indicate that DMT is not accomplishing its mission. Thus, it can be held accountable in regard to its social mission. This implies that accountability is a core element when measuring the social impact of a social enterprise.

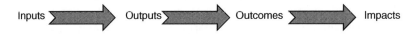

Figure 14.1 Inputs, outputs, outcomes, impacts.

The second component—evaluation—refers to the systematic study of quality, success, or worthiness.[9] Social ventures can employ continuous measures, rating scales, or binary measures to evaluate their social impact. Continuous evaluation implies that the measure used facilitates the counting of outcomes. For example, we can count the number of people treated for addiction to a particular substance or the number of lives saved by a particular treatment. A rating scale may be used if it is impossible to count the outcome. For example, the outcome can be described on a five-point scale from totally ineffective (1) to highly effective (5). Finally, a binary measure may also be used to measure outcomes. In this case, the measure focuses on whether the outcome is bad or good, effective or ineffective, yes or no. The basic standard for a proper evaluation includes four qualities: utility, feasibility, propriety, and accuracy.[10]

The third component—outcomes—refers to the end goals of the social venture. After all, the purpose of every social venture is to create social value. Finally, the fourth component—effectiveness—refers to the extent to which the social venture accomplishes its stated goals. This was discussed in detail in Chapter 12.

1.2 Understanding the Steps in Measuring Social Impact

Gaining an understanding of social impact should start with knowledge of a social venture's theory of change.[11] This refers to how the enterprise envisages the future and how it intends to get there. It is basically the social venture's logic for change. The theory of change diagrams inputs, activities, outputs, outcomes, and impacts in a way that shows the pathway has been well mapped.[12] Kickul and Lyons suggest three steps to consider when measuring a social venture's impact:

1 Define the social value proposition (SVP).
2 Quantify the social value (translate it into numbers)
3 Monetize the social value (translate it into dollars and cents).[13]

These three steps are explained below.

1.2.1 Define the Social Value Proposition

In their analysis, Kickul and Lyons contend that a social enterprise must start by describing its value proposition.[14] This is the potential impact that the social venture will have on its beneficiaries. It can be described in the social venture plan and is similar to a commercial venture's value proposition. Put simply, it is a yardstick against which the social venture will measure its impact. It may be defined in concert with key stakeholders.

Although it is important for social ventures to determine what impact their actions are having on their intended beneficiaries, doing so is not always easy. An interesting issue relates to the definition and measure of "success."

• What is success for a social venture?
• How can it be defined and measured?
• When is a social venture a successful endeavor?

These questions are important because social needs are endemic and often difficult to address fully—hence the construct of *wicked problems*.[15] It is difficult to solve wicked problems completely. They will always exist. Therefore, it is important for the social venture to operationalize the needs it must address and how it will measure its success. Some social needs will only ever be reduced, rather than solved completely. Take the example of the social venture We Care Solar. Despite the availability of the technology and the dedication of its staff, it will only reduce the number of maternal deaths during childbirth in developing countries. The same is true for social ventures that tackle corruption. Completely eliminating it would be impossible.

1.2.2   Quantify the Social Value

Once the social value proposition has been defined, the social venture must quantify its social impact. To do this, it is important for the social venture to follow three steps:

1   Identify three to five indicators of success.
2   Measure those indicators.
3   Track those indicators over time.

Identifying the indicators of success will help the social venture to develop a metric for measuring social impact. Although there is no ideal number of social indicators, three to five should be easily manageable. Attempting to measure more than that could dilute the social enterprise's efforts and confuse managers, whereas measuring only one or two could give the impression that the social venture is not particularly concerned about its impact.

Once the indicators of success have been identified, they must be measured. This requires the development of internal instruments. Finally, the indicators should be tracked to provide useful information to managers regarding the ongoing performance of the social venture. This can be represented on a dashboard—a user interface that organizes and presents information in a way that is easy to read and interpret.[16]

1.2.3   Monetize the Social Value

Why is it necessary to transform the social value into dollars and cents? The simple answer is because doing so increases the credibility of the social venture and its managers. Monetizing the social value can also attract investors and donors,[17] as it can be used as proof that the social venture is generating a positive social return on investment. For example, the Mercy Project's mission is to eliminate child slavery in the Volta Region of Ghana by convincing families to send their children to school instead of using them as free labor (see Chapter 7). If a decent high school education translates into $200,000 in lifetime earnings in Ghana, then this could represent a monetization of the Mercy Project's social impact. However, if the children were to leave their parents and go to the larger cities to become street beggars, rather than finish their education, the Mercy Project would not have achieved its expected impact.

Monetizing the social value could also indicate whether the social venture is using its financial resources efficiently. As indicated throughout this textbook, the trend in social entrepreneurship is for social ventures to address social issues while also remaining financially solvent.

1.3   Benefits of Measuring Social Impact

What is the benefit of measuring social impact? What does a social venture gain by measuring its impact? By measuring outcomes, social entrepreneurs can become more aware of which of their programs are working and which are failing.[18] Measurement can also help social ventures make a strong case to their constituencies to support their actions. Social impact reporting can help social entrepreneurs:

- enhance performance;
- access extra resources; and
- build organizational legitimacy.[19]

Measuring and reporting social impact can generate invaluable feedback for the social entrepreneur. So, when impact is measured, it becomes an integral part of the way the social venture is managed. Measuring social impact can also facilitate access to valuable resources. Without measurement, potential donors will be unable to differentiate between effective and ineffective social ventures. Therefore, measurement can help social ventures to build a convincing case that a certain program is working and, therefore, worth funding.

By so doing, measurement helps to resolve the "problem of lemon," which is widely discussed in economics. George Akerlof popularized this concept in the early 1970s.[20] A problem of lemon occurs when there is an asymmetry of information between buyers and sellers in any marketplace. For instance, in the used-car market, uninformed buyers are unable to determine the true value of a vehicle, but they are wary of buying a defective car (a lemon), so they tend to pay an average price (somewhere between bargain and premium) for whichever one they purchase. This actually tilts the market in favor of the lemon-sellers, because they tend to achieve higher prices for their useless vehicles than they would if they were dealing with well-informed buyers. Similarly, in social entrepreneurship, investors may have incomplete (or no) information about the social impacts of specific social ventures. Hence, they may invest in one without knowing if it is having a positive social impact or not, which will tend to mean there is less money for those that *are* having a positive impact.

Measuring social impact can also help a social venture to gain legitimacy.[21] It does this by providing evidence that certain social entrepreneurs are at the cutting edge by using the latest tools to assess their social ventures' impacts. For example, in social entrepreneurship, the trend is now toward sustainability and social accountability. By measuring its social impact, a social venture is able to demonstrate to key stakeholders that it is employing the latest management practices effectively.

Measuring social impact can also improve management control. Bagnoli and Megali have proposed a multidimensional framework comprising three reference fields for management:

- economic–financial performance, linked to the determination of general performance (profits, value added, etc.) and analytic results (production cost of services, efficiency indicators, etc.);
- social effectiveness, to measure the quantity and quality of work undertaken and to identify its impact on the intended beneficiaries and the community; and
- institutional legitimacy, verifying conformity with the law and the organization's own mission statement.[22]

The authors use Ulisse—an Italian social enterprise created in 1998 through a joint project between the local health organization and some third-sector entities to create and develop services for the community—to illustrate the importance of these three components when assessing the success of a social venture. Ulisse was perceived as successful because it performed well on all three indicators.

2   Tools for Measuring and Reporting Social Impact

Several tools are used to measure the social impact of social ventures. Some are applications of management tools to the social entrepreneurship domain, whereas others have been developed specifically for social ventures. This section reviews five of these tools:

- cost-effectiveness analysis (CEA);
- cost–benefit analysis (CBA);
- social accounting and auditing (SAA);
- blended value accounting (BVA); and
- social return on investment (SROI).

These tools were selected because they are quite popular and they provide a decent account of social impact measurement.

2.1   Cost-Effectiveness Analysis

What is the impact of investing in fighting malaria in Africa, India, and other tropical areas? If one were to put this question to the Bill and Melinda Gates Foundation, the answer would probably include the number of children who are not infected or dying of the disease. Measuring the impact of such programs in monetary terms would be rather difficult. Hence, potential lives saved is often measured instead.

A method that can help capture the success of such programs is the cost-effectiveness analysis (CEA). This compares the relative costs and outcomes of two or more courses of action. It is different from cost–benefit analysis (see below) insofar as it does not assign any monetary value to the measure of effect.

CEA is expressed as a ratio where the denominator is the gain from a specific measure. This ratio is sometimes informally termed the "bang for the buck."[23] Examples where this method is used include years of life, number of lives saved, and number of people brought out of poverty, but the most commonly used outcome measure is quality-adjusted life years (QALY).

The purpose of CEA is twofold:

- to combine appropriate measures of outcomes with costs so that program and policy alternatives within the same domain can be ranked according to their effectiveness relative to their results; and
- to side-step the uncertainties about how to value different aspects of program benefits by looking at the ratio of benefits to costs without reducing them to common units.[24]

CEA is often visualized on a cost-effectiveness plane consisting of four quadrants (see Figure 14.2). It has two dimensions: cost and effectiveness. As indicated in Quadrant III, cost and effectiveness can both be low. This situation implies that the program does not cost much but is also ineffective. Meanwhile, in Quadrant IV, a program costs a lot of money but does not yield any substantial benefits for beneficiaries or the community. Quadrant I indicates a program that is both effective and expensive. Finally, Quadrant II represents a program that is both highly effective and costs little money. In terms of efficiency, such a program provides the requisite benefits at a reasonable cost.

Cost

Effectiveness		Low	High
	Low	III	IV
	High	II	I

Key:
I: More effective/more expensive
II: More effective/less expensive
III: Less effective/less expensive
IV: Less effective/more expensive

Figure 14.2 A cost-effectiveness plane.

The CEA method is often used when it is impossible or undesirable to monetize the impact of a program's benefits.[25] Its principal advantage is that it does not require translating the social value proposition into dollars and cents. Therefore, social entrepreneurs do not have to analyze financial data to determine whether their programs are having positive social impacts. Its main disadvantage is that it can measure only one aspect of a program at any given time.[26] This can be a limitation because it is important to use a metric that is common across the board to allow aggregation of results when assessing the impact of a social venture.

A social venture's mission should always be considered when measuring its social impact. What is measured should be contingent on the venture's objective(s). As indicated earlier, impact measurement is affected by the social venture's theory of change and its operational strategy or logic model.[27] The theory of change is the venture's rationale for how its actions will ultimately achieve its goals and mission. So a complex theory of change will undeniably increase the difficulty of measuring social impact. A social venture's operational strategy is the second most important factor when assessing its impact on society. A social venture that has a focus strategy will concentrate its resources on solving a specific social problem. The Mercy Project is illustrative here (see Chapter 7). This social venture directs *all* of its resources to eliminating a particular problem—child slavery—in a particular region of Ghana. Although the same problem exists in other parts of the country, the Mercy Project focuses only on the Volta Region.

2.2 Cost–Benefit Analysis

Cost–benefit analysis (CBA) is popular in finance, economics, and economic development projects. It monetizes both the benefits and the costs of a program in order to compare them and establish which are greater. It also provides an accounting measure for evaluation. If the benefits of a program are greater than its costs, the direct implication is that the program is worth pursuing. If not, then the program is likely to be discontinued. CBA also helps a decision-maker to compare several programs and determine which are better and should be continued and which should be terminated. Variations of these methods have been used by several nonprofit organizations. For example, the Robin Hood Foundation (www.robinhood.org) uses a benefit–cost ratio, while the Center for High Impact Philanthropy (www.impact.upenn.edu) uses costs per impact as a measure of social impact.

The purpose of CBA is twofold: to help decide whether a program or intervention is of value to the decision-maker and to compare the program to alternatives and choose the one with the greatest measure of merit.[28] The output from CBA can be measures of net benefits (benefits minus costs), also known as the net present value (NPV); the ratio of benefits to cost (benefit–cost ratios); or the internal rate of return (IRR), which is the rate of growth a project is expected to generate.[29]

2.3 Social Accounting and Auditing

Social accounting and auditing has a long history in both for-profit and nonprofit organizations. It is an umbrella concept that is used to capture all forms of accounting that go beyond the economic. For example, terms such as "social responsibility accounting," "social audit," "corporate social reporting," "employee and employment reporting," "stakeholder dialogue reporting," and "environmental reporting" are all used under social accounting.[30]

Social accounting and auditing (SAA) takes into account both economic and social impacts. In so doing, it organizes the inputs from stakeholders into a report about an organization's social impact.[31] Social accounting assesses the social impact of nonprofits by including social inputs and outputs that accounting statements normally exclude.[32] It is a way for a social venture to demonstrate that it is meeting its stated objectives. Indeed, social accounting has contributed to social ventures and other nonprofit organizations through social capital, citizenship, community cohesion, relational assets, social wellbeing, quality of life, and social and economic regeneration of communities.[33]

Mook has proposed a nonprofit integrated social accounting (NISA) model that takes into account the particular objectives of nonprofit organizations (such as achieving their mission and remaining viable), their specific characteristics (e.g., the engagement of volunteers), and their economic, social, and environmental impacts. She proposes a conceptual framework that incorporates four elements:

- economic and human resources;
- economic, social, and environmental value creation;
- internal systems and processes; and
- organizational learning, growth, and innovation.[34]

These four dimensions must be captured in an organization's reporting practices.

Social accounting could be considered as a precursor to blended value accounting.

2.4 Blended Value Accounting

Emerson coined the term "blended value" to describe the combination of economic and social outputs.[35] For Emerson, organizations create both economic and social value regardless of their legal status. In reality, both economic value and social value are connected. Therefore, it is more appropriate to use the construct of *blended value*. Emerson suggests that the core nature of investment and return is not a tradeoff between social and financial interests but rather the pursuit of an embedded value proposition that is composed of both.[36] This conceptualization of the value created by organizations must allow them to become more innovative in their financial and accounting reporting, leading to a more holistic view of reporting. In such reporting, economic and social values are integrated.

Since Emerson proposed the concept of blended value in the early 2000s, several authors have expanded on his work and explored the role of blended value accounting (BVA) in evaluating the impact of social ventures.[37] According to Nicholls, BVA can be concretized within a spectrum of reporting practices that do not represent a prescriptive set of logics or a static overall reporting schema, but rather a conceptual space in which reporting innovations that allow experimentation and new learning can emerge.[38] For social ventures, using this technique implies that they report both financial outcomes and social outcomes. Therefore, BVA can be used by social entrepreneurs to report social impact.

One of the tools that is used in BVA is social return on investment, which is discussed next.

2.5   Social Return on Investment

Social return on investment (SROI) derives from the concept of return on investment (ROI), which is used in commercial entrepreneurship. It was pioneered and promoted by REDF (Roberts Enterprise Development Fund) and represents an attempt to measure the economic and social value of a social venture. It has two parts: enterprise value and social value.[39] Enterprise value relates to the net revenues from the business side of a social venture, especially when the social venture is a hybrid or for-profit one. It is calculated by subtracting the costs of goods, services, and operating expenses from the value of sales. Hence, for social ventures that rely entirely on philanthropic giving, donations, or grants, enterprise value can always be negative. Social value is the value that the social venture generates for society,[40] or the extent to which it adds value to the beneficiaries and/or the community it serves.

The SROI tool was created in the hope that it would provide a credible methodology for the financial calculation of the often unreported benefits of work integration activities that could then be set against program investments to form a more holistic cost–benefit analysis.[41]

2.5.1   Understanding Social Return on Investment

Social return on investment has three main aspects. The first calculates the full blended value of a project. (As we have seen, the blended value combines enterprise/financial value creation and a monetized representation of social impact value.) The second establishes the financial investment in the project. The third calculates the blended return on investment (combining the enterprise and social returns). The enterprise/financial value represents the economic value created, whereas the monetized representation of its social value consists of transforming the social venture's social impact into financial figures to facilitate the computations.

In calculating the social return on investment, some social entrepreneurship scholars suggest that three other issues must be considered.[42] First, organizational boundaries must be set. This implies that a clear picture of the range of stakeholders and the key objectives of the social venture must be developed. Doing so will help to identify the materiality of outcomes. Second, an "impact map" to clarify how impact is achieved (or will be achieved) must be drawn. This process consists of linking inputs to outputs to outcomes to impacts (see Figure 14.1, above). In this model, inputs represent the total cost of the project, outputs are the simple quantitative effects (such as number of lives saved), outcomes are the direct and indirect changes in target stakeholders and their communities, and impacts are the changes that are discounted by a deadweight analysis (the extent to which outcomes would have happened without any intervention by the social enterprise).[43] Third, appropriate indicators or financial proxies must be identified to capture the elements within the impact map and monetized values.[44]

SROI analysis, which is based upon conventional accounting practices, provides both a quantified ratio of social return on investment and qualitative evidence that provides a framework for increased transparency and accountability.[45] Such analysis is the set of practices necessary to generate meaningful SROI figures and other quantified social metrics.

One may wonder why social entrepreneurs should analyze SROI. To answer this question, it is important to visit the mainstream financial literature, and especially studies of return on investment. In finance, the importance of return on investment analysis is explained in two ways. The first relates to the meaning ascribed to ROI. It is a relative measure of a company's success and is used to compare companies within a given industry to one another and to their own individual performance over time. The second stresses its value as a management metric. Indeed, managers are expected to maximize ROI because it reflects a company's strength, so shareholders are always interested in it.[46]

2.5.2 Measuring Social Return on Investment

To measure social impact using SROI, the New Economic Foundation (NEF) developed a multidimensional approach that was designed to be as widely applicable as possible.[47] It focuses on four areas:

- stakeholder engagement;
- materiality;
- impact map; and
- appreciation of deadweight.

In stakeholder engagement, stakeholders' objectives should be central to the SROI process and mirror sustainability reporting. The area of materiality indicates that the analysis should focus on those areas that stakeholders deem important. The impact map area comprises a cause-and-effect chain from inputs to outputs to outcomes to impacts and entails developing a pathway to understand how the organization enacts change and thereby achieves its mission. Finally, the appreciation of deadweight consists of calculating the proportion of outcomes that would have occurred regardless of the organization's inputs.

SROI is computed using the following formula.

SROI = Value of Benefits/Value of Investment

Table 14.1 Areas for measuring social return on investment

Area	Actions
Stakeholder engagement	Identify stakeholders' objectives to mirror sustainability reporting.
Materiality	Focus the analysis on those areas that the stakeholders deem important.
Impact map	Use a cause-and-effect chain from inputs to outputs to outcomes to impacts. Develop a pathway to understand how the organization enacts change and thereby achieves its mission.
Appreciation of deadweight	Calculate the proportion of outcomes that would have occurred regardless of the organization's inputs.

2.5.3   Importance of Using SROI as a Social Impact Metric

Recently, several organizations have been created to facilitate the widespread use of SROI. Examples include SROI UK and the European SROI Network (ESROIN). These organizations are refining the SROI methodology and advocate for its use throughout Europe, the United States, and South and Southeast Asia.[48]

Measuring social return on investment could also imply measuring outcomes. Several social entrepreneurship scholars contend that outcomes can be measured as internal objectives (achievement of a mission and stated goals) or as external objectives (client/user satisfaction).[49] For example, measurement might involve evaluating:

- the success of a program of reinsertion of disadvantaged people, integrating them into the open labor market, and improving their life prospects;
- the utility to individuals of a post-university training program, measured in terms of employment outcomes;
- improved mental health at the end of a support program; and
- higher artistic/cultural understanding as a result of social tourism.

Such measurement allows the possibility of controlling whether the social venture accomplishes its mission.

The NEF advocates a ten-step approach that helps social ventures to articulate a way of measuring social impact clearly.[50] These steps are summarized in Table 14.2.

2.5.4   Limitations of Social Return on Investment

Despite its international recognition as an effective measurement tool for social enterprises, SROI remains underused and undervalued due to some significant practical and ideological barriers.[51] It could even be difficult to assess the effective social return on investment of a social venture. As a consequence, the results of SROI tend to underestimate the benefits that are produced since not all outcomes can be easily monetized.[52]

Table 14.2 New Economic Foundation's approach to measuring social return on investment

Step	Actions
1. Planning	Understand and plan the scope of the study.
2. Stakeholders	Identify and gain inputs to understand their goals and objectives.
3. Boundaries	Prepare background information; learn more about the main target group.
4. Analyze income and expenditure	Is financial information reported in a way that links it with economic, environmental, or social objectives?
5. Impact map and indicators	Understand stakeholder participation through inputs, outputs, outcomes, and impacts.
6. SROI plan — summary to date	Determine the timetable for collecting the remaining data, completing calculations, writing reports, and sharing findings with stakeholders.
7. Implementation	Implement the plan and data collection.
8. Projections	Determine for how long, if at all, projections can be justified.
9. Calculate SROI	Create discounted cash flow. Use sensitivity analysis to identify areas that will yield improvements in social value.
10. Report	Present results in a manner that reveals the study's subtleties, limitations, and assumptions.

Moody and colleagues recently studied the use of SROI in four social ventures, two in the Netherlands (Care Farm Paradijs, a therapeutic farming enterprise for seniors and youth with autism; and VitalHealth Software, an e-health solutions enterprise with social impact goals) and two in the United States (the Wellness Center at the Pan American Academy, a school-based center that caters for medically underserved children; and the Pennsylvania Fresh Food Financing Initiative, a public–private partnership that provides fresh food in low-income neighborhoods). The researchers found that SROI was rarely used in any of these social ventures because of its complexity and the time, money, and expertise that were required to measure it.[53]

In addition to the issues, the measure can be "abused" by social entrepreneurs who use it to claim that their venture is having a positive impact when in fact it is not. For example, the chief executive of Teak, a UK charity, used SROI to gain access to important resources.[54] This case illustrates the tendency for some unscrupulous social entrepreneurs to game the system for potential benefit. As Emerson has acknowledged, nonprofit managers know that a program is good and fight for it even if they suspect the returns and use of resources are marginal at best, since they justify their efforts on the basis of perceived social intent, thereby confusing programmatic intent with documented social impact.[55]

Despite these limitations, social return on investment could prove useful for social impact management.

3 Social Impact Management

Social impact management can be defined as a field that focuses on the study of the impact that a given intervention has on society. Interventions can range from technology to improve people's lives to social changes that create new ways of living. For instance, mobile banking is gaining traction in most parts of Africa and is changing how people interact and receive money. On a continent where very few people have bank accounts, mobile banking has made the transfer of money much easier. For a social enterprise, social impact management entails devising the best means to combine various resources, facets, and stakeholders to ensure that the venture has a positive effect on the community.

3.1 Areas Included in Social Impact Management

The box below outlines the main topics of social impact management. As it indicates, social impact indicators must be defined upfront. They must then be operationalized—that is, translated into measurable outcomes. For instance, the social venture must define what is meant by "success." This could mean number of lives saved, number of hungry people fed on a daily basis, or number of crimes prevented. Such operationalization will serve as a metric that will facilitate measurement. Once the metric is developed, the social venture must formulate strategies to accomplish the stated objectives and implement them. Actual results must then be recorded, analyzed, and compared to agreed standards. The actual performance could also be compared to external benchmarks to indicate the venture's position within the social landscape. For example, is the social venture doing well compared to others that are addressing the same social issues? Such comparison will indicate whether there are gaps between actual performance and specific targets. In case of gaps, their sources must be identified and corrective actions must be taken.

Social Impact Indicators

1   Define social impact indicators.
2   Operationalize social impact indicators. This implies transforming social impact indicators into measurable outcomes.
3   Develop strategies to accomplish stated objectives.
4   Implement strategies.
5   Record results.
6   Compare results to stated objectives.
7   Determine whether there are gaps between stated objectives and actual performance.
8   Identify sources of gaps.
9   Take corrective actions.

3.2   Tools for Effective Social Impact Management

Developing and implementing an effective social impact management system requires the use of several tools that have proven records in management. For example, social impact management could start with a social impact assessment. This is a methodology that is used to review the social effects of development projects.[56] It is defined as the process of analyzing, monitoring, and managing both the intended and the unintended social consequences—positive and negative—of planned interventions (policies, programs, plans, projects) and any social change processes generated by those interventions. Its primary purpose is to bring about a more sustainable and equitable biophysical and human environment.[57] Applied to social entrepreneurship, social impact assessment implies the analysis, monitoring, and evaluation of a social venture's social impact.

Social enterprises are using the internet to develop tools such as shared measurement platforms that are designed to measure their performance and social impact. These are systems that allow organizations to choose from a set of measures within their respective fields, using web-based tools to collect, analyze, and report on performance or outcomes inexpensively. The benefits of using these tools include lower costs and greater efficiency in annual data collection, expert guidance for less sophisticated organizations, and improved credibility and consistency in reporting. An example is the Success Measures Data System, which is used by more than two hundred community development organizations and provides web-based tools that enable each organization to track, analyze, and report on any of fifty outcome indicators, all for an annual fee of $2,500.[58]

A social impact management system should also include the management of stakeholders. Indeed, stakeholder inclusion is critical in facilitating connected thinking from which a framework for increased transparent accountability can be created.[59] Doing so helps a social venture address the concerns of all stakeholders and garners their support. As indicated earlier in this chapter, social impact management can use the dashboard approach, which consists of frameworks that combine evaluation of social, economic, and environmental performance within nations or regional geographic areas.[60] An impact management system must also rely on evidence-based management.[61] Evidence from programs that work should be tabulated and used as examples of best practice.

A social impact management system may benefit from the use of big data and analytics. Such resources are rarely utilized in social entrepreneurship, which has led some scholars to advocate for their adoption.[62] The use of data and statistics pertaining to social programs and their impact could serve as tools for measuring the social impact of social enterprises. Social analytics derived from business analytics, which refers to the extensive use of data, statistical and quantitative analysis, explanatory and predictive models, and fact-based management to drive decisions and actions.[63] Business analytics is concerned with using data to create value for an organization.

Managing social impact carefully is important because while the test of business entrepreneurship is the creation of a viable and growing organization, the test of social entrepreneurship is changing social systems that create and maintain a problem. The organizations that promote such change may become smaller or less viable as they catalyze societal transformation.[64]

Summary

This chapter discussed the importance of measuring the impact of social ventures. In so doing, the chapter identified the benefits of measuring social impact and presented five methods that are used to measure social impact: cost-effectiveness analysis; cost–benefit analysis; social auditing and accounting; blended value accounting; and social return on investment. Finally, the chapter discussed social impact management as a way of monitoring the social impact of a social venture.

Key Terms

Analytics; blended value accounting; blended social value; blended value; cost–benefit analysis; cost-effectiveness analysis; dashboard technique; shared measurement platforms; social accounting and auditing; social analytics; social impact management; social return on investment; social value proposition

Review Questions

1 What is social impact?
2 What are the benefits of measuring social impact?
3 What are the advantages and disadvantages of cost-effectiveness analysis?
4 What are the advantages and disadvantages of using the cost–benefit analysis for social ventures?
5 What are the main differences between the cost-effectiveness method and cost–benefit analysis?
6 What is social return on investment?
7 Why should social entrepreneurs quantify social impact?
8 What is a social value proposition? Why is it important for social ventures to define one?
9 What are the advantages of monetizing social value?
10 Define blended value and explain its importance for measuring the impact of social ventures.

Application Questions

1   VisitTRASI's website at http://trasi.foundationcenter.org and identify three tools and three resources to measure the impact of a social venture whose mission is to improve literacy in a developing country.

2   Go to www.youtube.com/watch?v=38fefskOejk, watch the video, and answer the following questions. Why is social impact measurement important? To what extent can social impact measurement help improve the performance of a social venture? What are the two usages of results in measuring social impact?

3   Suppose you have recently established a social venture whose mission is to raise the literacy rate among girls in the rural areas of India. How would you measure the social impact of your venture?

4   Identify a social venture in your community. Identify the metrics that this social venture is using to measure its success and social impact.

5   Suppose that you have been hired as a consultant to help a social venture measure its performance and social impact. One of your tasks is to help the social venture develop a social impact management system. How would you go about developing and helping to implement this system? Be specific.

Application Case 1: Eileen Fisher and the Making of Organic Clothes

For social justice advocates, everyone's basic human rights should be respected and everyone should be entitled to social and environmental justice. These principles underlying social justice are epitomized by Eileen Fisher, Inc. (www.eileenfisher.com), a privately-owned company that acts more as a social venture than a for-profit company. Eileen Fisher started the company Eileen Fisher, Inc. in 1984 with $350.00 and a basic idea; women's clothes should be simply designed. Fisher had a vision of women's clothes that were made of simple shapes that were easy to coordinate, like men's attire, but were also elegant and comfortable.[1] Eileen Fisher Inc.'s mission is to inspire simplicity, creativity, and delight through connection and great design.

From humble beginnings, the company has now become a brand for women's clothing, sustainability and social impact. In fiscal year 2015, the company had over 300 million dollars in revenue. The three pillars of Eileen Fisher, Inc. are: 1) environment, 2) human rights, and 3) economic issues. On its website, the company notes that its vision is for an industry where human rights are not the effect of a particular initiative, but the cause of a business well run. Where social and environmental injustices are not unfortunate outcomes, but reasons to do things differently. The vision for human rights programs is to provide people with dignified work that will enhance their livelihood which will in return empower them socially and economically.

Eileen Fisher, Inc. employs more than 1200 people and has over 65 stores in the United States, Canada and the United Kingdom. It has a goal of being a company that is 100 percent sustainable.[2] Because the use of fabrics tends to lead to pollution, Eileen Fisher, Inc. is working hard to strike a balance between sustainability and profitability. For the company, it is a constant balance between maintaining profitability while improving environmental and social impact.[3] Protecting the environment is done through recycling. For example, the company recently introduced the *Green Eileen Initiative*, which consists of mending used clothes and reselling them. When customers no longer want their Eileen Fisher clothes, they can send them back to the company where they are fixed for resale in new *Green Eileen* stores.[4] The company expects its recycling total operations to reach one million by 2020. It also intends to use mostly organic linen, free of pesticides and synthetic herbicides. Eileen Fisher, Inc. supports and donates to groups that are involved in environmental advocacy and research, child protection, recycling, human trafficking, and women's empowerment.

In order to contribute to the global economy, the company pledged to use the most sustainable fibers. It initially started by designing clothing that is durable and resilient. Although the company is a for-profit venture, it supports nonprofits and non-governmental organizations (NGOs) that extend and enrich their work on human rights and the environment. Its donations to environmental and human rights groups are based on the priorities of its socially conscious work and are the end results of internal nominations. The company audits its factories for compliance with Social Accountability 8000's strict labor standards. In India, the company has launched *The Handloom Project*, a six-year investment program designed to empower weavers in rural communities. It trained workers at its key suppliers' factories in China to voice their rights. Since 2005, it has invested in an alternative supply chain in Peru that pays fair trade wages.[5]

Discussion Questions

1 Identify Eileen Fisher's key stakeholders. Do you think their respective interests are well served? Yes? No? Explain.
2 Identify Eileen Fisher's social value proposition. How compelling is it?
3 How would you measure Eileen Fisher's social return on investment?
4 Assess the social impact of Eileen Fisher. What metrics would you use to measure its social impact?

References

1 Be a don't knower: One of Eileen Fisher's secrets to success. Huffpost Business. May 15, 2015. *http://www.huffingtonpost.com/matt-tenney/be-a-dont-knower-one-of-e_b_7242468.html*. [Retrieved on April 14, 2016].
2 Fashion icon Eileen Fisher talks about creating sustainable fashion. Huffpost Style. February 11, 2015. *http://www.huffingtonpost.com/karim-orange/fashion-icon-eileen-fisher_b_6315600.html*. [Retrieved on April 14, 2016].
3 Business as a movement: Social consciousness in the fashion industry. Bard MBA in sustainability. February 21, 2014. *http://blogs.bard.edu/mba/2014/02/21/business-movement-social-consciousness-fashion-industry*. [Retrieved on April 14, 2016].
4 Business as a movement: Social consciousness in the fashion industry. Bard MBA in sustainability. February 21, 2014. *http://blogs.bard.edu/mba/2014/02/21/business-movement-social-consciousness-fashion-industry*. [Retrieved on April 14, 2016].
5 *www.eileenfisher.com*. [Retrieved on April 14, 2016].

Application Case 2: The Community Shop: More than Just Food[65]

Community Shop (CS) is a retail discount food and household product store that was introduced in the United Kingdom in the form of its members-only store in Goldthorpe, Barnsley, in December 2013. Based on similar models that have worked successfully in

Europe as "Social Supermarkets," the business plan of Community Shop is uncomplicated: it sells goods, wholesome foods, and household products sourced from surpluses in supply chains at a discount of up to 70 percent. Community Shop's parent organization, Company Shop, is the UK's largest commercial redistributor of surplus stock and food. It works with retailers, manufacturers, farmers, and brands to ensure surplus products are redistributed ethically for human consumption, when otherwise they would likely end up in landfill.

Established in 1985 by founder John Marren (who is originally from Barnsley), Company Shop handles above 30,000 tonnes of surplus stock each year. Surpluses are caused by various reasons—forecasting errors, seasonal promotions, package damage, and labeling errors—that prevent mainstream retailers from being able to sell them. Community Shop only sells food that is wholesome and within its use-by date; it does not stock alcohol or tobacco.

Community Shop stores were rolling out nationally by late 2014. Ultimately, Company Shop aims to open about 20 Community Shop stores across the UK. This would provide support for 10,000 members (possibly more) and potentially provide millions of meals to people who need them. Each shop contains a maximum membership of about 500 people, with the membership of each Community Shop structured to ensure that only those who are actually in need are able to purchase the redistributed products. To become a member of the pilot shop in Goldthorpe, applications were only accepted from people living in defined areas who could prove they were recipients of government benefits (proof of address, signature, and benefit receipts). Future stores will adopt similar models, targeting anyone receiving one or more types of UK benefit, such as Income-Based Job Seeker's Allowance, Pension Credit, or Council Tax Benefit. Members' benefit status is checked every six months to ensure they are still eligible.

Not only does Community Shop ensure that cheap, healthy food and household products reach people who may be living in or on the cusp of poverty, but the store provides access to other services via its "Community Hub." While some Goldthorpe locals see the opening of Community Shop as attracting further stigma to the area, Community Hub is active in providing solutions to their socioeconomic problems. This program of wider support provides services including skills and employment training, curriculum vitae writing skills, budgeting and debt advice, and cooking classes. In this way, Community Shop underpins its provision of discounted foods to alleviate hunger among the economically disadvantaged by contributing solutions to other wide-scale social issues, such as poverty and unemployment. The services and advice provided by Community Hub can be viewed as vehicles to inspire people, raise their self-esteem, and help members achieve financial independence and go to shop at mainstream retail stores. In turn, this may ultimately provide space for more members to join. As their slogan states, Community Shop is "more than just food."

In 2014, Company Shop won the "Community Partner Award" at the prestigious Food and Drink Federation (FDF) Awards for its products and services. It already works with several retailers and top brands, including Morrison's, Asda, Marks and Spencer, Tesco, Tetley, the Co-operative, and Nestlé, and its already significant support within the food retail sector continues to grow. For these major retailers and brands, this environmentally responsible action (not sending perfectly good products to landfill) generates reputational benefits due to their associations with Company Shop. While the Community Shop's enfranchisement operations are still in their infancy, it is likely that future stores will achieve the same success as their counterparts in Goldthorpe and throughout Europe, as this is a socially and environmentally responsible enterprise that provides solutions to food poverty and services that can help individuals become financially independent.

Discussion Questions

1 Consider how the concept of "social supermarkets"—like Community Shop—could be successfully scaled in developing countries.
2 Identify Community Shop's social value proposition. How compelling is it?
3 How would you measure the social return on investment of Community Shop?
4 Assess the social impact of Community Shop. What metrics would you use to measure its social impact?

Notes

1 Kanter, B., & Paine, K. D. (2012). *Measuring the networked nonprofit*. Thousand Oaks, CA: Jossey-Bass.
2 Nicholls, A. (2009). We do good things don't we? Blended value accounting in social entrepreneurship. *Accounting, Organizations and Society, 4*(6/7), 755–769.
3 Kendall, J., & Knapp, M. (2000). Measuring the performance of voluntary organizations. *Public Management, 2*(1), 105–132.
4 Paton, R. (2003). *Managing and measuring social enterprises*. London: Sage Publications.
5 Nicholls, A. (2009). We do good things don't we? Blended value accounting in social entrepreneurship. *Accounting, Organizations and Society, 4*(6/7), 755–769.
6 DiMaggio, P., & Anheier, H. (1990). The sociology of nonprofit organizations and sectors. *Annual Review of Sociology, 16*, 137–159.
7 Nicholls, A. (2009). We do good things don't we? Blended value accounting in social entrepreneurship. *Accounting, Organizations and Society, 4*(6/7), 755–769.
8 Emerson, J. (2000). *The nature of returns: A social capital markets inquiry into elements of investment and the blended value proposition*. Social Enterprise Series Number 17. Boston: Harvard Business School.
9 Brooks, C. A. (2009). *Social entrepreneurship: A modern approach to social value creation*. Upper Saddle River, NJ: Pearson/Prentice-Hall.
10 Brooks, C. A. (2009). *Social entrepreneurship: A modern approach to social value creation*. Upper Saddle River, NJ: Pearson/Prentice-Hall.
11 Kickul, J., & Lyons, T. (2012). *Understanding social entrepreneurship: The relentless pursuit of mission in an ever-changing world*. New York: Routledge.
12 Bloom, P. N. (2012). *Scaling your social venture: Becoming an impact entrepreneur*. New York: Palgrave Macmillan.
13 Kickul, J., & Lyons, T. (2012). *Understanding social entrepreneurship: The relentless pursuit of mission in an ever-changing world*. New York: Routledge.
14 Kickul, J., & Lyons, T. (2012). *Understanding social entrepreneurship: The relentless pursuit of mission in an ever-changing world*. New York: Routledge.
15 Rittell, H. W. J., & Webber, M. M. (1973). Dilemmas in a general theory of planning. *Policy Sciences, 4*(2), 155–169; Weber, E. P., & Khademian, A. M. (2008). Wicked problems, knowledge challenges, and collaborative capacity builders in network settings. *Public Administration Review, 68*(2), 334–349.
16 Palpanas, T., Chowdhary, P., Mihaila, G., & Pinel, F. (2007). Integrated model-driven dashboard development. *Information Systems Frontiers, 9*(2/3), 185–208.
17 Kickul, J., & Lyons, T. (2012). *Understanding social entrepreneurship: The relentless pursuit of mission in an ever-changing world*. New York: Routledge.
18 Tuan, M. T. (2008). *Impact planning and improvement measuring and/or estimating social value creation: Insights into eight integrated cost approaches*. Seattle, WA: Bill and Melinda Gates Foundation.

19 Nicholls, A. (2009). We do good things don't we? Blended value accounting in social entrepreneurship. *Accounting, Organizations and Society*, 4(6/7), 755–769.
20 Akerlof, A. G. (1970). The market for lemons: Quality uncertainty and the market mechanisms. *Quarterly Journal of Economics*, 84(3), 488–500.
21 Nicholls, A. (2009). We do good things don't we? Blended value accounting in social entrepreneurship. *Accounting, Organizations and Society*, 4(6/7), 755–769.
22 Bagnoli, L., & Megali, C. (2011). Measuring performance in social enterprises. *Nonprofit and Voluntary Sector Quarterly*, 40(1), 149–165.
23 Tuan, M. T. (2008). *Impact planning and improvement measuring and/or estimating social value creation: Insights into eight integrated cost approaches*. Seattle, WA: Bill and Melinda Gates Foundation.
24 Tuan, M. T. (2008). *Impact planning and improvement measuring and/or estimating social value creation: Insights into eight integrated cost approaches*. Seattle, WA: Bill and Melinda Gates Foundation.
25 Kickul, J., & Lyons, T. (2012). *Understanding social entrepreneurship: The relentless pursuit of mission in an ever-changing world*. New York: Routledge.
26 Kickul, J., & Lyons, T. (2012). *Understanding social entrepreneurship: The relentless pursuit of mission in an ever-changing world*. New York: Routledge.
27 Kickul, J., & Lyons, T. (2012). *Understanding social entrepreneurship: The relentless pursuit of mission in an ever-changing world*. New York: Routledge.
28 Tuan, M. T. (2008). *Impact planning and improvement measuring and/or estimating social value creation: Insights into eight integrated cost approaches*. Seattle, WA: Bill and Melinda Gates Foundation.
29 Karoly, L. A. (2008). *Valuing benefits in benefit–cost studies of social programs*. Santa Monica, CA: RAND Corporation.
30 Gray, R. (2002). The social accounting project and accounting organizations and society: Privileging engagement, imaginings, new accountings, and pragmatism over critique? *Accounting, Organizations and Society*, 27(7), 687–708.
31 Mook, L., Richmond, B. J., & Quarter, J. (2003). Integrated social accounting for nonprofits: A case from Canada. *Voluntas: International Journal of Voluntary and Nonprofit Organizations*, 14(3), 283–297; Gray, R. (2002). The social accounting project and accounting organizations and society: Privileging engagement, imaginings, new accountings, and pragmatism over critique? *Accounting, Organizations and Society*, 27(7), 687–708; Brown, L. (2000). The cooperative difference? Social auditing in the Canadian credit unions. *Journal of Rural Cooperation*, 28(2), 87–100.
32 Richmond, B. J., Mook, L., & Quarter, J. (2003). Social accounting for nonprofit. *Nonprofit Management and Leadership*, 13(3), 308–324.
33 Haugh, H. (2005). A research agenda for social entrepreneurship. *Social Enterprise Journal*, 1(1), 1–12.
34 Mook, L. (2014). An integrated social accounting model for nonprofit organizations. In E. Costa, L. D. Parker, & M. Andreaus (Eds.), *Accountability and Social Accounting for Social and Non-Profit Organizations* (197–221). Bingley: Emerald Group Publishing.
35 Emerson, J. (2003). A blended value proposition: Integrating social and financial returns. *California Management Review*, 45(4), 35–51.
36 Emerson, J. (2003). A blended value proposition: Integrating social and financial returns. *California Management Review*, 45(4), 35–51.
37 Manetti, G. (2014). The role of blended value accounting in the evaluation of socio-economic impact of social enterprises. *Voluntas: International Journal of Voluntary and Nonprofit Organizations*, 25(2), 443–464; Nicholls, A. (2009). We do good things, don't we? Blended value accounting in social entrepreneurship. *Accounting, Organizations and Society*, 34(6/7), 755–769.
38 Nicholls, A. (2009). We do good things, don't we? Blended value accounting in social entrepreneurship. *Accounting, Organizations and Society*, 34(6/7), 755–769.

39 Brooks, C. A. (2009). *Social entrepreneurship: A modern approach to social value creation.* Upper Saddle River, NJ: Pearson/Prentice-Hall.

40 Brooks, C. A. (2009). *Social entrepreneurship: A modern approach to social value creation.* Upper Saddle River, NJ: Pearson/Prentice-Hall.

41 Nicholls, A. (2009). We do good things don't we? Blended value accounting in social entrepreneurship. *Accounting, Organizations and Society, 4*(6/7), 755–769.

42 Nicholls, A. (2004). *Social return on investment: Valuing what matters.* London: New Economic Foundation.

43 Nicholls, A. (2009). We do good things don't we? Blended value accounting in social entrepreneurship. *Accounting, Organizations and Society, 4*(6/7), 755–769.

44 Nicholls, A. (2009). We do good things don't we? Blended value accounting in social entrepreneurship. *Accounting, Organizations and Society, 4*(6/7), 755–769.

45 Rotheroe, N., & Richards, A. (2007). Social return on investment and social enterprise: Transparent accountability for sustainable development. *Social Enterprise Journal, 3*(1), 31–48.

46 Olsen, S. (2003). *Social return on investment: Standard guidelines.* Berkeley: Center for Responsible Business, University of California.

47 New Economics Foundation (2005). *Measuring value creation in social firms: A do-it-yourself training manual for SROI.* London: New Economics Foundation.

48 Tuan, M. T. (2008). *Impact planning and improvement measuring and/or estimating social value creation: Insights into eight integrated cost approaches.* Seattle, WA: Bill and Melinda Gates Foundation.

49 Desa, G., & Koch, J. L. (2014). Scaling social impact: Building sustainable social ventures at the base-of-the-pyramid. *Journal of Social Entrepreneurship, 5*(2), 146–174; Dees, J. G., Anderson, B. B., & Wei-Skillern, J. (2004). Scaling social impact: Strategies of spreading social innovations. *Stanford Social Innovation Review, 1*, 24–32; Bradach, J. (2003). Going to scale: The challenge of replicating social programs. *Stanford Social Innovation Review, 1*(1), 19–25; Taylor, M. A., Dees, J. G., & Emerson, J. (2002). The question of scale: Finding an appropriate strategy for building on your success. In J. G. Dees, J. Emerson, & P. Economy (Eds.), *Social entrepreneurs: Enhancing the performance of your enterprising nonprofit* (pp. 235–266). New York: John Wiley & Sons.

50 New Economics Foundation (2005). *Measuring value creation in social firms: A do-it-yourself training manual for SROI.* London: New Economics Foundation.

51 Minar, R., & Hall, K. (2013). Social return on investment and performance measurement. *Public Management Review, 15*(6), 923–941.

52 Manetti, G. (2014). The role of blended value accounting in the evaluation of socio-economic impact of social enterprises. *Voluntas: International Journal of Voluntary and Nonprofit Organizations, 25*(2), 443–464.

53 Moody, M., Littlepage, L., & Paydar, N. (2015). Measuring social return on investment: Lessons from organizational implementation of SROI in the Netherlands and the United States. *Nonprofit Management and Leadership, 26*(1), 19–37.

54 Dey, P., & Teasdale, S. (2015). The tactical mimicry of social enterprise strategies: Acting "as if" in the everyday life of third sector organizations. *Organization,* February 23. http://org.sagepub.com/content/early/2015/02/23/1350508415570689.full.pdf+html, retrieved on March 31, 2016.

55 Emerson, J. (2003). A blended value proposition: Integrating social and financial returns. *California Management Review, 45*(4), 35–51.

56 Barrow, C. J. (2000). *Social impact assessment: An introduction.* London: Arnold; Vanclay, F. (2014). *Developments in social impact assessment.* Cheltenham: Edward Elgar.

57 International Association for Impact Assessment. www.iaia.org., retrieved on March 31, 2016.

58 Kramer, M., Parkhurst, M., & Vaidyanathan, L. (2009). Breakthroughs in shared measurement and social impact. www.socialimpactexchange.org/sites/www.socialimpactexchange.org/files/Breakthroughs%20in%20Shared%20Measurement.pdf, retrieved on March 31, 2016.

59 Rotheroe, N., & Richards, A. (2007). Social return on investment and social enterprise: Transparent accountability for sustainable development. *Social Enterprise Journal*, 3(1), 31–48.

60 Emerson, J. (2003). A blended value proposition: Integrating social and financial returns. *California Management Review*, 45(4), 35–51.

61 Rousseau D. M. (2006). Is there such a thing as evidence-based management? *Academy of Management Review*, 31(2), 256–269.

62 Desousa, K. C. & Smith K. L. (2014). Big data for social innovation. *Stanford Social Innovations Review*, Summer, 39–43.

63 Davenport, T. H., & Harris, J. G. (2007). *Competing on analytics: The new science of winning.* Boston: Harvard Business School Press.

64 Alvord, S. H., Brown, L. D., & Letts, C. W. (2004). Social entrepreneurship and societal transformation: An exploratory study. *Journal of Applied Behavioral Science*, 40(3), 260–282.

65 Sources for this whole section: Crossley, L. (2013). Revolutionary "social supermarket" opens with branded goods 70% cheaper than the likes of Tesco and Asda ... but only people on benefits can shop there. *Daily Mail*, December 9. www.dailymail.co.uk/news/article-2520750/Community-Shop-social-supermarket-opens-goods-70-cheaper-Tesco-Asda.html; Cocozza, P. (2013). 'If I shop here I've got money for gas': Inside the UK's first social supermarket. *Guardian*, December 9. www.theguardian.com/society/2013/dec/09/inside-britains-first-social-supermarket-goldthorpe-yorkshire?, both retrieved on March 31, 2016.

Glossary

Affective commitment An emotional attachment to the organization.

Affiliation Process of creating separate units in other geographic locations that are loosely connected to headquarters.

Agency theory A theory that assumes that because of goal conflict between the agent and the principal, the former will not always act in the best interest of the latter.

Alertness Attitude of receptiveness to available, but hitherto overlooked, opportunities that leads people to discover what could add value to the human experience.

Assumption sheet A sheet of paper that includes the statements that an entrepreneur makes about the reasons underlying the need for financial and other resources.

Autonomy Ability to take responsibility to use one's own judgment as opposed to blindly following the assertions of others.

Balance sheet A financial statement that describes what a firm owns and owes at a specific period in time.

Balanced scorecard An instrument used to measure the performance of a firm that includes both financial and non-financial elements.

Benchmarking A strategic management technique used to compare a firm's business processes and performance metrics to industry bests or best practices from other industries.

Blended accounting value The combination of economic and social outputs.

Board of advisors A panel of experts who are asked by a firm's managers to provide counsel and advice on an on-going basis.

Board of directors A panel of individuals who are elected by a corporation's shareholders to oversee the management of the firm.

Bootstrapping A process by which an entrepreneur finds ways to avoid the need for external funding through creativity, ingenuity, cost-cutting, or any means necessary.

Branching Process of creating separate units in other geographic locations that are tightly connected to headquarters.

Brand A set of attributes, positive or negative, that customers associate with a firm.

Branding Process of developing a brand.

Business analytics Use of data to create value for the organization.

Business concept A set of favorable events involving customers, consideration, connection, and commitment (the 4 Cs) that have the potential to become a successful business.

Business model The content, structure, and governance of transactions designed so as to create value through the exploitation of business opportunities.

Business model design   Process of creating the content, structure, and governance of transactions designed to create value through the exploitation of business opportunities.

Business plan   A written document that describes the current state and the presupposed future of an organization.

Buzz marketing   A form of word-of-mouth communication which emerged as a reaction to the fact that more and more consumers are critical towards traditional advertising.

Calculative commitment   An attachment to the organization because of tangible benefits, such as pension, salary and the like.

Capacity building   The process by which an organization strengthens its internal capabilities.

Commercial entrepreneurship   Entrepreneurial activity directed toward the creation of economic value.

Compassion   An orientation and an emotional connection linking an individual to a suffering community.

Competitive intelligence   A strategic management tool used to garner useful information about the competition, the market and the technology that can be utilized by managers to make strategic decisions.

Corporate social entrepreneurship   Social entrepreneurship occurring within established for-profit companies.

Corridor principle   A principle that states that once an entrepreneur starts a firm, he or she begins a journey down a path where corridors leading to new venture opportunities become apparent.

Cost-benefit analysis   A method that monetizes the benefits of outcomes of a program along with its costs in order to compare them and observe which are greater.

Cost-effectiveness analysis   A method that compares the relative costs and outcomes of two or more courses of action and is expressed in terms of a ratio where the denominator is a gain from a measure.

Creation theory   An entrepreneurial theory that assumes that opportunities are created by the actions, reactions, and enactment of entrepreneurs.

Crowdfunding   Process of soliciting external financing from a large audience, the crowd, in which each individual provides a very small amount, generally through the Internet.

Design elements   The conceptualization and configuration of the business model.

Design themes   Describe the sources of the model's value creation and the holistic gestalt of a firm's business model and facilitate its conceptualization and measurement.

Design thinking   An iterative, exploratory process involving visualizing, experimenting, creating, and prototyping of models, and gathering feedback.

Discovery theory   An entrepreneurial theory that assumes that opportunities are exogenous, independent of the entrepreneur and represent objective phenomena.

Dissemination   Actively providing information, and sometimes technical assistance, to others looking to bring an innovation to their community.

Effectiveness   The extent to which an organization accomplishes its core objectives.

Efficiency   The extent to which the organization uses fewer resources to accomplish its core objectives.

Entrepreneurial actions   Set of activities to perform to implement an entrepreneurial opportunity.

Entrepreneurial choices   Decisions related to which opportunities to pursue and which ones to disregard or delay.

Entrepreneurial marketing Marketing activities performed in early-stage ventures that are conceived as an innovative, risk-taking, and proactive.

Entrepreneurial mindset A way of thinking about the business that captures the benefits of uncertainty.

Entrepreneurial motivation Willingness to start a new venture.

Entrepreneurial outcomes Results of acting on entrepreneurial opportunities, such as the number of successful new ventures, the economic or social value added or the contribution to economic growth.

Entrepreneurial thoughts Cognitive processes that lead to the discovery or creation of entrepreneurial opportunities.

Entrepreneurship Entrepreneurship is commonly defined as the relentless pursuit of opportunity without regard to resources currently controlled.

Environmental scanning A strategic management tool used to analyze the external environment of a firm.

Executive summary The summary of the content of a business plan; generally between 1–2 pages.

Feasibility analysis The process of collecting and analyzing data to assess an opportunity's perceived practicability or difficulty.

Financial feasibility Process of determining whether the entrepreneur has or can garner the financial resources needed to transform an opportunity into a viable business.

Financial vulnerability Extent to which a firm is likely to be severely affected by financial shocks.

Financial vulnerability index A measure of the financial vulnerability of a social venture.

Fixed mindset A view that one's talents and abilities are a set of traits.

Formal institutions Institutions formally created to regulate actors' behaviors within a society, such as laws, rules, and constitutions.

Goal setting theory A theory that argues that the goals are the main drivers of human behavior.

Growth mindset A view that one's abilities can be developed through effort, dedication and hard work.

Guerrilla marketing An approach to marketing that relies on bootstrapping, creative use of available resources, and a highly targeted mix of innovative communication techniques.

Hybrid social ventures Social ventures that pursue both economic and social value creation.

Income statement A financial statement that reflects the results of the operations of a firm over a specified period of time.

Industry/target market feasibility Process of determining the market and industry an entrepreneur intends to enter are attractive.

Informal institutions Institutions, such as norms, beliefs, customs, and traditions, that affect individual behavior.

Institutional environment An environment is comprised of relatively stable rules, social norms, and cognitions that guide, constrain, and liberate domestic economic activity.

Institutional profile Set of characteristics of a country's institutional environment.

Market segment A particular group of customers that a firm is targeted for its products or services.

Market segmentation   Process of dividing a market in groups of customers based on certain characteristics.

Marketing   The process of planning and executing the conception, pricing, promotion, and distribution of goods and services to satisfy customers and accomplish organizational objectives.

Marketing mix   Set of tools a firm uses to produce the response it wants in the target market including the four elements of product, price, promotion, and place.

Marketing orientation   A marketing method based on an understanding of the needs and desires of the market and establishing long-term relationships with beneficiaries and other key stakeholders.

Marketing plan   A written document that describes the marketing strategies of an organization.

Microfinance   Provision of financial services to populations typically excluded by mainstream banks and represents a social innovation to alleviate poverty.

Mission statement   A written statement that describes the 'raison-d'etre' of an organization.

Model   A schematic description of a system, theory or phenomenon.

Moral engagement   The extent to which social entrepreneurs are deeply committed to their ideals and feel morally obligated to pursue them.

Motivational plan   A written statement that describes how an organization intends to motivate its employees.

Need for achievement   Desire to attain an inner feeling of personal accomplishment, which is satisfied primarily by an intrinsic sense of success and excellence rather than extrinsic rewards.

Need for power   Desire to be in control.

Normative commitment   An attachment to an organization on moral grounds.

Opportunity   Entrepreneurial opportunities are situations in which new goods, services, raw materials, and organizing methods can be introduced and sold at greater than the cost of their production.

Organizational feasibility   Process of determining whether an entrepreneur has the human capital and other non-financial resources to launch a new venture.

Outside-In/Inside-Out Analysis Model   A strategic management tool used to analyze factors that are both internal and external to a firm.

Paid employees   Individuals who are salaried employees in a social venture or a non-profit organization.

Passion   A strong inclination toward an activity that people like, that they find important, and in which they invest time and energy.

PEST model   A model that analyzes the political, economical, social and legal environments of a firm.

Porter's Five Forces model   A strategic management model that analyzes the influence of five distinct factors, competitors, buyers, suppliers, substitute products, and barriers to entry on a firm's actions.

Product/service demand   The quantity of the product or service that customers will ask for.

Product/service desirability   Extent to which the product or service addresses a particular need or problem the customer faces.

Product/service feasibility   Addresses the question of whether the entrepreneur is able to produce and deliver the product to customers.

Psychic income The satisfaction of performing a job that makes a difference in the lives of others.

Public relations Creating awareness of a firm's products, services or activities by informing the public through the media, including journalists, bloggers or radio hosts.

Pull theory People are attracted into entrepreneurial activities because they seek independence, self-fulfillment, wealth, and other desirable outcomes.

Purely commercial enterprises Businesses that are market-driven and provide economic value by supplying goods and services to customers who pay market prices.

Purely Philanthropic Social Ventures Social ventures that rely exclusively on external sources of funding such as donations and grants.

Push theory A theory that suggests that people are pushed into entrepreneurship by negative external forces, such as job dissatisfaction, difficulty finding employment, insufficient salary or inflexible work schedule.

Quick Screen Model A three-component strategic management tool used to assess the external environment of a firm.

Relational marketing Marketing activities directed towards establishing, developing, and maintaining successful relational exchanges.

Revenue model Model that specifies how a firm would generate income.

Risk assessment Identification of the potential risks that an organization may face.

Risk propensity The tendency to take risk.

SCALERS Model A seven-component scaling model that contends that explores the conditions under which a social venture may scale its activities.

Scaling Increasing the impact a social-purpose organization produces to better match the magnitude of the social need or problem it seeks to address.

Scaling deep The process of deepening of a social venture's knowledge of the market and focus on developing and becoming expert in providing the required services.

Scaling up The process of expanding a social venture's products or services, or the extending its activities to other geographic locations.

Self-efficacy The belief in one's ability to muster and implement the necessary personal resources, skills, and competencies to attain a certain level of achievement on a given task.

Shared measurement platforms Web-based platforms that are aimed at measuring the performance and social impact of projects.

Signal detection theory A theory that describes the relationship between perception and reality when it comes to opportunity, and recognizes that people sometimes see opportunities that are not there or fail to see those that are present.

Signaling effect Sending of information about oneself to another.

Social accounting and auditing A concept that is used to capture all forms of accounting that go beyond the economic and takes into account both economic and social impacts.

Social alliances Strategic alliances that involve social ventures.

Social analytics Extensive use of data, statistical and quantitative analysis, explanatory and predictive models, and fact-based management to drive decisions and actions.

Social angels Wealthy individuals who provide funding to social-purpose ventures.

Social auditing and reporting Process of communicating the social and environmental effects of organizations' economic actions to their key stakeholders. (Also known as social accounting and auditing.)

Social bricoleurs Social entrepreneurs who focus on discovering and addressing small-scale local social needs.

Social business model Rationale for a social venture to successfully address a social need while remaining sustainable over time.

Social constructionists Social entrepreneurs who exploit opportunities and market failures by filling gaps to underserved clients in order to introduce reforms and innovations to the broader social system.

Social engineers Social entrepreneurs who recognize systemic problems within existing social structures and address them by introducing revolutionary change.

Social entrepreneurial motivation Willingness to start a social venture.

Social entrepreneurs individual who create and run social enterprises.

Social entrepreneurship Entrepreneurial activity directed toward the creation of social value.

Social finance The supply of capital to charities, social ventures, and businesses with a social mission.

Social franchising Social franchising is a hybrid growth strategy in which a parent social venture's products or services are franchised and the social franchisee pays some royalties.

Social impact The explicit social benefit that a social venture provides to its intended. beneficiaries.

Social impact assessment A methodology used to review the social effects of development projects.

Social impact bonds Bonds issued to undertake socially-oriented projects.

Social impact management The study of the impact that a given intervention has on society.

Social justice Perceived fairness among members of a community.

Social marketing The application of marketing knowledge, concepts, and techniques to enhance social as well as economic issues.

Social Opportunity Assessment Tool A four-component tool used to determine the viability of a social venture opportunity.

Social return on investment (SROI) Monetized social benefits of a social venture.

Social utility Impact on solving a social problem.

Social value proposition Indication of how well a social venture would need a specific social need.

Social venture capitalists Venture capitalists who fund social ventures.

Social venture concept A set of favorable events that have the potential to become a successful social venture.

Social venture landscape The external environment in which a social venture operates.

Social venture opportunity Situations in which new products and services can be can be created to address social needs.

Social venture plan A written document that describes the current state and the presupposed future of a social venture.

Social ventures A venture created to address a social problem. Is synonymous of social enterprise.

Social venture sustainability model Rationale of how a social venture will be financially viable over time while accomplishing its social mission. Synonymous of social business model.

Stakeholder Any group or individual who can affect or is affected by the achievement of the organization's objectives.

Statement of cash flow A financial statement that summarizes changes in a firm's cash and expenses for a specific period.

SWOT analysis   A strategic management tool used to assess the strength and weaknesses of a firm as well as the opportunities and threats presented by the external environment in which a firm operates.

Type A ideas   Ideas that involve identifying a new market for an existing product or service.

Type B   Ideas that involve the creation of an entirely new product or service.

Type C ideas   Ideas that involve the creation of new processes for producing and delivering existing products and services.

Viral marketing   A form of marketing that uses social networks, such as social media, family, friends, neighbors, or colleagues to draw attention towards brands, products or campaigns by spreading messages, mostly through word-of-mouth marketing, like a virus.

Vision statement   A written statement that describes the long-term goals of an organization.

Volunteering   The process of giving time freely without pay to any organization that has the aim of benefiting people in a particular cause.

Volunteer management system   A set of policies and procedures aimed at attracting and retaining volunteers in a social business and/or a non-profit organization.

Volunteer resource manager   A manager who hires and oversees the work of volunteers in a social venture or a non-profit organization.

Volunteers   People performing activities out of free will, without remuneration, and benefiting others.

Wicked problems   Intractable, complex, difficult to solve problems.

Window of opportunity   Period during which the entrepreneur can provide maximum value to the customer before circumstances change or reduce the value to the customer.

Index